Author, historian and newspaper columnist Ed Syers comes equipped to take you *Off The Beaten Trail* in Texas. As novelist William Edward Syers, his first novel, *Seven, Navy Subchaser* was critically ranked among America's best war novels and was cited particularly for its authenticity. His current historical novel, *The Gun*, ends three years of on-the-ground research through Texas and New Mexico.

In World War II William E. Syers served as a Commander with the U. S. Navy.

Syers spent seven years and traveled almost 100,000 miles completing the Texas exploration he calls *Off The Beaten Trail*, covering virtually every road in the state in search of the story behind Texas heritage. The work first appeared as a feature column in most of Texas' major papers, was subsequently rewritten in three softcover volumes, which exhausted seven printings before this single-volume revision.

A Presbyterian valedictory alumnus of San Antonio's Main Avenue High and St. Mary's University, as well as The University of Texas, where he edited both the Daily Texan and ex-student Alcalde, the former advertising and public relations executive moved his family to Kerrville's Hill Country in 1959 to devote full attention to writing.

OFF THE
BEATEN TRAIL

WILLIAM EDWARD SYERS

Copyright 1971
by
Texian Press

F
391.2
S 98

Published by

Waco, Texas

Binding by
Library Binding Co.
Waco, Texas

To Wm. A. Blakley

A Texian

Foreword

A people with no reverence for the heritage left them, a philosopher once observed, will indeed leave nothing of themselves to be remembered proudly.

Some years ago, *Off The Beaten Trail* set out for a reflectively proud look at Texas, border to border and prehistory to yesterday: what to see and, most particularly, to feel wherever we stand upon this land. It is from the *feel* of our forebears' land that we draw their strengths, that we rediscover the state of mind that has distinguished Texas from a mere geography, and that has given meaning to the identification, "I am a Texan."

Many of the sketches that follow were originally published as our back roads unfolded them (our superhighways do not). This volume attempts to correlate these sketches in divisions that I hope will prove self-explanatory, to catch up many threads into a pattern that is recognizably Texan, to bring the whole fabric forward chronologically, and to provide both map and index for those who care to share the exploration.

There is not room here to acknowledge *Off The Beaten Trail's* indebtedness to many — historian, librarian, the Texas press and, above all, the many old timers whose recollections are reflected in the following pages. One acknowledgment at this point, however, may be appropriate, may set the tone for the remainder of this work. It was orginally titled *Until Daylight to the Wattor*; let it speak for itself.

The casual reader may wonder if *Off The Beaten Trail* paints the old Texian several sizes too heroic. Was his land truly that uncompromising? Was he himself truly as spare-spoken, as indomitable as all that?

Take that ranger, Ed Westfall. Now did he really crawl thirty miles, blind and half dead, for a week up the Leona? Was the Karankawa truly that savage, the Comanche that unrelenting, the Spanish *conquistador* that dauntless? Wasn't the ordeal of Jane Long perhaps exaggerated? Don't we really, in fact, add a little with each retelling?

Suppose we trail four Texas Rangers, a hundred empty miles west of frontier San Antonio one fiery August afternoon, 1844, eight years after Alamo. They have read scant Comanche sign and now noon it under the stubby bluffs near where U.S. 90 today crosses Nueces Canyon, beyond Uvalde. Two have ridden, bareback and naked, to cool in the clear stream below.

Indian fighter Kit Ackland stretches in camp's scrub shade. His partner, an eight-year veteran at age twenty-two, is lean, heavy-shouldered Rufe Perry, standing camp guard. In moments now, Perry and Ackland will face the ultimate horror — sudden close-quarter Comanche, an arrow-whipping, death-screaming engulfment from boulder and brush.

Perry is shafted through the shoulder; Ackland, through the jaw as he comes up, yelling hoarsely . . . as the rangers' new Colt five-shooters blast them free . . . as reeling, stumbling, darting, they back for water . . . as Ackland is hit twice again, Perry, in stomach and head . . . as they seem to break clear, floundering in the river, then swarmed again . . . as their two companions, knowing them down for dead, escape, galloping naked.

They are not dead. Lost to the other, each burrows in a vast raft of flood timber. To survive, he must wait out the Indian. Then, without horse, food or gun, he must cross a hundred scorching miles. When? When he can rise to his knees.

This story of Perry and Ackland has been recounted over many a campfire. Years ago, Ranger A. J. Sowell wrote it into frontier epoch. Has it grown with retelling?

Ranger Rufe Perry's granddaughter by marriage, Mrs. E. R. Sitton of Houston, copied one of those accounts. She wanted it for her grandchildren today and sent it to me, for yours. She copied it word for word as it was first told.

It traces Rufe Perry, riding San Jacinto dispatches at

age fourteen, through every frontier fight to his long later command of Company D, Frontier Battalion, Texas Rangers, west on the Concho. It is Rufe Perry's diary, now riding into Nueces ordeal.

Decide for yourself if we add, in the retelling.

"We got as far as the Newaces. Just on this Side I saw the trail of a horce. I fowloed it until I was Satisfide that thair was a man on it.

"I toald the boys to camp up on a bluf but they Campt cloast to some thickets. I toald them when I came to Campt that an Indion would not have Campt thair and I thought that thair Indions not far off.

"I went up on a hill in order to look oute but Saw nothing. I had prsentment that thair was Something rong but after eating our dinor James Dun and John Carolin went to the river to go in bathing. They had just got of thair clothes when Acklin and myself was attacted in camp by aboute 25 Indions.

"We both jumpt to our feeat. I toald Kit to hoald his fior until wee coold get to our horces but hee fiored his gun killing one in his tracts . . . The shot I recevd was through my left Shoulder while I had my gun leveld on one. It made mee fior a little Sooner but my Sight was good and dound him. They wair not over 30 steps from mee. I had one of Coalt's first 5 Shooters. I Shot that 4 times and I am Satisfide that I did not miss a Shot.

"The next Shot I got was through the belley. The third was in the temple cutting an artree that bled So that I fainted from the loss of blud but I soon came to and got to whare Dun, Carolin was at the river. We was joind thair by Acklin.

"When he puld the arrow oute of my Shoulder leaving the Spike in whitch was cut oute two yars after. I caut hoald of one of the horces tayls and went a cross but I fainted again . . . The Indions made a Second Charge on us. They run of and left Acklin and me taking my gun, pistol with them. They had the horces.

"I run to a dence thicket whair I lay down with the woond in my face down in the dust and little Sticks. It stopt the blud.

"I did not lay long beefoar the Indions got all a round the brush. They Staid but a Short time then went away. I remaind until dark when I started to the wattor aboute 200 yards.

"It tuc mee from dark until daylight to get to the wattor.

"I was nearley famisht for wattor. After drinking all I wanted and washing my face I fild one of my boots with wattor and crauld in a hoal whair thair had bin a tree blown up. Thair I staid all day. After dark I Started for San Antonia.

"I did not go over 3 miles beefoar I laid down to dy as I thought I cold not go aney further but after laying a while I got up and Started a gain.

"I was all night and a part of next day getting to the leona a boute 10 miles from whair I started. I traveld then when ever I was able to go day or night. With oute aney thing to eat but 3 pricley pairs apples.

"I got to San Antonia on the 7 day aboute dusk. By the time I got to the Squar I met a grate meny for I was like one risen from the dead as Dun and Carolin had toald that I was dead an Acklin woold dye.

"Acklin got in the next morning afer I did but was all rite. In 2 weeks he was up.

"I was taken to Nat Lewis Stoar whair I remaind for a month. Then I was taken to another place whair I Staid too months longer beefoar I was able to ride."

William Edward Syers

Kerrville, Texas
September 1, 1971

Table of Contents

Part Five: A Lodging Place

Part Six: Ghosts and Treasure

Part Seven: A Number of Things

Part One

Beginning of Years

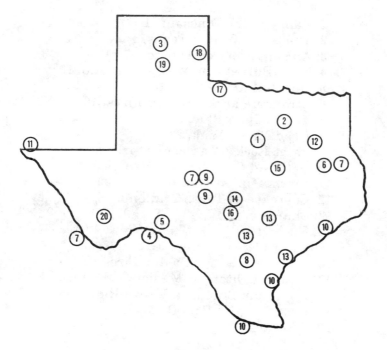

Before the beginning of years
There came to the making of man
Time with a gift of tears
Grief with a glass that ran.

Swinburne

Valley of the Dinosaur

There are two ways to look on the beautiful and old country of Glen Rose. Either takes you far indeed from your city's rush.

An hour southwest of Fort Worth, this little town tucks into lazy hills, flower-valleyed blue in spring and torched sumac red by fall. The Brazos gathers broad and, down from the upland shade, the Paluxy glides over slab rock bottoms.

The old resort, with its mineral baths and iron-sulfury drinking wells, bends south with its stream and, bypassed now by the highway, leisurely awaits rediscovery. This will come, for secluded about are dozens of excellent campsites where you can fish, swim, rock hunt, or simply contemplate beauty. Any of these provides one way to travel far from city tumult.

Another way is to look very closely along the wooded Paluxy bottoms.

This — as few sights anywhere — will fix man's metropolis in focus: a minute dust speck this side of a bottomless chasm of time.

Footprints are in the stream's rock bed — scores of them — many, clear as though imprinted just yesterday. Their size is awesome. But it is their "yesterday" — the truly old Glen Rose — that staggers the senses. To comprehend, consider them relatively one year old . . . and Texas has been a state just 28 seconds.

They are from the upper Mesozic Age of Reptiles. They were left by giant, claw-taloned or elephant-footed dinosaurs, who thundered this swampy way 135 million years ago.

1

Almost wherever the Glen Rose outcrops along the Paluxy, there are tracks - distinct underwater or weathering away on ledges, unpreserved. Some of the clearest are massed four miles west of town, where the stream wanders a low-rimmed valley toward chalky Adams Bluff. Here is Blue Hole, banked south in great slab tumbles and across in a thirty-foot slope, crested in live oak and pecan.

Through paleontology's old eyes, Blue Hole's valley was once shallow swamp, mud-flatted, bordered with giant reeds, strange palms and weird, cypress-like trees. Its waters eased the thirty-ton weight of the monster brontosaur — seventy feet from tail to flat serpent's head — the "thunder lizard" who could stand on your crushed house, smash your car at the front curb with his tail, and stare beadily over a three story building in your back yard.

He could gulp today's man in two bites, but for his frightful time, he was a relatively harmless vegetarian among deadly neighbors — cousins of the meat-eating tyrannosaur. By this swamp lived the forty-foot killers, lizard nightmares who stalked erect on great clawed feet, whose body became all head and whose head was all colossal crocodile jaw, studded in dagger teeth.

As you look across the swamp, glinting in the leaden sun, a brontosaur lumbers over a shallow mud flat toward a deeper lagoon. From the jungle crashes a waiting carnivore, who must catch and kill before his prey reaches deep water safety. Across the shallows, hunter and hunted plunge monstrously, crushing down the brontosaur's half-bathtub tracks, slashing in the taloned, eight-foot stride of the killer behind.

The tracks remain as centuries tick into eons and, as the earth changes, the Cretacious mud becomes marble-like Glen Rose limestone: flight and pursuit now etched deep in solid rock. New York's American Museum of Natural History called it the most dramatic dinosaur trail ever found, quarried fifty feet of Paluxy bottom for the major exhibit in its Hall of the Dinosaur.

Eugene Connally, graying and soft-spoken Glen Rose historian, and Charlie Moss, who has farmed Paluxy bottoms and known its tracks most of his seventying years, showed me the spoor of Somervell County's monster herd.

At White Bluff Crossing, a mile above Blue Hole, we counted thirty tracks of varying size under two feet of water, where they hold up best. Across the formation's slab they stalked, to disappear with it under the over-burden of more than a million centuries.

In many of the splayed tracks of the killers, you can put your foot in the gash left by a single terrible talon. One huge brontosaur track, deep in the rock, has trapped catfish at low water. It will hold a half barrel.

"But let air get at 'em," said Charlie Ross, "and they're gone. Come a freeze, and the whole rock busts. That one yonder'll go in a year."

Over the years, Glen Rose has been prodigal with its prehistoric treasure. They cut out biscuit-like slabs of rock with single tracks and gave them away, ruined others trying. There was defacement and always weathering as new tracks were upturned by floods. They helped quar-ry the Paluxy bottom to send to New York and to Texas Memorial Museum in Austin.

What oldtimers had thought were potholes or elephant tracks were, to science, proof of what some had doubted: that the brontosaur, despite his tremendous weight, could walk. This one ran...for his life.

I've seen both Austin's and New York's excellent ex-hibits. At both, you are quite aware that is what they are — exhibits. Not so with these stone footsteps. You need pretend nothing. You know you stand where they walked. It is that knowing and looking that shakes your earth and dwarfs you.

And so you wonder what Glen Rose will do with its Di-nosaur Valley.

With Texas waking to tourism and the Paluxy hills superlative for outdoor families, Eugene Connally believes his town must do something, get help somewhere.

"Actually, people don't know what is here right now."

Here now - and forever weathered away tomorrow - with-out some help. There is, in those giant footsteps that flee and those that pursue, a sense of reality that is not exceeded in Colorado-Utah's Dinosaur National Monu-

3

ment. Glen Rose merits help.

Why not start at Blue Hole, where the American museum crew left off? The tracks show pursuit right to the bank. With the slab, they go on, below you.

For little more than the price of a highway cut, a roadside shelter and some preservative, we could follow that trail a little farther. Perhaps far enough to solve the riddle now hidden.

Did the killer catch up?

5 Million B.C.

The Great Wall of Texas

Once upon a forgotten long ago, there was — closely northeast of today's Dallas — a great city with mighty walls of crude-hewn rock. The huge rectangular stones, close to a ton each, were struggled into place much as Cheops' ancient hundred thousands built his pyramids, and the Han Dynasty, the Great Wall of China.

Perhaps these Texas walls buttressed against a prehistoric sea or forbade enemies or were temples and palaces for a Mayan kind of culture. If they were, the kingdom fell, as civilizations do. The massive walls yet lie deep below the hackberry and locust and the black waxy, rolling land that is Texas' smallest county — Rockwall.

That there was such an ancient city was the theory of practical mystics like aging Joe Wanderer, and of curious and careful men like Dr. James Glenn, Rockwall's Presbyterian minister, and of legend lovers like many of us. It is a belief shared by few geologists. They say that the walls beneath Rockwall were caused by nature: specifically volcanic lava flowing into upward fissures and hardening to what they call dikes.

I won't debate geology's wisdom. I only question Rockwall's. They can sink a few laterals and let us curious go

4

below to look at their walls and conjure up our own visions as to whether the Great Wall of Texas really was...or wasn't.

I drove U. S. 66 northeast of Dallas, scarcely clearing its fast-marching reach before I was on the shiny new service station and the cutoff to bypassed Rockwall. Then, briefly north up the old-treed hill and into the community, quiet around its square.

I walked the square from the hardware store and the saddle shop to the Rockwall *Citizen.* Dr. Glenn was away from his church, across, making his minister's calls. Finally, I found Joe Wanderer. He lived in the crowded little room behind his Mobil station, back there with a lot of growing things and the musty sense of recollections tucked away in old drawers. He was a heavy set eighty with a good, seamed face that matched his name, which matched his living since he came from the old country and tried Arkansas and Arizona before he moved to Garland, then Rockwall. A striped gray cat, old and tolerant, was all his family.

Mr. Wanderer was eating a bowl of cucumbers when I came in and asked about the wall. He studied me, making up his mind if I had come to make fun or to listen. Then he told me about the wall.

As recently as the forties, you could get to it, lots of places. They had mapped eleven sites where it lay as deep as forty feet or extruded and ran from hillsides. He showed me hard-to-argue pictures. The walls lay plumbline straight, their great stones tiered five or more courses deep, two inches of yellow-gray sandlike mortar between. Beveled tops and mortises fitted many such walls which had been exposed by cuts made by lore-seeking laymen like the Fort Worth group in 1949. The cuts are filled now.

The courses staggered their great stones, one centering above the mortised joint of the two below, the way you lay brick or tile. Where excavators had removed some, they found the rock veins in one stone cross-running to its neighbors'. It was hard to see how this ever could have been a single tabular flow, cracked into precise blocks by the weight of centuries.

Mr. Wanderer showed me strange designs which you could believe had been carved into the rock face. A turtle, part of a woman, some indecipherable. Between Rockwall and Royse City, they had found a carved serpent's head. The Mayans worshipped serpents.

"Dr. Glenn knows a lot more about this," said Mr. Wanderer.

"He's out on calls," I said.

"I spent some money printing up his book." He handed me a folder. "I spent some money digging until they stopped me. I thought we could have a tourist place and give the money to the orphans."

He thought this ancient city, deep below his town, was once a seaport, but the other folks thought it is just part of Balcones Fault, which crosses Rockwall.

Later, he rode with me northeast to see all that's left. The excavations are filled. The few great stones are heaved around, out of place. Little to show.

Even the arched fieldstone doorway at the Tom Canups' place — on the old Dallas road — is closed. When I was a kid, you could walk down the stairs and see part of the wall. Then it got to leaking and it cracked, and they closed it.

Later, I heard from Dr. Glenn. The onetime enthusiasm about what might lie below Rockwall was gone. The geologists had this whole thing carefully pinned, a million years ago, to a natural phenomenon. It's Balcones faulting, which is Cenozoic Tertiary, and that's give or take five million years.

I doubt that Joe Wanderer was ever convinced. He pointed to those course-layed, roughly even stones that made a wall, made a two-foot window in one. Maybe Balcones could have slipped and still allowed men time to quarry the rock and build walls additional to nature's.

"They think I'm crazy," was the last thing he said to me. He was looking at me with old eyes. Did I?

I sure don't. I think maybe Rockwall is, for letting geologists write an epitaph — a million years' pinpoint accuracy — to a tourist's stopover in a now bypassed town. Let them dig down; let us look. For we, who like to look also like to believe.

We know they finally found Troy. And they may yet find Atlantis.

10,000 B.C.

Ancient Story of Alibates

Anerica's true industrial colosus, 35 miles north of Amarillo, is largely unknown to you and me, and with good reason. We have been here only moments of its formidable working lifetime: more than twelve thousand years.

It has excited American archaeology three fleeting decades. So, from us well-meaning vandals, they've had to lock it secret. It rims the rugged and broad Canadian River canyon in country, until today so remote, even the wind seems lonely.

This is Alibates — to science, a complex of five hundred fifty cliff-edge flint quarries and adjoining minertown pueblos: this continent's foremost link to man's dim past. To you and me, Alibates of the immediate future should become one of America's most dramatic and intriguing national monuments. It will center one of five large recreation areas shorelining Lake Meredith, which began filling in 1965.

There it will be: one step literally from the Twentieth Century into man's deepest-known American shadows — the hundredth century before Christ. More important, here only in all America, you can turn and back trail man up the millenia to his todays.

Most important is the way you will do it — as Amarilloan Henry Hertner showed it to me. Like many a High Plainsman, this businessman is an intent and articulate his-

7

torian in country where they are still writing it. He drove me to the lofting Canadian rims where all Americans came for weapons and tools seven thousand years before the pyramids.

For one moment, contemplate that trail. Walk it, from Montana, Minnesota or California in the deadly age of the fierce-tusked mammoth and giant bison!

Now, you're ready for Alibates' long trail into time.

You leave today outside — the handsome stone and glass pavilion, bluff-perched over the lake, reaching hazy to the rims of Big Blue Canyon, far across.

Just within, a band of frenzied, aboriginal Americans are flung — spear and stone cudgel, kill and die — on a bog-trapped but fearsome ice-age mammoth. These shaggy-haired, half-naked hunters are Clovis Man, at Blackwater Draw, New Mexico, 10,000 B.C. Over west central U.S., his identifying broad spear point focuses him in time.

Yonder is Folsom Man, two thousand years later, on the kill of giant bison. His splendid flintwork ranges him far across mid continent. All about, in life-sized diorama, they march toward you: Nebraska's Scottsbluff Man, Wyoming's Eden and Dakota's Angostura Man. There is this state's Plainview Man, pegging his pronghorn . . . only 5,000 B.C.: ten centuries before the wheel.

Finally, the historic plains pueblo builder who ventilated and insulated his fine rock and adobe kivas between the crusades and Columbus. Yonder he builds.

And all, with one incredible thing in common. They are at work or kill with the best "steel" of their day - Alibates flint. All of them had to come here, for nowhere else was quarried the razor sharp, beautifully-splashed flint rainbow that is Alibates — a three-square-mile, jewel-like slab outcropping these cliffs.

Today, an archaeologist can examine a flint fragment and tell you with certainty if it is Alibates. So could any of the fierce-faced hunters about you, across all the centuries of time while these quarries yielded their thousands of tons and, with their fragments, flecked their hills to a glitter.

The pavilion level below takes you into the cliff quarry itself. There, the aboriginal gouges and batters his treasure from the outcrop. Elsewhere on the lower level, he heats, cools, flakes and chips - fashioning weapon points from the deadly fluted Folsom to the bullet-shaped Angostura.

He crafts his tools: four-bladed knife, two-edged scraper, notched hammerstone and his awl, so fine pointed it can drill a necklace of tiny California shell.

Outside, round the bluff on the trail, you realize the enormous amount of chipped-away flint tailings he left down the ages. In every color, shape and thinness, they cover the ground, in places, several feet deep.

The trail bends a half mile to a high, wide mesquite flat. Here is a hundred room pueblo, yet unexcavated, its rock wall outlines clearly defined from Coronado's time. Below and toward the lake, a lesser pueblo has been excavated and found to have been a kind of market place.

Here appeared thousands of artifacts from red Minnesota pipestone, California shell, Yellowstone obsidian, Arizona pottery. From afar, they were brought to barter for this one ageless necessity to Indian — Alibates flint. Here, apart from the quarries, Alibates' miner - manufacturer - merchant worked and lived.

"You could call this a kind of prehistoric Pittsburg," I said finally to Henry Hertner. The slim and graying Panhandle vice chairman for this monument, an ex-Aggie from back in John Kimbrough's day, nodded:

"Or Damascus...or Babylon." Then he grinned. "Or their Cibola."

Nothing else in America approaches it archaeologically, he said flatly. Nor more dramatically shows the continuity of man's dim past on this continent.

Leaving, we stopped on the highest ground, where one lone wood windmill marks today's only intrusion on this otherwise virgin land. We were a mile from the quarry. The flakes were all about, tinting every color. I picked up a blank for a hammerstone, a point that had sheared, one bead from a California shell necklace. I looked back. Behind us was only the jagged haze of the canyon and the strange-glinting empty cliffs. The monument we saw is yet to come.

Come, it must. A wise National Park Service will not allow this one total story of man to escape; and, as the lake fills, boat and car traffic will descend on this longest American story ever told. Without adequate exhibit and protection for what is there? Well...we can take it from there.

And almost certainly would.

8,000 B. C.

They Buried Him West of Del Rio

They buried him west of Del Rio, with the affection and perhaps the ceremony due an esteemed leader of their community.

They dressed him in his best. For sentiment, they put in things he had liked, also practical things he might need, journeying.

You pass his grave on U.S. 90 today, near where the Pecos Canyon cuts for the gorge of Rio Grande. The land looks as it did then: jumbled and rocky-hilled to distant blue mountains, scruffy with thorn and berry bushes. He was buried in one of the caves midway up the sheer, four hundred foot cliffs.

From a distance, above or below, you can see the caves. Neither ranchers nor science wants you in them, but the Ed McCarsons in Comstock or the Guy Skileses at Langtry can tell you their story. It is worth the stop, for this was no common burial.

This man was a great fisherman among the Basketmakers, among the earliest-known South-westerners — a race so prehistorically dim, it has been but guessed at until recently. Like many others in those high canyon caves he was buried — give or take some centuries — several thousand years ago.

It long has been surmised that the first Americans

10

crossed a land bridge from Siberia to Alaska. But only in recent decades have archaeologists been able to link prehistoric man here with his shadowy European counterpart. The Basketmaker may be such a link.

The Fisherman now lies in a reconstructed grave at the Witte Museum in San Antonio. Witte expeditions in 1933 first attracted attention to this shadow people, and University of Texas scientists have recently probed the scores of shallow, water-scooped caves along the border canyons from Big Bend to Devil's River. The Basketmaker's image is becoming clearer.

Long earlier than the cliff pueblo dwellers, he was yet a remarkable craftsman. From fibers and grasses, he fashioned thread and rope, wove intricate basketry in checkerweave or herringbone; and he knotted incredibly stout and true nets.

It is sobering to think back to when he did his work. By comparison, the pyramids are moderns and our Texas flag has stood to the winds brief minutes.

The Basketmaker — this Fisherman — was better with flint and bone than the modern Comanche. His weapon was the bow's forerunner, the notch-ended, javelin-hurling, atl-atl. He wrote pictographs on his cave walls with a brush or "ball point" of bone, fitted with a self-inking manganese stub. He fished, hunted, gathered, and farmed a little. Hundred century-old seed were found, rawhide pouched.

To the children he loved, he gave painted pebbles and shells for playthings. When they died — as so often they did — he buried them with care, wrapped in matting of lechugilla fiber. He sensed his hereafter, for he broke his child's A-shaped, woven cradle. From its grave, the cradle's spirit would follow the little one's.

This Fisherman was buried in a ceremonial fur robe. With him went his pipe, his devilshead cactus fish hooks, his rawhide tobacco pouch for cedar foliage. They put in his flint tools, a basket of food, a brush to paint his messages, and some carrying baskets. Then they "killed" his excellent hooped fishing net and sent it with him. Over all this went matting and the ashy dust of his cave.

The dry desert air virtually mummified each cave's secret, so that scientists — by carbon tests and others — could focus in time's calendar, a long-headed, small-statured race who likely preceded the ancient Mayan cultures of Mexico.

At the San Antonio museum, the Basketmaker's life and times are well documented. But you should visit his land. At Comstock and Langtry, they can show you hundreds of the artifacts he left behind.

More than that, his home. Down Rio Grande from Langtry, you can make out the smoke-stained mouths of the ancient cliff caves. You are a half mile from Roy Bean's "Law West of the Pecos" and, ironically, the same distance from where these other men bowed to an earlier and more inflexible law — that of survival.

Farther down, where the Pecos comes in below the new highway bridge there is an even easier view. From a well-appointed roadside park, you can count caves toward the canyon mouth at the lip of a spur gorge, and up the cliffs northwest. Somewhat incredibly, this well-marked park neglects to advise that, directly below where you stand, there is the ample entrance to a cave dwelling of these earliest peoples. It would seem a major point of interest for the wayfarer. It seemed so to the Smithsonian Institute. This cave, they excavated.

Perhaps one day we will let you down to the cave, let you stand in it, much as it was, when older eyes looked across the canyon.

You'll know it really isn't the same. But the rocks across and the sky will grow old, and even the wheeling bird. And you will feel the awesome weight of the long time since they buried the Fisherman west of Del Rio.

How to Dig the Past

This isn't to expose you and me for the pair of history-wrecking vandals we are. Simply, I've discovered it's more fun not to be.

Take this cave—shallow-scooped and perching the bluffs remotely back from Devil's River. You and I could enjoy it, poking around awhile. Its hundred-foot-wide mouth is a spectacular picture window, fifty stories up a canyon wall. And, take my word, the rim path down has its moments.

Shoveling away ten feet of layered floor, we'd find enough "arrowheads", all right, some quite deep. Likely, we'd skip most of the rubble — broken, pencil-sized sticks, nondescript flints and wadded fiber, some sooty smears, bits of bone and straw, like torn sombrero brims. I'd keep the big point near the bottom — for a paperweight. Good relic-hunting, sure enough!

But, swimming or fishing later, off our big-shaded camp, we'd remember the cave best for its vast view. Now that was something!

It was, indeed — in the perspective shown me recently by a team of Lubbock area amateur archaeologists. We glimpsed a relatively skilled American who has looked from this same picture window for nine thousand years.

Aside from twenty-four identifiable and time-telling point types, what did you and I miss, shoveling out ninety centuries? That wad of fiber-pouched mescal beans, for one. The beans were chewed for a technicolor trip about the time Caesar visioned a Roman world. Some centuries

13

earlier, a mother slipped off skillfully-woven sandals, thonged at toe, instep and heel. She put away her boy's tiny bow, still strung today.

That smudge was a wayfarer's campfire, the time of Egypt's pyramids; the meal, javelina pork. Careful dusting would have shown one of our sticks, an atl-atl's spear foreshaft, still fitted to its point. My paperweight was spearhead for far-ranging Plainview Man, carbon-dated 7,000 B.C.

And all the rest — fine Z-twisted cord and stout netting knotted from it; checkerweave mats and basketry that can match today's; sleek bone awls, thorn needles, and the same gouging tool that, earlier in Europe, put an eye in the needle and clothed man to survive the Ice Age. We really missed the relics.

Also, we forever destroyed the whole picture.

With a skilled team, this cave becomes methodically different from ours. It recesses a half-dome fifty feet back from the cliff lip, where three quarter-inch screens swirl dust devils in the high canyon wind; and from the screens each artifact goes to a precise classification carton. Across the floor, stakes grid five-foot horizontal squares; and from above, a level line gives vertical reference.

The dusty, purposeful people about? Some wholesome families, from teen-agers up, like yours and mine. Their South Plains Archaeological Society, as others in Texas, has four watchwords: disciplined excavation, recording, analysis and reporting — to the pros at our university science centers.

Complicated? They're really charting a three-dimensional jigsaw. And archaeology - man's infinite unwritten history - gets one page here, accurate as possible. This could be any one of the hundreds of shadow sites in Texas - pueblo to midden and cave to mound - from Panhandle to coast and mountain to pines.

To Texas archaeology, our cave is Val Verde Dig No. 213, in rugged back country between Juno and Comstock. Exact location? It's closed to all but the qualified team

14

headed by Floydada insurance man Jim Word - one of the rare and wise breed who relaxes and finds fascination really exploring our past. In spare time, his team has worked this cave for two years.

"Some day, we'll have good teams all over Texas." Jim Word knocked dust from a battered hat and squinted a level over the pit in Grid Five. From it, he would trace the width of the time-layer designated Zone Three. "Do it right, you really enjoy it."

"Suppose I'd do it right," I suggested. "How long before I could help?"

"Right away." From the level bubble, Jim ran his tape. "Under supervision."

Presently in Square Seven, Zone Three, Val Verde 213, I gingerly brushed free a small sandal, dating about with Rome's fall. My partner was pretty, freckle-faced Charlene Bandy, who was to enter Brownfield High the next year. Checking from over our shoulders was her dad, who also likes the fishing and freedom from his business phone out here. Somewhere close by, he was sure, were the burials that will tell much more of the man at Val Verde 213.

You look at that sandal and think how short is Texas' four century written record. Before water filled the Lewisville Reservoir near Dallas, they traced one of America's oldest, some forty thousand years back. But what really lies behind our curtain? Europe has gone back a half million years.

Back at camp, you consider today's archaeologist, with his new, close-dating techniques, developed these last fifty years. Pro or amateur like Jim Word, he is an intelligent, curious, patient, and relaxed man. No ulcers. No skepticism. I know that sandal cut me to size.

Want to give it a try, maybe work into a team? Then contact your local archaeological society; they'll help you from there. If you don't know them, write the University of Texas Archaeological Research Center in Austin. They do. They even hold schools for beginners like us.

And, after you've worked a site right — say like Val Verde 213 — you'll find each day's swimming, fishing and relaxing even more fun.

You will know a little more about the American who splashed, fished and hunted this water, ninety centuries before you.

1542 A.D.

Strangers at the Sacred Fire

The oldest capital of this land of the Tejas is not Austin, nor those short-lived others, not by many a century. It is an Indian temple mound in the broad, timbered valley between the Angelina and Neches Rivers, 35 miles west of Nacogdoches.

That it was spiritual Mecca to the handsome, industrious and once highly advanced Indian known to early Spaniard as *Tejas*, none know better than Jacksonville historian Jack Moore. Much of the forested Tejas triangle between Frankston, Nacogdoches and Crockett, he has researched, mapped and explored afoot.

For how long, Mecca? University of Texas archaeologists are yet painstakingly threading this. They can trace three civilizations to shadows perhaps as deep as Mexico's goldsmiths and pyramid-builders. From this mound — earth instead of rock — a temple looked to the sun for a sophisticated civilization, long before Europe's knights crusaded for Jerusalem.

Like a half-block, broad-topped river levee, the pine-tufted mound lies south of Texas 21 at road edge. Texas forestry's Indian Mound Nursery, close by, grows seedling pine and cottonwood in neat rows. Once the land grew nearly all your supermarket vegetables before Europeans knew of such as corn, tobacco, squash, pumpkin or the rest. Across to the north beyond the farm buildings, are two lesser mounds on private land. But this one lofted the temple.

16

It has been excavated, shifted, replaced. Of the thousands of artifacts it yielded (aside from burials and building remains), you can see some of the really singular handicraft at the University's Memorial Museum in Austin, from gorget to urn to effigy pipe.

So don't dig. You can find more, anyhow, standing on top and looking back on time...just as the tribal spiritual chief, the *Grand Xinesi*, came from his temple's eternal fire and gazed on his city, one of the latter mornings in the life of his civilization.

A good morning, thought the *Xinesi*, even for the old and wise. With this season of the bud softly on, there came the growing smell from river forest and field. His temple, higher than any flood should reach, was like the town buildings circling about, only grander — fifty feet across. Wall poles, bent to a dome lashing, were interwoven with cane, grass-thatched outside and plastered within: white — for purity.

From the eternal fire by the centered altar, sacred smoke rose, chimneyed east, for messages from its spirit father at the sun...or perhaps beyond.

About the town square were the other beehive buildings, blue inside for sky's beauty. Here lived the chief warriors and elders. Directly across was the council house for each day's meeting. Beyond were the lesser houses, dotted with farms which the community worked together. He could see them in the east field today, singing the rhythmic growing songs. Good, the sound of singing work.

In the houses, finished with new-plastered walls, the women weaved mulberry or feathered cloth; mended, worked the buckskin golden, the buffalo and bear robes, supple and warm. Since first call by the crier, day-long cooking had begun: bread, nut butters, meats, flours. Yonder they glazed pottery, fashioned tight-meshed cane platters and basketry.

The very young were with each family's eldest and, far across on the playing field, the boys were practicing for the coming festival's races and games.

17

The *Xinesi* contemplated today's meeting. All would be heard until done, then they would finally follow the elders as they should. He would counsel as always; there should be pleasantly little. The neighboring friendship pacts were again firm. Treaties were renewed as far as Choctaw and Alabama and, it seemed, north even beyond Shawnee. The buffalo hunt was arranged for another season to the far west plains.

Town affairs? Not too much. A house-raising and a new field to discuss. A marriage to approve if each family elder consented. No quarrelers nor impudent young to banish, no lashings. Perhaps a third wife for the young chief's house yonder, for he proved rapidly. He might be chosen war chief when his uncle joined his ancestors.

Ended even was the blood right feud with the village north. The *Xinesi* had counseled well; it was wiser to take the gifts and the captive as substitute for the son who had killed. Sacrificial fire had accepted that substitute; the back-and-forth family killing could end.

It seemed too good that, once again, no war pole would be drummed and danced erect to splash red and black. They had besought all aid wisely, last time: fire to burn and water to drown enemies; snake to strike and storm to blind. Deer had granted speed; bear, bravery; panther, cunning; and dog, loyalty. Sacred smoke had bathed their warriors to turn enemy arrows.

They had killed one and lost one; the war was over fairly. Bad to spill Indian blood. All things, the *Grand Xinesi* knew, were either good or bad.

He crossed the temple matting. The eternal fire glowed red under its consecrated walnut logs. About the altar were the great glazed urns with bear oil, corn or tobacco for incense prayer; the ready wood, the delicately wrought bottles and pitchers. Beyond the benches, on the tall rawhide shelves around the wall, were the rest: basketry with sacred pipes and knives, his vestments hanging — feathered cloth and pale buckskin, the robes, his neck and head ornaments, serpented staff and power pouch: things of the spirit. He took only enough for a pleasant, uncomplicated meeting.

He summoned his assistant; this evening they would remove some of the sacred ash to its rest behind the temple. There was too much here; the fire was not pleased.

It flickered as though a harsh wind had come. Through his lifetime he had watched this fire as forgotten ancestors had watched it — even from the first ancestor who brought it to a temple, the old tales said, somewhere below him in the mound. He regarded his sacred fire. It was not good for the fire to be displeased, guttering so.

Should it ever cease to burn, his nation would die.

He found the council gathering early about a runner from the east.

"We shall have visitors within seven suns," the war chief told him.

"You have ordered that they be met and carried with celebration to feast — as is our custom?" the *Grand Xinesi* asked.

"I have. These are strangers. They wear strange garments."

"All come here," the *Xinesi* replied, "as they should. Even strangers must know we are of the nation, strong in many allies and friends."

"They know indeed we are *Tejas*." The other's eyes were lidded. "They come looking for us."

"Well, then . . ."

"Their faces," he heard the other say, "are white."

The Lady in Blue

This is the story of Texas' infinite journey, more than three centuries ago. It is not Cabeza de Vaca's ordeal nor Coronado's search. Neither is it a story for skeptics.

From Nacogdoches' redland pines to Rio Grande sierra, smoky over Presidio, is reasonably far, some seven hundred miles. But travel it five hundred times and begin each journey a world away in Spain. There, you have an odyssey!

With this one, you trace the thin edge between history and legend; and you follow this land's most mysterious pilgrim—lovely, dark-eyed, Maria de Agreda—our perhaps miraculous "Lady in Blue."

Sixty years before Paso del Norte's first Texas missions, Maria knew those western mountains. Eastward, toward today's San Angelo, she visited the earlier-than-Comanche Jumano at their Paint Rock Concho River cliffs. Far east, she saw beehive huts and pines of the Tejas.

Throughout a decade, beginning in 1620, old story travels her across all this, scores of times — this blue-caped nun of Spain's mountain village, Agreda.

Impossible? Not to her patron church of St. Francis, whose Christianity she must help send to Texas. And not to Indians awaiting her there. To both, Maria was real...and miracle.

Her physical being, you see, never left her convent in Spain.

Born in 1602 to devout parents in Agreda, Maria entered

convent at sixteen, a time when New Spain glittered with riches and Franciscan mission challenge. A time when conquistador and padre, uneasily allied, have been in New Mexico scarcely a decade.

New Spain dazzles the girl with deep eyes. But hers is the discipline and reward of St. Francis: give utterly to help the poorest. Raptly she contemplates the faraway Indian — a soul, she feels, most in need of all. More and more she fixes her mind upon the Indian. And now, indeed, she sees him!

Outside drifts word of her — lying near-lifeless for long periods. She confesses simply that she has been with them — coppery people in mountain, plain and forest; in skin tent or thatched. She teaches in her tongue; they understand in theirs. For this decade of the 1620's, her visitations increase: dozens, scores, now hundreds. She wakes in total recall of explicit detail, even to Franciscan brothers now there, unknown to her. Can this be true bi-location?

The church must seek proof. Has she been seen across the sea?

In his dusty mission refectory, down Rio Grande from Santa Fe, Fray Alonso de Benavides awaits his replacement, now after ten years remotely north here. He ponders the Indians camped outside the mission; shortly he must tell those patient Jumanos there are not yet enough brothers to staff the mission they ask, far east. A pity! Each year they have trudged an emptiness to ask that mission.

But now the supply train — first in four years — and with it, New Mexico's new *custodio*...and news of Spain. No, Fray Alonso knows nothing of the young nun of Agreda, not even her village. He listens more carefully. He calls for the Jumanos.

They point to the picture on the refectory wall - an elderly nun of Mexico City. It is one such as she... but young and beautiful, in the sky's color. Yes, she has come to them in their village; in fact, it is she who has sent them to him asking the mission each time. She comes from the sky.

21

Why had they not told him this? He had not asked.

Excitedly, the *custadio* sends two priests to accompany the Jumanos as far, ultimately, as Concho's painted cliffs. They return bringing startling word. A procession met them ... hundreds ... bearing a rough cross ... seeking baptism ... miraculously familiar with the *doctrina*. No! No, they had never seen a priest; only the Lady in Blue!

More, in the Jumano village were messengers from tribes far east. She had sent them!

Returning to Spain, Fray Alonso must ask more help for the Jumanos...and for those of the forests somewhere beyond, those called *Tejas*. But first he must see the Nun of Agreda. He finds her, scarcely twenty-nine, in coarse gray and white habit with a long sackcloth cape...blue. In her convent he listens in growing awe.

With incredible detail she describes the land he left and its people. How could she know the one-eyed captain and old Fray Cristobal Quiros? Yet she details the temporary mission he sent to the Jumanos. Of course, she sent the party to meet them.

He shakes his head; he can recognize the great river mountains she describes — they flanked his trail back to Mexico. He knows nothing of the forests she speaks of, the ones far to the east.

But he reports to his church, "I am absolutely convinced!"

Equally convinced is that Franciscan order. Truly, Maria de Agreda has been transported. She is convent abbess here; there, she must be the Lady in Blue.

Over the years that Franciscans march that New World north, they remain certain of their Nun of Agreda, even after she dies at 63. Fifteen years later, the white missions of Paso del Norte are begun; Jumanos come again up the river seeking churches. And across where Rio Conchos slashes Mexico for Rio Grande, today's Presidio will remain from the early river-reed jacals — Jumano-built with a knowledge saved from their long ago Lady in Blue.

And far to the east, now searching La Salle's French fort, another Franciscan, devout Fray Damian Massanet, will plan what is to become Nacogdoches, Mission San Francisco de los Tejas. He has met a Tejas chief who shows him — this year of 1690 — an altar and cross passed on from a Tejas father. Fashioning it was taught that man by a beautiful woman who came from the sky and wore its color.

An infinite journey?
Of course, we skeptics can write it off. An Indian tale to get gifts, not Christianity. A too-vivid imagination of a young girl, fervent in her early vows. And a need to believe by those long ago, wilderness-walking padres.
Not bi-location. Not a literal projection of image and voice across space!
No, the Lady in Blue isn't for skeptics.
Well . . . leave them to television.

Early 1700's

Dead Man's Tank

South of San Antonio is Atascosa County with its twin cities of Pleasanton and Jourdanton. Below them is where Dick Wiley has lived a long, long time near a forgotten and bypassed village, once called something other than its present name, Christine.
Dick Wiley and I, and a few of us who like legend better than statistics, are convinced he lives near a settlement as old as San Antonio's Presidio de Bejar.
Atascosans refer to the south pasture of the Wiley farm as their greatest mystery — Dead Man's Tank. The name is gruesomely precise. In 1928, digging a stock tank, Mr. Wiley cut away a bank which, when carefully excavated, revealed the charred ruins of a log fort, an immediate count of sixty-eight skeletons — some, babies not yet teething. Arrowheads were imbedded in their skulls, even in their open, screaming mouths.
University of Texas and San Antonio museum people determined the age of these skeletons, as well as the

burned fort — all crumbling at air's touch — to be three centuries, give or take some decades.

Some years ago, a Houston historian, Clement Hoyt, located a Spanish map of the early 1700's. Here,where the Camino Real crossed from the Frio to the San Antonio, there was an early mission, fort and smelter.

Mr. Wiley, who looks and talks like Frank Dobie, believes that this was an early mine-seeking outpost from earlier Spanish missions like San Juan Bautista, across the Rio Grande. There is no question in his mind but that there was one fearful massacre that left the settlement as lost as sacked Troy.

He took me the mile or so through the fence gaps to the lower mott of elm and oak. We walked the last part, for underbrush is thick and the trails are few. The few Texans who knew of it have forgotten this place.

What is called the tank is actually a perfect-circled island two hundred feet across. Around it is an old moat that time has filled approximately fifteen feet. A draw drops down to it and when heavy rains came, back in the twenties, Mr. Wiley noticed the way the water backed up. Seemed to be a dam that flooded everything but what looked to be an island. A little cutting would make a good stock tank.

He brought in his worker, Juan Vasquez, told him to cut away that bank. Juan walked around the moat, began to study the trees. There are faint marks today on those trees.

One that points to water, one to buried treasure and one, Juan insisted, that pointed to "many dead." Juan said the marks were priest-made; he couldn't dig. Finally, dig, he did; and the first cut uncovered the old bank-imbedded granary, eighty by twenty feet.

"Skulls came rollin' down that bank like coconuts," said Mr. Wiley. "I got the sheriff. When the museum folks told how old they were, he quit worryin'." Mr. Wiley reflected. "Sheriff first looked at me funny, all them skeletons. I said, 'Look here, Sheriff, I wouldn'ta used a bow and arrow. Not on that many.'"

The old Spanish map showed the original plan. A forted island, protected with the flood of a moat, dammed up. Across the dam, a granary, heavy-logged. Near the granary, a smelter. They found the ruins of all three. Charred corner joints. Burned earth and slag twelve feet deep with silver traces.

And the skeletons around the island fort, even in the outlying fields. Stone axes and close-range arrows had done the work. The biggest and most pitiful mass of debris had been trapped or thrown into the sunken granary and everything fired.

"Must've caught 'em by surprise," Mr. Wiley thought. "Moat must have been empty. Why they were turnin' a hog's hindquarters on the fire in the fort when it happened. We found the fireplace and the whole bone."

How does he figure a fort? The Spanish map. The priests' tree signs, faint in the upper oak bark. And the age? The map again. And what those museum people told him.

What connection had it with San Antonio? Mr. Wiley didn't know, but it dead-centered Camino Real, heading there. On the way to Alamo, Santa Anna camped in that grove a mile atop the rise. He could not account for the presence of the smelter either; the nearest hills would have made a hard day's ride northwest. But they *had* found the ashes and silver traces. They *had* found the charred log remains of a fort, built the way the Spaniards constructed their first ones in Texas. They *had* found those skeletons.

What were his plans for Dead Man's Tank? He wasn't sure, getting along in years. But he'd be glad to take folks down there and walk them around that filled-in moat, show them the burned ground, the granary bank, the cut-away dam. They could look up and, like him, see those Lipans come pouring through the trees.

He guessed he'd let folks make up their minds, by themselves.

I have, mine.

Mr. Wiley lived in a mighty old town.

Paint Rock's Massacre Story

Traveling westerly for San Angelo, you'll find the two quiet towns of Menard and Paint Rock, forty mile neighbors, more or less on your route. They are musts for however brief your visit.

On the pecan-banked San Saba, Menard has one of our state's least known, yet — in many ways — most important Spanish mission-presidios. Much of its significance derives from the macabre — the manner and results of its death.

To the north, Paint Rock's Concho canyon walls show an intriguing record of Indian pictography. This primitive calendar-almanac-newspaper binds these two locales with at least a two-century knot of time. I hope you come on them as I did, and in the same order.

I dropped in on Menard's Bob Weddle. Former Dallas United Press staffman, he writes with a taut pen and today edits a weekly so that he can stick with book writing. He has published a detailed study on *The San Saba Mission*.

The mission was anchor bastion on the third, last and most northwesterly surge of the Franciscan friars into the lonely land they called *Apacheria*.

In 1757, San Saba was the most heavily-garrisoned outpost of all — a hundred toops mounting presidio guard. Yet within a year, its log-built mission was burned, two priests and seventeen others murdered, the beleaguered garrison driven out.

Affronted Spanish arms took one year to muster the most formidable punitive force yet thrown against the

Indian. Presidio San Saba saw them launched in a drive that was to secure New Spain's frontiers forever, then saw them reel back from near rout at the Red River.

The western missions were abandoned. Presently, the whole century-and-a-half Franciscan effort had collapsed. After that, few ventured as far as San Saba. Of course, Jim Bowie carved his name in the archway in 1831 when he was lost-mine hunting. But then, that was Jim Bowie.

How does the Paint Rock story connect?

The pictograph cliffs lie on private land owned by the family of Mrs. Ellen Hartgrove Sims, a lovely and lively lady who took me through a mile of canyon and fifteen hundred cunieformed Indian symbols for which there is no Rosetta stone.

The road is easy, dropping below the eastern thrust of limestone blocks which rim a hundred foot high bluff with square-faced rock tablets. The rock is minutely covered with the careful handiwork of ancient men who recorded their boasts, their hopes, their drouths, their battles and victories, their despairs and deaths. Many, Mrs. Sims concedes, even the archaeologists can't decipher.

She stopped us under one that needed no guesswork. On an upper ledge was the sprawled body of a skirted frontier woman. Ahead was a shield with two crossed lances. Below, two scalps. Then some sign which Mrs. Sims thinks meant the prowess which destroyed a lonely wagon once headed west.

There are recurring turtles. They could be a warrior's amulet. They could mean slow tribal travel the direction of the arrows. The same is perhaps true for the birds which fly perpetually against their rocky sky. There are countless painted hands, possibly an Indian abacus. Marching vertical lines — armies?

Mrs. Sims showed me the Indian's deathly fear of his ultimate enemy, starvation. There were stalks of corn and bright, bright sun and grasshoppers. There were happier signs of turkey and buffalo, times of the full belly.

There is a vivid red devil, horned and tailed. There is a wedding gone wrong: the bridegroom standing on his head, the bride running off with somebody else. There is the same strange circled cross which has turned up in the bushman caves in Europe and Asia, even in the Bible's land of Ur. It meant power.

And, of course, Mrs. Sims showed me the defacement that finally locked her ranch gates to free entry. Names painted on the wall, scars left by a rifleman.

How old is this? Three hundred years, her best guess. But them, those fading old ones . . . There could have been others fading when they were young. And yet others.

Finally, Mrs. Sims showed me the two pictographs I most wanted to see. I knew their date precisely: 1758. One showed a Spanish mission afire. The other showed priests being murdered.

Bob Weddle had told me to look for them. The Indians had made two mistakes, his research showed: showing two towers on the mission instead of one, showing three priests killed instead of two.

Bob figures that in the lust of Indian killing, it was easy to get confused.

You can see the Paint Rock story; it has been reopened. And, of course, I recommend seeing the mission-presidio, then the cliffs, in the order I did.

It isn't often you can find the story of a book reviewed by rock-painting Indians two hundred years earlier.

Tattooed Cannibals of the Coast

"They drive a stake into the ground...kindle a huge fire...bind the victim."

Writing his report, the distressed padre felt cold sweat under his cassock, and his quill trembled. Yet he must assess Spain's mission hope with these coastal savages of Tejas, now after a half-century's trying. He set his jaw.

"As soon as the discordant notes of the cayman are heard, they begin to dance and jump about the fire, making a great number of gestures and terrible grimaces, and uttering sad, unnatural cries...

"Dancing and leaping and with sharp knives in their hands, they draw near the victim, cut off a piece of his flesh, come to the fire and half-roast it, and...within sight of the victim himself...devour it most ravenously..."

These were the Indian orgies, each time they ran away from the mission. Fray Gaspar Jose de Solis stared, sickened, at the parchment — his Texas coast inspection, this *Anno Domini* 1768. He had related their three-day dances to exhaustion: gourd drum, toneless reed flute and reptile horn...marijuana, peyote and yaupon-crazed shrieks...upside-down roastings...on totem sticks, skulls of their enemies!

He finished. *Their enemies? All mankind!* They were depraved beyond hope!

These? The Karankawa! Tattooed cannibal giant then astride all the Texas coast from today's Galveston to South Padre's tip. For them Fray Gaspar foresaw only oblivion.

29

To be utterly erased today, the Karankawa cast a long, grisly shadow across written Texas history, for — holding the coast — it was he who greeted all comers, from Galveston-enslaved Cabeza de Vaca to three-century-later Stephen Austin. To both — and all between — Karankawa spelled absolute bestiality.

Up Matagorda Bay, La Salle's pitiful survivors knew them for coppery-naked, near-seven-foot giants with persimmon wood bows no other could draw: tattooed ghouls reeking with alligator grease, mud and shark oil, and cowering or murderous on whim.

To colliding explorer and searching mission priest, they worsened — to gutteral-grunting, fire-dancing cannibal. Fray Gaspar was echoed in the early 1800's by hardbitten Jean Lafitte: "Demons from hell! They ate two of my men!"

Then demons to all men. To civilized Tejas, as to Comanche they were "killers" . . . "carrion eaters". Stephen Austin summed them finally and prophetically:

"They are the universal enemy of man. There is no way...except extinction."

The American Indian fell; these were obliterated.

The last coastal Texan drifted, his ranks thinning, toward Mexico. Legend says he burned his boats on Padre's south tip and committed racial suicide. Other accounts, no less grim, face him near Rio Grande City in the 1850's, with Mexican Indian cannibals.

In all events, the Karankawa is hard tracing. The University of Texas' Memorial Museum displays a diorama and artifacts in Austin. Down the coast — west Galveston Island to Copano Bay — granite markers fragment his story. On South Padre's resort tip, Realtor Bill Greene shows a portrait of old fisherman Emilio, said by some to have been last of the Kronks, tottering to mend nets for Port Isabel boats.

I think you can discover the real coastal Texan, just over the Padre causeway from Corpus Christi. This is Louis Rawalt's "Coastway" - a weathered frame mecca for fishermen and tourists. Rawalt is a lanky and quiet fisherman and scholar who came here from World War I and study at the Sorbonne. None know Padre better; few can equal his archaeological exploration of it: painstakingly, these last four decades.

Dusty history relates a vast Spanish treasure fleet, storm-wrecked in 1553, its survivors killed down the dunes to one priest who finally reached Tampico. Rawalt has silver and gold reales — 1553 — from that fleet. From that first Karankawa-Spanish collision, he can take you forward, with iron or bottle glass points, to the 1800's.

Or back to incredible shadow — the Aransas focus, now believed well over ten thousand years ago. Along the route, you may see a people developing to first rate craftsmanship and diligence. Here is an icepick-thin flint awl, a carefully beveled knife, an excellent whetstone, a perfectly rounded, smooth hide polisher.

Among the scores of points and tools is a tiny Perdiz "arrowhead", a quarter-inch across the base and delicate as an amber snowflake. It predates the crusades.

"It wasn't for any use," says Rawalt. "Some granddaddy made it for the kids."

His favorite piece—a true enigma—is a beautifully carved serpentine figurine from the La Venta Mayas: up somehow to these Texas Phoenicians from the dim, advanced cultures of Yucatan and Central American jungles.

His oldest artifacts are the shell tools of the Aransas, a conch-center awl, a scraping adze that carbon dates over eighteen thousand years.

When did the terrible Karankawa come? Rawalt shakes his head. But there was a skilled and diligent race here once — at least abreast of their times.

And cannibalism? He finds no truly-old evidence of it.

"Some of de Vaca's men, in order to survive, practiced it." Rawalt shrugs. "I'm not sure the Indian didn't pick it up, then turn it to his own ritual."

And he rejects the idea that the last of the Karankawa mass-suicided on Padre. "They went into Mexico. They had trouble there. What happened to the last of them? Well, it didn't happen here on Padre."

What did happen on Padre leaves you, as always in dim past, with guesswork.

There were people of relative skill, for a long time in what had to be a land of plenty. Food from the sea and game on abundant coastal prairie. Yet ultimately, this man of the coast plumbed the pit of blood-lusting depravity. You'll leave Louis Rawalt without a why for that.

But you wonder if, somewhere along the way, that forgotten man walked through too much abundance...first to laziness . . . then apathy . . . then decadence — even the thin shell of his civilization fallen away to savagery.

And so...to oblivion.

Worth thinking about, isn't it?

1830

Kiowa Sign at Hueco Tanks

Lonely Hueco Tanks are what you discover in them - ancient oasis and trailmark, one waterhole east of El Paso; giant-jumbled rock fading hundreds of Indian pictographs. Perhaps you'll find the thank-prayer of Kone-au-beah, Kiowa brave.

You hunt crag, crevice and cave, the mile-across, four hundred foot high devil's rockpile that jags dark against pastel desert. You find hidden springs, overhung rock potholes for timeless cisterns, broken canyons and, all about, old Indian sign — each a story. I could never find it, but there should be one for Brother Wolf and Brother Comanche, and for a kind god, Tai-me.

Dying alone, across where the hills rim morning, one Kiowa brave had time to contemplate them all...and how they came upon him.

This early fall of the 1830's, his band of ten warriors had come raiding the adobes of Paso del Norte. Straight into ambush! Then a desert race for life with too many horsemen, fast as they. Their mustangs made the ances-

32

tral rocks, old beyond memory...the blind canyon, the cave overhang with its clear pool. But muskets thundered close; the last horse pitched, dying with his rider, into their pool of water.

Within the cave, Kone-au-beah's braves fought back, an arrow only to count. Thirst came and friend Dagoi, darting gloom for the pool, brought water with a shatered leg. Then night fires sprang the outer rims and made the cave mouth death!

Kone-au-beah tried the thin, rear crevice. The enemy was above, dropping serpents that rattled death. Time closed in. The cornered Kiowa knew what we call siege. Six hungered, thirsting days! Finally, they had no choice.

Break clear...or die in the open like warriors.

Guarding emigrant trains west in 1849, Captain Randolph Marcy sighted his trail on the cortorted rock. *Hueco*—for the cistern holes—was Butterfield's last stage stop to El Paso, middling the way west from St. Louis to California.

Those hurried travelers glimpsed the red, white and black Indian paintings, the carved petroglyphs: white snake and headless woman, grotesque hunters leaping a rabbit dance. Other sign of plenty: antelope, red deer. Perhaps famine in grasshopper yonder. Leering face masks, insects strange as the giant scorpion with human head or the great dragonfly, eternally awing his dark rock sky.

But Indian sign meant Indian, and so these paused no longer than to write their own names on Hueco rock - traveler Argus, 1849; Pinkerton, 1853. Scores more, as years and wayfarers passed. In 1920, Smithsonian Institute estimated two thousand pictographs — an intense concentration of almanac history. Underneath, atop, within...wherever Indian fancy. Great age was ascribed by some, perhaps relating to pre-Incan Peruvian cave signs. Many were modern as Apache, and Kiowas.

And over these years, El Pasoans camped the big-rocked, shady canyons, picnicked the pools, called for state preservation against steadily increasing vandalism.

33

East of El Paso, 25 miles up U.S. 62, is Hueco's turn-off — eight miles of fair gravel. The rock crouches a broad valley sloped to gentle mountain. Round its north shoulder is the stone ruin of Old Butterfield's stage stop, beside one of the old natural cisterns. It is hard to tell if this could have been Kone-au-beah's cave, for these latter years have added something else, to no advantage. A make believe ghost town. And, aside from litter, the rest of the ruin is defacement. Over many a faint symbol from the centuries, you can read "Johnny dates Mary '63" in a dozen variants. It is a sad thing, the careless destruction of old story.

Somewhere written on the rocks, for example, must be the end of Kiowa Kone-au-beah's saga.

That darkest hour, his men broke across the dim-fired cave mouth. *Mejicano* guns were orange eyes and thunder. Helping Dagoi, Kone-au-beah saw two friends fall, felt the hot fist strike his thigh, stumbled on. Now, the shadowed rock wall, and up!

Dagoi could not climb. "Tell my father!" he cried out and put his back to the rock. Kone-au-beah looked on his boyhood friend a long instant...and went up.

From the dark beyond, he heard the guns for Dagoi; then he was down from the rock, running the night desert. Pain was knife; leg was broken stick. Yet on he ran. Too slow! Too slow for his brothers to escape!

Before first light they left him as he demanded, when he could not rise. Round his body, they walled rocks. Pull them down on him when the thing came finally to eat him.

He waked to Sun, felt it go. Sun burned his eyes, made him smell his wound and feel it crawl. His tongue choked. Could he reach his knife to finish it? He waked again to night wind. Wind? or the eagle bone whistle of his good god, Tai-me?

It was Tai-me's voice. "Have courage. Help comes!" He felt cool rain loose his tongue, wash his eyes to see. See clearly! Above him, sharp ears, thin muzzle. Wolf! He could not reach his knife.

Could this be *Brother Wolf?* Into Kone-au-beah's hole he came; and presently, the Kiowa felt him licking the wound, as he would his own. A long time, this; then beside him, curled to warm. Warm beside him the whole night through. The brave waked to Sun. Wolf was gone.

Yet back again with dark, Brother Wolf cared that wound and lay close. And Kone-au-beah waked, once more alone, to struggle with Sun. The third night, Brother Wolf rose and howled long, then again and again. Then he was gone.

Above him now, Kone-au-beah could see the broad face, eyes glittering, silent in the night. It was Friend Comanche, the Kiowa remembered last.

They bathed him carefully, then salved him with buffalo tallow. Finally, they fed him broth - the thin, keen strength from stripped, dried hump. The Kiowa remembered little of the travois on which they trailed him, up the slopes and over the passes, finally to the shaded waters and teepees of his people.

There the Comanche left him. They also left him a symbol of Tai-me. He had talked much of Tai-me, it was told him; even of Brother Wolf and Brother Comanche. And Kone-au-beah lived and grew old and wise in years, as a man should.

Such wisdom would return him to the rock, one day, to leave his thanks. So it must be there.

Our trouble - all our Hueco Tanks these days - is correctly reading good sign.

And painting over what we cannot understand.

Cherokee at Texas Trailend

Meandering the forested hills near Tyler and Jacksonville are some little back roads which tourist-minded East
Texans should mark as a trail. There is beauty, spring
to winter, and up those Neches woodlands, a poignant
story known to very few.

A wayfarer crosses the last Cherokee nation, a million-
acre piece of Texas between the Sabine, Neches and
Angelina Rivers. Our infant republic ceded it to the Indians by an 1836 war-time treaty and, after independence,
felt compelled to take it back.

I would call it the Cherokee Trail, for where it ends
— in a broad valley northwest of Tyler — there ended the
proud Cherokee people as an independent nation. That
the Indian still claims this land is another story — for the
lawyers.

The trail was shown me by graying, soft-spoken
Jacksonville historian, Jack Moore. He knows the Texas
Cherokee as do few; and, to him, the trail begins at wooded,
red-hilled Alto and Rusk, to the south, veers east to Henderson, then north to some drowsy little villages that today
are called Noonday and Teaselville and Chandler.

Originally, the Cherokees were Allegheny Mountain
Carolinians, aristocratic southern cousins to the Iriquois
and Hiawatha's Hurons. They felt Anglo pressure early:
in the American Revolution they found themselves fighting on both sides.

Trying to adjust as driven westward — to Tennessee and

Georgia, then Arkansas and Mississippi — they modeled on the U.S.: government, schools, even a written language. They would co-exist ... if they could find some land they could hold.

In the early 1820's, before Stephen Austin's colonists, they settled in East Texas. A red-headed, tall-standing, freckle-faced half Scotsman — already old in Cherokee war councils — led them to the new lands Mexico offered colonists. He was a deep mixture of Scotsman's independence and Indian's need for solitude. All he wanted for his people was to be let alone. He was known simply as Chief Bowles.

To Mexico City went Cherokee emissaries for land grants in the country triangled today from Mineola to Longview, across the top, down to a southern apex between what is now Crockett and Nacogdoches. They got promises.

From the restless, expanding *Tejano*, they got promises, too. One, they could believe; it was from their blood brother, Sam Houston. This could finally be their land. With Texas in the balance between Alamo and San Jacinto, Chief Bowles held his fifteen hundred horsemen in check — men who could have raked Texas from the rear.

Perhaps the chief secretly hoped Texan and Mexican would just destroy each other. But he had Sam Houston's sash and sword and a treaty signed by his nation and the Texans — done in the creek bottoms near today's Henderson. Then the war was over and an angry Bowles learned that the Texas senate had refused Houston's treaty.

Finally he learned of a new president, Mirabeau Lamar, who suspected an alliance between Mexico and the Texas Indians. And from his village, near today's Alto, he learned of the Texan army coming to drive the Cherokee once more from the land.

Five hundred *Tejanos* were coming with strong names like Rusk, Burleson, and Albert Sidney Johnston. From the red oak, sweet gum and pine bottoms where the Indian had built his mounds for centuries, Chief Bowles began a last retreat for his people. Through the little strung-out Indian villages, he fell back — past now Rusk and Jacksonville. Finally, with the Neches at his back, he stood.

At a high, wooded prairie just above where Tom Kirkpatrick's corner grocery stands today at Teaselville, the Texan army camped. Six miles north, in the walnut grove east of little Noonday, Chief Bowles made his last campfire. Then he sent down the Cherokee word.

They would go no farther. They would fight.

Three miles northwest of Chandler, where an iron stake marks the ground in the back yard of Bayless Allen's place on Battle Creek, the Cherokees made their first stand — late afternoon, July 15, 1839. They carried away their dead — too many for those they took of the Texans. Through the night, they fell back along their river.

By morning, they stood again—this time near the Neches headwaters on the William Harper place, just over the new Dallas-Tyler highway. From the high, broad hill by the Harper's redwood and brick house, they were beaten into the bottoms where the trees curve along the river.

Old Chief Bowles saw his warriors die as long as they could, then break and flee. With the sash and sword Sam Houston had given him, he stayed to die.

You can find all these places, even without the markers that should be there. And, pressed close by the forests or looking high from the uplands, it is a fine drive. In the spring, there will be the smell of awakening land; in the summer, the lazy sounds and even to late fall, the blazing colors - from sweetgum's scarlet to sycamore's gold.

But of the places to stop and ponder the way it was, my favorite is the old land where Chief Bowles halted with the river at his back and sent his answer to ultimatum that he must leave Cherokee land.

A war chief who deserts his people, he told the Texans, dies by Indian code. To stand and fight is to die in the Texas guns. So, for an old man, it is really a choice of how to die. It was his considered judgment to die as an Indian.

He was like Horatius at the Bridge: "And how can man die better, than facing fearful odds...for the ashes of his fathers...and the temples of his gods?"

There was one difference. Horatius lived in a day when Romans held their bridges.

1840

Charge of the Light Brigade

Used to be, any Texas boy could recite *The Charge of the Light Brigade* from the first half-a-league-onward right into the mouth of hell, where they rode back, but not the Six Hundred. We knew there never was another cavalry charge like that one.

We were wrong. There was one in Texas that was bigger, faster, better-ridden, as desperate of purpose and as foredoomed to defeat as that which the British chasseurs hurled at Balaklava.

To trace its seven hundred mile sweep today, you trail dusty names like Council House, Linnville and Plum Creek. You course from San Antonio to Port Lavaca's coast and back to Lockhart, near Austin; then far west to Colorado City.

To find where they fought and why, you visit a quiet Catholic bookstore, a forgotten town, and a hill overlooking a state park's golf course. You turn time back, not long after San Jacinto — four summers, as Indian reckoned it.

You see, this cavalry is Comanche.

It is March 1840. From the new northwest frontier capital, Austin, comes President Lamar's no-treaty, iron-fist Indian policy. West of Alamo's rubble, where the city grows in adobe and rock by old San Fernando, San Antonio listens carefully. This town is still number one Comanche target.

Down from the hills to talk prisoners and a now empty peace, the Comanche hears it, too. Straight to Bejar's low-ceilinged council house ride the nation's twelve top chiefs and their party of sixty-five, half women and

39

children. A trap? Stoically, they pass three companies of *Tejano* infantry by the courtyard. Their leaders meet inside.

Inside in the closeness, it goes wrong. Captain Howard moves his company in, jams elbow to enemy elbow. Sullen quiet, showdown ... explosion! Texans count fifteen dead and wounded; the Comanches are wiped out.

This Indian Alamo stands directly opposite San Fernando's twin towers - today, ironically, a Catholic bookstore operated by the gentle Pauline Sisters. Very near where Sister Josephine talked with me, Captain Howard took a knife in the stomach and his Comanche assailant was brained with a musket. By the door, Captain Dennington fell with a squaw's arrow and, toward the courthouse, Judge Thompson, playing with an Indian child in the old courtyard, was riddled even while laughing.

Toward the tall new bank on the corner was the old rock house where they trapped the last Comanche survivors, burned them into the open and the rifle muzzles. A milky, marble wall plaque tells some of the story. It does not begin to plumb the eternal vengeance which the Comanche swore that night in the hills above San Antonio.

The bookstore, of course, is where the charge of this light brigade really began.

Into the summer, scattered furious skirmishes play sudden lightning in the thunderheads building northwest; in August, the thunderclap! Out of the hills pour a thousand Comanche horsemen — a red and black-daubed, buffalo-helmeted, wild-riding, flint-tipped flood: the great Comanche assault — so lightning fast, it races ahead of its own alarm.

Down, the riders sweep, past Austin, past Bastrop and San Marcos...even Gonzales and San Antonio, now behind to the west. Each town might have been engulfed; the breakthrough instead drives on and on, southeast.

Two hundred miles deep into colonized Texas — far outside *Comancheria*— the brigade lashes thunderstruck Victoria, sprinkles her with dead, fires buildings and surges on. Straight for the coast! Straight, incredibly, for one tiny and scarcely-known town — the little, new Texas port, Linnville.

Just up the tidal flats from Port Lavaca, opposite where Alcoa's shiny domes and globes glint across the bay today, Linnville is annihilated before she recognizes that horizon-wide, dust-wrapped half moon, hammering out of the morning sun. She runs screaming into the surf, some to die there, others to make the boats and watch their town torn apart with a searching fury, then burned.

Why? Now the riders are vanished — the wheeling-back, cattle-milling, loot-streaming horsemen. With all Texas as target, they hit this one pitifully unready town!

Then they rode back.

Behind them, across the vast woodland, couriers from Ben McCulloch and Old Paint Caldwell have fanned out, galloping, to rouse the settlements. McCulloch hits them at Texana, below today's Edna; but they throw him aside.

Yet McCulloch expresses back the startling word that they really shun a fight. They are falling back to their hills, straight up the valley between the Colorado and the Guadalupe. Then, bar their gates to the north!

The gate slams closed at Plum Creek, last barrier before Austin's frontier. From the big hill above Lockhart's park and golf course, you can see the long roll of country — now patched in farm and timber — where they ran and fought and ran.

It was a strangely different Comanche who fought that day. His cavalry was half-hearted; he tried instead to herd away horses and cattle. He went into battle unfamiliarly decked in what he had brought from Linnville — frock coats buttoned backward, ribbons streaming, bonnets and stovepipe hats.

He did not even fight well. He held grudgingly, then broke into running knots that bled their way finally to the hills. Two months later, Texans would pursue far west up the rivers and smash a major Comanche village near today's Colorado City.

He was still thirty-four years of savage fighting from finished; but this great charge across Texas, begun so

41

furiously, had collapsed in weirdly-garbed riders who died, already beaten...their medicine run out. A puzzler!

An even bigger puzzle, you say, in why the long smash at unknown Linnville?

Plum Creek was, as customary, Texas rifle against Comanche bow. It was supposed to have been Comanche rifle, too.

I told you it was like the British at Balaklava. Up there, you remember, somebody got the wrong signal. That charge was ordered straight for the guns.

So was the Linnville assault. Guns aplenty were supposed to wait the taking at that little Texas port. It was calico and haberdashery instead.

1841

Enchanted Rock's Long View

Enchanted Rock, we call it — this giant, gently-rolling, pink granite dome that dominates Hill Country's Llano valley, south toward Fredericksburg. Climb it, which you can with leisurely ease. America has loftier views, but few search so far.

From the broad, flat top, you see rearing Bullhead and Smoothing Iron above lesser rims northwest; and the wind keens down the blue wall of Riley Mountains to the east - a mighty vista. But not really what you ponder.

Perhaps the secret begins with that plaque near the top. In 1841, our first great ranger, Captain Jack Hays, singlehanded, held this naked summit against a hundred Comanche, circling its three-mile-round base, far below.

Ask any combat rifleman where and how he'd fort, to hold for one day up there. Oh, he'd stop a lot of them, but some one of even a dozen determined bowmen — from boulder or crevice — would get him within two hours. He'll shake his head at a hundred. Those warriors didn't really attack.

42

Which brings us to what you truly see...and it is through old Indian eyes. You are atop the fearsome spirit rock where ghost warriors walk the dark, where death fires dance the moon, and the devil's voice — deep below — can condemn or save your people; though, from oldest time, you have appeased with blood sacrifice of your fair and young.

That's first glimpse from atop. Now look from below.

The Charlie Moss Ranch, along Sandy Creek's rivulet, is some two thousand acres. You can dayhunt or birdwatch or go rockhounding. Along a half mile of deep timber is a good private campground. Across Sandy, a white-arrowed trail winds through sheared, house-sized boulder formations like Queen's Chair and Council of Witches and, toward craggy Turkey Peak or the lesser domes, a score of others, unmarked. The trail mounts the rock — a pink granite umbrella that could cover a seven hundred acre town, fifty stories high.

Geology's billion year calendar can tell you that all this Texas granite hub — fifty miles across to Lake Buchanan — surged molten from earth's deeps. It stopped short of volcano, then waited eons to be worn exposed. Only Georgia's gray granite Stone Mountain is mightier than this pink dome.

And science, of course, can explain the other things, the strange ones...but that's for later.

All this, pretty Mrs. Ruth Moss explained carefully, then turned me loose up Jack Hays' trail. Sure, I could manage the climb; she'd seen some eighty-year-oldsters make it.

That first climber, Tennesseean Jack Hays? A hundred miles west of then Austin frontier, this autumn, 1841, the dark, hawkeyed ranger knows what he rides for. He is cut off by Comanche, while surveying. He drops sad-dlehorn compass and Jacob's rod and the chain, and he hammers straight for the round mountain.

Up it, saddled, then afoot, he carries a brace of Navy Colt five shooters and his rifle. He has a clear fire field down much of the slope. But most of all, he knows he has something extra that will let him hold until help comes.

What is it that stops the Indian below?

As do we, the Comanche knows there was an earlier people. Earlier even than Lipan or Tonkawa. Remotely, he understands that a man's rock temples must sacrifice to his gods — just as Cortez saw it on the bloodstained pyramid tops in long earlier Mexico.

He knows that east and north, Indian nations from long ago, lacking rock, have built earth mounds for their pyramids. But here, west, is a startling rock awaiting! Nights, it whispers and shows lights. Even is there tale that phantom warriors guard the top.

From the old ones, he knows that, since the beginning, all other peoples have appeased the spirit beneath the rock, in sacrifice of their young — burned in the boulders at the base. He knows that once came a time of empty belly, and some chief took his daughter to the heights and offered her to the devil-spirit below.

It was not good medicine. Nights, that dead chief was condemned to walk the mountain. Even the skeptical Comanche knows that no Indian now climbs the great red rock . . . and lives. Bellied flat on the cold granite, Jack Hays knows he can get the few braves who dare to try.

That intrepid Ranger Hays fought and survived is fact. The rest, of course, is Indian legend. It is easy to shrug off the latter-day Comanche and what he never quite believed from the old people, yet feared to doubt. You shrug it like Jim Bowie's lost mine, down below to the north...and the phantom warriors whose tomb your footsteps drum hollowly, the devil voices from beneath the rock and finally the old chief who walks like eternally-warning Sisyphus.

Science can explain easily. A creviced granite mass, heated days and chilled nights, will shift with deep whispers. The slit caves atop and up the sheer west sides are simply split-off faults. That tomb-hollow feel under your feet, the mountain's north front — an old granite layer splitting loose.

The ghost lights? Granite's mica and perhaps moonlight

on the rainpools that fleck the slopes and stand wind-rippled atop.

Indomitable John Coffee Hays might never have admitted that he had something working for him on that summit. But he did.

Look close at those low boulders and wonder the countless sacrifices since before the Druids. And above the last line of precarious cactus near the top, you'll find something else. Sure, they're potholes, water-worked for centuries in eternal granite.

But back and forth, don't they make precise moccasin prints - an Indian walking his tragic vigil?

Enchanted? Or, to the Indian, *Forbidden Rock*?

1845

Waco's Great Council Grounds

If our really old Texans could come back, they might tell you that we overlook one of the singular "capitals" of our land — down the broad and fertile valley of the Brazos, just east of Waco.

A mile north of little Harrison Switch, toward Marlin, are loamy bluffs back from Tehuacana and Trading House Creeks, meandering for the river haze. Atop a mesquite-crowned point, a fallen gray marker rests above the long valley. Distant yonder is the timbered bend of the Brazos and Waco's horizon beyond.

On the quiet point is no trace of what the marker recalls: a half-dozen log buildings, a century and a quarter ago. The buildings comprised Republic of Texas-approved John F. Torrey's Trading Post — beads, calico and cloth for buffalo and deerskin and Indian peace.

In enigmatic understatement, the marker adds, "Here, the Indians signed treaties and received presents until 1854..." Look more closely at that slumbering valley. *Capital* isn't the word. But perhaps you can see the shadows from the last assembly here, for this was the Great Council Grounds of this once empire of the Tejas.

Guy Bryan Harrison, Jr., Baylor University's distinguished Texas historian, routed me to the grounds. It was easy for him because, a century ago, these were family lands; and no one knows better what is out there.

What is out there is age-old boundary of the Brazos — between the plains hunters west and the master farmers and craftsmen, east, a boundary that has stood since the time when Europe was young. That here was common council ground both early Spanish and French discovered. For how long before that, archaeology one day will tell us. But that's another story; we hunt the latter days of the land below.

Here was drawn the first major Indian treaty for Stephen Austin's colonial Texas, the last for Sam Houston's Texas Republic, and the first for America's twenty-eighth state. Here, to the last red man as to his forefathers, is where one came for his most solemn and hopeful treaties.

Stephen Austin learns of the grounds early as 1824. To treat with costal Karankawa, inland Tonkawa, Waco and Tawakoni, Texas' first frontiersman Strap Buckner will march Austin's peace party from their colony beachheads, 150 miles south.

Then in two short decades, America avalanches west, thrusting ahead the strange faces of Indian remnants. In Texas, Indian fights Mexican, Anglo . . . even Indian, for the land.

Now, this late fall of 1845, Sam Houston tries as relentlessly for Indian peace as for American annexation. Peace or Indian chaos! His once Cherokee friends are beaten from the East Texas they took from Caddo. West, the Comanche ranges the hills he wrenched from Tonkawa and Lipan Apache. Yet into Texas pour more and more tribal fragments — Kickapoo and Delaware, Chickasaw and Pawnee. Houston, traversing Texas, pieces a jigsaw agreement calling for one more great peace parley. Let it be

46

on the Great Council Grounds of the Brazos. Let red and white really prove it better to trade than to fight. Over the wide valley already stands Torrey's Trading Post, a symbol that Houston earnestly wants peace and trade. And so the Indian comes. From this bluff, you can see the vast camp, its last assembled morning.

Under cold smoke wisps, this first November light, dogs stir to scratch; ponies to graze the deep grass; mules to shift their packs. As far as the river glint a thousand teepees; in them, chiefs and braves of twenty nations and tribes from ancient Caddo to newcome Shawnee. Three thousand of them, this mightiest peace talk ever in Texas. They have spoken and listened and passed the pipe.

Listening, the white man has wondered, "When will they steal and kill again?" And listening, the red man has pondered, "When will they keep their word and leave us our land?" ·

But peace it is — however uneasy — this last great council of the Republic.

It seems short-lived to the new State of Texas. U.S. commissioners are here, then travel west with the advancing U.S. fort-lined frontier. In a half dozen years will come the last date on the marker, 1854, and its ultimatum: reservation west for all Indians.

You wonder if frontier-wise and friend-to-Indian Sam Houston did not see it all coming that last November morning. Perhaps not in the immense terms of an America emerging from the Mexican War: a sudden continent wide, an America of forty-niners storming for California gold, of buffalo hunters, railroad builders and new towns, hard behind.

Perhaps he saw things to come in the very faces about him. Who were these shadow nations on the Great Council Grounds, this last time in the Republic?

Here was Caddo, Hainai, Anadarko and Kichai, with tattered old claim to their land of Tejas. And with them, their west allies, Waco and Tawakoni.

Here, too, other remnants: Delaware from distant Alleghenies, Shawnee from Ohio country, Chickasaw and

47

Biloxi from Mississippi, shattered Cherokee from long ago Carolinas, and Pawnee down from the plains with Wichita yet to come, and angry Comanche, saddled in from the west. All of them swept ahead of frontier's surge — a surge, Houston had to know — would keep on.

Would keep on, finally to the reservation ultimatum; and the red man's desperate reply: "The Great Spirit did not make me a Reservation Indian."

And like Houston, the Indian had to see it coming, had to know he rode away from something singular when he left the valley this last day.

Capital is not quite the word for this valley.

Something more between a hoped-for United Nations and an actual Appomattox.

1846

Fredericksburg's Easter Fires

Across our land, we symbolize Easter's promise many wondrous and beautiful ways. But few have more meaning than Fredericksburg's Easter eve watchfires, leaping the night rims round that Hill Country pioneer town.

There is beauty in the high flame spangles from Cross Mountain and the dark lesser hilltops. Old custom, too — each eve for well over a century. And in the old-world-steepled town below, happy pageant. At first glance, this is pageant that strangely mixes German-Texan frontiersmen with Comanche warriors, and both with Easter bunnies and wildflower paint and eggs in youngsters' grass-tucked nests for finding before church bells tomorrow. Strange?

There is dual significance in those watching fires. The first ones on these hills ringed our remotest western settlement in dread. They were Comanche watchfires that seemed to promise death.

You travel an old road to find their ultimate promise — thanksgiving.

As for many a Texan today, that road began in Germany — a steady colonist stream in the 1830's, then floodtide with statehood. *Adelsverein* — Society for the Protection of German Immigrants — provided finance and order, bought grants, straight off the new Texas maps, up the river valleys...unknowingly straight into the deadly heartland hills between the Llano and Colorado, where only Comanche held title.

Edging those hills, colony anchor New Braunfels was as dangerous, this 1846, as frontier capital Austin. Old frontiersmen knew that, from there, you shot your way in and got out fast. But the purchased grants lay beyond; and a strong-faced, brilliant and incredibly patient colonizer proposed to settle them. Former German baron, he was now red-bearded, thirty-four year old, plain Texan, John Meusebach. Through sixteen days of ordeal, he led his wagons into those hills, settled one hundred twenty men, women and children in the remote Pedernales Valley, and named their tiny outpost for Frederick the Great.

Their ordeal was only beginning. Three months' oxcart for sea-borne supplies at Indianola! More colonists coming, with little food awaiting them, and crops still seed in the ground. Cholera would take one in ten; Comanche poised doom for the rest. Fredericksburg, near nothing but Indian, tottered. Then, forget this western folly; leave this wilderness! Would Meusebach lead them back from these hills?

He would not. He'd go deeper...in peace, and in search of treaty. *Treaty!* With warriors who believed no white man's treaty-word good? That was exactly what he proposed.

Terms were simple. Fredericksburg colonists would again buy land to till — this time from Indian; would interfere with no Indian hunting. Comanche and colonist would protect each other within treaty bounds. Lodges of one would be open to the other, trade of one offered the other. And offenses by either would be reported and punished immediately. The Texas government shook its collective head. Trust the Comanche?

That, said the red-beard, was the key. Trust! He believed his people could earn equal trust. To prove they came in peace, his riders would empty their guns, face fifty-to-one odds, go into wilderness no one ventured, unarmed. His column, scarcely thirty, rode west.

Let Fredericksburg not expect him under two months. If treaty talks went well, he'd ask permission to explore the wilderness across the Llano, even the San Saba—empty almost a century since Spain was driven out.

Under its circling hills, the defenceless settlement knew its men would be gone a long time. Forever? They'd know that, if the rims emptied death on them!

Now, over the hills, winter moves toward spring; below, Fredericksburg waits tense, knowing it is watched. By lonely day, the heights seem empty, looking down; by night, the terrible eyes are there atop — Comanche watchfires. These are signals to Indians west, where Meusebach is alive, or even now, may be dying. Perhaps the fires answer signals from the west. Perhaps even now they tell Fredericksburg's fate. *How do you read them?*

No way to read them, thinks a distraught mother by her children, restless and tossing in bed.

"Are there Indians by the fires, Mamma? Hush and sleep! Where is Papa? When will he come home, Mamma? *Hush and sleep!* Then, what is up there by the fires?"

Far back, the mother gropes for answer. Have they forgotten Easter is coming? Have they forgotten how the Easter bunnies gather the colored flowers and make paint for the eggs? Haven't they seen the blue and pink and yellow flowers over the hills now? What else then, but fires for the bunnies' kettles?

"Then is Easter soon, Mamma?"

Soon, she says; and they sleep. And, like all the waiting mothers in the small houses, she watches the night fires and prays on her knees. *Let it be soon!*

It is nearly three months. Then John Meusebach rides in with every man. He has explored between the Colorado and Llano. West of today's San Saba, on that clear river, he has Comanche word. They will try the colonists' word!

This treaty — almost unique in our history — stands. Texas Ranger Jack Hays trails in, puzzled. He fights Comanche everywhere west, yet crosses this line to instant peace. And two years later, when Fredericksburg battles cholera, it is Indian who brings meat, honey and bear oil to help the ill.

The peace collapses ultimately, but not by either hand here. Fredericksburg has made it, impossibly remote and alone...and unmolested. Thereafter, from that first Easter, Meusebach's people will climb the circling hills to make the promise good to their children: that only good looked down on them.

Fredericksburg will welcome you any Easter you can come. The pageant will tell its story and the hill fires will stand like close stars. Your youngsters will know the bunnies are up there, for nothing but good can come from the promise of those fires. Their message, when you think of it, never changes.

You remember the Second of those Two Great Commandments, before an Easter long ago: "Thou shalt love thy neighbor as thyself"?

Wasn't that what made for Meusebach's miracle: real trust and a real try?

1860

Two Daughters at Medicine Mounds

Like most old things Indian, they're easily overlooked or missed outright, and they can leave you puzzling.

Below Quanah, where our Panhandle corners north, first glance dismisses them for four low hills rimming the Pease. But keep watching as you circle south or east. They stand apart in spaced-out line; cedared hills, all right, yet they seem something more—pyramid, mosque, canopied temple, square basilica, all in a row.

From the river's red shale breaks to the south, you can

51

see how they formed—eroded tips of the long mesa that walls across from the west. You can see how, around that wall, centuries of buffalo, trailing greener seasons south, veered to their brief pass. With always hunter following, until this was worn trail; and that first, highest pyramid, way-marker and lookout tower...at its base, ancient campsite.

Look very closely. There are teepees, silver in morning twilight, cold smoke-plumed in the early chill. Outside, one man moves about, a listless shadow. Shortly now, he will leave legend a name for these hills—the great Medicine Mounds.

He stirs, sleepless in anguish, this chief. Forgotten, the buffalo hunt; for these days past, all his wisdom has struggled for the life of his daughter—so nearly a woman, so fair and good. But he has lost; within his lodge, she burns as with fire. Exhausted, his charms; his pouch, near empty. This Sun will take her from him.

Sky lightens east. He walks apart for the shadows round the mound's foot, for there, none can see him fling down in dust, crying within like a woman. Within himself crying, "Can she not be saved?"

It is within that he hears the voice, "Climb. To the top! Speak there!"

He is up the steep hillside, as Sun, paling sky, climbs to meet him. Atop the highest rock, he has crushed his herbs once more for potion. As sun rims fire, he stands erect and, across the morning wind, cries out for his daughter's life.

Then, down to the still-dark camp. Within his teepee, he lifts her head to drink. Even as he holds her, his bare arm feels the fire leave. Deep into her father's eyes, she looks once, then rests slumbering. She will heal!

Outside, Sun slants across the waking camp. Silently, the chief gazes where he had climbed high. It stands like the great rock temples, told of forgotten ancestors, far away. He must summon his people; the Great Spirit truly has touched them.

And so, the long time after—father to son, and people

to people—these are heights of the Great Spirit. Upon them wind lengthens life's breath; to their summit for the warrior, storm gathers strength. In silence on the summit, thoughts dance like falling waters or run deep like clear pools. Here is camp for Indian prayer. Temple Rock! Medicine Mounds!

Today you can circle the mounds from U.S. 287 near Chillicothe and drive to within a half-mile of them on Farm Road 1167 toward the little town that took their name. The best view is along Bob Brown's fenceline where they wall the back of his Medicine Mound Ranch

Young and gracious Mrs. Rhonda Brown isn't sure which of the four strange shapes intrigues her most. Artifacts are heaviest around the tallest or first pyramid. The Browns, however, leave them alone for archaeology, which has traced man deep into their shadows.

Deep perhaps as that Indian daughter, saved in legend.

You turn to history for another daughter here...and a different ending.

In wind-bitten cold, this December morning, 1860, Peta Nocona's Comanche have camped on the Pease River near the mounds. Breaking camp now, they will trail west for canyon sanctuary, for Nocona senses pursuit. His warriors have just slashed deep as Weatherford, with many horses and scalps carried back for trophy. The chief is proud; his wife and children ride with him. They will elude any pursuit!

Nocona does not know pursuit already is upon him. Unseen across the hilly breaks, unheard in the shrilling downwind, a ranger leans his saddlehorn to study the camp. Indian-wise young Captain Sul Ross knows his quarry; he carries the wound from their last battle. His sixty horsemen are outnumbered, but surprise is their ally. They will attack.

The ranger captain sends a small troop circling to cut Indian escape. Then his right arm flashes charge. Over the crest they pour, two hundred hammering yards for the camp that is thunderstruck with surprise, Colt and carbine fury.

Down, the teepees...down, the plunging mustangs, spilling as mounted...down, the highscreaming Indian that scatters straight into waiting ambush. Across the shattered camp, Ross wheels; yonder is his real quarry—Chief Nocona, a rider doubled behind, another galloping beside, racing for the shelter of the river breaks. Bent low, Ross rides them down, lets his men take the off-rider. It is Nocona that he wants. And that shot . . . *has him* . . . saddle-emptied!

No! Plunging to rein about, he sees Nocona somehow on his feet, whipping arrows . . . feels one rear his horse . . . snaps a shot over the withers . . . sees the chief's bow arm smashed useless . . . sees him yet stagger forward, trying with the lance. Vaulted clear, Ross puts two balls through his chest . . . reels him back against a tree. Will Nocona surrender?

The chief stabs feebly with his lance. Ross signals and trooper Tony Martinez blasts with buckshot. Savagely quick, the Battle of the Pease is but scattered pursuit.

That other rider? She holds a baby. Peta Nocona's wife. She is Cynthia Ann Parker. A quarter-century earlier, she was the nine-year-old daughter, Comanche-wrenched from Fort Parker's logs, far east.

She will go "home to her people", live briefly, never knowing that her son—that off-rider— made it, finally lived out his life in peace to leave his name for the town just north.

That son, Quanah, will insist throughout his life—and be believed by many—that his father, Peta Nocona, escaped the Texan guns at the Pease. In any event, he was effectually finished there.

And so you puzzle the medicine of those enigmatic hills. If Peta Nocona sought that medicine, it was denied him.

One Indian girl was saved, the story goes, by a father's prayer. Could this chief have asked to save what was torn from another father? Or only to conquer? Or did he climb the heights to ask anything?

Or were these mounds, in those latter days, become more campsite than temple?

A Captain Stands; A Kiowa Rides

Our Panhandle high plains spill east to Oklahoma in the red-jumbled, hilly breaks of the Canadian and Washita. From far-north Wheeler, up U.S. 83, you conclude it a lonely land, unlikely either to history or her heroes. Amarillo historian Ernest Archambeau can tell you there were both.

There was an army captain and his ambushed wagon train that, for nearly five grim days, promised only an Indian-crushed Alamo. Yet a Travis who lived.

Across in Oklahoma, the sons of the Kiowa can tell the same story—Indian-viewed. They know a ride to match Jim Bonham's.

History yet unrecorded? Too recent. We forget that our green-glistening Panhandle—within oldest generation's memory— was final Indian battleground. And this furious fragment of it was near the tiny village Gem, triangling east from Wheeler and Canadian today, where Gageby Creek seeps sandy to the Washita.

A lanky Vermont captain. dug in by the wheels of his shot-up, forted wagons, is certain death stares him, feathered from the close gravelly rims. He is about to draft a letter to his commanding officer, much like that from Alamo's Carolinian, Travis. The Indian—a Kiowa who knows his people's time is done—is about to fling himself over his pony.

Two men—neither expecting to live—at destiny's crossroads. What brought them there?

Far away this September, 1874, big city New York reads paperback Wild West and jails machine politician Boss Tweed. Chicago rebuilds mightily from her fire. Texas, war-rebounding, drives cattle and promises real cities at San Antonio, Houston and Dallas. But here on the high plains is bitter end for an Indian empire that was.

From every direction, army drives to corral Comanche-Kiowa remnant. From northeast rumble Nelson Miles' wagons. From south, Ranald Mackenzie's columns that, these next few weeks, will finish it at Palo Duro Canyon. Still other troops, east and west! And this moment all Panhandle is confused snarling battle. Into one this clear, cold morning of the ninth, jogs a supply train headed south for Miles, under the Cap Rock near today's Pampa.

Captain Wyllys Lyman double columns his thirty-six wagons and flanks his hundred Fifth Infantry foot. A dozen cavalry ride point. Corral, if hit. His mission is to get supplies to Miles.

A mile short of the Washita, where the red hills rear like forts, they are hit by Kiowa horsemen, perhaps five hundred, in one screaming, engulfing wave!

Captain Lyman will hold almost five days, despite the fury of that first charge. His sergeant, closing the front gap, dead as he yelled...the lead wagoner, toppling...the mules going down...his lieutenant, racing to hold the rear, hit, pitched...the red-daubed wild circle beaten back from the very wheels.

But Lyman has his fort now, this day and a half later. Only the *splaaat* and long whine ricochet tells him they are still all about. He has fed and watered his men canned tomatoes from the wagons. Midnight now, he must get a scout through, get a report through. It has the restraint of a man who does not expect help in time.

"Sir: I have the honor to report that I am corralled..." He lists his casualties, estimates five-to-one odds, advises he has "only a small pool of rainwater for the men which will dry up today..."

Then doggedly, he holds. Water, a hundred yards distant; death, the first dozen feet. Twilights, he watches the Kiowa whirl his wagons. If only his scout got through...

He had a mission. He must hold. He must get the wagons through!

Strangely, from the spitting crests above, the Indian knows his time has run out, too. Yellowlegs, west and north, say his riders. Soon he will be quarry, not hunter. This fourth day, the stubborn, thirst-dying ones will not come out to be killed like warriors. No choice but to run for the canyon west.

One young brave knows a choice. He has already ridden to the wagon-wheel gun muzzles. The choice a man makes finally, is for his soul. Since he must die, it is how!

They call him Botalye; he is a breed with Mexican Comanchero. He is young, untried. He watches Yellow Wolf, the great one, don his feathers. They pull Yellow Wolf down. He watches Bear Paw and hears: "I will ride through them. Once, before we leave." They pull Bear Paw from his horse. Such a ride is death!

The young Kiowa manes his pony with red. Carefully, he places two eagle feathers in his hair. Down the long slope is the wagon-fort, trenched on both sides. They lie dead-silent, waiting, those trenches. But Botalye has a mission, too.

He flings to the saddle and, hugging thigh and arm, thunders for the wagon-fort. Not outside, where the others fell, but straight between the guns!

He knows the Kiowa watch from the hills. He clings low, under his paint. He can see the eyes of them, swinging their guns. He is through . . . up . . . churning sand where they call Kiowa acclaim, then without looking, he is back into the gantlet.

This is his proof of soul—defiance! He feels the eagle feather shot from his head. He feels the paint hit, the pluck and whisper of death and sees the faint white faces, sighting, shooting. Safe again, he turns as Yellow Wolf grabs, shouting: "Nobody rides more than twice; you have done enough!" But he is gone once more.

He is between them again. Heat's sear on his hand on the reins. His white sheet knotted, burst and gone, a hot iron across his cheek. He has made it another time, with one eagle feather. They clutch. He beats them back. Once more! *Once more!*

He pulls up, this last time, where he started. He could have touched the gun muzzles. They were in his face. They took his last feather. But they missed!

In false dawn, Botalye's Kiowa rode away. A day later, cautiously, so would the wagons. . Ernest Archambeau can tell you that the Vermont trooper made good his mission. He held on when he should have died. Instead, he got through to Miles. He was decorated.

So was the young Kiowa. His sons, reservationed today, know him from the Indian plaudit—the new name, "He-wouldn't-listen-to-them."

Yes, that empty country you pass today, has its history...and its heroes. It proved two of them. Both with a mission they made good.

Beyond that, it's point of view.

1874

Last Camp at Palo Duro

They were right, that Tennessee family, camped beside. We ought to talk more about big and rugged Palo Duro State Park and its fine campground.

The Tennesseeans liked the startling view of chasm from above and, deep within, the rearing, tinted canyon walls. They liked the tall cottonwoods at the water crossings, the pleasant young park rangers and the neat showers on the little mesa—beyond the grove at the fifth crossing of these Red River headwaters.

They stowed their trailer tent and came over for coffee, waiting while their kids hiked, hallooing back. The kids had been to the great purple spine of Devil's Slide and around the minarets to the Lighthouse in Little Sunday Canyon.

Their dad asked about the thousand-foot battlements of Fortress Cliff, dark against morning's pink sky, then wished they had allowed time for the park horses. Presently they left for Amarillo and east on U. S. 66.

"People ought to know more about this," he had said. "It's a fine camp."

I got to thinking how little we really tell them. It should be a fine camp. In Texas, it was the Comanche's last.

It is easy in the canyon quiet to turn the calendar back to the day it was...

Autumn of 1874 will end Texas' longest war—thirty-four years of Comanche no quarter. As the low gray walls of San Antonio's Council House saw it begin, the jagged reds of Palo Duro see it ended. Ended—as it had to be with Comanche—when that greatest of all light cavalry ceased to exist.

Never more than a few thousand, they had—like no other warriors—stood against all, from Texas Ranger to yellowleg trooper. Now but a few hundred, together with tatters of once proud Kiowa and Southern Cheyenne, they will yet hit hard and run, so long as their plains have horizon. That is very little longer.

They do not know that army columns from north, east west and south are strangling that horizon. They know only that across their land is no sound but gunfire.

Their last chance is the great hidden gorge that few but Comanche have seen. Winter comes soon, so it may yet hide them and turn back the yellowlegs, freezing.

So this is their camp on a late September false dawn. And on it, high against a cold, dark sky, Colonel Ranald Mackenzie's Fourth Cavalry look down from Palo Duro's southwest rim.

At the precipice overlook inside the park entrance today, the corraled horses below look like ants. You look down much as did those stiffened troopers nearly a century ago from the point of Cito Canyon, ten miles south. Then you could have flipped a pebble on the teepees beneath—shiny silver dimes in the canyon night. But how to attack? That narrow path would dizzy a goat! The troopers' rim view is grim.

You can judge the Comanche view from the little mesa with the showers. Below, where the canyon bends, Cito slashes from the west. Cottonwood and stream, the floor between has changed little, except the teepees are gone.

On this morning they stretch three miles to Cito's mouth. Just over the thin stream from your mesa are the silvery lodges of Iron Shirt's Cheyenne and, farther, those of Lone Wolf's and Sky Walker's Kiowa and on...past the Buffalo and Antelope Comanche of Wild Horse and Shaking Hand.

Smoke hangs dying over the cold teepees, and the gaunt dogs are not yet astir to scratch. Toward the west wall, the great mustang herd drowses, standing. Beside those lodges most lately up, are pack mules hobbled and still burdened. These are of warriors, in this very night from the fighting. The camp sleeps exhausted.

All but the lodges where Red Warbonnet guards beneath Cito's wall. He will warn if troopers ride up the canyon floor. Then there will be time aplenty for warriors to climb the cliffs, shoot down, and turn that ride to death. He knows where to watch. Not the west cliffs. Only a driven Comanche would dare his horse down that. He scans the cliffs toward the sun, for it comes soon.

But Red Warbonnet never sees that sunrise. He dies under A Troop's first rush...from the foot of the unwatched dark west walls.

Markers—even the "near here" kind—could tell much along trails over that strangely decisive battlefield: A Troop's headlong assault up three miles of village-strung canyon . . . Mackenzie himself, heading H and L Troops, close behind . . . frenzied first panic of rearing pack mules, spilled lodges, squaws screaming for the bluffs . . . Iron Shirt and Lone Wolf rushing up and Wild Horse shouting them to the high boulders as planned...an excited captain ordering the heights stormed, and Mackenzie—come for no Little Big Horn—thundering countermand...L Troop's bugler, shot from the saddle as he trumpets recall . . .

60

Troops D, I and K checking the Comanche circling to seal the rear ... finally A Troop galloping back ...

Back with Mackenzie's one battle objective—two thousand Indian ponies—driven ahead. And out of the canyon by the cavalry's dark route in—the west precipice path!

It's better to walk or ride the ground—far better, if marked — but from that low mesa you can see nearly all of what finished the Comanche. Look at the vaulting cliffs. You can understand his mistake. He had lived by the horse...and it beat him.

Fourth Cavalry's horse—this one morning, on a path a mustang would shun!

And come—not for Indian—but for his mounts!

In his last, burning village, the Comanche knew he faced reservation. This first time in thirty-four years he had nowhere and nothing to ride.

Walking back from Cito Canyon take a last look from the mesa and finally from the cliff edge as you leave. They were right, those Tennessee campers.

We ought to tell more about Palo Duro!

1880

Wild Rose Pass

Overawed by the lofty grandeurs of Berthoud, Donner, or even Raton, we Texans write off, as picayune, our own mountain passes. This is error, as Fort Davis historian Barry Scobee, or any true Mescalero Apache, can tell you.

North up Texas 17 from our West's great fighting fort, now a restored national monument, the spiring Davis Mountains march to a mighty wall that overlooms endless flatness to horizons beyond Pecos and far east of Fort Stockton. Here is magnificent and storied Wild Rose Pass.

The way to look on the pass is from its top, within the

crags. North, you see a canyon, wrenched wide at its bottom to lower a broadening grassy valley. On each side, thousand-foot cliffs rear, V-ing out like fluted Gibraltars.

Whether smoky with winter's low clouds, rain-veiled or thunderheaded the other seasons, the high view is for you; for here you stand when these were the Apache, not Davis, Mountains; and what you see is through Mescalero eyes as he watched the end of his empire come at him from far below.

From below? The west-driving American saw water, the one feasible highroad to California, the pink and white, cliff-climbing beauty that named the pass and...the deadliest point of ambush between 1850 frontier San Antonio and the Pacific.

He saw ambush because you fought from *your* fort—the pass! But that was long ago.

Now you are ready to leave your land as the white man decrees, but you take a last look from this gate you guarded and think back how it happened.

When you were very young, you remember the old, old tales how once the first intruders came this way. Their robes were iron that nothing could hurt. But they passed, and all they really left were the horses you rode well for such a long time.

Then, for all the memory of all your forefathers, there was only the *Mejicano*; but he stayed below the river to the south after he learned that no one — not even the arrogant Comanche — invaded this land of the mescal-eating mountain fighter.

While young, you remember laughing when you learned another was coming—the *Tejano*. Beyond the rising sun, he was taking Comanche land. You laughed for your blood enemy's troubles; but the old ones worried, saying: if Comanche falls, what stands between our mountains and the new man? Being young, still you laughed.

Then came the day you saw them first. Greatly armed, they seemed a war party yet only peered about. For two suns from these cliffs, you thought to attack. They camped under this very rimrock. Uneasily, you let them pass—west, from your mountains. How could you know this was a young topographic lieutenant—later Confederate General Henry Whiting—who named the pass "Wild Rose", its brook, "Limpia", and set the road west —thus finally Fort Davis—and wrote the date, March, 1849?

Nor could you know that his report dispatched the four-mile-long army train to blaze that road and put the Third U.S. Infantry in El Paso, September, that year. Nor that orders immediately sent Butterfield Overland's high-wheeled, wild-muled Concord stages racing mail up the road weekly as America took her new West.

It was only remembering the end of laughing. The old ones were right: you were between two rocks. Time had come to fight for your mountains and your life.

The first fights were with the racing wagon and the riders, rushing this pass again and always again. You killed some; they killed more. But the strange fear was of the big man who led them through, almost alone. He was *Wallecky* to Comanche and Lipan. The white man called him Bigfoot Wallace. He came through, scornful as Sioux, knowing no Indian could kill him. You fought him; you could not stop him.

Then the great battle. The horse soldiers, like a river, through the pass! Every Mescalero shot them for three suns, died while shooting. Yet the soldiers made a fort, the very place in the trees well beyond, where your father played when young.

You had no way to know this was U.S. Eighth Infantry, spiking in Fort Davis, point of no return—east or west —fall of 1854.

From the pass now, across all your mountains, you struck at everything. Burn! Drive away with Apache warning on your kills. You caught the longknives more than once; and one time you remember the young boy who struck the drum—twelve summers perhaps. Angry with your dead, you let your squaws drive pine splinters in him and fire them to test him against Indian bravery. He died well enough; you left him in the rocks.

Then there was the time it seemed you might hold. The crazy white man fought himself, some wearing the color of smoke; the others, that of night sky—striped yellowlegs. Then the yellowlegs were back, and there was no end.

With Espejo, you trapped some and had their animals to eat and ride—for no longer could you hunt buffalo; they were gone. Finally, with Victorio, you fought the last battles; but the yellowlegs waited at your waterholes and there was no food—nor across the *Mejicano's* river. Your chiefs were dead. Behind your pass now was a great city the white man called Fort Davis.

And what was left to you? Squaws! Perhaps thirty warriors—half, untried. By now, perhaps you knew it was the year of the white man, 1880.

So from here, atop the pass, you can see where it began: the end of your time. But what really marked the sign? The great army's first wide trail through your gateway? Or was it *Wallecky* — the man alone, scornful, unstoppable? You saw him riding that bend of the river . . . how many times?

Was it the time you watched him after the night fight when you lost your brother? You watched *Wallecky* ride straight through your pass. You saw him, flat-bellied on the top of that strange wagon, point his rifle. And high on yonder crag, five times higher than an arrow's flight, he shot a young deer that fell like a star. And he dropped it, shooting in such fashion, that he could take it without pausing.

You asked your last brother, now dead: "Have we a warrior who could do that?" And he replied, you remember now: "No, not even with his gun."

Barry Scobee, graying and perceptive, more than anybody is Davis Mountains and its forts—the one he saw restored and the one he revealed. He pretends he is no romanticist, but is—if he can document it. He will not tell you where the Mescalero saw his Texas empire die. His excellent book, *U.S. Fort Davis* may, depending on how you read it.

I think he can stand atop Wild Rose Pass, show you the few blooms left, and also the second fort. He knows —and most of us can only guess—that here is where the Texas Apache stood and knew his medicine had run out.

Part Two

The Color of History

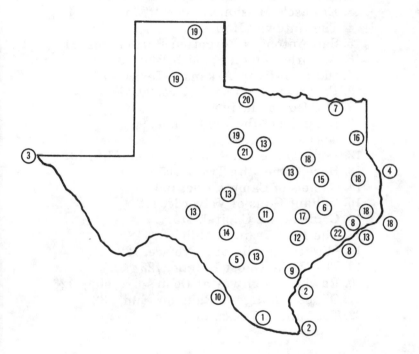

*"The years by themselves do not make a place historic.
It is men who give the color of history to a place, by
their deeds ..."*

Simeon Strunsky

Aged Penitas

This is a tale of two tiny villages. I must take you first to the one, so that you may feel what could be more than a myth of the second.

Just south of Mission, where Valley palms leave off for the long road to Laredo, there is a little chapel, La Capilla de la Lomita. This lies in heavy woods close by the Rio Grande and is one of our state's least-known missions.

Its sandstone and adobe walls, its mesquite sills and sagging belfry show age. Inside the white, unlocked doors, silence rests on straight-backed pews; above the pulpit, the words are in English to the left, Spanish to the right.

Outside, there is a grotto, a miniature Lourdes, and past the statuary mother of Oblate missions, where bricks were set aslant for a long-forgotten flowerbed, there is a hexagonal sign. It tells you that the Oblate fathers made this a way station a century and a half ago, when these cavalrymen-priests covered their border in hundred-mile chunks, riding from hacienda to jacal.

La Lomita is not really old as we count missions. Yet, in the stillness, you can hear the whisper of what may be the oldest settlement in Texas—one hundred fifty years before Ysleta, up El Paso way.

The settlement, legend says, was called Penitas; but let's get to that.

Back in the middle Eighteenth Century, Spanish Franciscans were determined to missionize all this great river boundary, from the mountains of Paso del Norte to the mouth, at Point Isabel. Their string of river missions, both sides of the lower Rio Grande, have about disappeared.

Some decades behind them, the hard-riding Oblates would come. And, given them for a way station would be a ranch with buildings that were old even then. This was La Lomita. Under the weight of time, it flourished, fell to disuse, was partially restored. But the railroad had passed it and there was a new town with only its name—Mission.

Yet today you can stand within the desertion of the little chapel and a feeling steals on you that, even before there was a ranch here, there was something else. A cruder chapel? About it, jacals for dwelling? Some kind of ruin, some trace that brought those moderns of the Eighteenth Century to where Spaniards had walked and worked and prayed, back in 1530?

This is our second village—mythical Penitas.

Consider history a moment. You remember the massive Narvaez New World expedition; it followed Columbus not so very much and Cortez, by no time at all. It came to storm-smothered ruin. One nobleman, Alvar Nuñez Cabeza de Vaca, made it, swimming to shore somewhere near Galveston. Some eighty Spaniards, he reported, made it, too. Four of them struck out to find Mexico, down the coast.

Then came winter. Only fifteen survived weather, starvation and the deadly whim of the Karankawa. De Vaca and two others were too ill for escape; but twelve men did manage it, fleeing along the coast toward what we now know as Rio Grande. When the indefatigable de Vaca reached home in Spain after nine years' ordeal of wandering, he recalled clearly that those men got away.

Legend and some authorities hold that some of this little band or the earlier one reached the Rio Grande, found friendly Indians, erected a crude mission (there were two priests), Christianized, called their settlement "Penitas" and, as all men and their works do, passed with time.

So, go first to La Lomita. Perhaps you'll feel an age much deeper than the old walls of the chapel. A guess, yes; but towns have a way of settling where older towns preceded them. And legend says that somewhere near here, original, tiny Penitas lived out its life.

Original Penitas because, a very few miles down Rio Grande, you'll find a village by that very name. And old as it is—it ranks with any from Reynosa to Ciudad Mier—this Penitas of the here and now is not likely the ancient one. Spaniards put a town where a town had been and a chapel where once a chapel was; and the ancient one was very little more than the crudest place for worship.

Today's Penitas, just a little west and off the highway below the big Central Power and Light building, is an out of the way, drowsy clutter of little dwellings. Some are old adobe with hard-packed yards and colored with the rare blues and pinks that you find only in Mexico.

At Penitas' post office, I inquired of Mr. Romulo Martinez as to his city's age. He was sixtying with a good lean leathery face and honest eyes. I had found the right man, not simply for his immediate cordiality, but also because he was of long lineage and his town's authority.

"It is, in truth, an old town, is it not?" I asked through the little post office grill.

"Very old," Mr. Martinez said agreeably.

"Have you heard it said that the town is the oldest of all along the river?"

"It is possible," Mr. Martinez agreed.

"Some tell it," I pursued, "that possibly the men of Cabeza de Vaca established a village near here. Perhaps as long ago as the year 1530."

Mr. Martinez seemed to weigh the years, sold two stamps to the lady who had come to the window, then regarded me with friendly Latin tolerance.

"For knowing that," he said, "One would require a long memory, would you not agree?"

71

White Island's Odyssey in Horror

At a map glance, you might dismiss Padre Island for little more than a long, thin sandbar. Encounter it mile by mile, however, and you come closer to focus: an almost endlessly vast sea of shifting dunes, an incredibly varied treasure fetched up daily from the ocean. You are still far from knowing the white island.

It is so easy to become lost in search for the *things* it has hidden or in pondering its very vastness. And in so doing, you overlook its story; and that will match anything that Tortugas or Hatteras could tell. There is no way to know how much has been erased by the enigmatic sand, but some pages have come down intact or relatively so, and one of them has few equals in the telling.

It has to do with a centuries-ago Spanish padre stumbling into Tampico, half-dead of hunger and thirst and arrow wounds, with a 1904 treasure hunter who swore he had seen a sunken treasure galleon below Corpus Christi and whom no one believed. And quite likely it has to do with the recent discovery by salvage divers off Padre's beach of one treasure-laden ship indeed. And yet none of these is the heart of the story; you go far back for that.

Go back before the Civil War's strange fights, when Confederate ox-wagoned "cotton forts" ran a sniper gantlet from Corpus to blockade runners off Brownsville, before the 1845's when Ben McCulloch's rangers galloped the long beach highroad to prove that Zachary Taylor's army could march it for Mexico, before the days when Lafitte took treasure at sea and beach pirates took it ashore, luring coasters aground with cattle-bobbing lights pretending buoyage, before Spain's eighteenth century island-long roadway, waymarked with mahogany stakes.

Go back even earlier: the full-rigged prime of the buffeting Spanish Main and treasure galleons loaded to the gunwhales. Of the rich hulks somewhere beyond Padre's pounding surfline, this is one story.

It is also the first recorded island-long journey, and it is an odyssey in horror.

The year is 1553, scant decades from Columbus'voyages, and crest of Aragon's golden flood—the rape of Aztec and Inca empire. Annually, the old Cortez beachhead, Vera Cruz, launches New Spain's tribute home. Now weighing anchor is the greatest fleet of all: twenty treasure ships plus convoy. Aboard are two thousand Spaniards, from priest to adventurer, even the beautiful Doña Ponce de Leon. This is a convoy of great importance to Spain, for King Charles V is at war with France, and the wealth is needed.

The *flota* touches Havana and, homeward bound, sails east . . . into hurricane. Three vessels finally make Spain; the rest are hurled, foundering, across the Gulf. The remnant washes on Padre's long beach, about Mile 20, south of today's Corpus Christi.

Three hundred survivors reach shore, regain some strength, learn gradually that they are on a broad, dune-mountained finger of land. Panuco (Tampico) they tragically believe but a few days south. It will take forty days and every life but two.

Presently, from the sandy hills about, materialize weird-painted savages who proffer food, then—with starving Spanish guard dropped—let fly their arrows. Screaming, women and children rush for the shelter of dunes and there is momentary victory for the few salvaged Spanish crossbows. The Indians fade, make no pursuit when the fugitives flee south, their first dead dotting the beach.

Twisting through the dune labyrinth, hugging the sandy canyons, shunning the naked beaches and open valleys,

Spanish hope rises. Perhaps there will be no pursuit!

The Indians did hold back, where the dead lay. Later, in horror, the fugitives will know why.

Hope is short-lived. Far ahead, among the women and children, a boy drops screaming. His mother bends beside him, dies, her back feathered. A burly rear-guard captain, cursing the mocking, empty dunes, takes an arrow through the throat. A padre stumbling to him, falls across his body. Even the crossbows are gone now.

Yet in this grisly gantlet, the pursuer remains invisible. Where? In these twisting canyons of sand, *where?* Atop yonder dune? Lurking beyond the one ahead. *No! Merciful Father! Right behind you, bow full-drawn!*

Down the jumbled, shifting sand, desperate mile on mile now: terror by night, agony by day. Eyes are baked and lips split. Thirst-crazed, some rush to the beach and die, feathered there. But nemesis stalks from the north; they stagger south, paying each mile its dead.

Someone reckons that the hunters—in a macabre Atlanta's Race—might be delayed by clothing, anything ornamental, left behind. They buy time with nakedness. And now the sun sears but the arrows still sing from nowhere. Clustered bodies drop behind and, each time, there is brief respite again.

Even yet, the Spaniards do not realize they are cattle in a pen their herders know. They are beef or game, take your choice. They are leisurely driven, for sport or ceremonial feasts take time.

The white island ordeal is ended two weeks from the day the once happy voyagers washed up on its long sands. Every woman and child is dead. All but a few men die in the crossing where Padre ends on Boca Chica and again at the Rio Grande.

Of those who stumble on down Mexico's coast, all but one man, Fray Marcos de Mena, will perish before reaching Panuco. This stout brother, though riddled and delirious, lives to relate in Vera Cruz what happened to the great fleet.

It will be confirmed by salvagers sent the following year. Don Francisco Vasquez, steel-tough with a gambler's mind, had turned back midway down the island. Almost certainly he would soon be dead, as would the others. Yet . . . a thin chance! Go back to the treasure wrecks. For treasure, Spain will surely come looking.

From the coyote, Vasquez learned to dig for water, found Padre's strange fresh caches. Night cloaked the awful way back, and finally he made rude shelter in one ship's superstructure. There was food from the sea, and water barrier to the savages; in time he was alone. Salvagers found him alone; he lived to share what treasure could be raised.

He, with de Mena, also left proof of the first journey the length of the white island—a four century old odyssey that, though omitted by history, likely will remain unequalled.

Proof also to us map-watchers of what the map dosen't show. Padre is not, as it appears, a narrow bar of sand. On such a bar — without miles of dunes to hide them — the terrified fugitives would have been cut down in a very few miles.

Of course, you can argue that the Indian was notoriously frugal with his game.

1598

El Paso's White Missions

Beyond Sierra Blanca, you slope into the long, rich mountain valley of upper Rio Grande and, an hour northwest, the fast-spreading metropolis, El Paso.

It's easy to rocket straight into this Texas combination of Denver and Old Mexico. The mountain skyline pulls; the highways are excellent. New Interstate 10 is non-stop, non-town, along the ridge over the valley. Lower, in the green and gold and old cottonwoods and sliding-by towns, U.S. 80 rides the river route.

Going straight in is a mistake. You bypass Farm Road 258—a quiet, shaded valley loop that fringes the Rio

Grande and is the most intriguing fifteen miles of highway in all Texas.

It connects this state's three classically beautiful white missions—at old Ysleta and Socorro, and sleeply San Elizario. More, it is storied ground that with some authority, can debate Santa Fe as to white man's real beginnings in western United States.

El Pasoans pridefully call this their Mission Tour and have marked it well.

Just below where today's Ysleta high school youngsters await their school buses these late afternoons, you come suddenly on the heart of Texas' oldest community. It is a fenced-in, block square compound dominated by the restored church in the center. You are welcome.

The mission is cream-colored, its left side sheer, sloping over to a cross-topped silver dome where pigeons cluster. To the right is the old bell and to the left, granite history recounts that, after flood and fire, the walls stand today on original foundations laid in 1682—first of all Spanish missions in Texas.

Inside is a many-statued altar, heavy in brass, light in lace. Around the pastel blue walls, the stations of the cross are told—from Pilate's decree to the tomb—in Spanish.

East of the mission, where the wire-sided cotton wagons stand still wispy from their harvest, is the plot first broken by Tigua Indian plows in 1681, and cultivated—from maize to grape to cotton—almost continually since.

From Ysleta, the road runs columned in big cottonwoods, with the adobes and new bricks set back in heavy-bearing fields. You pass people walking as they have since the road was dusty, western Camino Real. Socorro is three miles.

Its mission, shortened to La Purisma Church, is classically simple in line. It is snow white as its Jesuit pastor, Father Apton Zuniga, firmly believes missions should be. He showed me the original hewn roof beams supporting slant-set saplings, painstakingly replaced in a rebuilding after flood, just as first laid by Indian hand. He showed me the little museum of old paintings and documents and, in the sacristy, the rare, hand-carved statue of St. Michael.

Legend has it that the statue was planned for a New Mexico church. Ox-carted, it reached this spot in 1838; but here it bogged, and neither oxen nor men could move the cart further. Whatever may say ecclesiastical record, Socorran parishioners know that St. Michael was intended here—and here he guards in the left transept.

Six miles beyond Socorro's ancient cemetery, the road bends at Nacho's Place, and you are in the adobe around San Elizario's plaza. It is worth a close look, for this village was the first hub of El Paso County in the mid 1850's.

There is the sagging old courthouse, little bigger than your double garage and west of it, the still usable adobe jail—once the only Texas carcel west of San Antonio. Across is the low, beam-fronted building that has been Spanish Governor's Palace, a three-generation school, and now a dwelling.

The white, four-belled mission facing the plaza has a later look than the others—more like San Antonio's Franciscan work. And it, like Socorro and Ysleta, is in daily use by parishioners.

Old as Ysleta's and Socorro's near three century visible history, this valley land turns Spanish pages still earlier. From dim time, there had been an Indian crossing at the river here.

Thus, here had come earlier Spanish explorers—Coronado, Espejo—but they had come only to search and had returned across the mountain-desert wilderness south to Mexico.

In 1598—two decades earlier than Plymouth Rock and scarcely a century after Columbus—the Spaniard came to stay. It was Ascension Thursday, April 30, that he crossed the river. (Some say at Socorro; more, at present-day San Elizario.)

He was Captain General Don Juan de Oñate—one of

Mexico's most powerful, whose wife traced directly to Hernando Cortez and to Montezuma. Oñate came with colonists, the cloth and armor—a four-mile train.

Across the river, he drove in Spain's cross and took possession of the land of the Rio del Norte "without exception whatsoever." Then he moved to colonize. At this crossing, Oñate based the white man's first armed garrison outside of distant Florida. And from his Spanish train came America's first domestic cattle.

The captain general's colonizers followed the river far into the country Coronado had explored. This first governor of New Mexico founded in 1610 what would become Santa Fe.

Ironically, seventy years later, the bloody Pueblo revolution would drive Spain from all of Mexico. Flung back on this riverbank where their forebears had started, those refugees and the Indians who followed would found Ysleta and Socorro.

And so that quiet and shaded strip of road really swings full circle. Driving it, you may be sure of one thing. Where this state's three white missions stand aside today—somewhere in there—is where it all started: Santa Fe and everything west.

It is country not to bypass.

1806-12

The Gateway House

East of San Augustine, in the red, rolling pineland that is the oldest part of Texian Texas, you wind leisurely past the classic old homes, some handsome new ones; and presently — beyond sleepy little Milam— you cross the quiet. wooded Sabine into Louisiana, on the road to Nachitoches.

At the river, running dark from upland rains, there is a girdered bridge and, to the side below, a park of oak and gum and cushion pine. Across the road is a neat store and just away, beside a bent old mulberry, there is a house beside the Texas road.

The house is solid, roomy one story. Siding, in some places, covers the original dovetailed log walls. The little sign reads, "Gaines House, 1812."

They are glad for you to come inside, for this is more than one of Texas' oldest houses. This, with its worn-bank crossing below, is the eastern Texas terminus of the greatest highway of them all—El Camino Real. Even more, Gaines Ferry (or Crossing) ranks in its way with Plymouth Rock. Literally, it was the great gate that opened Texas and everything west.

For centuries, they crossed here. First the buffalo, then their hunters—tribe on tribe—until the Spanish found the east-west trail of the Caddo Confederacy. The French found it, too. For nearly as long as we have been a state, French cannon were at now Nachitoches. But through these years, the Sabine crossing—midway—remained fairly quiet.

It was when Jefferson paid Napoleon an astronomical fifteen million dollars for a "wilderness Louisiana" (stretching to the Rockies) that this remote river bank became the door to the West. First came near war with Spain who claimed that Texas yet remained in her empire.

In October, 1806, Spain threw an army along the west bank where the bridge stands today. On the east bank, where Louisiana Highway 6 begins, were the deadly American long rifles that, in nine years, would rout the British at New Orleans. In this showdown, American colors remained on the Sabine, although frontiersmen angrily insisted their true boundary was the Rio Grande.

Still, the drive west has begun. Virginian James Gaines had soldiered to the Sabine in 1805. Now, in 1812, his strong log cabin stands defiantly across the river in Texas. Gaines Crossing is to be historic rendezvous for Americans who believe the western land is theirs.

First comes a secret frontiersman-adventurer army, allied with Mexicans in revolt from Spain. The Gaines

79

House is first stop in Texas for nearly a thousand Americans who will fight a bloodier struggle than the Texas Revolution and will carry all the territory to three desperate battles around San Antonio (Rosalia, Alazan, Medina). Except for American-British war behind them, they might have won. Instead, they are nearly destroyed. The Gaines House that mustered them sees one man in ten escape across the river the following year. History writes off the Gutierrez-Magee Expedition.

Similarly it writes off the second assault, crossing here. From Natchez in 1819 comes Dr. James Long. Three hundred Americans capture Nacogdoches, most of the upper country. Again, James Gaines rallies reinforcements to the newly-proclaimed republic, at Galveston almost enlisting Lafitte's volatile aid. However, once more the house by the road at the crossing sees its defeated army flee.

For a time this door to Texas sees peaceful entry. Mexico, free of Spain, seems free of tyranny, briefly welcomes the flood of settlers crossing here. It is short-lived welcome. South is Santa Anna and north, revolt.

And now come new faces to Gaines Ferry: a young lawyer with a tragic marriage behind him in Alabama; a Tennesseean who is more frontiersman than congressman. Travis will meet Crockett at the Alamo.

Another Tennesseean will come this way. It is at San Augustine that Sam Houston is elected to the command that will lead him inexorably to San Jacinto.

And in the last desperate days preceding that battle, one more crossing at Gaines Ferry—little-known but possibly what tipped the scales. Across northeast Texas, the angry Cherokee masses. A signal from Santa Anna could obliterate the republic from behind.

Into Texas canter U.S. troopers, taking battle stations at Nacogdoches. Indian war is faced down while San Jacinto is fought. This intervening American column swings a long, dusty line down Camino Real. At its head, General Pendleton Gaines passes his brother's house by the river.

San Augustine engineer-historian Steve Kardell drove me to the old house by the side of the road. With the lake, there's talk of looping a new road wide of the historic

crossing. Steve didn't think the highway people are planning one of those jet-stream, non-stop supers.

"I think they'll leave Camino Real pretty much alone.
Particularly here." Steve ran a hand through crew-
cropped, iron-gray hair. "I think they should."

So do I.

Let tomorrow's wayfarers have, as their first sight of
Texas, the old Gaines House—as near as possible to where,
for a century and a half, it marked the way.

How we got here—to build roads and dams—is one thing
not to forget.

*Author's Note: The Sabine River has been dammed, and
the great Toledo Bend Reservoir now forms the Texas-
Louisiana boundary here. From its century-and-a-half
foundations, historic old Gaines house has been removed
to the west bank of the lake.*

1812-13

San Antonio's Forgotten Battlefields

The farmer by the door of Ella Lee Jasper's whitewashed
concrete block grocery had his hat back over the sweat,
rolling a Durham. He allowed me the tolerance of country-
man for newcomer. No, he hadn't read what the monument said—there across the highway in Johnson grass
—which, of course, he had.

This grocery is in little, drowsy Losoya, just south of
San Antonio.

Walking away, I asked Mrs. Jasper's young son, Charlie,
about the marker, and he agreed that the Battle of Medina
must have been an awful fight, the way it said; and I
asked him if he knew anything about Rosalia—the unmarked one in the San Antonio-Salado bottoms under the

81

hills a little east, and he said he wished he had studied more Texas history. He hadn't any idea that three thousand men had died within a mile of where he lives.

Next time you're in San Antonio, you can—with a little effort—take a tour into its violent past, which is known to few citizens of the Alamo City and to almost no other Texans at all. It is not the Mission Loop, although San Antonians have marked their Franciscan heritage well.

However, this tourist-wise city has never used the second string to its bow. Nobody is shown San Antonio's battlegrounds, and there are many. We get to stern, gallant Alamo, then stop. I want to take off my hat and stand a moment in silent salute to Travis and his men, then look beyond.

For a San Antonio battleground tour would include eight beside the fortress church, more than any other American city. Some were brief fire fights like Concepcion and Grass Fight, near the missions. Some were reconnaissances in force like the storming of Bexar, right down Main and Soledad to the plaza. There was also 1840 Council House, downtown, where Texan and Comanche struggled hand-to-hand indoors. There was Salado, north by Fort Sam Houston, which drove back Mexican invasion six years after San Jacinto decided "peace." There were three others.

You can encompass these battlegrounds with an expressway loop that, already existing, starts south for Laredo, laterals across to the Valley highway (U.S. 281), and circles up to finish on U.S. 81 bound for Austin. It would be easy to mark turnoffs as well as the contested ground itself, even that which is downtown.

This loop also would include the three battles which were bloodiest, least known, and most nearly successful. All were fought a quarter century before Texas Independence, and nearly won it.

Rosalia. Alazan. Medina. Let's look at them now.

It is 1812-13; Jefferson's, Madison's, Monroe's America regards its Louisiana Purchase as everything west. There is a shrouded alliance which, in the Sabine country of

82

the Louisiana border, gathers an army of Americans—some freebooters, some dedicated men—Mexican patriot-revolutionists, and confused Indians.

This Republican Army of the North sweeps across Texas in successive victories at the Sabine, at Nacogdoches, then Goliad, and finally, the prize of Bexar—Rosalia to win it, Alazan to hold it, slaughterhouse Medina to lose it.

Had Americans not been diverted to Jackson's struggle against the British, this forgotten war would have occupied a larger page in history. It was decided in early victory and final defeat in the three relatively unmarked battles of San Antonio.

How would you mark that first one, Rosalia? At Mrs. Irene Delgado's little house on Salado Creek, a plaque should recall where the Americans crossed at night. Another, beyond, where twenty-five hundred Spanish were routed from the ridge. Others, where Luckett's sharpshooters picked off Spanish artillerymen, where the Indians took the brunt of cavalry charge, where Americans marched to within thirty yards of the blazing Spanish line, then rushed it. There should be many others.

Then there is Alazan, weeks later as a new Spanish army moves up from Laredo. Here, the battle was fought almost beneath today's balconied expressway, down where the creeks jumble together in the stockyards, near the neat plants of Gebhardt and Roegelein. Here, nearly a thousand Spanish troops fell at the breastworks, left their welter of dead, fleeing down the old Laredo road.

August 18, 1813, the last Spanish army comes up, four thousand strong. Most American leaders have gone home, sick of the massacres following Rosalia and Alazan. Kemper, Perry and Ross will not be our Houston, Travis and Crockett.

Two thousand Republicans, fortified with aguardiente, march into ambush at Medina. One in ten gets home to American Nachitoches. San Jacinto is still a long way off.

And for all this desperate war, which pitted more numbers in battle, alive and dead, than the Texas Revolution, there is one dusty, forgotten granite marker on a farm road into Losoya.

Ella Lee Jasper can tell you of the graves she found up where the Medina joins the San Antonio, of the rusting Spanish arms turned up when they made the cut for the new bridge.

San Antonio historians—if they work at it— can tell you a lot more.

Much always can be told, and should be remembered, when many men die, believing something.

1813

A World Fell on Spanish Bluff

The lieutenant couldn't know he was about to bequeath Texas a little-known and strange monument to martyrs—tragic as Goliad. He only knew his orders.

"The prisoners, Teniente? Shoot them!" His colonel had reined in by the trees on the river bluff to watch flame sweep the town. "How many, did you say?"

"Perhaps eighty, Comandante." Behind a young mask, the sweating, jackbooted dragoon shut out thought that the prisoners believed themselves also soldiers. Now grimly he asked, "And those of the town?"

"Leave not one man." The colonel glanced where his cavalry herded them, straggling along; and the lieutenant stiffened in his saddle. Possibly three hundred from that town. Old ones...and very young: how could all of them be traitorous?

"Save your ammunition, Teniente." The colonel tapped his saber against a trooper's lance. "Let this obscenity of a town feel Spanish steel!"

Saluting, the young officer wheeled his troop. He wished he had never known the name Trinidad, in the province of Tejas.

84

Today, few indeed know this Trinidad that was. Not the Henderson County community on the Trinity, but the one, once called Spanish Bluff, downriver where Camino Real crosses rolling woodland meadows from Madisonville to Crockett. There is a marker west of the bridge, but old timers cannot agree exactly where Trinidad perished, and with reason. On Spanish Bluff came no ordinary death to time or change. It was sudden as Indianola's, but the storm's fury was man-made, like Goliad's; and unlike both, as final as ancient Troy.

Even more ironic, Trinidad was killed by the very men who built it and who, for its eight years beginning in 1805, believed its destiny might challenge their other four outposts: San Antonio, La Bahia, Nacogdoches and far west Ysleta.

Trinidad's destiny? A whole world dictated this, and that was the irony of all.

It is fall of 1805 when New Spain's northernmost governor, purposeful Don Antonio Cordero canters a long column up the royal road east. He must found a fort and city that will endure. He knows some of what is happening across the crazy world.

Napoleon holds powder-keg Europe, from Portugal to Prussia, but—counterblockading—England holds the sea. A brash America, timing Europe's preoccupation, suddenly buys Louisiana from a France who cannot reach it . . . and pours west. Unable to stop it, Cordero knows, is his once proud Spain.

Still proud New Spain? Stretched thin, Argentina to Mexico, she must yet check the American who has settled across to the Sabine. Nacogdoches? Too close to the Americans! Then make Trinidad anchor bastion. Cordero will send hundreds of loyal colonists to buffer all his eastern front.

Within a year, Trinidad's strong log walls garrison four hundred troops. Up go depots and granaries; and down both river banks—bluff and bottom—spread cabin and rancho to graze the great cattle herds. Mexico streams colonists steadily. At Nacogdoches, 90 miles east, the

slipping-in Anglos smile and call it all "Spanish Bluff."
But behind it, New Spain feels more secure.

Now, the winter climaxing wrong guesses, 1812-13, and
a world turned upside down. Napoleon is in freezing retreat from Moscow. Shattered Spain is free of France
but can scarcely aid England's Wellington, crossing to
draw the noose; let alone, her colonies. Venezuela to
Mexico—afire with America's revolution! Now from the
Sabine comes the buckskin rifleman himself. Allied with
Mexicans! All insolently proclaiming "freedom" and
"Republic of the North." A growing, menacing, green-
bannered army of more than a thousand. Nacogdoches
falls; then in hard fighting, coastal La Bahia.

Some probabilities, a grim New Spain knows. Hold San
Antonio or lose all Texas. If America's rumored thousands
pour in, lose even Mexico!

One certainty, a furious New Spain knows best. Who
helped these invaders? Who based their army, supplied
them for three strength-gathering months? Who marches
with them now, to Bexar's very gates?

Trinidad—built to stop them!

For Spanish Bluff, this world has a last irony—American
error.

Mexico cannot yet go it alone, and the Southwest's frontiersmen move too soon. Their new nation has misjudged
the speed of French collapse, is at war with an England
now able to overrun most of the North. Washington will
yet burn before New Orleans holds with Andy Jackson.
Forget reinforcement from the Sabine! Embattled America writes off the Gutierrez-Magee Expedition.

There had been enough to take San Antonio and hold
it in two bitter battles. But now, variously disenchanted,
half the Americans have gone home; the remaining fifteen
hundred allies growl discord. At bloody Medina, Spanish
ambush crushes what is left of the alliance. Two hundred
survivors flee for the Sabine; the Anglo half makes it.

The rest, Spanish cavalry has cornered in the town Spain
decreed just eight years earlier. On the Trinity bluffs,

Colonel Ignacio Elisondo gives the order. The prisoners are manacled and shot into a ditch below the flaming town. Every male is herded to a big hill upriver and "to save ammunition," cut down.

That hill is likely the slope rising north of the marker opposite white-framed Antioch Church. At little Midway, white-haired and pert Mrs. Elisha Clapp believes this, and she remembers her forebears who ran Texas' first ferry, below. When they cut the bridge approaches, she remembers all the old Spanish relics from Black Bluff.

And the town? Somewhere in that great bend was Trinidad, but you'll find no trace. Spain erased her bluff in fact and in history.

So call all that bending river valley Spanish Bluff. For even stranger than that somewhere here is a forgotten tomb of martyrs, is how it became forgotten. That was because there was simply no one left to remember. Failing and frustrated, Spain was about to leave. Americans were yet to come.

Mexicans? Searching for freedom, it was they who were martyred here. Was it simply Spain's fury, loosed on them? A little more complex. Take a long look down that valley.

From Moscow to Madrid, Paris to London, and Washington to Mexico City, the world fell in on Spanish Bluff.

1816

Old Red River, Arkansas-Texas

Your map doesn't show the road, but you'll find it anyhow. Wandering fifteen miles of wooded Red River bottoms northeast of Paris, it crosses what was capital of an empire, unique in Texas.

"When you get lost," said the Kiomatia lady cheerfully, "just ask somebody. You'll find your way." Kiomatia is a wayside grocery and white house in tall oaks. It is also part of that empire, and where your road begins—a sandy lane striking for Texas 37, at the Red.

On the way, along the big-timbered riverbend, you find an old plantation that the forest has beaten and, by it, a vine-choked marker. You have reached the site of Jonesborough on Pecan Point—the point being those sleepy bottoms you crossed from tiny Kiomatia. And why singular, this land?

Little known today, here was our first Anglo settlement. Stephen Austin's father asked Pecan Pointers the way to Texas. And here, up the Red in 1831, wide-ranging Ben Milam landed a New Orleans steamboat when they were barely venturing the Brazos, south. Here passed Sam Houston on his way to Texas.

In fact, everybody knew Pecan Point and old Jonesboro...except for one thing: exactly where it was. Today, you'd roughly bound its one time Red River domain by Texarkana and Marshall east, Gainesville and Denton, west. Jonesborough—seat of one vast county!

Miller County, Arkansas? Or Red River County, Texas? Until the mid-1840's, both!

As always with Texas boundaries, you begin with how much Louisiana Thomas Jefferson bought from Napoleon in 1803. The Rio Grande debate—which once had an infant Texas republic looking north into today's Wyoming—overshadowed another treaty-line, equally open to argument.

That was what John Quincy Adams and Spain agreed was Rio Roxo—separating them; but their 1819 treaty left frontiersmen to guess whether it was today's Red River, or the southerly Sulphur. The country between was big—most of thirty-nine Texas counties today. You weren't sure, however, whether you lived in Arkansas or Texas.

Immediately after San Jacinto, President Sam Houston asked a joint U.S.-Texas survey. Six years later, the Republic of Texas approved the line, happily picking up land. In 1845, with Texas a state, U.S. approval made it the line of today.

For the few years after San Jacinto, though,

Jonesborough seemed capital in fact of a "Free State of Confusion." It was nothing at all to find Arkansas courts running full docket in town; and just down the road at new Clarksville, Texas courts arguing the same cases. A U.S. marshal rode into Jonesborough to serve Arkansas papers in Miller County. A Texas sheriff from Red River County promptly arrested him.

And more than one Jonesborough roof sent one son to Little Rock's Arkansas legislature, and another to the Republic of Texas congress.

What really happened to those people?

Down the old road from Kiomatia to Jonesborough, you strike the once plantation lands of the Claiborne Wright family, among Pecan Point's 1816 earliest. That year, they had flatboated the Cumberland, Tennessee and Mississippi, finally laboring up the Red to the new land Jefferson had opened west. Two youngsters, Travis and George, saw their father—like the others—stake both sides of the river.

Now, the year 1819 brings uncertain word. This new Spanish treaty! Which, the American riverbank? Arkansas Territory's new Miller County claims both sides, including most of today's Oklahoma. The boys' dad is Miller County's first sheriff.

But two years later, America's word is that the north side belongs to the Choctaw nation. The Wrights and Miller County move south; Jonesborough tops a thousand population. Below it is wilderness to Spanish Nacogdoches and San Antonio and to some scattered colonies those Austins finally got started.

Now, in troubled 1836, the boys are grown. Trouble indeed! South of the river—their land—may be Republic of Texas. At a place called Washington on the Brazos, far south, men will meet...maybe declare independence.

At Little Rock, far east, they are readying a constitution for America's twenty-fifth state—resolutely still claiming Miller County.

Only one thing for a straight-thinking Red River family

to do. From their Jonesborough home, Travis Wright will represent Miller in Little Rock. Brother Gorge saddles a black mule and rides for San Jacinto. He stays to represent Red River County, Congress of the Republic of Texas.

Unusual? Not at all. Nearby, the James Latimers have done the same thing: the father helping draw Arkansas' state constitution, the son signing Texas' Declaration of Independence.

At Kiomatia — like Paris and Clarksville, one of the communities that grew from Jonesborough those days — it was all perfectly clear to pleasant and pretty Mrs. Ernest Boulware, who put me on the right road from her husband's grocery. Their family forebears were like the rest who settled Red River country. They came to stay, whichever government that boundary commission put them with.

It's an interesting road those old timers left. State of Determination is a better word for what it crosses.

If you aimed to run a government...well, you just ran both, until the government figured where it was.

1832

Freedom Boots at Velasco

The boots, of course, are gone now. They were there, though; side by side they stood there, waiting as though to be claimed, to be filled. We'll come back to them, and first, look at the land where they were left.

Below Houston, from Freeport's seagoing high bridge, you can see a lot of country: our Gulf coast's industrial sprawl against the horizon, and all along the surfline, the color-splashy beach resorts. Also, something more.

Aside, just over the bridge toward the sea, is a new historical marker. Near here was old Velasco, once the seagate to Texas. Today, Velasco's traces are spilled under the booming complex we call Brazosport—a half dozen bright new cities that have sprung from magnesium to marvel chemicals—all above the weathered remnants of our first towns. At this old mouth of the Brazos, Stephen Austin's first colonists landed in 1821.

Now, the old river mouth and the beach to either side is a carefree skelter of kids with surfboards, of sunup fishermen working the jetties, of tent, trailer and beach house up Surfside's new road that jumps to Galveston Island, east. A new Brazos channel is cut through to the west; this old one now reaches inland to dock this great, growing port.

A little distance up what was the original river is the red-roofed U.S. Coast Guard station. There's your second marker, for you stand on the site of old Fort Velasco. Take a long look. Almost forgotten today, here is where Texans' fight for freedom actually began; here is where a treaty said it ended.

What is it like, across Austin's colony, this year of 1832 when it began? Velasco, together with Anahuac around Galveston bay, are Texas' two ports: stark log cabin and shack along the beach and up the river that reaches inland to scattered frontier settlements.

The settlements are flung away west to Goliad and Bexar, north at Washington on the Brazos and San Felipe and faraway Nacogdoches, with a scant few between—all of them growing, swelling with colonists that pour west from the United States. Today, the colonists cross by land, for these ports are closed.

Closed ports? A Mexico, scarcely free from Spain, fears America plans a Texas grab; she has begun to distrust her Anglo settlers. And these colonists that she herself brought suddenly face import duties and taxes they cannot bear. They see nothing of the democratic institutions they thought promised, and—most of all—they fear convict-conscripted garrisons that enforce what now seems to them, tyranny. There seems one hope: a man emerges in Mexico who promises democracy and a fair deal for all. The colonists, along with many a Mexican patriot, resolve to support that man, regardless of deepening trouble.

Trouble is deep enough: one of their firebrands, William Barret Travis, is jailed with others at Anahuac. Texans will free him—if necessary, shipping over cannon they hold at tiny Brazoria, just upriver from Velasco. They will have to run Fort Velasco's guns; that log bastion barricades the river mouth.

Texans declare for the man in Mexico who talks freedom and democracy, and advance on that fort. Its commander, Domingo de Ugartechea, bars their way. Down the Brazos, past where Dow Chemical's towers stand today, steams the schooner *Brazoria*; and from three sides of the river-bend fort, the land force attacks.

In eleven hours of storm-torn, night-to-daylight fighting, the fort surrenders. Both small armies, scarcely a hundred fifty men each, count fifteen per cent casualties. But here at Velasco, as at Nacogdoches a scant month later, Texans and Mexicans now declare for the man of democracy in Mexico. It looks like peace.

That man, however, is Antonio Lopez de Santa Anna, dictator-to-be.

Now it is four years later and everything west burned flat—Gonzales and the Alamo, Goliad and Refugio—and Sam Houston grimly falling back to a riverbend in the San Jacinto. There seems little hope for the Texas provisional government, its back to the wall like its buckskinned army.

Yet on this very instant, this infant government has suddenly the incredible prisoner, Santa Anna himself—ironically, the symbol for whom Velasco had been stormed those long years back. And even more ironically, the site to sign liberation's treaty—that same Velasco.

Prisoner Santa Anna, aboard the old *Yellow Stone* , is taken past Galveston — too battered for negotiation — around the coast to what briefly will be capital of Texas. The *Yellow Stone* moors alongside the old fort where it all started for these colonies.

Two treaties are signed, one secret. The public one clears Texas of invading troops. There will be an armistice to set terms for lasting peace. The secret treaty will free Santa Anna to Mexico where he will see to recognition of Texas freedom.

That neither Texas nor Mexico held to the treaty and left the issue for a long later U.S.-drawn document at Guadalupe Hidalgo is not the point; old Velasco is. There began freedom's fight and there, supposedly, it ended.

I drove down from the high bridge to look over the old land. The marker by the bridge tells of a Velasco that was Confederate port when blockade runners tried to sustain the South. Little is said, either here or at the Coast Guard station, that here the fight for freedom began, and here it ended.

Perhaps that's as it should be; perhaps the fight hasn't ended. I thought that as I looked at the boots. Under the steel plaque by the highway, neatly to either side of its post, they stood. They were scarred and worn—G.I. boondocks.

There was no way to tell whether their fight was World War II, Korea or even Viet Nam's jungles.

No, perhaps the fight hasn't ended.

1836

The Horse Marines

That obscure bard, "Anonymous", began his scornful ditty, "I'm Captain Jinks of the Horse Marines. I feed my horse on corn and beans." To him, such cavalry was a joke and Jinks always ran when the shooting started.

And Mr. Webster's big book is equally skeptical: "Horse Marines: (1) a member of an imaginary corps of marine cavalry; (2) anyone as much out of his element as a mounted marine would be on shipboard."

93

Neither of these scribes is quite on target. In 1836, thirty Texas Rangers ambushed and captured three fully-manned ships at anchor in Copano Bay, just above Rockport and midway down coastal Texas.

Nor was Captain Jinks around at all. It was Major Isaac Watts Burton whose horsemen boarded schooners, *Watchman, Comanche* and *Fanny Butler*, and took $25,000 prize cargo east eventually to Galveston.

Beginning with historian Henderson Yoakum, this incredible cavalry troop drew the title, "The Horse Marines." The name has stuck, and it is fact. "Imaginary corps", indeed!

All this happened, I believe, near the little town of Bayside at the deep upper reach of Copano Bay. There is a plaque, one of those steel-historied tablets, which tells you this is old-storied land. The plaque is on the bluff over the water. Opposite is a venerable eight-columned mansion whose stately widow's walk argues with TV antennae reaching above; and around the curving bay-front is the little town.

The steel tablet records that, in 1519, Spain's Alonso Alvarez de Pineda stood atop the bluff near here: first European to chart the Texas coastline.

I think we could add a second plaque about the Horse Marines, because Pineda knew a port when he saw one and the earliest maps—like Parrilla's of the 1700's—show that El Copano was an excellent port. It nurtured the Refugio mission just above, La Bahia, a little beyond, and even Bexar, far within the interior.

And old Copano, whose ruins are still visible on private land beyond Bayside, is where Burton's cavalry took the navy.

Incredible was Burton's feat, you can see how events led up to it. Santa Anna's army, this spring of 1836, was pincer with one claw south on the Refugio-Goliad line, the other north from its Alamo and across to reckoning at San Jacinto. Chartered privatiers were at sea with supplies and munitions for an army far from base, even after that army had been erased at Buffalo Bayou.

With a four-ship Texas Navy and fourteen hundred miles of coastline, General Rusk called in cavalry to hold the beaches. Major Burton drew the soft underbelly, the logical landing port—Copano: a straight shot into Refugio and then east as far as Santa Anna had intended going.

With San Jacinto behind, the Ranger cavalry actually had the drop on anything inbound. Burton hovered over Copano, rode to its bluffs when the first ship, *Watchman*, lay to, off the bar. Down to the beach clambered two Rangers, making distress signals. Aboard the anchored schooner, up first and uncertainly, went American and Texan colors.

"Keep signaling," said Burton. "They'll show the other colors."

Now up went Santa Anna's ensign. The ambushers waved them in, confronted the *Watchman's* captain—ashore in his long boat—with carbine and pistol.

Sixteen Rangers took over the boat, rowed back. Ship's crew, glad for the assistance, helped them over the side, surrendered scant moments later. One privateer out of business!

Burton was to get his prize to Velasco, but the winds were contrary, and *Watchman* waited two weeks. Now in came *Comanche* and *Fanny Butler*. Cavalry man Burton had his captive captain signal over the two new skippers. Then he had three ships.

Fledgling Texas took her prize cargo—a fortune for her empty treasury—and returned the ships to their owners.

And that, practically speaking, was the end of seagoing invasion supply against the little republic.

From Kentucky, Edward Wilson marveled for U.S. consumption: "I suppose you'd have to call them 'Horse Marines'."

If you want to drive to where it happened, check the old timers in Rockport, or old Lamar, across the bay. This will lead you eventually, as it did me, to sleepy Bayside.

There, I suggest you visit at the little blue and white Gulf station and grocery, where former Chicagoan Earl Willis holds forth. He is a heavying, jutjawed and graying Scotch-Irish-Cherokee who was an Illinois tool and die man and who took a long look at California before he moved to Texas to stay.

He is a Texan now, restless as Burton was when he took those ships. His only objection to the Copano marker is that they left out the Horse Marines, and he thinks it all really happened just around the bend of the bay, where private fence guards the old ruins and says "keep out".

Ask him. He might just take you there by boat.

1839-40

Republic of the Rio Grande

Atop the north bank of the Rio Grande, near the two Laredos' International Bridge, is a small white building, unobtrusive among grander structures about. Little noted and less known, this plastered adobe and rock is, at the same time, one of the most remarkable, historically, in our land.

Hurrying south, turista-bound, you round old San Agustine Plaza, its bandstand and shady benches for watching the Sunday promenades. The granite marker yonder recalls Villa Laredo's 1755 beginnings. Cornering the plaza is its silver-steepled patron church, and across, the tiled and mission-arched new hotel backs lushly on the river.

The neat one story beside the hotel is Laredo's Historical Museum and, across the front above three heavy, dark doors, Texas' six flags stand to the wind on festive days. Look again. There is a seventh. It is similar to Mexico's red, white and green, yet when it first unfurled here, that flag intended a vast difference.

For two wild-dreaming, harried years — 1839-40 — Mexican and Texan allied themselves — patriots and freebooters in both ranks—to create a new nation: most of Mexico and much of the United States now west of the Mississippi.

This was the Republic of the Rio Grande, and this building, its only real capitol while it struggled and failed for life.

Laredo's museum chairman Mrs. Marie Kraut took me through the little capitol—a building some date as old as the 1760's. That age closes quickly on you: mission-thick walls, heavy-beamed ceilings and sagging floors of brick, aslant. In the rear *cocina* is the big fireplace cookery and heavy sandstone water filter. Most of the furnishings—the *recamara's* delicate lace, mesquite wood cradle and rope-bottomed bed—suggest substantial Mexican home more than statehouse (coming as they did from old Laredo families like that of founding Don Tomas Sanchez).

Laredo historians have done splendidly in marking and describing each room's content. And warming to the shrine they own, they press now for any period piece that will recall that January 17, 1840, when the already embattled republic announced its nation to the world.

There was a constitution somewhat like ours, a proclamation against dictatorship in government, a declaration for each man's dignity through his own electors. In essence, neglected North Mexico seceded from Santa Anna, certain that the oppressed would rally round, from the mountains below coastal Tampico to the ocean of the Californias.

A North Mexico attorney, Jesus Cardenas, was president with a small cabinet. General Antonio Canales would command the hard-riding rancheros, the other allies that must arise, and whatever Texans would join.

Texas? Officially neutral; actually sympathetic. The republic was as much at home north of Rio Grande as south.

The great map mural within the entrance sala is my favorite part of the old capitol. For here you grasp the

97

really incredible scope of the war this republic endeavored to fight.

It was not so much the size of forces engaged (though occasionally opposing armies could muster more than a thousand each). It was the length of land—the wild, lean and limitless distance they marched and fought for.

Study the map and visualize that country as it was then. At San Patricio, near Corpus Christi, gather forces. Win a battle in the emptiness below Ciudad Mier, on the river. Lay siege to Matamoros, where the river empties. March the bone-bare land, living off it, to Monterrey, then back to the river once more. Travel as far as Austin for Texan recruits; not beyond, for there is nothing but Comanche.

Now drive deep below Monterrey to Ciudad Victoria, start over the mountains for San Luis Potosi, double north through impassable canyons, as far as Saltillo. Then, for the last time, recross the Bravo; the republic is finished.

What was it like, along the way? Battles won, lost, never joined. Fight for food, water and guns where thorny arroyo blows dust, where wind rattles the high passes, where heat is solid and thirst, crazing; where trails crawl for peaks only the sun reaches. To win, your allies must rise from that empty land.

They rise, even come over from the other army, for they want to live as free men. But even more, they are men who want to live, and they leave you by hundreds when it seems you may lose, and they must die for it.

And the *Tejano*? He seldom loses. But he will fight his own way or not at all. He marches under his own single starred flag, not the republic's. Whose republic does he really plan this great nation to be?

A handful of Rio Bravo rancheros and Texans win their last fight below Saltillo, even as their recent allies turn on them—perhaps believing their chance to live lies best in the republic's death.

After Saltillo, the only road now is north to the river. There is no more Republic of the Rio Grande, nor empire from ocean to ocean. Where you stand, measuring the thousands of gaunt miles theatering this struggle, the republic's little capitol becomes just another building—emptied of proclamation, constitution and dreams.

Until Laredoans restored it.

I don't believe the map shows all the republic intended. Had it succeeded, as even Texas President Mirabeau Lamar briefly thought it might, it would have been a sprawling nation to match size with anything North American.

But under what name, you ask yourself; and directed by whom?

Another story entirely: perhaps why it was foredoomed to die.

1840

L'Affaire Pig

To most everybody, the Longhorn steer is the rampant Lone Star symbol. However, we had another four-legged hero who rooted for Texas, and there is a storied old house in our capital that recalls his heroics.

This is the French Legation, Austin's oldest building and a colonial gem maintained in authentic Gallic elegance these days by the Daughters of the Republic of Texas. It is shaded in a high-walled, box-hedged garden perching a hill east of the capitol.

Its square-columned portico and dormered windows have looked down on a capitol building since the first log stockade in 1840. You can visit any day and sense how it was, that fourth year of our republic.

It was quite a year: among other crises, a time when France tried to buy Texas with a loan. And just might have, too, had it not been for what has become obscurely known as L'Affaire Pig.

What was the world of this upstart young republic?

She was target of the U.S., driving west; of England, to slow the American drive; and of France, who still remembered LaSalle's empire. To the south, Mexico smouldered to return her lost province. To the west, Comanche!

Texas herself? A brawling, dreaming, over-reaching, visionary's world, which some felt should outstrip the America others wanted only to join.

The new capital, Austin? Last year she had been Waterloo's seven families under the violet rim of the Comanche hills across the Colorado. Now she was nearly a thousand, strung along Congress Avenue's mud and dust frontier. She was President Lamar's pretentious two story and Sam Houston's dirt-floored log hut. Hub of town was Tennesseean Richard Bullock's half-block-long inn at Sixth and Congress.

This capital of Texas was abuzz with plans gamuting from conquering Mexico to annexing California. And she was flat broke. Across Europe, Texas bonds went begging.

Into all this journeyed a French Charge d'Affairs with an entourage of three servants, a Parisienne chef and such persuasive credentials as rich-bodied cheroots, driest Peyregueys and hors d'oeuvres that awed and dumfounded Texans. He was set to lobby for a plan as intricate as his name: Comte Jean Pierre Isidor Alphonse DuBois de Saligny.

The plan was this: France lends Texas seven million dollars to clear her debt. In return, France gets three million western acres—key ones militarily—and will garrison them with ten thousand troops, more than Texas had expelled under Santa Anna. Into Texas Congress went the Franco-Texienne Bill.

And into Bullock House went Saligny, waiting for completion of his hilltop legation. This, he specified, would contain a dominant entrance hall suitable for entertainment and halving off into parlor and bedrooms; stairing down at the rear to a proper wine cellar and up to alcoved quarters for his lackeys. Hardware and millwork was from France. It was elegance, and is today.

Saligny and two-fisted Bullock spent little time in working up a warm disregard for each other. The Frenchman found Bullock's Texians, boors. The innkeeper found Saligny's cheques rubbery.

Then the count moved to his residence, met Bullock's pigs, and the diplomatic pouches shuddered.

Around the count's garden was a fence of wood palings. Inside was corn and, with daily punctuality, Innkeeper Bullock's pigs. Every morning, the angry count informed the Texas secretary of state, it required two hours to replace the palings rooted out by the hogs. Did Texas want this loan? Had she forgotten he was brother-in-law to France's minister of finance?

The Texian pigs continued unimpressed by protocol and palings alike.

Name of a name! raged the count. Had they not even entered his house, eaten his towels and state papers and thoroughly demoralized his day? At this juncture, Saligny counter-attacked. Assault the hogs, he told his servants. Kill any invading Bullock pig! And the servants obeyed.

Innkeeper Bullock caught a Frenchman downtown and whipped him. Then he cornered Saligny himself, who reported to the Texas State Department that he had completely unnerved the Tennesseean by coolly refusing to brawl.

Here, the Texas archives are freighted with reams of diplomatese that would do justice to a full-blown U. N. debate. Boiled down, however, the question was simple. Would Texas punish Richard Bullock for his uppity pigs? Did Texas want that loan?

She wouldn't and she didn't.

Innkeeper Bullock continued one of Austin's respected citizens and eventually Saligny went his huffy way, leaving Texas to what he knew her fate: invasion, bankruptcy and collapse.

So far as is known, the Bullock pigs lived happily ever after, finding other corn. And all that is left of the storm and fury that singed the docket of those years is exactly what is left of the French plan to garrison an army in Texas: one delightful old home with a long memory.

I have been thinking there must be a moral in all this. One, certainly, is that diplomats can take themselves too seriously.

Of course, another way to read it is that hungry pigs on the prowl are respecters of nobody's fences, whatever the summit meetings.

One thing's certain. These rooters were Texians. As long as that's the case, it's good enough for me and most of the Longhorns I know.

1842

Long Three Miles to Monument Hill

The oak is on the square, and the shaft on the hill, high over the town at the river. The signs in shady old La Grange say they are three miles apart.

You should not see one without the other, for the resolute old tree and Monument Hill are as inseparable as beginning and end. Walter Freytag took me to the oak. He looks like a scholarly, graying Glenn Ford and his history is as precisely ordered as his post office. He knows the trails from Fayette County's oak, since the beginning.

Here, they mustered against Indians, or to join Sam Houston or Hood's Texans or Roosevelt's Rough Riders or Fort Sam's old Indianhead Division.

"Even World War II," Walter Fretag recalled, "this is where we all started." He showed me the granite markers that were to salute the veteran tree on La Grange's next San Jacinto Day. For the men she sent out, he wrote the legend.

After that, I went up to Monument Hill and the trees on the bluff over the sweep of river bend. There is a great shellstone shaft and granite crypt for some who left the oak. There is a long, long view.

Something other than three miles.

Many who see this beautifully small state park confuse it with the times of Alamo and Goliad; it dates later. The first men here mustered under Fayette's oak six years after Santa Anna's surrender.

It was that confused time of struggle: Texas to survive as republic; Mexico to reconquer a province. General Adrian Woll's fifteen hundred invading troops held San Antonio; sweat-caked horsemen hammered the alarm across the settlements.

Under the oak, Captain Nicholas Dawson saddled Fayette's men and, swelling to fifty-three as they rode to the guns, found Woll's army beaten and retreating—directly over them!

Dawson and thirty-five men were buried where they fell to cannon and lance. Later, Fayette's hilltop would send for them.

Now rage sweeps Texas. From Santa Anna's Mexico, three invasions! Texans in Mexico's prisons! Beyond reason, Texas will invade a nation twenty times her size. Fayette's oak musters again. Captain William Eastland rides them out, every man with a score to settle. Their captain, too: Dawson was his cousin.

A wise President Houston maneuvers the angry little army until most cool off and go home from a wintry Rio Grande. A hard core stays; in it, Eastland's company.

Christmas morning, 1842, two hundred sixty Texans incredibly storm foreboding Ciudad Mier, forted with two thousand troops. In they batter, house by bloody house...day...night...day. Then, ammunition gone, they surrender on terms—Eastland's men last.

They will not forget the real terms: the bleak, 130-mile march to Matamoros; two weeks' walking cold desert to Monterrey. And now 150 miles into Saltillo's mountains and south to the adobe-walled courtyard prison, Hacienda Salado.

No sane men attack, barehanded, a company of guarding bayonets. Yet the guards go down. Up the saddles! Freedom is 300 miles north. In a week, they nearly make it. But they have eaten their horses and, waterless, drunk their blood. Lost and delirious, they are recaptured, marched back to Salado in irons.

Into an earthenware pitcher go 159 white beans, seventeen black ones. Captain Eastland sees most of his men draw white. His is black!

When it is over, the remaining Texans toil the length of Mexico, finally to the great dungeons of Castle Perote, near Vera Cruz. Two years later, they are freed.

Back in Texas, one man cannot forget the last sight of Salado. He remembers that boy trying to hold his hand steady and write his mother that he has ten minutes to live. He remembers the old one who tried to joke, and the one with freckles who kept saying it was a long way home. He remembers the graves they left.

He is Captain John Dusenberry, Texas Rangers, Zachary Taylor's United States Army, advancing on the Rio Grande—past Palo Alto's cannon and Resaca de la Palma's bayonet charge.

Now strangely they stride the same ground they knew in stumbling despair before. Matamoros...Mier...then across to Monterrey, and house to house. These are map points, battle objectives to cockaded American troopers. To a handful of rangers with long memory, this is the old road to Salado's adobe walls and the men who drew black beans, the men still there.

At Monterrey, Bigfoot Wallace knows he has captured the man who held the pitcher with the life-or-death beans. They are getting closer! After savage Buena Vista, below Saltillo, Captain Dusenberry is certain that Hacienda Salado has to be next.

But the army halts, for the war has moved far south, battering from Vera Cruz to Mexico City. Zachary Taylor's troops will penetrate no farther.

A flying column, then? A handful of rangers on one lightning sweep behind the lines to Salado? Their Texan commander says no, then pointedly looks the other way.

Down the long valleys under the mountains, they gallop. Ride by night, circle the towns; enemy cavalry is still in the field!

A second time, Salado prison is burst. Dumfounded guards are ordered to open the graves. Four long boxes are slung to mules and, as suddenly as they came, the cold-eyed gringo riders are gone!

At General Taylor's headquarters, a strange request is made and granted. In their muleback boxes, the men of Salado's black beans will march with the army. And yes, they will go home with it.

They do, a half year later. Captain Dusenberry is detailed escort to the boxes. By ship to Galveston, they go; then by wagon to La Grange. From there, to the hilltop.

Three miles from the oak?

Infinitely farther, if you measure miles.

Infinitely closer, if you measure the men who rode to bring them home.

1853

Here Comes the Train!

Remember the clickety clack of the rails? The clickety clickety clack of the rails, the spilled back dingdingdingding of the grade crossings, the *whooooeeee* of the whistle up ahead, the leathery luggage smell of parlor car, the prickly opulence of chair car velour, the adventurous lurch of diner eating, of coal smoke's smell, the mysterious blurs of light that were night towns beyond your pullman window?

Who wanted to sleep, anyhow? "Catching" the train was a lifetime's milestone. And in our total picture, so was catching the train in the life of Texas. It shattered distance, it bound up empire; everything about it was of giant proportion as Lone Star trackage untimately became America's largest, and its land grant bounties once were bigger than the state of Indiana.

Railroads built and they destroyed. A ruthless bypass could wither promising cities and create others, could metropolize a Houston instead of a Harrisburg, could nearly erase this state's leading city of the 1870's, Jefferson, and very nearly eliminate Fort Worth, saved from the panic of 1873 only when its entire population built, almost bare handed, the last 26 miles to their depot.

The American railroad was born when Baltimore determined to compete with New York's Erie Canal and in 1828 began 14 miles of westward track, and a horse-drawn carriage foreran the famed B. & O. line.

Railroading came to Texas almost three decades later when San Jacinto veteran General Sidney Sherman in 1853 launched the Buffalo Bayou, Brazos and Colorado from Harrisburg's tidewater docks. Civil War found Texas with eleven feeble companies and not quite 500 miles of track, mainly southeast and east; the war bankrupted every line. But in the two decades following, over five thousand miles of rail went down, and the high iron boomed on for destiny, with almost enough trackage to girdle this planet.

Look elsewhere for those historical mathematics. It is with the spinoff of such mammoth industry that we are concerned: Texas' most extraordinary line, perhaps her most extraordinary railroad journey, and unquestionably her most extraordinary "spectacular" to promote that growth. These were, respectively, a 100-mile long right of way without crosstie or track, a locomotive that took three years to reach its destined depot, and a staged head-on crash that obliterated two sixty-mile-an-hour trains.

You can trail this history at Weatherford's railroad museum, near Fort Worth, or at San Antonio's Texas Transportation Museum, where Rod Varney recalls "Tillman's Lane", a strange Hill Country line of sixty years ago. To consider it first adjust your perspective. By 1911, a quarter century's off-and-on building had pushed a Frisco subsidiary, the Fort Worth and Rio Grande south as far as Menard, aimed for Kerrville and feeder lines to the cattle country hills about, still transportation-isolated.

"The F.W. and R.G. struggled to serve counties like Sutton, Kerr, Edwards, Mason, Kimble and Schleicher," Varney recalls. "Southern Pacific, Santa Fe, and Texas and

Pacific were tough competition. A line south from Menard just seemed a loser. So Frisco's stock agent, E. F. Tillman, came up with an idea."

Tillman fenced a lane from Sonora to Brady, 100 miles long, 250 feet wide, with holding pastures, wells and windmills. He bought "right of way" from a dozen ranches. He had sixty thousand dollars invested, not a foot of track, and he opened for business.

In the black! Down Tillman's Lane for Brady's end of the line came the cattle, up to fifty thousand at a time. For ten years, into the Twenties, that beef-walking railless road paid. By then, Santa Fe made Sonora from San Angelo.

But in the meantime, Tillman had made himself a cattleman's walking railroad.

Two other San Antonians, Sidney Langhard and Sam King, tell of the old shore-hugging Gulf and Interstate, from Beaumont to Port Bolivar, across from Galveston, and the 80-mile, three year journey of Train Number One.

The G.&I. went out behind Engine No. Four, the morning of September 8, 1900. Down to High Island it rolled, then along the coast...straight into the eye of the terrible Galveston hurricane. Eleven miles short of Port Bolivar, wave and wind halted it, half buried in the sand.

Three years later, funds were found to dig out the train and repair track. Back to Beaumont went Engine No. Four for repairs. Then the resolute road announced that any tickets not punched before the end of the 1900 run...well, they'd be honored. Several of the surviving passengers made the trip.

"On the morning of September 23, 1903," says railroader King, "Train No. One chugged into Galveston, three years sixteen days and ten minutes late."

Tyler's Arthur Bishop recalls America's greatest staged railroad wreck. It took place on a fall afternoon in 1896 on a Missouri Kansas and Texas siding near West, between Waco and Hillsboro.

"The Great Train Wreck was widely advertised," Bishop recounts. "The railroad advised that excursion trains

107

would be run to the scene from Dallas, Fort Worth, Waco, and other points north and south. There was no town where it happened, just a siding called 'Crush' in honor of William Crush, M. K. & T. passenger agent, with whom the idea reputedly originated.

"Came the big day; excursion trains were packed. 'Crush', with its refreshment restaurant tent, its sideshows, lemonade stands, temporary wooden jail and two hundred special constables, became a one-day town. The crowd, estimated as high as forty thousand, was fenced almost a mile from the point of impending collision, but, of course, some worked in for a closer look.

"At the appointed hour, the selected engines (ready for junking by the road) with an engineer at the throttle of each, slowly puffed toward one another. These were two potbelly stacked, 35-ton locomotives: 1001's bright red train and 999's green, each with six box cars. Underway, the engineers jumped clear."

For ten minutes, the trains crawled, gathered speed, and finally hurled toward collision. It was cataclysmic and, despite precaution, there were injuries in the terrific explosion: flying fragments shrapneled the area, far as a half-mile distant. Then the shaken excursioners went home.

Old railroaders argue that the era of the gandy dancer and his high iron epitomized a time of America's brawniest ambition. No matter how skimpy his bankroll, a railroader saw only the most distant horizon in his line's name. Maybe track made it no farther than a creek eight miles from town, but in its blazoned name, it went down as Northwestern, Texas and Mexico International.

One tiny line had proposed to reach from the Gulf to Albuquerque (and all points west), and announced itself as Gulf, Texas and Western. Its skeptical passengers, watching it play out in a West Texas shortline, renamed the G. T. & W. alternately (but with affection) "Getcha Ticket and Walk" or, on cinder-smeared arrival at way stations from Seymour to Mineral Wells, "Getcha Tub and Wash."

Logically, the G. T. & W. tied in with another horizon promiser, the Weatherford, Mineral Wells and Northwest! The W.M.W. & N.W. met "Getcha Ticket and Walk's" challenge with its own localism, "Water, More Water, and No Whiskey!"

Nonetheless, the railroad era in Texas, as elsewhere, was a distinctly American time. It was a time when a man could dream the farthest horizon...and name that horizon. And it was a time when his neighbors bet on him...but salted down important sounding words...until he got there.

1858

Camels of Camp Verde

One of the most singular pages in Texas history is folded away in the hills northwest of San Antonio. It is the story of how the camel got the Army mule's job, and lost it again.

Near Kerrville is a gentle valley with sleepy hill rims and a clear stream, heavy-banked with cypress and pecan. Back from the crossroads and the water is an erect old stone two-story with a sign: Camp Verde Post Office and Grocery.

Camp Verde—despite claims all the way from old Indianola and Fort Davis to Arizona and California—was the Cape Kennedy of its day: launchpad in the mid-1800's for U.S. Second Cavalry's bizarre experiment with a camel corps.

A granite marker says so. Across from the store that, alone, is Verde's downtown district today, it also concludes that the experiment "proved impractical" and was abandoned. Impractical? Try a visit with history-minded Joe Stooksberry, who likes his retirement, his country store and its visitors. Ask him what really happened to Verde's camels

In 1846, Zachary Taylor's army is hammering from the

109

Rio Grande deep into Mexico. In Taylor's van is a brilliant colonel who has seen victory in every battle but supply. The great wastelands whip the Army mule and its wagon.

No ordinary soldier, the colonel knows this war will unlock all the west. Another arid vastness to subdue, protect and provision. Mules, he determines, cannot do the job. What then? He toys with the idea of dromedaries, forty years before the British will claim to have been first with a modern camel corps at Khartoum.

A decade later he is no longer a colonel, U.S.Army, but secretary of war under Franklin Pierce. He maneuvers congress into a startling appropriation of thirty thousand dollars—object: American cavalry, camel-mounted, for the western deserts.

An Army-Navy team is commissioned to horsetrade with pashas and beys from Asia Minor to North Africa for the best one-humped dromedaries and two-humped bactrians alive. Texas will be test site. The secretary well remembers Texas.

Navy Commander D. D. Porter's book-length report brings the War Department its first hoped-for good news. The thirty-four camels stand up to seafaring better than horses and mules. Homeward bound, Porter takes no chances, though:

"April 1st, 1858: Curried and brushed the animals as usual: washed hindquarters, legs, etc., with warm water and castile soap. At 2 p.m., Smyrna Mare No. 6 calved a fine male calf, the largest and strongest of any born as yet..."

Two thousand Texans chuckle when the strange beasts stilt ashore at Indianola. What a joke on the sweating cursing cavalrymen! Imperturbably, Army Major Henry C. Wayne counters with the first of many demonstrations to come. He loads one dromedary with well over a ton of hay. The camel rises easily and ambles for the barn across the beach.

"Lordamighty!" breathes a top-booted horseman up front. "That'd take two mules and a wagon, easy."

"Four!" The hawk-faced mule skinner corrects with authority. "Lookit that sand! He don't sink in; he jus' tip-pytoes!"

"She ain't no *he*! An' she's meaner'n the devil hisself!" The trooper is dour, rubbing his wrist where Smyrna Mare No. 3 took a quick nip. "Mister, the cavalry has plumb gone to hell!"

Major Wayne's reports to the secretary of war become more detailed and exhuberant with his caravan's progress north. From camp at Victoria, a pair of camel's hair socks go to Washington City, plus word the camels have recovered from voyaging. From San Antonio, he predicts that, in ten years, the race will spread across the continent. By late August, Wayne's troop is home, at Camp Verde's caravansarai, faithfully modeled to Arabian scale and complete with nine-foot walls.

Wayne out-reports the Navy, slaps spurs to his superlatives: camels thrive in this climate...two full mule teams play out on a San Antonio test haul; the camels saunter ahead on schedule...troopers are accepting (with less profanity) the animals...heavy rains mire the wagons hopelessly; the camels simply strike out over the mountains...the herd grows rapidly...desert-testing exploration near Fort Davis kills mules and would have got the men, too, except for the camels...camel-borne light artillery can go anywhere an Indian can; think how this will abbreviate the western campaigns; think of the troopers' lives this will save...the mule is obsolete in the west...tomorrow will see...

Eighteen Sixty One! The Second is gone from Verde. The handful of men who remain wear gray. They know nothing of camels, care less.

And the secretary of war? He is now Jefferson Davis, president, C.S.A.

Joe Stooksberry led me out on the long front gallery. Up the valley, the bluffs steepen to make a canyon. A mile up there is a private ranch where the ruined outlines of the old caravansarai are still faintly visible. The ranch house is a reconstruction of the old officers' quarters where Robert E. Lee was once billeted and Major Wayne wrote reports to Jeff Davis. And the camels?

"The ones that had gone west," Mr. Stooksberry squinted. "After the war, well...they just let 'em die out. Arizona, California saw some. Some ran wild here several years. Most of 'em," he pointed at a cliff up the canyon. "That's Camel's Bluff. Or Camel's Leap."

"They pushed them over?" It was hard for me to believe. Ungainly, ill-tempered, stupid...granted. But the record was there: they were incredible workers. "Why?"

Camp Verde's postmaster, merchant and most accessible historian pushed his hat back on graying hair, ran his hand across his jaw.

"Who thought 'em up?" he asked mildly. "Sure wasn't U. S. Grant."

"Okay, but the monument says they were 'impractical'."

"All things considered," said Mr. Stooksberry, "do you know of a better word?"

1861-65

Valiant Guns of Valverde

The stubby old gun stands silent by Freestone County's court house columns. You figure its lost cause a century ago and pass it for nothing more to tell.

Look again. Few Texas cannon ever knew as strange or grimly valiant saga. A recent historical plaque close beside salutes the veterans for which it still stands guard: Confederacy's Valverde Battery—six guns that Texans shot like rifles and fought nearly two thousand miles from New Mexico mountain to Louisiana forest in two now nearly forgotten invasions.

Tall, white-haired Llewellyn Notley, retired schoolman and Freestone historian, took me to the Fairfield square, east of Waco. By the glinting, three-inch muzzle loader, trunnioned to wagon-wheeled carriage and trail, we traced the guns of Valverde across their long war, beginning 150 miles up Rio Grande from El Paso.

With First Bull Run yet echoing east, this February 1862, U.S. Colonel Edward R. Canby orders the battery into first action—to block Confederate invasion west.

From the beginning, a Louisiana brigadier, H. H. Sibley, conceives Confederacy's great chance to be west —California's gold and blockade-proof ports. Jefferson Davis agrees, but—already brigading Texans for Virginia, Tennessee and the Mississippi—leaves invasion to the state's scant home guard alone. Sibley has marched west, late 1861, with less than three thousand "mounted rifles"—two troops of them with no guns—only ten-foot pennoned lances.

Behind them finally is ten weeks' empty march from San Antonio—waterless, forageless, wagon-shattering miles. Then north in bleak February, where Rio Grande cuts shrub-grizzled rock. Rations? Live off the land!

Now at Valverde ford, a sea of sand-duned cottonwoods and lava rock, Canby's Federals bar their way, even force the river and pin them with artillery they must take or— starving, freezing and without water—surrender. Raguet's lancers charge the guns on the left, are shattered.

And now the Texas center, dismounted, hurls a quarter mile at the deadly battery across, straight into the muzzles...falling all about...their colonel...and major...yet on: a gray flood with shotguns, engulfing, knife-to-pistol, swinging the pieces point blank on blue...ramming with their flagstaffs...and routing Federal wreckage in the river.

They have Valverde's guns! Yet no supply. Then on to Albuquerque, even wintry Santa Fe. Up the Stars and Bars! Up, too, grimly retreating smoke columns—Union depots. Down now to mouldy biscuit, wormy beef. On then, far around the Rockies' snowstormed east flanks, for depot center Fort Union. Down moves a fresh Union army.

Under the mountain shoulder of Pecos River's wilderness headwaters, Sibley's advance column—less than a thousand — storms snowy Glorietta Pass in six hours of brutal hand to hand fighting. With late March dark, the battered Texans again have swept the field.

But it is dark indeed! To their rear, unguarded, their

remaining supplies, a hundred wagons, burn in the canyon night, their six hundred mules bayoneted beside. Incredibly to these plainsmen, a second Federal column—Colorado mountaineers—has crossed the heights and descended a sheer cliff to bleed their victory white. Their decision writes itself: fall back!

Down Rio Grande, trailing clots of burned-out wagons, buried guns and used-up men, they dodge into mountain to escape trap. For almost two weeks of sand, rock and gorge, the Texans rope and drag what they have sworn to bring out—the guns of Valverde. A shadow army crosses Rio Grande, toils on for San Antonio, another six hundred miles.

Half a brigade trails in, nine months after leaving. Angry veterans like Tom Green, William Scurry and William Hardeman know they whipped everything but distance and starvation. Yet they can show but one prize—the sleek Valverde Battery. Then make it symbol! Command it with young Captain Joe Sayers (who will live to be governor) and Lieutenant Tim Nettles. They took it at the muzzle; already their gunners can bullseye their first salvos.

The war is not over for the guns of Valverde. Now they're across in Louisiana, now trying to relieve pressure on Vicksburg. Now General Magruder calls for them, retaking Galveston, New Year's, 1863. By spring, they capture Gunboat *Diana* on Louisiana bayous, hold the rear at Camp Bisland and Vermillionville, as Union General Nathaniel Banks invades, this spring of 1864: a juggernaut of 35,000 men and river fleet with Gettysburg's gunpower, up the Red for Shreveport and Texas, beyond.

A third their numbers await in a clearing just over the Louisiana line, near Mansfield. But long-waiting names, these—Scurry, Hardeman, Green. And Valverde Battery, Captain Nettles commanding, after Sayers' wound moved him to staff.

Even as all Confederacy trotters—Lee exhausted in Virginia and nothing between Sherman and the sea—Banks' sprawling army is thunderstruck at Mansfield, again at Pleasant Hill, and reels back on New Orleans. At tiny, forested Mansura, the guns of Valverde fire their final

114

shots on retreating invaders. But it is last gasp. Shortly, Lee's remnants face Appomattox; two months later, Texas yields trying it alone.

Ironically, a now General Canby accepts Trans Mississippi's surrender. On the ordnance list to recover are his first guns from that long ago rocky ford, far west.

He will never see them. Captain Nettles has fought them too far, too long, not to know their cost. In Texas Confederate heartland, near Fairfield, he buries the last surviving gun. It will come out finally to signal South's hope in Grover Cleveland's election.

And so it stands today, in its way a monument. Not for war and its horror, but for men's courage: for that quality, whatever the odds, to stand by your guns.

A salute from old Valverde!

1862-65

Confederate Capital

Northeasting, to fish Lake o' the Pines or to adventure Caddo's water wilderness, you can circuit the gleaming, new-look rim around Marshall and never see the Old South city you leave behind.

You miss the old Confederate square, the brick-cobbled streets named for heroes. You miss the staunch churches and the proud-columned old homes, back in the red-hilled shade. You miss part rococo, part sleek new growth and part long memory. Mostly, you miss the sense of our little known and extraordinary capital city.

Marshall, Texas...capital of Confederate Missouri.

And, although not recognized as it should be, the truly final capital of embattled and last-ditch Confederacy.

I saw the Marshall that no one knows with slight, white-mustached and ramrod straight Colonel Chesly Adams. He's an authority on the U.S. Field Artillery, the heavy machinery business and most of all, old Marshall. Perhaps you'll like the route he selected for me.

You cross the leisurely square to handsome new Hotel Marshall. It abuts an abandoned annex that was long ago Capitol Hotel. From the grassy square, a gray granite Confederate rifleman stares at you; not far from his statue, old Peter Whetstone produced a jug of whiskey from a spring, thereby convincing Texas Republic commissioners that this woodland was not too dry for a queen city northeast. That was 1842.

By the 1860's, Marshall is all this, vying with San Antonio, Houston, Galveston and nearby Caddo port, Jefferson. All about are great-columned brick homes or handsome Texas colonials, for this is cotton plantation country. On this square, the Capitol is a three story hostel, one of the handsomest west of New Orleans. Banquets are solid silver, soirres, lamplit elegance. The French grillworked hotel is where you go to get the news; today it is tense.

Far south on Rio Grande, a U.S. colonel, Robert E. Lee, has left off chasing border bandits, upriver to today's Eagle Pass. He has gone home to search his soul for Union or Virginia. He decides...and thunderbolt strikes the land! That square yonder will muster company on company—Lane's Rangers to the Bass Greys, from the Texas Invincibles to the Clough and Hill Avengers.

Within Capitol Hotel now echoes grim news north: over the rolling Missouri woodland, a true brother-to-brother war! The pro-South governor, staff and state militia are falling back as government in exile: Arkansas...soon Texas.

And now in July 1862, the governors of Arkansas, Missouri, Louisiana and Texas hold their first conference. Most of their men are east with Lee; what to do, west of the Mississippi? Their conference ground is easiest common capital—Marshall.

Then comes the Vicksburg they feared: the Mississippi River gone and the Confederacy divided. They meet again in Marshall; 1863 Trans-Mississippi is a separate, desperate Confederacy. They scrape together everything from post office to ordnance, even a paper treasury.

General Joe Shelby's Missourians hammer vainly for their state. Governor-in-exile Thomas C. Reynolds sets his capitol and mansion in frame bungalows, three blocks south of the hotel, where the Marshall Medical Center and pharmacy stand today.

There are times it seems they may hold, even as late as 1864, when they rout the massive Federal army short of their gates and Shreveport's. But inevitably to bare-handed men comes Appomattox. Lee is out of troops in Virginia, this April, 1865. Marshall's Confederacy, fighting alone and still uninvaded, must consider what to do. Rumor has Jeff Davis on the way to Texas to keep on; he does not come.

A month later—May 15—the Confederate governors meet for their last time.They have rejected separate peace terms; and, two days earlier, far south near Brownsville, Texans have won Palmito, last battle of the war.

But at this capital is chaos: no cannon, horse, food or ammunition. And from the worn few that stream home comes the simple word: "we're give out."

This last Marshall meeting declares terms by which they will surrender. But by early June in a gunboat off Gal-veston, Trans-Mississippi will sign an Appomattox docu-ment. The separate Confederacy is finished.

Not quite finished are the Missourians, who have never been home and who believe they face standing shoot-on-sight orders. These ride southwest; a thousand of them reach the Rio Grande.

At the foot of today's Main Street in Eagle Pass, two hundred yards below the bridge now there, they prepare to cross into Mexico. At sundown, July 4, the last Con-federate battleflag is sunk to bugle, echoing the deserted walls of Fort Duncan.

Strangely they cross the river where Lee patrolled, long years before. Most will get home, but their cause and its last capital is done.

It seems unfortunate that Marshall demolished the old

Missouri capitol a few years ago, overriding every effort by historians like Colonel Adams.

Still, I believe the city yet has its last Confederate capitol. Colonel Adams and I conjectured where those Marshall conferences must have been held. History's memory from that tortured time is not certain; some believe the site is old Hall Plantation, toward Longview. Others feel it had to be the old hotel.

I crawled up the fire escape with Marshall Hotel's maintenance man, Ozie Woodkins. Together we explored the rooms, stripped some years ago. Where the cream plaster has fallen away, the raw red brick showed old, and the musty rooms—however remodeled—still seem to echo those forgotten voices of men on a lost cause.

I am not one to advise a history-proud city as Marshall. They have lost one capitol; I suspect the other stands unmarked and empty over a discount store, just off the old square.

1865

The Last Train to Millican

The road bend into drowsy little Millican is where you watch for the train. Over the rails south of Bryan, it is express-thunder—a horn blast spilled back on the crossing's clang-clang-clang, echoes fading for Houston or Dallas.

At the bend, you watch from the neat drive in grocery of Mrs. Lula Cowen. There are a couple of wayside stores and, up the low hill, a scatter of frame houses and a white steeple against the Brazos bottom haze.

"Just below is where they turned the engines around." Bespectacled and hearty Mrs. Cowen says it matter-of-factly. Millican today doesn't watch for its trains with the intensity it once did.

That was a time when a new boom town marched raw-

118

boarded over the hill, and the red-dusty streets milled
ox-teamed freighters with troops in gray; when cotton
lined the tracks deep in bales and stretched beyond in
a white plantation sea.

It was a time when the train puffed the 80 miles from
Houston—as far as they had laid the tracks before capital
went back North. The new plaque beside Mrs. Cowen's
grocery explains it simply.

This was Millican, Texas, Confederate States of
America.

Millican's strange role will last six years, and it comes
by accident. Little more than a log stage station, the town
has anticipated its first train arrival. From Boston and
New York—old hands at railroading—have come money
and engineering. From Harrisburg's Buffalo Bayou
wharves, one line crawls west for San Antonio; this one,
north, for the new towns of Waco and Dallas.

Now the raw line reaches Millican. At trackside, all
along, farmers keep wood stacked. Each ten miles, the
fireman loads a half dozen cords. The big-bellied stack
belches embers that can set a cotton car afire; but the
speed is better than that of a jouncing stage. A tied-down
whistle clears the cattle; and into Millican they pull, a
brakeman hopping cartops to set his handwheels on the
drums.

A great day for Texas! Already you can freight to Houston and deepwater, or on west another 70 miles to the
Colorado at Columbus. All of 150 miles of connected railroad!

Millican has no way to know that this year of 1861,
President-electsLincoln rides the Wabash nearly a
thousand miles from western Illinois to his Washington
inaugural. They only know their railroad stops with the
guns of Fort Sumter.

Slowly they realize the role chance dealt them. Here
must be distribution center for frontiers west. Here—with
blockade—trans-shipment point to run Confederate cotton
from the Mexican river port, Matamoros. And here, at
the Peach Creek tents of Camp Speight, staging area for

battlegrounds east. Here, literally, railroad's end of the line for embattled Confederacy.

Unaware there is more trackage in Chicago's environs alone than in all Texas, Millican watches the trains come in. Each brings news. One day, the news will say it is all over, and their city can grow normally.

But how goes the news?

First...men pouring east. Like those fire eaters from next-door Robertson County, shipping out for Sabine boat and New Orleans railroad to Virginia. Word from them? They're Company C, Fourth Texas, Hood's Brigade. Nobody'll whip those boys! Give us one good fight, they said; we'll be right back! The Millican train, it seems, must have sent at least half Hood's Texans.

The town builds on. Sanger Brothers, moving with the railroad, runs a first rate store—anything from ham to Navy Colts. Already, three churches and another building. And—where you're standing—old Bloody Boots Saloon.

Now, men come trickling back — not as they left. From Chickahominy's swamps . . . Second Bull Run . . . Sharpsburg . . . Gettysburg . . . Chickamaugua . . . Vicksburg. No, they sure weren't licked; they ran out of men and horses; and they never had enough cannon.

And now the trains come in, whatever schedule, No farmers to stack wood, and the fireman's old and slow. Half the cars are worn out. There is no iron to patch Texas' 150 railroad miles.

And crucial miles, these! U.S. Navy has sealed every Confederate port; whatever runs that blockade must make the impossibly desolate run to Matamoros. Millican's cotton piles deeper. Of what they get through to the wagon trains, half is lost on the last leg, running the empty coast or even Padre Island.

Desperately, they have hauled in English machinery and French millstones. They start a big cotton and flour mill at nearby Hearne. Can they finish in time?

From the west, Millican's used-up trains hurry gaunt horsemen to halt Federal invasion, below Shreveport. From the east, rumors trickle that Hood's army is a skeleton at Nashville and Franklin in Tennessee; Atlanta is gone and Lee faces Appomattox. Will Texas go it alone?

For nearly two months, she will; but the Confederate end of the line knows that the last train has reached Millican. Perhaps it was the train that brought Company C home.

Of the hundred twenty who started, five will walk it from here. They are not the boys who left. Of all those boys Millican's trains sent to Hood, one in five comes home.

Over the years, they will gather on the anniversary of their first battle, when they swept the Federal right at Gaines Mill. They will talk of how it was before they had nothing left but courage to throw against the Federals. They will gather until 1934, when no more can make it.

It seems no coincidence that their last fifteen meetings were near Millican. The red brick Bryan library is cornerstoned their last home; librarian Mrs. Hazel Richardson remembers them.

There was no place to meet where they started. No place at all.

In 1866, the railroad pushed north again; and the following year boomed a new city that would last. Most of Millican's homes went on the flat cars to Bryan, just as Sangers followed the train eventually to Dallas.

The last train was in. The end of the line had passed Millican, C.S.A.

Mighty Spindletop's Preface

Once upon a time in a now-forgotten kingdom, a man scooped a little earth away, better to take the dark oil from where it seeped. Carefully, he returned with his oil for its valued use among his people.

He was not the Egyptian preparing to embalm, nor the Greek, formulating cement. Nor was he from torch-lit Persian temple near the revered flame pits, where Russia today harvests petroleum along the Caspian.

This man was ancient East Texan—perhaps the one of mounds and beehived temples. Oil ornamented his body and, in his belly, cured greatly. Sixteenth Century Spaniards found him obviously long acquainted with the stuff's use—limited, as they well knew, only to softening leather and easing a *carreta's* axle.

This man, simple in his ways with nature, let oil come to him. But what of the early visionary who first dug for it? That Texan was hard on the 1850 heels of the Pennsylvanian who found he could derive a fair substitute for coal oil; called it kerosene, and dumped most of the rest.

You can trace the latter East Texan's beginnings any pleasant weekend meandering from the direction of Dallas, generally toward Houston—which, of course, is where any oil story should end.

Tucked off *Camino Real* between Nacogdoches and San Augustine, tiny and old Chireno is a jewel box of Texas Colonial with all the charm, in miniature, of either neighbor. What Chireno could do with her antique, legended Midway Inn, where Sam Houston convalesced after San Jacinto, her gingerbread house and the others is...well, another story.

You are here because, southwest in the rolling pine forests is Oil Springs, one of the beginnings you seek and, at Chireno's bank, tall, sandy-haired president H. V. Hall likes curious travelers and will map you there.

Believe me, you need that help, or a guide, for the pines press close on a Y-ing, crisscross maze of red gravel lanes that wander eight back country miles to where Nacogdoches County is certain of this state's first oil well.

There is a stout wood bridge over a creek, a small cleared valley the stream crosses, dark-stained. Up the west bank briefly is the oil spring that the Indian worked. Beyond the slope is where Lynis Barrett dug and lined his well, much like those that dot the farms hereabouts but reach, bucketed instead, for water.

Some say Barrett's well was 1859; others shrug. It didn't work. Who would want to hunt kerosene with secession almost on this cotton-growing state? But there is no doubt concerning the well sunk in 1866, the year after the war.

"They had a team of mules...round and round like an old sugar mill," Banker Hall recalls from his grandfather. "They just augered out their hole."

Twenty years later, beside Oil Springs, there was a crude skimming plant and Yuba Field that barreled out black oil, boomed awhile, then faded. Maybe elsewhere, like Brownwood, they could sell it for fifty cents a gallon to lubricate, and a dollar a pint to medicate. But reserves here were shallow and scant. The field and Texas' first crude refinery surrendered to the forest. Back in the mat of vine-laced undergrowth, two rusted iron tanks stand on oil-boggy ground in mute testimony to the beginnings.

Nacogdoches discusses a possible scenic tour to Oil Springs. And scenic beauty these forest lanes have, every mile. And history, too; you might as well try to take that proud city's Fredonian flag as argue this isn't the Texas first in oil.

Some San Antonians contend that an "oil well" on the

old Dullnig Ranch, now within the city's eastern limits, lighted lamps at a ball for U.S. Colonel Robert E. Lee. However, south of Nacogdoches 120 miles, where woodland thickens to Big Thicket's magnificent jungle, there stands a major contender for the Texas *first;* little, forested Saratoga.

If you would talk discovery in 1859, they counter that pioneer Andrew Briscoe reported oil in Big Thicket's glades fifteen years before. If you want to compare what remains, they'll show you the casing of what they believe to be the oldest still-standing oil well in the world...date, 1865.

Just outside town, it is an old, puddled-iron casing rim, a little above the soggy ground beside a tank battery that ranges from cypress staves to aluminum. This forest capital knew its latter day oil boom, too.

Lance Rosier, who knew more about Big Thicket than anybody, showed me Saratoga's well. It is on the Cotton lease, as it has been since John F. Cotton first went after oil.

"They drove in that casing with a pile driver." Lance kicked at the rim. "Mules pulled up the hammer, then let it drop. They said you could feel it all over the county."

Battering it down, inch by inch that way, finally had to strike sparks to the oil and, ultimately, out the top of the casing came a fire. Helping his father, a boy ran for his house, grabbed a quilt, smothered the flames But the next fire found an irate mother blocking his way. Use rags or gunny sacks, she told him. He'd ruin no more good quilts on stuff as worthless as that oil!

And, for her time, she was right. Who could know men like Daimler and Benz, Olds and Winton, were planning carriages that would need gasoline? Who ever heard of a kid named Henry Ford? Who wanted to blow up her house with nature gases?

You can pick up two more milestones driving for Houston's oil capital. At Corsicana, west of Nacogdoches, are some of the old buildings and a concrete monument to the state's first real refinery in 1898—about the time we set out to help Cuba free herself of Spain's dictatorship.

And, after Saratoga, swing east a little. On Beaumont's south edge, you'll find a red granite shaft noting Spindletop. Here is where the Twentieth Century literally roared in. It will be up to history to measure the echoes from that 75,000 barrel per day explosion; they are still reverberating.

While we're waiting for that tomorrow, put me in the corner with Texans Rosier and Hall. Mark those two hidden and forgotten beginnings. Both of them!

1874-77

The White Ghost Buffalo

From the Cap Rock to the Canadian—under all the vast Panhandle—there is a giant cave; and out of it, one night of furious storm, red-eyed buffalo will thunder from the earth and take revenge.

A shaggy white herd bull, mighty and terrible as the ghost he is, will lead them, and this will be the day the Kiowa nation rises again.

Since Kiowa legend decrees the herd must be as limitless as before the white man, there will surge from far-north Perryton and Dalhart—south to Abilene's mesas and beyond—a sea of sixty million trampling bison. Six foot giants, a ton each!

No one has found the cave and few talk of it, for the Panhandle folk, busy with rich land and fresh cities, have almost forgotten theirs is the capital of the buffalo empire—one that lasted a million placid years, then fell before the white hunter in one decade of slaughter—the 1870's.

On a few Texas ranches, like the *Quien Sabe* spread west of Amarillo, scattered head of the humped, bearded and heavy-shouldered oxen graze today. But the great ghost herd? The White Buffalo hides it underground, waiting his time.

Driving the High Plains—a geometry of endless green to crystal horizon rims—you find it hard to believe they ever were there, rumbling the earth as they grazed. Yet the great plains rancher, Charles Goodnight, once saw the main herd west of today's Amarillo. For two days it passed—120 miles long, 25 miles wide. Driving his steers into sheltered and curly-grassed Palo Duro Canyon, the rancher had to push ten thousand head of buffalo before them.

Goodnight saw the era of the Texas buffalo hunter—the most terrible massacre ever visited on the animal kingdom.

Where Midland glistens today, a lone guard once stood twenty-one days' vigil over ten thousand hides, awaiting wagons. East, near Albany, old hell-roaring Fort Griffin stacked them four blocks long, a block wide and higher than its frame buildings. Fort Worth saw two hundred thousand hides sold in just two days.

The slaughter reached a two-year peak in 1874. The vanishing herd walked dumbly through a leaden hail, no place to go but into the guns. Week-legged calves tried to nurse as their mothers were skinned and pegged. By 1877 it was largely over. In one year, the Santa Fe would ship east for rendering more than a million tons of bones.

Once, the buffalo had not been afraid. Man had come from river caves and met him with spears and stone axes. For meat and a robe, a hunter was swapped, more often than not.

The long-later Comanche and Kiowa (and tribes north), up on their Spanish ponies, clung to the kill-for-need hunt, but as their major sport. Their three-foot bois d'arc bows could completely shaft their quarry, but, as with all good danger, closeness counted. The kill must be hair's breadth from the hooves. It was that way, too, with the wild-riding Mexican cibolero and his lance. His racing pony leaned his thrust home, then swayed clear of the hammering herd...or didn't.

The frontier hunter took chance from the game. Briefly he tried cavalry pistol tactics, discarded them for the stand. Motionless and methodical downwind, his rifle dropped the herd from outside in. He stopped when they were gone—dead or stampeded. A good man could drop a hundred without moving his pony.

An impatient or greedy man simply herded a bawling, cataract over a cliff, then scavenged below. Nearly a thousand went off Buffalo Ridge, near Post.

Hunters went up to the plains in near-standard outfits. High-sided Conestogas were triple-tandemed, six men to the camp: the boss hunter with Spencer or Sharps, four skinners and a camp cook-guard. A hundred hides made a fine day.

The buffalo's death was every facet of his hunter's life. Hump ribs were roasted; kidney, heart and tongue, baked. Backbone fat served for bread. Saddle and hump made steaks, jerky or—tallowed down with dried fruit—pemmican. Hides provided tents, blankets. More than one man escaped the sudden, terrible blizzards by crawling into the wet red warmth inside a fresh-slaughtered carcass.

Hides brought him an average two dollars, yet he left two on the ground for each one he staked. He cured perhaps a pound of choice beef for each ten tons he left to rot. And he seldom cleared more than a hundred dollars for a long three months' hunt.

This was the truly prodigal Texan and his big kill. It wasn't profit that drove him, for aside from England's briefly-processed twelve-dollars-a-yard wool, the buffalo really left little more than a robe or a rug.

Yankee General Phil Sheridan told Texans it was important to wipe out the herds. Take the Indians commissary and his horse, and he was finished—more than the army had managed in fifteen years. Yet it is doubtful that the hunter ever looked down his long sights and saw the Panhandle empire he was building.

Kiowa Chief Stone Calf called him a senseless killer and told of the ghost herd that would come one day and haunt him. Stone Calf knew the entrance to the deep cave where the White Buffalo was building his herd against the day of vengeance. In all, the hunters trying hard for the strange albinos, shot just seven of them.

127

The last they saw, goes the story, led a strangely ghostlike herd in a wild run before a fearful blue wind. Below Perryton, where Wolf Creek falls into the sandhill breaks of the Canadian, the herd vanished into the storm.

Stone Calf died, fearing toward the end, that the great white bull had lost the cave entrance. I could find no caves —near Perryton nor south, along the Cap Rock—and, of course, you can say the Kiowa were a fanciful people.

You might have more luck than I. Try a solitary camp in the old and big cottonwoods along the Canadian. When the wind is right and the night makes lightning in the mountains, away west, you can hear something running the long, dark plain.

Who can say we know too much about caves, anyway?

1883-86

Rawhide Highway at Doan's Crossing

The sign says "Doans" and "road end". It was to have been great beginning.

The sign is fifteen miles northeast of Vernon, where pavement plays out against Red River's hilly banks, meandering Oklahoma boundary. There's an old adobe in the elm and willow and some weathered farmhouses scattered away.

Up from solid, lived-in-looking Vernon, you've come the final Texas prairie miles of one of our mightiest: the Western and Kansas Trail for Dodge City—last rawhide highroad for cowboy drover and his Texas Longhorn.

You can read the roll on him, yonder on the big gray granite marker—over half a hundred of the tall-riding brands: Richard King and Shanghai Pierce from far south; George Littlefield and Charles Schreiner, the Blockers, Dan Waggoner, Adair and Goodnight, and all the rest. Near the top is C. F. Doan. This is Doan's Crossing.

Over six million cattle and cowponies, and thirty

thousand riders hammered this road deep. For nearly two decades, beginning 1874, here was last stop before the three hundred mile Indian country push for Dodge's railheads, or far beyond to the Dakotas, even Canada.

Across the river haze, Oklahoma seems the same as the land this side—quiet farm and pasture. It nearly became America's most incredible highway gate—to a miles-wide, strong-fenced, river-bridged thoroughfare stretching almost two thousand miles for Canada. A highway for cattle!

Here was to begin—fed from Texas—the Great National Cattle Trail that Congress debated for three years of the mid eighties. Beef highway for northern and western ranges.

Recently opened, Vernon's regionally excellent Red River Valley museum tells much of Texas cattlemen. The planners knew Doan's place in any cattle story.

Texas had been cattle country since Spain, two hundred years earlier. Small herds drove New Orleans trails from Liberty before San Jacinto, then west with California's forty-niners. Distant thunder, though, against the torrent to come.

War's end left Confederate Texas with a Longhorn population ten times its men. In New York or Chicago, good steak brought thirty-five cents. That steak—six dollars a fat steer here—meant over thirty dollars, north. For near bankrupt Texas range, just one answer—the great trails north!

First, the Shawnee, over the Red at Old Preston by Sherman; then, driven westward by farm fences, at Red River Station above Nocona, linking the Chisholm from Abilene to Texas feeders. Finally, flood tide of the eighties, the trail here for Dodge.

Ohioan Corwin F. Doan's adobe, green-roofed yonder in the timber, marked westernmost, best and last crossing. Here finally, a dozen houses, two long barn stores with flour, grain, bacon, Stetsons, ammunition, and Colts —by freight-wagon lots. To quiet-spoken Doan, credit was universal—on a trail boss' word, and he knew them all. One after the other, they came: sinuous, mile-long, bawling, dust-churning, fifty-foot-wide, rope-like herds

129

...trailing behind point riders and lead steer, pinched compact by swing and flank riders, drag men tailing in stragglers...rattling chuck and hoodlum wagon for bedroll and ditty bag, clanging coffee and bean pot with iron oven for sourdough biscuit, rawhide cooney slung under for cookfire's wood or chips. Cattleman Doan knew those drovers, all right.

And here, they'd ride the river—high or low: that herd, a rope of rocking chair heads and horn and, across the other side, maybe lucky enough not to bust stampeding.

He knew them all—wet and dry, sweating or bone-chilled...first-trail, slatty kids, grizzled, dusty-eyed, bent-legged old ones who'd sworn to their last, two...five years ago...quiet hands or loud...maybe singing "Bury Me Not" or "Cowboy's Dream"...fast guns and easy-goers...the ones Dodge likker would mean-up or just get to dancing...the whole slouch-hatted, loose-vested, leather-chapped, jingle-booted, Durham-rolling, tobacco-chewing, dust-eating bunch—Texas drovers.

And he knew their ordeal. Not just heat, cold, thirst, mud and dust. Stampede—like that one on the Brazos that glutted the gully with two thousand dead beef...or the one here: eleven herds busting over thirty thousand head for a hundred miles and over a hundred cowboys, ten days of dead-beat riding to round them up!

And the river! Take it flooding high, and let that lead panic and turn it into a boiling, milling, crazy jam that got tighter and tighter and pushed under its center. They still talked about Bill Blocker swimming his big paint lead steer, hand on horn, right out of one just downriver, and about that kid that broke a jam, walking their backs like logs, walking across to one steer he knew was strong enough to free the center and lead it to the bank.

Then, from here north, add Indian, Jayhawker or just outlaw. Finally, the loading pens at Dodge and maybe a loose count or a bad price break; and, at last, pay and a thirst...and you had the Mastersons or Bill Tilghman waiting behind their stars, the dealers behind their tables, and the women wherever you found 'em.

Each year, the drives came on, better run...but farm wire pushed west. In 1883, Texas cattlemen called on Congress for a fenced-off right-of-way, clear to Canada. America's cattle industry backed it for the next two years.

Opposite Doan's Crossing would begin the Great National Trail—over free land. Fence both sides, an average three miles' width, bridge the rivers and gate for grazing, set handling facilities at all railheads. Cattle's highway! Were six thousand square miles too much for Congress to grant an industry opening America's West?

Too much, said Congress. Kansas farm marched west and Colorado strung wire east. No room between. A tremendous vision, this highroad...but too late. Northern ranges were nearly full; the railroads were coming.

So, across that river...well, just a dream, after all. Was it?

Go back and once more read the monument close by Doan's old adobe:

"In honor of the trail drivers who freed Texas from the yoke of debt and despair." Their Longhorns quit, only with range and market full, and nowhere left to trail.

Opposite Doan's crossing was the great highway, all right; and the beginning of the road back for Texas. It just was never marked with fenceline.

So skip that "road-end" sign.

131

Oilboom Ranger's Rainbow End

One day, I believe, a wisely introspective oil industry will really memorialize itself in its rip-roaringest boom town of all. This has to be a neat community, much smaller than it looks and deceptively quiet today, 90 miles west of Fort Worth.

To be certain you have the right boomtown, strike up a conversation with any oil field oldtimer. Begin with "Do you remember...?" then make up anything outlandish.

"Sure," he'll say. "That was Ranger in '18 or '19. I was there."

Or, with someone who knows her well, see the old Ranger yet there today. You can find traces of her, from the John McClesky and Nannie Walker discovery sites, to what was the world's longest brick highway, over the mud to Cisco; and from Merriman Cemetery, fenced about in millions-making derricks yet refusing to be sold for drilling, to the shadows of Gholson Hotel.

My guide was Mrs. Helen Murrell, a handsome lady whose information service at up-and-coming Ranger Junior College beats many a chamber of commerce. We picked up Hall Walker, a banker and business leader who saw it all—from Ranger's two million dollars a week gushers to the day she blew dry.

We stopped awhile at the foot of Main Street to recall how it started.

Spindletop has blown the Twentieth Century in—on oil. The other big fields, Sour Lake to Electra and Oklahoma, have given the engine time to catch up. But now there

132

is even a Model-T assembly line. For rowdy, unregulated oil, time now for the big one! World War I needs it.

Ranger is a one-street, board-fronted town under bare hills, with Saturday band concerts and traveling shows for entertainment. Ranger is lucky to be neighbor to big, prosperous, coal-mining Thurber.

Lucky indeed! Texas and Pacific Coal (of Thurber) is ready to try for oil on twenty-five-cent-an-acre Ranger leases. On a brisk October Saturday of 1917, atop a mesquite hogback on the McClesky farm. Ranger Pool's No. One blows wild—thick, green-black top crude. The marker is back from the road west of town.

"I was out here then," Hall Walker said. "Oil shot up and ran over the hill. We tried to dike it, but it just poured down that draw, all across the road."

In bare months, a thousand population mushrooms to 40,000—give or take, according to what time of a frenzied twenty-four-hour day. From Pennsylvania to Rumania, they come—roustabouts and carpenters, financiers and promoters, lawyers and land men, drillers and dressers, mule skinners and uniformed chauffeurs, gamblers and women. Rainbow's end is shack, tent and wagontop city. A hotel cot in the hall costs ten dollars, a lobby chair, five. You pay for a drink of water and sleep in shifts. If you sleep. All is bedlam in whip-cracking, drill-thudding, steam-hissing, shouting, sulfur-smelling, gas-flaring Ranger! The walks jam with land men, cards in hats and sandwich-boarded. Dirt streets jam, too—a quagmire to axles that are tugged by Percheron or Kentucky jack. You walk across, wagon to wagon, or sled Main Street's mud for a dollar.

Cabaret Row, down from the Gholson, has the Grizzly Bear, Blue Moose and Oklahoma, and five killings in one day. A judge fines a shooting seventy-five dollars. Evangelist Billy Sunday is down, exhorting the likes of Slippery Sal.

Everybody's pot-o-gold! After forty unbroken dusters, even Cowboy Evans hit. So everybody buys—Heavyweight Champ Jess Willard to John Ringling to Harry Sinclair to a new outfit called Humble Oil. Ex President Taft can walk downtown, unnoticed.

Who has time to notice? You listen through the cardboard walls and whiskey talk and beat the others to the leases. One lease changes hands three times one Friday, jumps from $150 to $15,000. A broke wildcatter kidnaps himself, finishes his well on his friends' ransom money, hits and repays. Another ties up a lease with a $500 hot check on Saturday, waits at the bank Monday morning with a $50,000 deposit from his weekend sale.

Ranger shoots the works...and the wells! Shooter Jack Rapp feels his well going, right under twenty quarts of nitro he is lowering. He catches the bomb riding up the gusher and can walk away. A driller in a twenty-five-dollar silk shirt celebrates his well, lights a cigar and blows his rig. An auto backfire levels an entire camp. One oil-rich farmer moves three times to get away from the stuff; it follows each time. Another, watching his well blow in, stands dumbly, trying to sweep the black oil from his doorstep.

Now, three years of this, night and day. Nearly a billion spent; over 80,000 barrels a day gushed at peak, a field spread to thirty-five counties: Ranger has plumb slopped over in oil!

Then came in the well that promised two thousand barrels a day. And the celebrating wildcatter, sober next morning and panicky; his well was dry!

They capped the wells or pumped. Rainbow's end, right enough.

Unchecked, unregulated, Ranger had simply blown her top.

For more than forty years now, Ranger has fought back the ghosts. Weeds have the dikes where the tank farms stood, the pipe racks at Prairie Oil, the foundations at Mid Kansas. Down has come many an empty-eyed building. And, even gaping as she does downtown, Ranger still looks ten times bigger than her 3,400 population.

Some new industries have come in. And at the junior college, engrossed in a building program, the research is sometimes Ranger's past; the talk is the town's future.

So this suggestion to the Ranger that looks ahead.

Ask the oil industry to start you modestly toward a real, life-sized historic museum, telling the Bunyanesque story of an industry learning how. Not quite a piece of Disneyland, but nearly. It could teach and show what an industry needs taught and shown.

You have some empty buildings, the manpower, and the desire.

For not too much money, you could put up something in Ranger we'd all buy gasoline to come see. And one day, I believe, a wisely introspective industry will really memoralize itself this way.

Where better to show the old days than where they were?

1941-45

Top Gun In Texas

Aging and broad-beamed, she drowses near Houston. She is obviously out-of-date. Yet, for your sons, the time to see her is now.

Below the sward and tall shaft of San Jacinto, she is moored aside the brown ship channel with one-inch steel cable. She has five 14-inch twin turrets, with *fives* and *threes* and clusters of 40s and 20s cresting bristled to her tripod fore and mainmasts. She could cover nearly two football fields, this once city of 2,000, ten stories tall. She is Battleship *Texas*.

From gangway to superstructure, the kids will swarm her. They'll swivel her quad mounts and whack her turret plate and yell, "BangIgotcha!" and shinny the ladders to her topmost bridges to sight across industrial stilts and scaffolds and tank farm thimbles to Houston's tips, beyond.

Those kids all over, she'll seem, at first, an armored Disneyland. She is more. She is still top gun in Texas;

it was not too many years ago that she proved it.

That was D-Day, Omaha Beach. She was a World War I battlewagon in a toe-to-toe shootout with Fortress Europe.

What chance had old Big T? She'd been that other war's best; but age had her slowed and clumsy...except at the guns. If she could live long enough to close the range, she'd outshoot anybody. This, her men knew from the beginning, when *Texas* flagged the Atlantic Neutrality Patrol and only Navy had the war. Survive...to shoot...to survive: *Texas'* credo.

Tough, gravelly-genial Jack McKeown knew it. He took me over the ship he now skippered. He saw her survive; forward on the bow, he could recall black ocean mountains avalanching to the turrets—the eleven straight days of North Atlantic's roaring cold hell, Argentia to Iceland, in the beginning. He could recall the typhoon off Buckner Bay that broke ships like sticks. That was Okinawa, at the end.

Within the superstructure at the old radio shack, you can feel how it was when she flagged the first invasion fleet above Casablanca; and when the North African French fought back, Texas closed to blast anything that moved.

It was from here she broadcast General Eisenhower's first war message: "Frenchmen of North Africa, the forces which I have the honor of commanding, come to you as friends...help us and the day of world peace will be hastened..."

Then afterwards, each time, she drove impossibly close to every major beachhead. She was old; she could be risked. She had to be the floating fort to move in, gun-to-gun, on the fixed forts and get them before they could sink her.

Her greatest test begins off Omaha, where the pebbled beach runs briefly to chalk bluffs—a warren of sunk-in, twelve-foot-thick concrete blockhouses. Above, the plane-streaked, red-shot sky; below, the horizon sprawl of in-crawling ships; and between, the ultimate inferno that

136

is cliff, zeroed beach, the dirty surf, its tearing wire and concrete jacks and its mines, scattered like gravel.

And men—to get through...and take those cliffs.

We have shoved *Texas* and the rest close enough to scrape bottom, and now they are blasting and blasting until the men can move ahead a little. But on the beach, they're hanging on by their nails, and inland air reconaissance tells that everything enemy that can move is coming up for counter attack.

Deep down in *Texas* is Lieutenant Commander Richard B. Derickson, gunnery officer. He takes an R.A.F. Spitfire's taut report: "Tank column, moving up, two nine zero three..." He scans for grid coordinate 2903; it is a crossing intersection, well inland. To where those tanks are massing, a mighty long shot!

Texas is a rolling gun platform, the long *fourteens* lifting, adjusting, offsetting...then letting go in one orange-flashing, ship-wrenching salvo. A long time later, it seems, *Texas* logs the Spitfire's Englishman:

"Oh, simply champion! Only one of the blighters left, and he's running!"

Nine miles. One salvo. Bullseye! Methodically now, *Texas* blasts out the cliff then the long guns behind, and—for the week to win Omaha—nothing enemy moves in or out, across the ten miles which Texas' guns own.

Next it was *Texas*, off Cherbourg's mighty forts —the port we had to take to land our heaviest stuff. The old battleship closed on the forts and their guns, big as hers. With her *fourteens* she drove in to three thousand yards.

Captain McKeown showed me where they blew *Texas'* navigation bridge apart. You could look down that gaping hole for three decks and see the guns still firing.

"You took three hits," I recalled, for the report read that way.

"We took eighty-seven," Jack McKeown said drily. "They called 'em near-misses." He looked across the slip toward San Jacinto's reflecting basin. "If this were Cherbourg then, well...the shaft there'd be their guns and there'd be nothin' but holes, far as you could see, round either of us."

"And the fort?"

"We got the fort." He squinted. "Mister, I told you; *Texas* could shoot."

After Cherbourg, and the robot bombs off Southern France, *Texas* plowed out to help finish it in the Pacific. She shot up Suribachi at Iwo and sawed through Okinawa's awful kamikaze curtain. Then it was over; she went home.

Finally, some Texas patriots headed by Dallas' Earl Hoblitzelle and Houston's Lloyd Gregory worked to bring her to last mooring here. Your admissions pay to keep her a shrine.

A shrine to what? To show our sons war? Not if you're sane and saw one.

It was what she did and how. She fought a war she couldn't. Yet she was one of the very few who made it, beginning to end. How? Refitted, she was slow and awkward. She carried *fourteens*, not *sixteens*. But new—and kept that way. Within her range...the mechanical equal of any.

By unrelenting effort, she made them the best. And she added a little more. To excellence, she added courage...resolve...and pride.

Qualities we can enshrine and show our sons, these days of our years.

Part Three

And Not to Yield

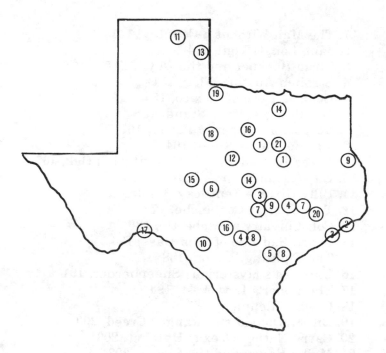

"To strive, to seek, to find, And not to yield."

Tennyson

The Man Without a Country

Remember Philip Nolan? If so, which one?

Almost anybody can tell you that Nolan was "The Man Without a Country." In the book, he was a treasonous, tragic American pawn, condemned to live out his last fifty years—far at sea—with never another word, written or spoken, of his homeland.

Strangely, there are two Philip Nolans: the fictitious one, a traitor; the real one, a stalwart of the Bowie-Crockett stamp and the first American to fight and die for Texas.

More incredible, the Nolan we remember was the man literally dreamed up by Boston author, Edward Everett Hale in a booklet, hoax-written to sound true. It was convincing enough. It destroyed a hero, left him indeed without country or even memory.

The true Philip Nolan was killed by Spanish cannon, March 21, 1801, and is buried in the rolling vastness north of Waco in a yet-unmarked grave.

The real Nolan first.

It is 1790. Washington's restless young America is probing west. A handsome, adventurous young Irishman appears on frontier's fringe—Kentucky, Natchez. New Orleans, even Nacogdoches. At nineteen, he has Erin's charm and brawn. One-handed, he can heft a barrel. Also he has the sponsorship of yet-untarnished American General James Wilkinson. He can come and go in New Spain at will.

A year later, he is across into upper central Texas,

141

genially horse-trading with Indians—from Waco's Tawakoni to the Caddos of Red River. Two years, thus. He has Sam Houston's at-homeness with the wilderness people, also a mapmaker's eye for the new land, but not yet Spain's suspicion that he may be studying her land too closely.

Now, it is 1797 and two long expeditions later. He has been commissioned by Spanish Territorial Governor Carondelet to venture the lands which Spain suspects only a crazy man would ride. She cannot colonize that wild country and can scarcely garrison it; yet Nolan explores it, bartering for mustang cavalry mounts. He roams south to Bexar, first Anglo seen there. He brings home more than a thousand horses.

More than that, he brings back sharply accurate topographical reports, rough maps. Texas indeed is rare, good land.

In mid 1799, he is called to Washington City by Vice President Thomas Jefferson. The upcoming president is almost ready to dicker with Napoleon for a Louisiana Purchase he believes to be everything west to Rio Grande at Santa Fe. Is Texas worth the argument? Will Nolan ride back once more? Will he report, immediately upon return?

One last time, Philip Nolan saddles up, mid-December, 1800. His last trip, he knows, has turned Spain against him, that he will ride Texas at his peril, yet he goes. Some twenty men ride with him for "horses"; he will confide to a few of them that the horses are a ruse, their purpose is scouting and mapping. Accosted beyond the Sabine, he shows Governor Carondelet's visa. He does not care if Spain's wind is up; he does not know there are standing orders at Nacogdoches, from deep Spanish Mexico, for Nolan, alive or dead— better, the latter.

March 4, 1801, Jefferson is president and in little Nacogdoches, Spanish Lieutenant Musquiz mounts a hundred troopers and a mule-drawn swivel cannon. Pursuing Nolan, he catches up at early sun, March 21, somewhere north of Waco.

The fight that followed was typical of the bloody struggles to come for this contested ground. Ordered to surrender, Nolan brandished his "free passage" and, in salty Irish, told the Spaniards to come take him. He held to his crude log embrasure and pitted his rifles against heavy odds and cannon.

Almost the first Spanish shell killed him. It was no longer important that some of his own men had defected, the last, with Nolan's own rifle. Survivors, in hopelessly outnumbered fighting retreat, finally to the desperacy of a cornered cave, surrendered some hours later to Spain's guarantee of "safe conduct." They were the first Americans to learn, in dungeon, the meaning of that guarantee.

Philip Nolan, buried where he fell, was first to learn it, dying.

Then why the contrived and traitorous pawn, Philip Nolan of Hale's "Man Without a Country?" The Boston author, born 21 years after Nolan died, knew of the maneuvers for Texas: Jefferson's, by government acquisition; Burr's, for personal empire. Decades later, Hale wrote his booklet while Gettysburg and Vicksburg were in the balance. He sought another *Uncle Tom's Cabin* to bolster sagging Union spirits and to moralize, as he later admitted, against men in defiance of central government. He selected the murky connection between Wilkinson and Burr, but he needed a tool that his plot could maneuver. He says he invented "Philip Nolan", never dreaming there was a real American by that name. It doesn't wash.

In truth, he took a gallant young man who rode out for Jefferson, to explore Texas for the United States. Hale invented treason for his Nolan.

I've tried to find exactly where Philip Nolan made his forgotten last stand. Historians differ. Some figure it Tehuacana, above Mexia, where Indians' camps stood for ages. Seventy miles west is the other site. It is near sleepy Blum, on the Hillsboro to Cleburne road. Houston researcher Lynn Bellah has it pinpointed there close by the Santa Fe tracks, below the schoolhouse. It is on the family land of Jim Carmichael, Hillsboro editor who, as a legislator, declined to claim the spot, because he wasn't sure.

Where Philip Nolan died, which is what I started out to find, is less important than why and how he died. You Central Texans gather up your geography, or Bostonian Hale will have written false epitaph on a gallant Texan.

Mark both places:

"Near here passed Philip Nolan, intrepid first American in Texas. Not 'The Man Without a Country', but a hero who came to explore one."

1821

Jane Long's Vigil

On December 21, 1821, twenty-three year old Jane Wilkinson Long bore a daughter—our Texian first-born. And so, near shaded old Richmond, where long later and last she lived, there is a marker to "The Mother of Texas."

Any salute to this lovely, dark-haired and gallant young woman is a good one. But, better than the Richmond stone, I like a monument that, to me at least, stands for Jane Long—wife. It is not easily found or recognized.

Drive Galveston's broad seawall east to the ferry across Bolivar Roads—three miles of deep and ship-stirred dark water that puts Texas 87 over to hug the coast for Port Arthur. Across, where the low peninsula is a scatter of stilted color far upbeach, you land almost under an old lighthouse—lonely, storm-darkened and, though abandoned now, still watching the sea.

Nearly all Texans drive on, for there are five miles of fine north jetty fishing just ahead; and beyond, fifty miles of splendid wide beach.

And so you miss the real monument to Jane Long. Under the oleander and palm fronting this 1872 tower, gray granite tells that this site was also headquarters for Dr.

144

James Long's expedition that tried—and failed—to free Texas, 1819-21.

In thundering understatement, it adds that here, Jane Long waited for her husband.

What was it like when she waited and walked that long ago, salt-cedared sand? No notched skyline across, nor towers and domes glinting up to Houston! Texas was empty wilderness with only names like Bexar to the west and coastal La Bahia and, far north, Nacogdoches—a world away.

Another world away and a half-dozen years before, she had been a laughing, brown-eyed Natchez belle of sixteen, niece of powerful General James Wilkinson, then suddenly and forever in love. Handsome young Captain James Long! Surgeon, favorite of Old Hickory Jackson—his "young lion" at New Orleans. Quick as breath, that marriage!

Even young as then, she had told him she would never leave him and had quoted Ruth's "Whither thou goest". Down deep, she feared his other love—the far horizons.

She remembered when he told her he had pledged everything—their Vicksburg plantation—to head an expedition to free Texas. Though he said no, she had to follow, soon as she could carry their two-weeks-old Rebecca...up Red River's forest wilds...into a month's delirium in her sister's Alexandria home, where she lost the baby...yet on by cart and horse to find him at Nacogdoches...to watch with him for help that did not come...to see the Spanish crushing up to shatter him, ruin him...everything, even his horse, lost...

And scarcely safe across the Sabine, he had to go back; thus, so did she!

So here to Bolivar Point and the mud fort...and the once again waiting, waiting for help from New Orleans...and even Lafitte's pirates sailed away from burned-out Campeachy across on the island...and with this fall of 1821 coming, only the dreadful, daubed cannibal Indians, the Karankawa, watching from there now...

Now, this last goodbye. She had begged to go; it was inflexibly no. Just a few weeks, he had promised, to sail his fifty-two men down and occupy nearly-deserted La

Bahia. Then a grateful Mexico, free of Spain, would give them all their dreams in Texas.

The weeks lengthened; the provisions ran low. The guarding handful deserted the fort. Watching the pass for her husband's sail she was almost alone. There was five-year-old Anne, and her Negro girl, Kian—who would not leave.

Kian would help, gathering shellfish. She would have to help in December. Sighting her long glass from the parapet, Jane Long could feel her third child stirring.

Across the wide breasting water from the island, she saw what she had feared most: Karankawa dugouts, bearing straight for the little fort. Stifling the cold in her stomach, she ran her red petticoat up the flagstaff and, ramming feverishly, loaded her brass cannon. The Indians must not know the men had gone; her husband had told her of the French schooner they had boarded and its crew they had eaten.

Her cannon bucked, roaring. Crouched, she saw them mill in confusion. She served a second salvo; frantically, the dugouts fled for their island. Weakly, Jane Long went down to the canvas shelter in the fort's corner. Soon it would be winter, and the Kronks would leave the island for mainland shelter.

Winter laid the lash that only rare icy nor'easters can bring this coast. Now, the ocean scudded greasy gray, the wind bit to the bone like hot iron, and the driftwood piles burned as fast as they were gathered.

The birds were gone. What matter! Very nearly so was the gunpowder. She tried to fish; the wind screamed and beat her. She felt her jaw hinges lock, freezing. She scooped for shells. Her hands cracked and split. Her eyes burned tears when she looked for the sail. She had to look for the sail!

Now drove sleet and snow. Through a world turned gray, Jane Long could see a bear stumbling from the mainland toward the island. The bay was frozen.

Kian was sick, desperately sick. Night came. What night? What matter? When it ended and the sail came, they would find only bones. But they would be in the fort! They would be where he had said to wait!

She wrapped Anne in her bed and then Kian; then sank into her own. In the guttering firelight, she saw the canvas sagging under snow, then spilling it. She brushed it feebly from her. Then she felt the pain.

In the darkest watches, alone, she delivered Mary James Long.

In the morning, Anne helped her mother gather shellfish and driftwood.

The cold broke in January, by February, there was sun enough to dry fish. Spring came, then summer. In July, she saw a sail—this one from the east. It brought her husband's old friend, Randal Jones.

He had no way to know that this valiant woman would come back to Texas with Austin's Old Three Hundred — and live out a long, quiet life near Richmond.

He only knew her husband was dead in Mexico. He knew she no longer needed watch the sea.

But Jane Long's monument should.

The lighthouse — not the granite — does.

1821-32

Strap Buckner and the Devil

In a way, it's too bad that La Grange folks can't tell you exactly where their buckskin giant, Strap Buckner, fought his last bare-knucks fight.

The bad part is that we disremember what most old time Americans and any Texian at all knew for sure: Strap had the mightiest one punch this country ever saw. Harper's Magazine, eighty years ago, figured him an even stand-off with Paul Bunyan.

And big! Legendary Strap needed four deerskins just

for shoulder room. He had gunpowder kegs for forearms and oak stump fists. One solid shot would drop an ox; a miss would flatten most men.

And Strap had an edge on Bunyan and the rest. Outside of Dan'l Webster, he was the only American ever to take on the Devil; and he did it first. Also, where Dan'l talked his way out, Strap stood toe-to-toe on a liveoak hill back from the Colorado.

Main thing, Strap was real—just as real as Dan'l. Fayette County's fiery, red-headed first Texian, he had a cabin up and plow down when Stephen Austin settled fifty miles behind his forest frontier. If Dan'l met the Devil, you can bet Strap did.

Take history's Strap Buckner first.

Virginia-born, with a Scotch burr in his tongue and an Irishman's under his saddle, burly Aylett C. Buckner hit Texas with 1812's first Anglo-Mexican wave: the ill-fated Gutierrez-Magee Expedition. Between times riverboating the Mississippi, he was back with every try for the country—to James Long's last, in 1821.

The expeditions fell back; Buckner stuck. Beautifully empty Texas gave him his breed's need—room to roam. Karankawa and Tonkawa Indian already knew him fearfully for "Red Son of Blue Thunder" when he went down from his remote cabin by the Colorado near today's La Grange, to see if Stephen Austin aimed to crowd him.

Those first few years of collision scattered stories that Buckner never denied: that he had "felt compelled to knock over" nearly every man in the colony, some three times. Later friends like Judge Thomas Duke and Josh Parker had learned to let his temper cool from explosions that instantly challenged rifles at ten paces. They found him prodigious in size, strength, appetite and thirst, yet well educated, fiercely honest and generous..."if irascible." For his bulk in a fight, they knew him as Strap.

Stephen Austin learned him, too. Wisely, Austin turned Strap from a one-man rebellion to a one-man frontier. Captain Buckner led the drive to clear Karankawa, and was first on the ancient council grounds below today's Waco, to draw an 1824 treaty with tribes northwest. With Aus-

148

tin's colonists, he stood against premature Fredonian Rebellion at Nacogdoches; finally with them again, joined revolt's issue in what would be the first shooting battle in the coming Texas Revolution.

Down from his forests in 1832's hot summer, he marched one of the companies against the coastal fort at Velasco. There, history leaves Captain Aylett Buckner.

But not legend, spun from those ten years of Strap's, up the trail from raw colony. Stories drifted back. Sure, he swung once and downed an ox. Who was it, saw that? Was it five men or six he knocked over in one frolic? Brought 'em round inside his cabin with the corn jug, didn't he, then knocked 'em over again? Six? *More like eight!*

Remember that Kronk redstick claimed he saw Strap stop a wildcat in midair? Just set himself and swung. Skinned that cat on the spot. Like as not a bear, too!

But it was the black killer bull, *Noche* they whispered most about, down the trail. The remote cabins knew that giant, crazy-eyed outlaw. Six foot spread of dagger horn that could cut down anything. It was like *Noche* had the devil in him, working closer and closer to Buckner's bachelor cabin, as though he knew they had to meet.

Strap came out, put down his gun, and set himself. *Noche* pawed and bellowed, and Strap bellowed back. Then *Noche* charged; Strap's swing was a lightning blur. You could hear it hit ten miles. That killer bull dropped, finally reeled away. But he lay there an hour after Strap was back in his cabin and half through a jug.

Must have been that jug or the next—they figured later—made him do it. Strap came out front, red hair flying, rared back and bellowed for the Devil hisself to come on! He was champion for the world, was Strap; and he aimed to protect it. Up there on the big stump, hollering to shake the hills, he flat challenged the Devil to duel.

That night was mighty black, the wind tearin' the cabin, lightnin' rippin' trees, something tryin' to get in...now gettin' in—down the chimney—horns and a face red as mesquite coals and a black forked tail. Would 9 a.m. do for the duel?

149

Strap just went on eatin', washed down a mouthful of cornpone from the jug, and reckoned it would do. He sat up with the jug, waitin' for mornin'; and a thunderous dark and awful mornin' it was, when Strap went up the low hill for the fight.

The Devil came for him, grinnin', and Strap swung and missed; the Devil was all at once a dwarf, laughin' and kickin' Strap's knees. Then Strap got hit, hard as even he could swing; the Devil was a man, that quick, as big as he. Then they commenced to pound one another; and the rocks gave way, and the trees fell down, and, tryin' to catch his wind, the Devil kept changin' shape: a snarlin' cat, a bear...even a black bull like *Noche*.

All day they fought, half-rootin' out that hill and rippin' out trees a mile around. Strap yelled to fight fair, but the Devil changed to wind and blew the hill at him. Strap threw it back, but the Devil exploded it with lightnin'!

And that's the way they fought through the night. Strap holdin' his ground, but gettin' mighty tired. The stars turned red and the moon went out. Through all that black dark, Strap had to hit everything everywhere, and he did...and got hit back.

With mornin' come, they figure the Devil saw Strap just wouldn't go down, so he grew two hundred feet tall and half that wide. Strap had to stop; he couldn't even reach the Devil's boots. He crawled on his bob-tailed gray and rode off three months to rest, knowin' he'd never mention this fight...where he got no better'n a stand-off.

He should have figured the Devil wouldn't let him off with a draw. One of the first bullets at Velasco had a name on it—Captain Aylett Buckner. You can guess what happened to that Indian who, far distant, had watched the fight and told of it just one time.

So you won't find the hill. That fight cut and cleared it to a field, like so many around Strap's shaded old home town. In a way, maybe that's good.

Who wants to look up the Devil, anyhow?

Particularly the way Strap tried it—on his own.

Stephen Austin's Flag

The flag is at old San Felipe, and you may never see another quite like it. It shows the good and true colors of Stephen F. Austin, "Father of Texas."

Our big and beautifully-timbered state park that is named for him lies in the bend north of where U.S. 90 hurdles the Brazos for Houston. Beside it slumbers what was first city of today's Texas and, open for a few years now, an excellent museum of Texas colony times that will let more of us discover our Anglo beginnings.

And perhaps discover more of the quiet fighter who caused those beginnings. His flag dominates the entering right hand wall.

The museum is the J. J. Josey General Store, well over a century old and carefully restored just as it stood on the colony's *Plaza de Comercio*. Across is the dog-run log replica of Austin's cabin, the bronze Austin statue, the old brick-walled 1824 well, the site of San Felipe Convention Hall, where Texans debated rights, then statehood, finally war.

Just below is the still-rutted ferry and steamboat landing where the first ones came up to sprawl their log cabins that San Jacinto's retreat must burn. To the south is the white frame church for Texas' oldest Sunday school.

But it is inside the museum, by his flag, that you sense Austin of San Felipe best.

For their historically dedicated park association, Sealy's Mr. and Mrs. Walter E. Hill took me through. The long room's wall shelves and quadruple-banked glass counters compactly display something of everything: smoothing iron to ox yoke, two-man ripsaw to whiskey barrel, cornmeal grinder to shoe last, blacksmith bellows to bullet molds to a 1793 copybook. Range is extraordinarily complete.

At the front goes a detailed diorama of the old town, from Noah Smithwick's smithy, edging the settlement west. Down the rambling, log-fronted street, Travis practiced law and waited for Bonham; Three-legged Willie, off to found the Texas Rangers, left freedom newspapering to Gail Borden. Here began Texas' postal system and provisional government; here, one time or other, came every great name from Houston to Bowie and Wharton to Rusk.

Yet above all came Stephen Austin first, long before. His desk is by the door below his San Felipe flag.

You cannot fit Austin's struggle for colony into this brief space. Virginia-born of a west-moving New England father, he took up that father's Texas cause in 1821, age twenty-eight. He would lay it down at forty-three, but his old Three Hundred, from coastal Brazos to Colorado, would key the lock for America, west to the Pacific.

At colony capital San Felipe, he put down Indian and land speculator, built a legal system, created a provisional self-government, bridged the clash of Latin and Anglo mind and method, spent himself thin to help a colony prosper, moderated the hotheads, and struggled to the last ragged hope for peace with Mexico, while still demanding the democracy his colonists had been promised.

He was in Mexico to this end when Velasco, Anahuac and Nacogdoches went for their guns in 1832. Even while the Texan "War Party" shouted for independence, he would seek representative statehood, journeying alone to Mexico City and nearly two years' prison on now-dictator Santa Anna's charges of sedition and treason.

He would return to the turmoil of San Felipe's colonial hub, the fall of 1835, with actual revolution's first guns echoing at Gonzales and Mexican troops staging to crush it in San Antonio. Now even the Texas voices that had branded him "vacillating", called desperately for him to lead. Vacillating? He had sought peace...with rights! Lead where? To war?

In his Bollinger Creek cabin, like the replica across... at his desk, like that beside, the quiet man crystallized a decision for Texas that we sometimes forget. You can read it in the flag he would design less than three months later — San Felipe's banner yonder. With decision locked, he acted.

A jumped-up, buckskinned "army" of three hundred call him to reinforce them at Gonzales. He must hold against heavy troops that will sweep west from Bexar. With a provisional Texas government roughed out at San Felipe, Austin rides for the Texan line on the Guadalupe.

And, with his "army", crosses it. . .straight for fortified San Antonio!

He lays siege to double his numbers, rallies in-streaming raw frontiersmen to ready assault on the city while he cuts its supply lines. Leaders as war-wise as Houston and Fannin fear he has blundered in this direct strike to the west.

We must fight east if not here, Austin reasons prophetically. More, the army must assault San Antonio. Will a more skilled commander head the attack? He will storm with the troops.

Does he really think to take a cannon-held city with rifles? Yes, says Austin.

He will not see the attack. The night he receives San Felipe orders to leave for Washington to seek U.S. aid, this intent man asks his war council once more to storm the city. The council declines.

Enroute Washington, he learns that Ben Milam has achieved what they told him was foolhardy. Yet the plan he forged has fired Texas to resist. Ironically, he will be far from his home when Alamo stands to the end, and Goliad. . .and finally San Jacinto. He will have helped lay groundwork for U.S. recognition, finally annexation. But he will never see it. For a long time worn and ill, he will live but half a year after Texas freedom.

So look at his San Felipe flag, designed while he traveled
to Washington. It holds a philosophy Stephen Austin lived and died for. Atop, the Union Jack for North
America's Anglo Saxon ancestry, thirteen stripes for the
colonial origins of his Texans; yet, below the jack, a Lone
Star for Texas. And, true to his colonization word, the
Mexican colors of red, white and green. Across all of it,
spring the final words: "Our Country's Rights or Death!"

We forget this moderate man was always fighter:
against wilderness, poverty, misunderstanding, greed,
bickering, and finally tyranny. At showdown, all other
avenues exhausted, it was Austin who crossed the Texas
Rubicon . . . and would have held at Alamo.
held at Alamo.

As Travis fired showdown's first cannon and Houston,
its last. . .

Then in patience, reason, honor and determination to
duty, the quiet and peace-loving Stephen Fuller Austin
surely loaded those guns.

1828

Goliad's Hero of Mexico

Remember Goliad?

It is a quietly withdrawn little town west of Victoria.
Below, on a 'hill over the river is massive, bell-towered
Presidio La Bahia, once the greatest Spanish fortress
north of Rio Grande; and, on a Palm Sunday morning
of 1836, last sight on earth for Colonel James Walker Fannin and his 342 Texas volunteers.

Goliad's memory stirs more easily now, with recent completion of a church-directed preservation project to raise
the battered, block-square outer walls, the gun-mount-
ing corner bastions, and the ruins of inner buildings
around the two-century-old chapel that is still in use.

Yet, remembering Goliad in the tragedy of Fannin's men

is only part of what is here to recall; no ground in America can recollect more of man's continuing struggle for freedom than can La Bahia. Here, before Fannin's command, were fought four battles. Here was struck the first declaration of independence in Texas; here, ratification of San Jacinto.

And here, most incredible of all, could be a shrine to Mexican freedom from foreign aggression; next to Benito Juarez, a man from Goliad did most to inspire it.

Who were the men who passed this way?

First, the priest and soldier to anchor New Spain's northeast frontier against La Salle's French. Thrice moved, in search of better, more defensible location, La Bahia in 1754 crests this highest hill to guard its neighboring missions: Espiritu Santo nearby, and now-ruined Rosario, two miles across valley. The missions fail; finally the fort, alone, guards this lonely eastern front.

Now come the early Nineteenth Century assaults, with Spain beleaguered at home, Mexico in revolt, and Jefferson's America pressing west for a Rio Grande boundary to her new Louisiana.

In 1812-13, almost a thousand Mexicans and Americans under Bernardo Gutierrez and a young Massachusetts West Pointer, Augustus W. Magee, sweep from Nacogdoches to seize La Bahia. There, Spanish reinforcement besieges them for three months of intermittent fighting. They break final Spanish attack and pursue their enemy to Bexar. But La Bahia's long deadlock has given Spain time; the early try for liberty wins briefly, then collapses in final allied disaster at bloody Medina, just south of the Alamo city.

The next two filibustering expeditions never pass the grim old fortress. Colonel Henry Perry, a Connecticuter who had ridden with Magee, falls back from an abortive raid on Spanish Mexico, tries to capture the presidio in 1817, and dies with his forty-four men just beyond its walls.

Four years later, Virginian James Long sallies from Galveston for a quick coup at La Bahia as, far south, Mexico fights free of Spain. Long seizes the fort but is surrounded and captured there, to die in Mexico.

And now, in 1835, with Texas freedom's first shot still echoing from Gonzales, Goliad's bastion is stormed by South Texas Irishmen under Ben Milam. Old Ben rides on to assault Bexar and die there, but by December, Goliad runs up her own flag, a bloody arm and sabre, underscribed *Independence*, which she proclaims seventy-two days before Washington-on-the-Brazos.

Then Fannin musters at the fort he has renamed *Defiance* . . . and waits too long.

Yet Goliad, who attacked first, proclaimed freedom first, will have her last word in the revolution. It is across the San Antonio bottoms that couriers, with Santa Anna's surrender treaty, overtake the Mexican coastal army under Filisola. Goliad, in effect, notarizes San Jacinto; Filisola leaves Texas.

But what of Goliad's hero, least known to Texans?

I talked with the man who has worked hardest to salute him: soft-spoken, white-haired Corpus Christian W. M. Neyland. The veteran realtor divides his time between the city he helped build and Goliad country, where he grew up.

Traveling Mexico in 1940, he noticed that he crossed almost every town on a *Calle Zaragoza*.

"Just as many of them as there are Houston Streets up here," he said. "And a horseback statue of General Zaragoza in nearly every city."

Any Mexican patriot could tell you that General Ignacio Zaragoza won the battle of Puebla over the French of Napoleon III and Maximilian. At the mountain gateway to Mexico City, the intent, bespectacled, thirty-three-year-old general was ordered to hold. With 4,000 poorly armed irregulars, he faced double that number of battle-tested Zouave veterans. It would take a miracle!

It took Zaragoza's brilliant tactics. Into an encircling trap, he lured Maximilian's forces and completely routed them. The date was May 5, 1862; and *Cinco de Mayo*, perhaps Mexico's greatest holiday, honors that young general.

156

All this, Neyland learned when, homeward bound for Goliad, he had looked closely at a Zaragoza equestrian statue in San Luis Potosi and, dumfounded, read the Mexican hero's birthplace: "January 14, 1828 — La Bahia, Texas."

Neyland came home to proof out what he had found, then to work with growing numbers of South Texans to salute this land's contribution to Mexico's roll of heroes. Ignacio Zaragoza had been born to a young Mexican officer briefly stationed at the presidio.

Today, his birthplace is marked simply by the foundations of a three room dwelling just outside the walls of La Bahia. After Texas independence, his family — like many a South Texas Mexican — recrossed the Rio Grande.

Yet it seemed appropriate to Neyland that young Ignacio Zaragoza first rose to fame in 1855, leading forces against the collapsing dictatorship of Santa Anna, the man who alone demanded death for Goliad's prisoners.

In May, 1962, Neyland worked with Mexican and American groups to celebrate the hundredth *Cinco de Mayo*. To Puebla's National Centennial Museum, eleven hundred miles distant, schoolboy runners relayed a torch and tube of earth from Zaragoza's Texas birthplace.

Goliad native Neyland believes his city's testimony ultimately must be to all the heroes who passed La Bahia's walls. He thinks that testimony will be completed only when the United States and Mexico join in a commemorative shrine to the Texan-born man of *Cinco de Mayo*.

When, to Latin America these days, we talk this hemisphere's freedom from foreign dictatorship, it makes sense.

Jim Bowie's Other Stand

For eighteen days from frontier Bexar, the buckskinned column— packmuled and heavily armed — had threaded the silent, forbidding Indian hills northwest. Strung out in weary haste now, they seemed more than eleven riders. They knew the big Indian war party was close behind.

They had struggled for the abandoned Spanish walls of Presidio San Saba near today's Menard. Bleak dark, this November 1831, caught them miles short. They forted what seemed most defensible: an oak mott for hidden camp, a rocky creek, a short rifle shot west. North was a block of shinnery, thick as hog bristles. Just within it, they hacked a path where a rifleman could belly flat and command the rocky, high-grassed flats to the low hills about.

With false dawn came their hunters. Two Texans went out to parley, took a volley instead. One big man shouldered up his companion whose leg was shattered. He ran labored, shouting, "Jim!" His brother's rifles snuffed the pursuit; he made the trees.

The two brothers — Rezin and Jim — knew they could forget the Spanish silver they hunted. Against twenty to one odds, they would stand. . .and leave a legacy. Most recall it for the younger brother and his legendary "Lost Jim Bowie Mine".

I think, particularly these days, the legacy was also something else.

Perhaps, like me, you've spent a silent moment or two contemplating the crypt room, just off Alamo's chapel.

You remember — from when we were kids — that Jim Bowie died on his cot here, right to the last thrust of his knife. We knew that like catechism and flag. But now, in our sophistication, have come hero-erasers who suggest: "Didn't Travis really commit suicide before the onslaught? Wasn't Davy Crockett a groveling drunk begging mercy at the end? Didn't Bowie truly cower under the covers before they bayoneted him?"

Take your children to study the "Lost Jim Bowie Mine", the one near Menard. Old story says he spent a year—about 1829-30 with the Comanche, found a great cache of Spanish silver. If he did, he took his secret to death in the Alamo.

Now, you can hunt Jim Bowie's "mine" a dozen places: from near Menard to August Oestreich's pastures south of Llano, or from Ben McCulloch's and Harp Perry's Packsaddle Mountain, below Llano, over the granite hills north, as far as Gatesville. In a way, you can find it best from my friend Bob Weddle, Menard author-newsman. He knows two sites, each claiming to be where Bowie, on his last search for treasure, had to fort and fight for life instead.

You can take the Fort McKavett-Sonora road, twelve miles to gravel meandering north up Dry Creek, where shortly you reach the "Silver Mine". Or you can try the other way from Menard, toward Brady, at the McCulloch County line. Take your choice between markers, for both claim Bowie.

Up Dry Creek, the "Silver Mine" is a honeycomb of shafts and a ghost of old shacks where an aged Comanche "princess" and a San Antonio lawyer sank a fortune seeking the lode. They thought they found the skeleton of one man killed in Bowie's fight. The Brady road marker picks the oak mott and shinnery by Calf Creek.

Neither site is likely to yield you silver, but rather the legacy of the Bowie stand. Its ordeal is graphic from a half-dozen accounts in our early history: the eleven Texans faced some two hundred Tawakonis, Wacos and Caddos, enraged with the Anglo who had driven them from their land.

David Buchanan, first to fall, was the man hefted in by Rezin Bowie. Then the Indians circled; they had learned to respect white rifles in East Texas.

Matt Doyle slumped with a bullet through his chest. Tom McCaslin, running to help him, fell dead. Bob Armstrong's rifle was shattered with the ball that took his arm and side. Bowie's men made their shinnery fort with seven defenders.

Through the day, they lay in their fire paths, squeezed off and rolled instantly, for Jim Bowie would recall you could cover an answering twenty shots with a handkerchief. The Texans cleared the creek, then shot at anything that moved.

They fired and rolled. Jim Coryell, too slow, had a smashed arm. Then they saw the fire; grass was a ten-foot curtain of flame that roared to the barrier creek. Then the wind shifted and drove the fire from the north, and up to the shinnery wall it swept, blinding with its smoke.

Who was left to fight it? Four riflemen, two loaders against inferno, from which the Indians must burst any instant! The buckskinned men beat down the fire with buffalo and deerskin. Their shinnery wall was gone; just burned twigs now! Around their fallen comrades, they shoved up dirt and rocks, drew their knives, and half-blind with smoke, awaited engulfment. Night came instead.

From the small, near hill they could hear the Indians' death song for their braves. Frozen-fingered and burned, the defenders hacked out enough rock to stand, by morning, behind a makeshift breastwork.

There were no more attacks. In their circular fort, the Bowies stayed eight days. Then they came out — what was left — and packed their men back to Bexar. They had taken ten times their toll; reeling in hunger and exhaustion, they were home in two weeks.

You can compare a very few stands. Billy Dixon's high plains buffalo hunters, long later, held an equally hopeless fort — and won. The Alamo, against the same twenty-to-one odds, fell. And Jim Bowie in it.

Cowering under the covers? Not on your life!

160

Not the man who held his ground on the San Saba. Nor Travis, nor Crockett, nor any of the Alamo's others.

That's the real legacy of the "Lost Jim Bowie Mine."

Forgotten Father Muldoon

The more you think about the monument in the quiet, old land just north of Schulenburg, the more extraordinary it becomes, the more mysterious its hero.

His career, those half-forgotten days when Stephen Austin put Texas together, was meteoric. He was an unknown priest, then Austin's right arm. He came and went, for eighteen years a riddle: now in Mexico, now Texas, wherever trouble was. He saved Austin's dream, then his life. Then this man deliberately walked off the edge. History leaves his page relatively blank.

The monument? It is gray granite like the sedate hundreds which centennial-grateful Texas raised for her founders. But for this Texas father, the shaft stands bare of the great seal. It was privately erected.

Coming up on U.S. 77 from Schulenburg, I pulled to the shoulder opposite the live oak park and the high-steepled church away on the hill and there, read the strangest memorial in our state:

"In Memory of the Forgotten Man of Texas History. Father Miguel Muldoon, Resident Priest of Austin's Colony. True Friend of Stephen F. Austin and his People."

The memorial commission was headed by L. J. Sulak of La Grange, an elder statesman in newspapering, practical history and the state generally. I drove over to visit. Enroute, I detoured twenty miles to the tiny and slumbering community of Muldoon and could find no one certain for whom his town was named.

161

Mike Muldoon was only half Irishman because his father had clouted an English soldier and departed for Spain, where he married. Young Miguel grew intellectually and spiritually and became a priest. He could choose service. The Irish in him picked the adventure of far-off Spanish Mexico; in 1821. Father Muldoon was chaplain to the viceroy in Mexico City.

The following year, young Austin arrived for routine confirmation of his father's grant — the beginnings of Texas. It was not routine, but delicately complicated; Austin's mission stretched a year, far beyond his money.

But the visionary had struck a spark in the adventurer. From Father Muldoon would come guidance, grasp of Spanish, shelter, food, financial help and an unwavering friendship to the day of Austin's death. Once ready to give up, the colonizer instead left with his contract. Father Muldoon stayed in Mexico.

Now it is 1829. Austin's colony is the hub of Texas, hundreds of Americans flooding in, taking the allegiance oath to Mexico and the land-granting vows of Mexico's religious faith. Father Muldoon sets first foot on Texas soil at San Patricio. And now San Felipe. In 1832 he is resident priest with tremendous attendant powers of state and church. He has become, in sudden fact, the second most influential man in Texas. But he wears his power gently.

He ignores his fifty thousand acre land grant in now Galveston, Wharton, Lavaca and Fayette counties. Instead, from Houston to San Antonio and wherever the frontier, he ceaselessly walks the vastness. Grayed now, fat and contagiously merry, he shows equal disregard for money, trappings, danger. As the law decrees, he baptizes and marries his frontier dwellers. As remote distance demands, he does so en masse, with seldom more than a log shack or a tree for church.

He is aware of whispers about "Muldoon Catholics" — vow-takers with fingers crossed. But if even Stephen Austin is a mason, the padre knows his own spiritual charge. There is impending storm enough that he must keep harmony among all faiths. Mexican and Yankee, Protestant and Catholic trust him.

Justifiably. Unarmed, he follows raiding Indians from their massacre to their wilderness, returns a captured wife to her wounded husband. At Anahuac, he offers himself hostage to Mexican troops against "good behavior" by fiery Will Travis. He almost averts the bloodshed at Velasco.

But 1834 has come, and the storm is bursting. Austin, on a last-ditch peace mission, is imprisoned in Mexico City — virtual hostage against Texan revolt. Magically first to reach him is Father Muldoon. The priest smuggles food and word from Texas, meantime leading efforts that finally free his friend.

Back to Texas, then to Washington for aid, comes a now-ill Austin. War flares and is over. Austin returns to a destiny that has somehow passed him. He consents to offer for presidency, not really wanting it. Father Muldoon paradoxically disposes of his now-secured land at a fraction of its worth.

Stephen Austin loses and is dead in three months. Now Father Muldoon looks at the Texas he helped build. Does she really longer need him?

He undertakes one more task for his adopted land. William Wharton, returning from Washington's assurance of annexation, represents all that Mexico fears most. Her gunboats have captured him.

The year is 1837. Fully gowned, Father Muldoon — again magically — appears within the Matamoros prison:

"Mr. Wharton, I bring with me the garb of a Catholic priest. . . If you are accosted, simply extend your right hand. . .and say 'Pax vobiscum'. Remember that you are a Catholic priest until you reach Texas."

Wharton walked to safety, and Father Muldoon, into eternity. History records that he returned by ship to Mexico in 1839. An informed Santa Anna waited.

According to Mr. Sulak, some say the roaming priest lived to reach Spain. But the newsman has studied Santa Anna.

163

"Forgotten man is right!" Mr. Sulak tapped his pencil. "He rescued Texans three times; you might say Texas, herself. Who went to help him?"

I drove on to our capital city, puzzling over the man, perhaps more over the monument. The great seal should be on that quiet and enigmatic gray marker.

1836

Jim Bonham's Rides

This has no intention of tarnishing Paul Revere, a stout American patriot who, as every schoolboy knows, made The Midnight Ride.

Instead, it's to saddle you up with possibly the most underrated man in the Alamo. His two desperate rides for help defy comparison. Yet mighty few of us realize what they demanded, those rides, from Jim Bonham.

In actual fact, Paul Revere made it about 15 miles from Boston, spreading the alarm as far as Lexington then was captured by the British. It was Sam Prescott who got through to Concord, which was the Redcoats' real target. Moreover, these sorties were into Massachusetts, pretty well populated for 1775, and those folks friendly, armed and awaiting the signal.

Each of Bonham's rides took him almost a week, carried him through enemy lines in a sweep across country pathetically empty of anything but Santa Anna's oncoming legions and the waiting Indian. Each fearful journey carried him more than 230 miles to plead and exhort for Fannin's five hundred troops at Goliad while there was yet time to save the Alamo. Each failed, but the dark-haired, handsome, tall Jim Bonham didn't.

There is no way to know the exact Bonham trail. Certain only is that he made the incredible journey twice in scarcely more than two weeks, reached Goliad both times, returned to report failure with Fannin both times, then died on Alamo's walls with his closest friend, Will Travis, the man who sent him out.

But you can piece together some of the known fragments. Follow your map and you can closely approximate his route, perhaps some of the now-gone places where he rested his gray and grudged himself enough sleep to keep going.

Follow your imagination, and you may guess at the thoughts racing his mind as he raced time across wintry, scrubby land, through gray, cold day or bleak, blackest night.

Follow him on his second mission from San Antonio.

Drive southeast down U.S. 181. Where pleasant, shaded Floresville now thrives, there was nothing but the motts of oak and the hacienda, *Palo Blanco*, of the friend of Texas, Don Erasmo Seguin. Bonham may have stopped there briefly. Or he may have pressed another thirty miles where the trail broke away near what is now hill-topped Karnes City. He might have sheltered in the jacales of now forgotten Alamita. Thirty miles more, and then Fannin and showdown!

To pursue Bonham at this point, you have turned east below Falls City and followed the back route straight for Goliad.

Riding, or in those quick-snatched rests, what crossed the young South Carolinian's mind? That first mission to Goliad. . . he had thought he had Fannin convinced . . . but that fine man with those fine troops was indecisive . . . yet maybe there was a chance that, even now, Fannin was on his way. . .

He remembered coming in to report his first meeting at Goliad . . . the shock in realization that bombardment of Alamo had already begun. . .hadn't really been so tough riding through it . . . it got tougher though: those four days of fighting. . .of watching the fort encircled. . .

Getting out this time had been tight . . . that patrol: that was close! . . . He wondered about the other couriers . . . if they got through . . . if they got help . . . Mexican lancers all over the country . . . they almost got him when he went to sleep in his saddle . . . was that last night . . . or was it tonight? . . . Was Crockett still cracking jokes? . . . was Bowie better? . . . Anyway, he had patched it up between Travis and Bowie . . . Old Travis was a stiff kind, even when they used to fish together . . . kids back in Carolina . . . hard for him to show friendship he felt . . . yet you couldn't pick a better best friend . . . Was Travis still firing those three shots a day to proclaim the Alamo still fighting? . . . Sure, he was . . . there was still time!

If Fannin moved, they'd break through, they'd hold! . . . Fannin had to move! . . . Damn that mesquite that whipped your face from the night! . . . Don't stumble hoss; I know you're tired . . . Lord it's cold! . . .

At Goliad you can see Fannin's fort, where the colonel told an exhausted Bonham that he had tried to move to support Alamo's handful, but had broken down, fording, just a few hundred yards downstream. His troops would have to remain here.

Bonham, as ordered, doubled back through Gonzales, 70 miles, then another seventy to San Antonio. A guess only, but his route probably approximated today's Cuero Road. Old Friar's Store was where Cuero is now. From there to Gonzales — nothing!

What was he thinking those terrible hours? He had to report that help wasn't coming. He wouldn't have to tell Travis they were all dead men.

Did he wonder what he was doing in Texas scarcely four months? His family ranked high in South Carolina. He was intellectual, well-educated. He was a promising attorney. All future beckoned, yet here he was in what seemed a lost cause through divided command, conflicting ambitions, jealousies.

I think, instead, he thought about friends. Will Travis. Duty. Shortly before noon, six days after leaving, he surveyed from a rise the hopelessly surrounded Alamo. Another more practical courier turned away and would live out the war. Jim Bonham galloped straight through astonished enemy lines to report within a fortress he knew he would never leave. Three mornings later, he was dead, across his cannon on the walls.

As I said, this takes nothing from those intrepid Minute Men, riding the nights when America was born. And after all, Longfellow lived up there, and he immortalized Paul Revere.

He should have known of Jim Bonham's rides.

1837

Three Legged Willie's Constitution Oak

Drowsy, coastal Columbus has a mighty oak on its old, magnolia-shaded square. Imbedded is a weathered plaque to a great Texas jurist. But its story ranges much of the state and all of man's quest for freedom. And it begins — and really ends — elsewhere.

Say...when the judge rode into Shelbyville, brisk as the October wind that flurried the pines and blew red sand devils round the northeast Texas log houses. It whistled the chinks in the dog-run inn where he rolled up in his blankets that night.

He lay awake awhile. It wasn't his leg; it was trouble in that wind! "Shelbyville will have no Texas court!" he'd heard around. "And no Texas constitution!"

He stretched out saddle strain. He had ridden a long way for that constitution: San Jacinto's cavalry charge ...before that, his Texas Rangers — north against Indians, south to cover Houston's retreat...and even earlier than Gonzales' first fight, the time he had pulled Travis from Anahuac's jail...

At San Felipe, some said he had started it all: naming Santa Anna a tyrant who had torn up Texas' and Mexico's constitution! Then, that July Fourth declaration he'd circularized across all Texas. Well...it was over; his best friends, dead. And he? He was a first judge with a constitution they'd fought for — like America's!

His had been a long, long ride; for how else to explain a constitution and this republic's government? How else but, mile by mile, cover all his circuit . . . a log hut at Harrisburg, that shack at Bastrop. Now he was up from Nacogdoches' Old Stone Fort. At least, his court there had boasted a building.

Columbus, he guessed, beat everything. Since the town had been burned with Houston's retreat, he had used that big oak tree. Well, he liked that oak court; he liked the strength it symbolized. And since you were just beginning to extend justice to all, the first order of business for a court was to talk awhile on the freedom that a constitution guarantees. A man could talk freedom fine under that oak.

And so, there in Columbus, the oak and its marker remember Judge Robert McAlpin Williamson. In the morning, Shelbyville would remember, too. For his right leg, polio-withered above the peg that he hobbled...Three-Legged Willie!

The leg came with youth; the name, with Texas. He rode into Stephen Austin's San Felipe in 1826 - a dark-haired, bushy-browed, strong-jawed, twenty-two year old Georgian. If you forgot the strange drape of his trousers over that stump of a leg — and the pain it etched on his face — you'd call him handsome.

San Felipe, strung from the Brazos smithy past Peyton's Tavern, clear to Stephen Austin's cabin, called him what came frontier-easy—Three-Legged Willie. He gave himself nothing on that leg but a cane. Rather, he defied it. He'd tap out Juba for buckskin dances, singing to his banjo, or he could quote Byron or Chitty on criminal law. He got his first buffalo on his back, breaking his pegleg on it.

Those earliest days, he practiced law and edited the first *Texas Gazette*, worrying his friend Austin with his masthead, "God and Liberty" instead of "Mexico is My Country." Yet he won election as alcalde and left the post to ride against Indians. Historians have pondered whether he became Texas' Thomas Paine or her Patrick Henry, for he flared the Texas fight. And though a devout man, he had a plain-spoken way in praying for rain: "Lord send us a bounteous one that will make corn ears shake hands across the row...not one of those little rizzly-drizzlies..."

He would become one of Buck Travis' closest friends: it was he who went for that friend, locked in Anahuac, stumping in and, in cold fury, demanding: "Let him go, or you or I will be a dead man by tomorrow!" Saddled despite the stump leg, he rode Travis out.

Then came war and, after Gonzales, Texas provisional government ordered him to mount the republic's first Texas Rangers. He held the north against Indians, as far as the desolate forts at now Marlin and Groesbeck. When Mexico's troops hit the Colorado at Bastrop, he had twenty-two troopers and the task of screening Houston's retreat and shielding settlers who had panicked into the Runaway Scrape. At Hempstead, he left scouting to gallop for San Jacinto.

Then he was judge of the republic seven months later. In a year, he rode a thousand miles' circuit. No, he gave himself nothing on that leg; just bit back the pain, and wherever he rode to convene court, talked on the strength of Texas' constitution, its guarantee of rights against tyranny. It was strong, all right: like that fine oak in Columbus!

And so, he waked to a chilly Shelbyville dawn. He knew this old freebooter refuge — the Neutral Ground, with allegiances to nobody. He stumped over and set up in the store, his bench a dry goods box. He called for his grand jury; outside the crowd growled defiance.

Now their spokesman, a burly and hard-eyed "lawyer" came forward. Shelby had met last night, he said. They had resolved that the court would not be held. Three-Legged Willie listened, then spoke very quietly. Defying a court established by the constitution was very unusual. He eyed his man:

"What legal authority can you give for such a procedure?"

169

The Shelby man flashed a knife, drove it into the bench. "This, sir, is the law of Shelby County!" Still gripping it, he looked into the judge's pistol muzzle.

"If that is the law of Shelby County," Three-Legged Willie thundered, "this is the constitution that overrides that law."

He laid the pistol on the bench and, without regarding the retreating lawyer, had the sheriff summon Shelby's first grand jury.

Then he spoke on the constitution.

Judge R. M. Williamson finished that first term, went on awhile to the republic's congress and finally retired at Independence in the Austin colony he had defended. There is a marker at his last home in Wharton and in the Austin state cemetery.

But the Columbus oak marks him best. Its bronze reads simply: "Beneath this tree, the first court of the Third Judicial District of the Republic of Texas was held in April, 1837, by Judge Robert M. Williamson." To make sure you know this lawyer-editor-ranger, it adds: "Three-Legged Willie."

Yes, the oak's best. You need a memorial that goes back a long time.

For Three-Legged Willie's fight for a constitution, what better than a living thing that was seasoned and strong when the English wrote their rights into Magna Carta?

1853

Ed Westfall's Long Journey

Any man, young or old, can tell you there is nothing new in hikes for toughened fighters. Some few may have equalled this one; not many.

Across the rich, green checkerboard of winter garden, north of Crystal City, it is 20 miles by straight road from tiny Batesville to Uvalde. Once, by thin trail in the deadly Comancheria brush, it was much farther. From a lonely, forted cabin on the Leona — following the river through a mesquite wilderness to then western outpost of Fort Inge — both cabin and fort gone now, more like 30 miles, that year of 1853.

Two men measured it, almost inch by inch. One was Bigfoot Wallace— to many a Texan, greatest ranger of all. The other, unfortunately overlooked by our own histories, was a man Bigfoot would have told you was at least as tough as he.

And so might the Comanche, who knew them both.

They knew Wallace, whose twelve years' trailing their chief's big moccasin track made *Tejanos* call him "Bigfoot." They also knew it was this other who killed that giant chief under the Llano cliffs. It was Wallace's friend they painted on those cliffs for all Comanches to remember.

He was tall, powerful Edward Dixon Westfall, who came from Kentucky and stayed ahead of the frontier so far, few Texans saw him unless on Indian scout. To the angry amazement of Comanche, he dared to live scornfully on their land — alone! Again and again they had tried; they could not kill him. But now, one more try!

171

For more than a day, they had fought that heavy-walled cabin fort in the mesquite clearing. The clearing was death; their first two braves had dropped instantly. Then they had fired and taunted; but the log walls waited ominously, showing a rifle ready for them. It would cut down the first to move. And soon more whites would come.

They could stay no longer. Perhaps, at least, they had killed some within.

They had indeed. Westfall's only companion, a French trapper, Louie, had blasted once with his shotgun, shooting through the cracked door. As he sighted again, he was hit in the chest. He jammed the door closed before he died beside it.

Ranger Westfall, firing through a slit in the logs, took a bullet through his neck. Blind with the impact and knowing he was dying, he still thought to wedge his rifle through the logs — a last, desperate bluff. Then he fell across the bed.

Whether on that bed three days or a week, Westfall was never sure. He remembered three things. If he rolled to his back, he would strangle in the bleeding. Yet finally came a time he could make out dim objects in the swim of light; he recollected that, for he might yet see! When he was able somehow to drag Louie's body outside, nothing happened. The Indians were gone.

Then Ed Westfall figured he had a chance to live. He might see to walk and crawl the 30 miles to Fort Inge. A heavy stick would support him and feel the way. He remembered reeling out the door. He fell once, crawled ahead to his feet and stumbled on.

Then the days and nights closed him in.

To follow him best, detour to Batesville by way of the town, Bigfoot, where Wallace lived last — east near Devine. There is a fine, down-to-earth museum of the old ranger's life and times and chairman Ralph Crawford knows this forgotten odyssey as well as any Texan.

He can send you to the point, south of Batesville, where Westfall started; and where, nearly a week later, Bigfoot

172

— scouting the country — rode down to visit his old friend. Short of the clearing, Wallace felt trouble — the sudden cold way a watchful man feels it come. He moved closer; then he saw it.

In the cabin was grim inventory. There had been a bad fight, all right. Somebody must have died on that bed. Bigfoot would send back to bury the Frenchman, but now he had to find his old partner. Striking trail up the Leona, he read Westfall's sign.

His friend was hurt bad: short, shuffling steps, heavy weight on a supporting stick, confused tracks where it looked like Westfall had fallen. Here! Crawling a piece, getting up. Here, he'd dropped to one knee and lain down.

Westfall had a water gourd and a pistol: each place he had been down, Bigfoot could read them pressed against the earth. Ed was hurt bad, just to lay on 'em like that, never move 'em.

His partner's trail crept the miles like a man blind drunk. There! He had tripped on that rock and fallen hard; there was some dried blood. Wallace set his jaw: that one hurt! He had stayed there awhile, then crawled on. Here he'd made a small fire; and again, a few miles beyond. Good! Had something — maybe coffee — too keep him going. Ed wouldn't backlight his own camp, no matter what.

How many nights? Now Bigfoot figured backwards, trying to judge the miles against the pace. He might have slept in that heavy cedar brake, early; or there in the shinnery of the Leona; or beyond, where he had crawled between the two big rocks.

Westfall was down more often now. Bigfoot moved slower. Don't pass him if he's give out and fetched up off the trail to die where they won't get to him!

It was that way right to the gates at Fort Inge. In the whitewashed rock hospital under the hackberries, Bigfoot found his partner. The Doc showed him the wound. It had grazed the jugular and creased the lung, Doc said. Plumb through! Doc said he'd come in, pretending to walk straight, but half-blind. He said Ed Westfall had no business living after he first got hit.

Then he said nobody that blind and dead could have

made it 30 miles. But damn if it didn't look like he'd make it, even see, when he came to.

Of course, Bigfoot could have told him old Ed would live another half century, sound as a dollar, same as he aimed to. No use tellin' docs, though; they didn't even know how to use a good prickly pear poultice.

After that, Bigfoot rode back to the Leona ranch to take care of his partner's horses. Riding watchful, it was a long way. A mighty tough walk. Bigfoot rubbed his jaw. Seven days and nights, Ed had kept a-comin'!

But then Ed Westfall was a mighty tough Ranger.

1874

Billy Dixon's Kentucky Windage

There are two monuments at remote Adobe Walls, northeast of Amarillo, where the quicksandy, miles-wide Canadian valley is a nick in the unnoticing, limitless plain. One marker tells the heroic five-day stand of twenty-eight buffalo hunters against seven hundred Indian cavalry. The other salutes the indomitable red man in the latter days of his lost cause — home and range.

There could be a third. Seems to me American riflemen would mark this spot, for here — even in the sights of us tin can marksmen — was fired what must go down as the most incredible single long range shot in history.

On the third day of Adobe Walls' siege, buffalo hunter Billy Dixon—mustached and raven-haired to the shoulders like a twenty-four year old Custer — was challenged to pick off one of a party of Cheyenne horsemen atop a butte east of the hunters' sod fort. Dixon squeezed off his Sharps Big Fifty — a shoulder-breaker for lesser men — and shot the Cheyenne from his horse. Range: seven-eighths' mile!

Yes, there have been longer shots. It is by comparison with one of them — peculiarly also fired in a fight for Texas — that you grasp fully the phenomenal blast from Dixon's buffalo gun. But that, in a moment.

174

The bloody, desperate fight at Adobe Walls, beginning dawn June 27, 1874, was caused, as customary, by white man's invasion of red man's land. One of those advancing treaties had set the Arkansas as deadline to buffalo hunters pressing south. More and more hunters dared to cross, finally raising a crude, sod-walled headquarters of three buildings — New Adobe Walls — near, along the Canadian, where an ancient mud-bricked village — Old Adobe Walls — had thwarted Kit Carson and his First New Mexico against Comanche and Kiowa, a decade earlier.

An Indian confederacy, dominated this time by Lone Wolf's Cheyenne, thundered out of the rimming morning sun to obliterate the hunters. They would have counted coup on sleeping men, but surprise was denied them. Even then, this would have been a smaller Alamo (odds were the same), but Indians never understood that engulfment of even mud forts must be under waves of infantry, however bleeding.

Horses could reach windows and barricaded doors, but their rawhide saddles were emptied by the grimy, sleep-bleared, tangle-bearded men who fought back, half-naked or in their drawers and barefoot. By early afternoon the buffalo guns had won. Indians were a mile away in the breaking short hills.

They were there the second day and gone by the fifth. The third, however, produced Dixon's riflery. Fifteen Cheyenne looked down on the little fort from a low butte almost a mile east. No nearer! They respected the Big Fifties.

Behind the walls, somebody said try a shot. They picked their marksman. Bat Masterson was good, but Billy Dixon, squinting from his barricade, was better. On that butte a man was barely visible — except the horse let you notice him. Dixon hefted the heavy, balanced Sharps. It would take some fine figuring, that shot.

How much figuring? Ten years earlier, consider another marksman with a similar shot. He is with Federal General Nathaniel Banks' Red River expedition, which was to overrun Texas with 35,000 men, but was thrown back by smaller forces, short of the border. April 1864 brought

175

Red River disaster and one piece of marksmanship.

Captain John Metcalf, West Pointer dedicated to proving long range sharpshooting, has been ordered to drop a Confederate general in camp, out of range across a stubbly, mile-wide Louisiana valley. Metcalf has twenty-four hours to ready for the shot for which he has devoted his entire military study.

He has a 30-pound, muzzle-loaded target rifle with a long 25-power telescope. A surveyor's transit gives him the precise 5,467-foot range to the tentpole, before which the Confederate officer will stand at tomorrow's reveille.

Metcalf takes fifty men to build his firing bay on the crest of the highest Federal hill. Down goes a firm, heavy-planked floor. To it is bolted a firing table, and to that is fitted a scaled swivel for exact elevation and traverse. Metcalf spends the night with ballistics and trajectory tables. Now he has the measured load in grains of black powder, his angle for range, wind, even drift. When the scope conters the Confederate, the barrel of the target rifle angles sharply into the sky. It locks there, no hair's breadth tremble to throw it yards wide of target. The captain squeezes his shot. Slightly over four seconds later, the down-arcing bullet drops the far-away officer, wounded.

Metcalf's incredible marksmanship rates Federal citation.

How could Billy Dixon, steadying on that corn-sacked barricade, squinting his open sights for a high piece of sky — while three days of close death dance his mind — make those same corrections? He had to lob his heavy slug over almost the same range.

I asked my Ingram friend, gunsmith-collector-marksman Al Kennedy. He knows the old Sharps, has a couple he likes to shoot.

To Al, every correction Captain Metcalf made with telescope, table, formula and gun-vise came easy to Billy Dixon. "Kentucky Windage," Al called it.

"What's Kentucky Windage?" Al snorted. "Well, it's by guess and by gosh and by ten thousand other shots with a Sharps...and with maybe some luck to boot."

If you get up to sprawling Turkey Track Ranch, between Stinnett and Spearman, you'll find the adobe walls returned to dust; but the markers are there and, away from the cottonwoods and hackberry on the watershed, the long-off butte. You're ten miles from pavement along a sandy ranch road.

Worth the trip, though, to stand in the Great Plains' quiet and wonder about that impossibly long shot.

Come to think of it, Billy's sharpshooting drew a citation that beat the captain's. Billy gave it, himself. He shrugged it off as a "scratch" shot. Doesn't quite mean an accident. Just means it'd be tough to do again...even for Billy Dixon.

1874

Two Guns at Comanche

Cupped within choppy hills, halfway between San Angelo and Waco, the old western town of Comanche boasts two little-known and strange-storied landmarks. They are a block apart on the west side of courthouse square. One is a doorway; the other, a tree.

You can link them in a way, because — long ago — both were defended with guns in defiance of law. The door was John Wesley Hardin's. The tree was gentle old Uncle Mart Fleming's. From that doorway, Hardin shot to kill, possibly in self-defense. Uncle Mart's rifle, without firing, held the axes from a gnarled old live oak that had saved his life as a boy.

Veteran, white-haired editor James C. Wilkerson can look directly across from the windows of his Comanche *Chief* office at Hardin's fatal doorway. A few paces to the northwest corner of the square, he can point a block south to the Fleming oak, a splended survivor in a sea of pavement that surrounds Comanche's courthouse. But, one story at a time.

177

Riding sweat-saddled into Comanche, the summer of
1874, John Wesley Hardin could look back on his twenty-
one years with probably no more explanation of his thirty-
plus gun notches than history has been able to adjudge.

Growing up on the worn-out heels of Southern defeat
and the influx of carpetbags, John Wesley, at fifteen, had
killed his first man "in self defense." Then came three
of Reconstruction Governor E. J. Davis' state police. Hardin drifted from Polk-Trinity's forests to DeWitt's brush
country. He had a growing price on his head. As Hardin's
toll mounted, fewer cared to try for it.

He drove cattle up the trail to Abilene, where he backed
down Wild Bill Hickok. Generally he was left alone with
his brooding, dark good looks, his volcanic temper, his
whiskey and poker, his lightning guns and his conviction
that he fought only when forced.

That he was about to be forced never entered his mind
as he loped into Comanche.

Earlier, near Brownwood, a cousin had bought some
cattle. The seller had neglected to advise that the beef
was still heavily mortaged. Despite the real owner's protests, Hardin took the cattle under his cousin's bill-of-sale
and his own guns.

Brown County's deputy, Charlie Webb, may have determined to get the cattle and John Wesley's bounty, too.
An unwise Webb rode into Comanche, close behind.

Legend says the two men met, apparently in a friendly
mood, near the square. Hardin and his riders had enjoyed
a good day racing their horses (who wanted to beat John
Wesley's horse, then collect from him?). Now they were
determined on the saloons and poker. Grim Comanche
was equally determined that this town was for raising
kids and not for Hardin's gunplay. This was the stage
set when Webb and Hardin agreed to a drink.

Some say Hardin went into the saloon first, his careless
back turned for the first time in his life. Others say he
laid a trap for Webb, following close.

Somebody yelled, "Hardin! He's gonna shoot!"

Hardin spun, and Webb was hammered dead into the
dirt, his guns unfired. Of the many turning points in John

178

Wesley's dark, strange life, here was the fatal one. He had killed Texas, not reconstruction law. He fled awhile — as far as Florida — but he was caught. Returned to Comanche's aging courthouse, across from where it happened, he drew twenty-five years in Huntsville, September 28, 1878 — age twenty-five. He served fifteen years, came out just old and slow enough to be shot in the back of the head by John Selman in El Paso.

The Comanche doorway had opened on oblivion to John Wesley Hardin.

In the summer of 1854, young Martin Fleming's father brought him far beyond frontier to look at family land grant. They pitched camp in the live oak grove which, in a few years, would become Comanche's square.

In the night came the quick thunder of Indian riders. Young Martin dived behind the biggest oak as the horsemen drove by, yelling. In the morning, he helped pull Comanche shafts from the bole of the big tree.

Except for occasional visits, he did not come back to Comanche to settle until after his service with the Confederacy. He lived quietly, prosperously and generously. Regularly, Uncle Mart, as they knew him now, visited the big tree that had saved his life.

Comanche was growing. Now, around courthouse square, even the thin remainders of the fine oak grove were getting in the way. It was time to take them all. The county court deliberated now-elderly Martin Fleming's plea to leave one old thing, one tree — his tree.

The court respected Uncle Mart as a Comanche builder and elder statesman. But the tree had to go, and they told him so. He told them his tree would stay.

In due process, the court ordered the square cleared. When the workmen got to Uncle Mart's oak, they found the tall, slim, black-hatted and graying man standing beside it with his rifle at full cock. The men left.

"Would he have shot if they'd come at him." I asked Editor Wilkerson.

"Nobody in this town would have come at Uncle Mart.

They thought too much of him. They just hadn't realized he was dead serious about that oak."

At the base of the old oak is a small white marble slab: "Uncle Mart's Centennial Oak." Each year it lights with this town's Christmas season. It is Comanche's growing monument.

And John Wesley Hardin's doorway? It is service entrance to one of West Texas' better drug stores. Walk in it today and you enter the prescription department where C. L. Huett — as he has for thirty years — works at keeping people well.

This entrance on an enterprise for saving life is, in a way, an ironic, unwritten plaque. And unquestionably one that John Wesley Hardin never figured he'd be remembered by.

1874

Colt Chivalry at Mobeetie

If you believe the sophisticates, the Old West of Gary Cooper and William S. Hart was all just amusing movie myth. But I like to think of a Panhandle town that once really knew Six Gun chivalry . . . and the night it came to climax.

In the lamplit, dusty mirror behind the heavy bar, he could see himself. He was tall, with twenty-one years' lean strength. Real silk, the bandana at his throat under a wind-darkened face. His gray sombrero was gold-braided and immaculate, and so, the hand facing of soft shirt, vest and trousers. Polished boots jingled silver-chased spurs. A newcome fool could have thought him a dude. But ask a buffalo hunter!

Catlike, he eased away from the bar; the heels of his hands pushing down to clear his gunbelt from the red sash round his waist. Now he must walk blind from the light, to where it puddled the dust outside and would back-light him. Outside, night crouched the little street; and, likely, so did ambush.

Why? She wasn't his girl! He'd told her time and again! She had been just a good, clean girl in trouble; and nobody else to step in. Now, desperate-woman-like outside, she had to see him. Quick! So a man walked out, a first-shot target.

His spurs tinkled against the saloon's sudden silence. He had to go out, all right. As elsewhere west, they knew him in Mobeetie. He was Bat Masterson.

Old Mobeetie lies in the cottonwoods east of Pampa. Above her, the Washita heads for Oklahoma, heaving the high prairies to a rolling green sea. There is a square rock jail, some tumbled cisterns, a few houses and the cemetery on the hill.

In the early 1870's, when Texas began east of Angelo, this was buffalo hunters' "Hidetown" camp, finally Mobeetie — the Indian name for Sweetwater Creek, before he lost it to the hunters and Fourth Cavalry, following hard.

Shortly it was Panhandle capital: a one street town of cottonwood pickets holding raw frame fronts against the wind. There was Lady Gay Saloon, the blacksmith's shop beside, and across the dust, the white frame hotel. Down the street were the other springing-up emporiums toward the fort they didn't need, because the Indians were through.

Down on this town rode a handsome young surveyor. To know the land, who better? Long before the troopers came, he had fought it and for it — at desperate Adobe Walls. Billy Dixon might beat him with a Sharps Big Fifty; nobody beat him with a Colt. Nor with dress nor courtesy.

His name was William Barclay Masterson.

He knew Mobeetie's women — the early, resolute wives and the others. One — from neither camp — struck a chord of sympathy. She was Molly Brennan: a plain, sturdy-limbed girl whose father repaired boots behind the Lady Gay.

181

Molly had a good white dress and, for some time, the frank admiration of Mobeetie's men. Then, what had been fun for Molly — looking for a man — turned to terror. A man found her. He was a hardcase ex cavalry sergeant with whiskey's red face, a slack mouth, and a killer's record. Even tough Mobeetie had watched in horror when he first laid claim to the girl. A stranger spoke to her; she had smiled. The sergeant, a bowie knife belted over two guns, killed the man almost instantly.

Right-handed, he feinted for his knife. The stranger's gunhand leaped toward it. The sergeant's left-handed gun swung up and went off, muffled. Thereafter, Mobeetie had the word: however Molly Brennan might hate and fear this man, it was death to speak to her. She was as fearfully alone as he was ambidextrous and deadly quick.

Quietly, Masterson heard the story, studied the girl and the man, then made his move. Passing, he tipped his hat. Later, he spoke to her. Then he chatted, laughing on the corner. One day he took her arm and escorted her across the street. He went into the Lady Gay where he knew the sergeant waited.

It was too quick for the trooper's eye. His knife was half-sheathed and his left hand still holstered. Yet he stared into the Bat's gun muzzle and froze. Contemptuously, Masterson whipped the barrel across his skull and watched him crawl away, humiliated before all of Mobeetie.

Shortly, Masterson knew his mistake. It was not, as Mobeetie insisted, that he should have killed. For himself, he had no fear of the sergeant's return. Any buffalo hunter an ex cavalryman could ambush ... well, he likely deserved killing.

His mistake was the open-faced girl in the white dress. Simply, she had told him she was his. But he had acted only to free her! Well, free ... she chose him! She couldn't help it. Yes ... even if he didn't want her!

Finally, she told him she wouldn't bother him any more. He wouldn't look round and see her, wherever he turned. But Bat Masterson knew he was not done with the sergeant; through the girl, the man had his blind side for sure. He finished the survey; still he waited. He must be here when the sergeant came back for Molly.

Now they told him she had come running desperately down the dusty dark street. She must see him! Now! Yes, outside . . . and hurry . . . *hurry*! It had to be, the man was back.

In the bar's dark mirror he saw himself clearly. Go outside to ambush because a foolish woman set it up. Stay here and let her die! He walked out the door.

Across in the shadows, the dim white figure screamed, was thrown aside and the night crashed blue. Bat sank to his knees. Into the light sprang the sergeant, leveling for the second shot - at the close-in range where he couldn't miss. His shot was muffled in the white figure flinging against him.

The third shot was Masterson's; it killed him.

Waiting for his thigh wound to heal, a somber young ex surveyor saw them bury Molly on the hill south of where the old windmill stands today. Then he rode on to Tascosa and finally a marshal's star at Dodge and long later, his memoirs. Of course, those memoirs were the kind of stuff that amuses the sophisticates.

Well, you take the sophisticates; I'll take Old Mobeetie's great cottonwoods. They cast long, strong shadows, like the tall men who knew them.

Short Sad Life of Sam Bass

Maybe Shakespeare had the line for Sam Bass, dying in Round Rock.

The outlaw had a rifle-torn middle, a shattered right arm, sweat-matted black hair and mustache, two days' agony and a square jaw, still locked. Would he talk?

Unless it was that deputy...he'd never killed a man. Would he tell anything else? A feeble "no." He was "goin' to hell anyhow," he'd take those secrets with him. He did. Before sunset, his twenty-seventh birthday, this July 1878, he took them straight into legend that Texas seldom tops: loot hidden from Hill Country's Longhorn Caverns to the Red River; a lightning gun that could initial, at gallop, a Belton oak. A dozen tight escapes, Breckenridge to Terrell; and haven, almost any barn, Denison to Waco. Didn't he tip twenty gold dollars once, for ham and biscuits he liked?

Handsome Sam Bass could hit every North Texas stage or train, yet share camp with a lost preacher's family. Touch the rich; give to the poor! In that song that survived him, a gun-slung Robinhood. Well, you decide about Shakespeare.

North of Austin, Round Rock's Luke Robertson was the best first-hand authority I know. At a jaunty 89, he walked straight with a carved cane and knew anything from old Texas to real dough bait fishing. Down Brushy Creek, he could show you where our ill-starred Santa Fe Expedition started, and how Sam Houston's riders — taking the capitol back from Austin — were stopped. His family settled here, those early 1840's.

But his first hobby was Sam Bass. Sure he was young when Sam fled, dying in his saddle...right by Mr. Luke's daddy, working a slip on Red Hill. Sam gave out in the brush west of the Robertson homestead; and the store where it started has been Mr. Luke's family's for three generations. Naturally, he studied Sam Bass. We retraced that wild, running gunfight — right to the cemetery.

"Old marker's knocked down." Mr. Luke leaned on his cane by Round Rock's new stone. "Handsome black-haired lady — sister, maybe — put the old one up. It kind of wondered, the stone did, where Sam took a wrong turn."

Sam Bass was born in Indiana, orphaned at thirteen, last Civil War year. He ran away from an uncle and, like many, made Texas by 1870. Through Denton County, near the Red, came the cattle drives and the railroads. Ought to be good money.

At twenty-three, he was a good cowboy — gun or horse — and broke as twenty dollars a month. Must be an easier way! He raced his fine-flanked Denton Mare; found you can lose. In 1876, he trailed up to Kansas, kept going to Dakota Territory's golden gulch at Deadwood. Even there, which was easier — dig or gamble? The tables got his trail money. Sam took the next step — his first, outside the law. His outfit lay for bullion stages, finally the Union Pacific. Half died; Sam got through, back to Texas...Denton County.

Recruiting the gang he'd lead to easy money — beefy Frank Jackson, skinny Sebe Barnes, runty Jim Murphy — Sam couldn't know he had just one year for legend.

Riding south, this next summer of 1878, he can only think back sourly on that year. The Cleburne stage netted eleven dollars; the Fort Worth-Weatherford, little more. Then, hit trains!

They would hit the Texas Central, down from Denison, the Texas and Pacific, three times near Dallas. Never what they hoped and paid for — Arkansaw Johnson dead

185

by the tracks, Murphy captured, the rest scattered. Too many squeezes; too little gold!

Now Murphy back; "jumped bail," he claims. Sam knows the awful hunch he has a ringer. Kill Murphy? His gun's needed. It'll get better, he promises Jackson and Barnes. They'll hit a bank. Waco? Too big and chancy. Belton doesn't feel right. They'll try Round Rock: size it Friday, take it Saturday; Sunday's his birthday!

They've got an edge, he tells them. Sure, law combs North Texas, but who knows them down here? For tomorrow's look-round, they just ride in...

Into ambush! Murphy had indeed turned, sent work from Belton. While they camp, sweat-lathered rangers ride the night from Austin and San Saba. One thing Sam Bass has right. Nobody waiting his gunsights tomorrow, will know the look of his target.

Round Rock's main street runs neat store fronts east today as it did, dusty and frame-boarded, then. By the signal light, Robertson's was a clapboard general store, next to the bank. Diagonally across, the old theater was saloon. Down the alley behind, the north trail left off in bushes where Mamie's Cafe stands now. There they tied their horses. With Murphy watching back trail, Bass, Barnes and Jackson ambled round for a drink. They'd ease over, buy tobacco in the store, size up the bank and town.

"Fellow told our deputy," said Mr. Luke, "that one man showed a gunbelt, hikin' his jumper to pay for the drinks. That's what he followed into the store . . . an illegal gun — not Sam Bass."

"One of you fellows got a gun?" said the deputy, up close; and Round Rock exploded. The lawman went down under three guns. By the door, the Austin deputy shot blind into smoke and — spun round, hit in the left lung — saw them make the street.

A wild street: a ranger running, bent low... others behind him...Bass, right arm smashed, shifting gunhands, yelling to circle for the alley...windows and cracked doors opening up...Ranger Dick Ware, firing deliberately, ducking behind a cornerpost that splintered where his forehead should have been...

186

Now, round to the alley and down it...Bass, holding his arm, buckling with a close-range Winchester; Jackson holding him up...the horses there, rearing in dust-spurting tumult...Sebe Barnes vaulting, forking saddle and right on over, into the dirt, shot through the head...Jackson hoisting Bass up in that lead storm, holding him there ...drumming up the trail from the smoking little town...

They made a mile and Sam gave out. Jackson rode on, into obscurity. Bass lay through the night in the shinnery, crawled a little way by daylight when they found him, took him in to die and maybe talk. He wouldn't talk, and it left a legend.

Who shot him? Hard to say: maybe a ranger, maybe somebody — long since gone — that Mr. Luke will let you call Jones...or Smith. Anyhow, that's not the moral. Legend is.

You can figure Bass outlawed Texas less than a year. A man would have to move mighty fast to do everything folks credit him, in that short time. That was Mr. Luke's notion. Could we have built Sam Bass all out of proportion — this gun-slung Robinhood?

If he'd talked, would he have told his real secret: What a savage, dirty, short...and hopeless life it is — once outside the law!

You decide if Shakespeare fit him. The line?

"Nothing in his life became him like the leaving it."

The Fighting Parson

Were I to teach Texas history, these frantic times, I'd spend awhile back-trailing from that sagging and forgotten saloon gallery where San Angelo thrives, church-steepled and neatly bustling today. At first glance, a raw page, rightly forgotten.

But look on the dusty, sunblistered town, across the river from Fort Concho as he did. The men — booted teamsters, buffalo hunters, riders — shuffled toward the saloon benches about. They'd recognized him, bearded, compact and clear-eyed, riding in from solitary camp: Winchester still holstered, but his saddlebag on the whiskey case with his Colt and his Book.

Oh, he'd heard them as he rode up; it was generally the same: "Oyez, oyez...oyez! There's to be some spang-up religious racket on this gallery...fifteen minutes sharp...by the fightin' parson...a reformed gambler, but now a celebrated gospel shark." It was their way.

"All you old rummers and whiskey guzzlers and card sharpers come out and mend your ways, or you'll all go to hell, sure as you were born!" He accepted that, because they accepted him as they did no other across Texas' western frontier, this year of 1880. Since they knew him as rawhide-bred as they, they'd listen.

He was Andrew Jackson Potter, Methodist circuit rider, age fifty; his text, the entire Bible. Scanning them, he could backtrail and see himself. Half his life ago, he couldn't read or write. Yet he knew he was about to shake some of them to their foundations, perhaps change a life, even as his had been changed.

Preacher Potter's backtrail touches all Texas, from the Sabine to the Canadian. It began, he knew, with a ten-year-old Missouri orphan, just after Alamo. No mother, no father, who'd named him for New Orleans' hero...no way to live except as gambler apprentice, horserace jockey, saloon swamper. Thus finally, a sixteen-year-old muleskinner on trains for the Mexican War and Santa Fe, California gold, Indian frontier, and nearly every dive from the Santa Ritas to San Antonio. At twenty-six, a full, worried life.

At Bastrop in the summer of 1856, he knew everything from quick-dealt monte to a fixed horsetrade, how to face a knife showdown to the shakes. He'd been able to defend himself with wagon tongue, rifle or his fists. He was unscathed. He knew himself uneasy.

Then came the camp meeting, arbored below Bastrop – three weeks of it and his buddies taken in. Five days he resisted, then went in on his knees and home to his wife. "Emily," he said, "I'm going to try to live right." That simple!

It had seemed that absurd, for a man who couldn't read or write. He'd learned how, poring over what he'd talk on today at Fort Concho - the Bible. He had learned to let what was in him do the talking.

He'd read that Bible over and over again, marching with Debray's Confederate Thirty-second, all the way from Hill Country's Camp Verde to Louisiana. He'd gone for wounded and dying at Mansfield and Pleasant Hill. Nights over there, this chaplain's troops had slogged in, sick of dying and killing, to hear him tell of a promised new life. Then, war despairingly over in muddy Houston, they'd listened to him tell that the new life was still promised; they just had to start over.

He could recall fragments, those years after war...a Big Thicket bandit he disarmed near Huntsville, talked to and turned free...a Comanche ambush above Del Rio that left him untouched...a Nueces gunslinger sworn to kill him: he'd just taken the man's gun . . . but in Boerne, he'd had to face a .44, flatten his man, then bail him from jail in the morning. Literally, he had dared to preach every

189

frontier brush arbor from Fort Clark north. They called him the Fightin' Parson; he knew the answer to that.

Sure, he could fight. But only to defend the life he'd dedicated. And on the western frontier that was his circuit, a man had to be able to defend himself, particularly if he rode alone to hit saloon step and buffalo camp — his congregations.

It's easy to surmise that Andy Jackson Potter's sermons were tub-thumping blood and thunder. What else from such a rawhide background? What else from raw man with only the will to try?

For an hour, though, the backwash of Fort Concho would hear him speak on his Book — from its beauty to its truth. He'd challenge any to call it false. Hear this unlettered man:

"If true...it puts each individual upon trial for eternity by a divinely prescribed mode of faith and consequent course of action. But if not true, it leaves us in darkness more dismal than the grave.

"With this question before him in unsettled state, and with the strongest possibilities against him, can any man safely neglect to search the Holy Scripture? Is it safe, is it agreeable to the common sense of mankind...to treat a question of such fearful import with indifference?"

Astonishingly, he could rally Bacon, Newton and Scott to denounce Voltaire and "his satellites, Paine and such as Hume..." Finally he attacked those who saw the Word as a "contrivance of an artful priesthood to serve their own interests.

"It imputes at the same time to these conspirators, the greatest acuteness and the utmost stupidity. To frame such a scheme, they must have infinitely surpassed all the world in talent for 3,500 years; yet so blind were they to their object as to sentence themselves without reprieve to a life of hardship, opposition and toil; for such is the general lot of the Christian ministry upon this Earth."

Are these the words of an unlettered man? How could he speak so to these others in buckskin, dirt, sweat and doubt? Yet he never faltered, our frontier's "real gospel

190

shark" from the Concho to the Canadian...and finally to his pulpit in Lockhart, when he finished his sermon, closed his Book, and at age sixty-five, his life on Earth.

You have to ask what gave illiterate Andy Jackson Potter his Pentecostal tongue. Was he a buckskinned Paul, a mulebacked Francis?

Or maybe one like you and me...and the sons we'd teach. If, shaken deeply enough, we'll try.

1881

Bandera's Mysterious Sheepherder

Almost everybody knows Bandera — jaunty as a creased Stetson — for its amiable and handsome guest ranches just northwest of San Antonio. Many, for its craggy battleground pass, toward Kerrville; and some, for its dimmer history — the brief Mormon camp, the ancient Indian one.

But few, even among today's Banderans, know its fragmentary role in one of the strangest, most mysterious and persistent myths in our nation's history. I learned of it from quick and bright Mrs. Jenette Saul, who publishes Bandera's *Bulletin*; she, from her frontier-historian father, Marvin Hunter.

If you rummage around in the Frontier Times Museum, a Marvin Hunter legacy that is priceless in itself, you can pick up the Texas thread of a tale that baffled America, decades after it was supposedly finished.

In the very late 1870's, Bandera is a thin scatter of dwellings and huts and the usual row of false-fronted establishments. There is a swelling flow of wagons, horsemen even men afoot as Texas presses west. Strangers are commonplace.

One stranger has put over on the E. M. Ross Ranch on Julian Creek. He is fine-featured, with dark, deep-shadowed eyes. He is well-mannered and quiet. He seems

191

content with the job he lands, herding sheep. His name is William J. Ryan.

Like many another western town, Bandera is looking for roots, and one of its favorite cultural pastimes is a community spelling bee. The sheepherder attends one and, astonishingly, spells down the entire town.

Banderans look at each other with the awed suspicion that the dark-haired, preoccupied stranger might just as easily have done the same thing in cultured San Antonio. Will he be teacher for their children?

In 1881, William J. Ryan, principal of Bandera Institute, has fifty students. Along with the basic courses, the school offers Latin, German, Greek! There is heavy emphasis on instruction in drama!

Ryan's personal life is succeeding as well. Though admitting to an age of forty, he is engaged to the daughter of one of Bandera's most prominent families.

Two years later there is no institute. Ryan has left as silently as he came. Just before the marriage, old-timers said, word got around that he was a fugitive from justice. What fugitive?

Shortly after 10 p.m., April 14, 1865, Washington's elation with war end collapsed in national agony at Ford's Theater. A dying Abraham Lincoln behind him, John Wilkes Booth had raced to Anacostia Bridge, bluffed his way across and, by midnight, was lashing his sweat-flanked dun across sleeping Maryland.

Johnny Booth! Brilliant, cultured youngest of the stage's greatest family!

He had a good start on the fifteen thousand men flung into all direction pursuit. But he had a broken fibula in his left leg. Always dramatic, he had leaped from the president's box to the stage. The leg would undo him.

One of his accomplices, simple-minded Davy Herold, caught up. The others, daily and one by one, were cornered. But incredibly for twelve days and nights, Booth evaded the closing cordon, even reaching Virginia (where he had expected all Dixie's acclaim but learned of horror and loathing instead).

On the Garrett farm near Port Royal, time ran out.

192

Surrounded in a tobacco barn by twenty-five troopers and secret service, Herold surrendered. For his last act, Booth stormed and defied. The barn was fired. Against orders, according to official later testimony, Booth was shot dead by Sergeant Boston Corbett.

Now came unaccountable official action that spawned the myth and the mystery. Frenzy of the nation demanded to see Booth hang, now at least to see his corpse. Instead, Secretary of War Stanton whisked the body secretly aboard a gunboat anchored in the Potomac, refused statements, allowed only a selected few to identify the man. Some confirmed it was Booth. But others came away convinced that it was not, shaking off realization of what twelve days' exposure, hunger and shock could do to a man. Rumors flew.

Stanton, moving fast and again unaccountably, now decreed secret burial. Eight men handled it, all sworn to secrecy. For the record, Stanton felt instant action necessary, for he feared the whole plot was high Confederate strategy to reopen the war. An amazing mistake on both counts!

"Was it Booth or was it concealment of a major blunder?" Some of the press asked it openly and on the street, despite mounting documentation, more and more knew that Booth had escaped. He was, of course, seen everywhere from Canada to the Orient. Men had talked with him. Most reports put him on the road for Texas, then Mexico, which, in fact, had been Booth's plan.

For decades, many an intelligent man was certain Lincoln's assasin escaped.

The Booth "escape" ended long years later. In the early 1870's, a drunken saloon keeper confessed to a young lawyer in Granbury, near Fort Worth, that he was Booth and, going mad with his terrible secret, would show proof.

The lawyer, Finis Bates, listened skeptically, forgot it. A quarter century passed. A derelict in Enid, Oklahoma wrote his confession as Booth, took poison. Bates went to Enid, determined that it was the man of Granbury, produced photographs and documents the suicide had left.

He finally wrote a book in 1907 which sold well but did not stand up under official authentication.

It must have puzzled the old time Banderans, though. The pictures Bates produced and those of Booth himself suddenly recollected their own picture of their long-ago sheepherder turned principal. Recollected mighty close!

One thing's certain, even were it not all just myth. If John Wilkes Booth didn't die beside that burning barn, his "escape" was far the more terrible punishment.

1882-1897

The Loner's Law West

"Señor Judge!" cried one distraught groom at this special-rate double wedding. "You have marry us the wrong wives, my brother and me!"

The burly, beady-eyed and white-bearded man straightened his alpaca justice coat. Over the bar he scowled. He spoke on the enormity of sundering conjugal bonds. But he would rectify their mistake. He granted immediate divorce. Then he officiated a second wedding. At each step, of course, a fee — now triple.

Then he doffed his coat of law for bar apron. Drinks, all round!

Who was to argue? Was not this fierce, big-shouldered old one, as his signs said: Judge Roy Bean - Law West of the Pecos?

The court and signs are there today, preserved by our state on the in-loop below where U.S. 90 hurdles the high Pecos gorge and touches the Rio Grande's. The town is brief, rock-windy Langtry, where the east-west railheads met in the 1880's beyond Del Rio, toward El Paso and California.

All is there — where he slept by a bed-chained bear — picket-bottomed porch to stovepipe chimney. All but the judge, buried in Del Rio; and which of him was fact and which, legend . . . not so long ago.

194

Of all who trailed Roy Bean to the Pecos, El Paso's historian C. L. Sonnichsen has done it best. Bean was an 1825 Kentuckian, down with the Mexican War, then gold-rushing California. He salooned it there and in New Mexico and, after Civil War, for nearly twenty years ran a "Beanville" down San Antonio's South Flores, where he wood-yarded his neighbor's timber and let the river help his dairy until a minnow swam one bottle. Then, at an indomitable fifty-seven, he started over.

He had a stiff neck from a misfired Chihuahua hanging and a one-volume law library - Texas Statutes, 1879. In 1882, he followed the rails just west of the Pecos canyon. From east, Irish micks; from west, California's Chinese. What a spot for a tent saloon! No law? He'd be that, too!

It was land nearly wild as the cave-dwelling man had known, ten thousand years before Bean. But at Vinegaroon, just over the gorge, then Eagle Nest Springs —today's Langtry—the judge set out to tame it. He sobered drunks, chaining them to his bear until they came alert to his heeding and fine. Always, the fine! He found a corpse with forty dollars and a pocketed Colt. He took the fine for the concealed gun he must also confiscate.

He could be brutal. He made one rustler stand for sentence — a long description of the beauty of passing seasons: the ones he'd miss, hanged to a mesquite. He could be kind: any down-and-outer had a refuge with the old man. He met the gun-toters head on. On ordered "pizen" from his bar. The judge produced a jar of embalmed centipedes and scorpions and poured out the alcohol.

"You ordered it; you'll drink it!" But a round of drinks let him off.

A wrong man? Or just old and expedient? In either case . . . Law West of the Pecos.

Perhaps a name dropper. He knew his town was named for an early railroader, but he doted on the calendar picture of the British stage beauty, Lily Langtry. A drunk sign painter got two "L's" in Bean's "Jersey Lilly," but the judge wrote her he had named his town for her. Touched, she volunteered a drinking fountain. Water, wrote the judge, was what his community couldn't drink. She saw her town only after he was gone.

It riled the old man that Langtry might doubt his a-vowed friendship with Jay Gould, who had driven the tracks west. He determined to meet the tycoon. There was a west-bound, Gould's castle in tow. It roared into Langtry, shrieked to a halt.

The judge sauntered from his Jersey Lilly and brought the New York party inside. For three hours, they toasted with Bean's specially-procured pink champagne, while Wall Street telegraphed frantically to know if Gould's train had crashed.

Roy Bean had only waved his red bandana at the engineer - emergency danger! Then he had met his friends-to-be.

Maybe appropriately, in the late nineties — shortly before his death — the judge scored his greatest triumph. He and Austin law had been at odds so long; now the capital said there could be no heavyweight championship fight in Texas.

Involved was reigning Australian, Ruby Robert Fitzsimmons and Irish challenger, Peter Maher. Dallas, then El Paso, were closed as sites for the fight. From lonely Langtry came Roy Bean's word: Send your excursion trains; the fight's here.

Fight-stopping Texas Rangers rode those trains, as did keg on keg of beer that Bean had ordered. Then the judge showed his hole card. Under the Mexican cliffs just below — but days from anywhere across Rio Grande — there was an ample sandspit, a ring erected, a pontoon bridge, to float over the excursioners.

Fitz finished the fight in two rounds; but Bean didn't start it until he'd sold out his beer at a dollar a glass. And the Rangers? This was international law. Best, just to watch.

A few years later he died — alone, as old men do. He had hung on one last jamboree in Del Rio, come back at age seventy-six and never survived it.

You stand by his Jersey Lilly and wonder. An out-

and-out rogue? Or just open with it? Or maybe one indomitable old-timer against the world? His Del Rio stone
carries no dates — apparently just what seemed important
to the old man:

"Judge Roy Bean — Justice of the Peace — Law West of
the Pecos."

For his time, it'll do for your answer.

1897

Cowboy Reunion

About now, Ol' Hub and Sam Graves ought to be somewhere beyond Abilene and the Clear Fork, headin' home.
Maybe you saw 'em, down to Cowboy Reunion at Stamford.
You'd remember: Ol' Hub, all cow sense on tippytoes,
and Sam, easy and proud in the saddle . . . ridin' out cham-
pions, when there wasn't a cowboy west of Fort Worth with
a plugged nickel for their chances. Well, let's turn 'em
and catch up.

Our state's Cowboy Reunion is three days each early July
— rodeo to parade and chuck feed to tall stories. It's in
Stamford, a sturdy-built town up the grassy, humpbacked
prairie from Abilene. Come reunion, it's recollection capital for all the riders since West Texas was fifty million
open acres, and beef saved us after Civil War.

Its purpose — as the old brands from Pitchfork to
Swenson's SMS can tell you — is to preserve the history and
culture of the real Texas cowboy. That's why Ol' Hub and
Sam and the rest ride down, year after year.

It was about 1880 with little west of Fort Worth but
horizon when a gangling Jacksboro kid, Sam Graves, met
Hub. He saw a smooth bay colt with ramrod legs, split
two thousand oak rails, grew, and had a horse. Hub had
a partner-friend with a quiet voice and a magic training
hand. They drifted west together, growing up.

197

By the time Hub was six, he was a sleek, compact twelve hundred pounds that could feint out a scared steer, stare down a bull, and pivot inside a lightning bolt. He also belonged to Sam's boss; his pay and Sam's weren't enough to keep them together. But Sam was along, so Hub kept going, whoever his rider. . .guessing, thinking with that rider. Cow sense, they called it. He'd learned it, easy enough. Hadn't he and Sam grown up together?

Let another cowboy brag that his pony could haunch down and stop a locomotive to a saddlehorned lariat. Hub could work, almost without rein. He proved it once, cutting a wild steer. . .after his rider dropped off the bridle. Hub had to jump a cedar clump and nip that steer's neck and just plain "fierce" him out. Well, a champion had to think. And West Texas, from Double Mountain to Palo Duro, knew him for one: the best cutting horse ever.

Too good for Sam to buy back. When he ranched off alone, over near Guthrie, he had to leave Hub behind. And that leaving was hard for the bay to figure. Well, he'd wait.

Sam bore a man's mind. You can leave what you love most, when you must. You can know you won't come back and wish for a way to make leaving easier . . . wonder how it'll be when Hub gets old . . . and you don't ever come.

So Sam left and Hub waited and did his job. . .in trail and roundup's dust and cold, on the night string; finally, down to riding line . . . for the wire was coming, this end of the century, and the open range was gone. Along with Hub's youth.

He was out to pasture, grubbing it in the hot-gullied cedar under the Cap Rock. Hub was nearing twenty, and it was a long, hungry time since he'd seen Sam Graves.

In his *Big Ranch Country*, Wichita Falls historian J. W. Williams traces, among most other cow country things, barbed wire's coming on the West.

At dusty old Haskell, as from Abilene to the Panhandle, they sensed the end of open range and its free-riding cowboy. Reunion — chance for Four Six riders and Matadors and Spurs to talk old times — had to come. It was summer,

1897, that Haskell rallied almost the first; and it echoed from that cowtown's *Free Press* to Fort Worth, even to the Kansas City *Star*. From railhead, fifty miles away, fifteen thousand would come. A main event would be contest to determine the greatest of the West's cutting horses, last of the free range breed. Purse: $150 for the champion!

Nobody thought of Ol' Hub. Except an aging Sam Graves, still ranching under Guthrie's Cap Rock. He came looking, found a gaunt, rib-slatted bay in the brakes, so poor you could hang your hat on his flanks.

Sure, he could enter that horse. But what a shame to drag him down. He'd be up against fiery youngsters and riders good as Sam Graves ever was. Sam took the old horse home, fed him soaked oats, gentled him and brought him easy to where he could feel them think together under his saddle. Nearly a month, he searched Ol' Hub's memory, then set out for reunion and cutting contest's showdown.

And Hub? Weak-legged and slower. . .but thinking again with his rider. Knowing that rider's rein before he felt it. Why not? He'd waited for him so long!

They lined a mile around Haskell's make-do grandstand and grounds. All the rest had run off; it was time for the cowponies. Old timers set their jaws and hated to see it happen to Ol' Hub. They'd known him in his prime; but who'd seen him these ten years past? Sure, he'd been great; now he was old. . .*old!* Look what he was up against!

Kent County's Boley Brown would chute first. Nobody rode better than Boley and he was up on a six year sorrel, all strength and fire. And that Childress rider on the dun. They set the "roundup" — a little herd of heifers, wild as bucks. A man had five minutes flat. Cut as many as he could, one at a time. Deliver to the two counters by the gate. Miss any, it scored double against you.

Boley Brown got nine, fast as lightning, but his sorrel overshot one. Then the Childress pony lashed out and lost his first. Now it was Ol' Hub's time.

Out he came. Not fast, but straight in, like he owned that herd. He cut for a brindle, right in the middle. His old legs straining, he feinted and blocked and took her out. Great! But too slow! Yet he was back again, Sam Graves' legs dangling and reins near limp. . .just talkin' to Hub. The old bay had a second, now a third. *There!* he blocked that one, just putting out a forefoot. And that one. . .he stared down, threw a shoulder, then headed!

Across those grounds, they were on their feet, yelling. Hub was up to six . . . seven . . . time running out on that deliberate pace. . .Sam Graves talkin' him in like they were kids again. And time! Exactly eight cows to the cut. And none lost!

Ol' Hub picked his way out, Sam Graves up; and the both of 'em knowin' they'd thought it through. The mark stood, but what stood most were all those yelling proud riders who'd seen it happen. Not speed or power . . . but an oldtimer on heart, head and belief!

Of course, the purse went for oats for Ol' Hub's last days; not many but none finer. And of course, Cowboy Reunion, now down to Stamford, will be a continuing tradition, long as men can ride down to meet — even in nowadays blue pickups.

You might have seen 'em, Ol' Hub and Sam Graves, headin' home. They'll be back next year. . .and the next. They come back in memories . . . which is what makes reunions.

Also Texas tradition.

1900

Bill McDonald and Ranger Creed

Used to be, any Texas boy could tell you right off who was fastest gun in the West, whether his nominee was Hardin, Hickok or Bill Longley. For the same reason that nobody remembers the first name of the sheriff of Nottingham, it was harder for us to pick our state's greatest lawman.

Actually, it isn't easy to make this latter selection, for down history's long hall, the Texas Rangers count many stalwart names: black-bearded, Indian-fighting Ben McCulloch and prodigious Bigfoot Wallace; red-headed Sam Walker who helped design Colt's revolver and intrepid first captain, Jack Hays; writer-doctor-fighter Rip Ford and leathery, fearless Lee Hall, or, for that matter, the lawman's ranger, slim, soft-spoken Leander McNelly.

No, it isn't easy at all yet perhaps there was a ranger who spoke and lived a creed for all this elite band.

Walk a wintry street in Quanah, west of Wichita Falls, near century's turn. A tall, wide-hatted, blue-eyed and full-mustached man strides lankily against the cold, squinting the gusty dust, flexing his gunhand against the chill. He is Captain Bill McDonald, Company B, Ranger Frontier Battalion.

He is about to leave his outfit the creed by which it serves, and has, since its beginnings.

Those beginnings knew Indian border "rangers" early as 1823 in Stephen Austin's coastal colony. Texas Rangers were formalized short months before the republic and held its frontier against Santa Anna south and Indian northwest. Uniquely in American military history, they spearheaded Zachary Taylor from Palo Alto to Buena Vista, and Winfield Scott to Mexico City. Over the years to come, they would stand nemesis against bandit, riot, feud, outlaw, rustler or gunslinger.

It was over the span from Texas reconstruction ordeal to the more solid ground of the 1900's that William J. McDonald stood tall. Across from Mississippi to Rusk County at fourteen, a year after Appomattox, Bill McDonald grew inexorably toward law enforcement. By his early twenties, he had been teacher, grocer, deputy and small rancher. His friend from Mineola, Jim Hogg, helped him be what he most wanted — a ranger.

His career would trail across all our state — from the Sabine to Brownsville to the Panhandle. He would wolf hunt with Teddy Roosevelt and bodyguard Woodrow Wilson; yet he had broken rustling out of Amarillo, banditry in Wichita Falls, riot in coastal Texas, and mutiny at Rio Grande's tip. He had a lightning gunhand, true enough; but he used it only to disarm. Quietly, for example, he had backed down Bat Masterson at Sanderson.

He had a dry wit about him. Off the train to put down a riot in Columbus, he was confronted by citizenry horrified to see but one ranger. Legend gives Bill McDonald's drawling answer: "Well, you ain't got but one mob, have you?"

Warned against singlehandedly confronting such a mob, he said wryly, "I'm pretty good at single-handed talkin'." He was.

Later, when 25th Infantry's Negro troops rioted and shot up Brownsville in 1906, McDonald alone would walk into Fort Brown with a pump shotgun, face twenty level rifles and the command to halt or be shot. He prefaced his reply with sulfur, then snapped, "Put up them guns!" The troopers dropped them, and an officer of the 25th would summarize for posterity: "Bill McDonald would charge hell with a bucket of water!"

Which, in fact, stated the case for most rangers.

But it was Quanah, where this one lawman wrote out a clearer creed for them all.

Call the rustler Miller (not his name). Company B's captain had word that the hardcase was in town with two gunslingers, avowed to get him. "Then I'll do him the favor of meetin' him halfway." The tall man's eyes iced and he started angularly for the saloon where the three should come out.

There were four; Quanah's sheriff walked them out, found himself sudden shield when Miller ducked behind him, snaking for his gun. McDonald beat him. Carefully missing the sheriff, he put two bullets in Miller's vest pocket (where a tobacco plug and tally book stopped them) . . . and fury broke.

The ranger took one shot through his coat, another in his left side. Down sprawled the sheriff to duck fire and scramble away. Spreading out, sprang the two gunmen, drawing and shooting. For the staggering officer, Miller leaped to finish it, ramming his pistol for McDonald's body. The ranger's left arm swept up the gun to powderburn his face and rip his hat. Then, reeling, he drove a third shot to finish the rustler.

But in that crossfire fusillade, McDonald was hit now in the upflung left arm, now in the right side. . .spun around, eyes hazed. . .the ground reeling. He hadn't strength to trigger his gun to full cock. His left arm limp, he tried to thumb it with his right. He couldn't and he had but seconds.

He whipped the gun to his mouth. Spraddle-legged and knees buckling, he caught the hammer with his teeth, snapped it back, then swung on the spread-out gunmen.

They were gone, running.

They knew he would have cocked it again with his teeth . . . or boot . . . or saloon post. They would fall. He wouldn't go down!

He did, only with the rustler finished and the field held.

In a few weeks he'd be saddled again. It would take age and pneumonia long years later to stop Ranger Captain Bill McDonald.

Our greatest? Who's to say? And it isn't the point.

What is — for all rangers and our lawmen — every lonely day they serve, is that this captain proved a creed that raw, wintry Quanah street. Many times he had put it into words:

"No man in the wrong can stand up against a fellow that's in the right . . . and keeps on a-comin'."

1900-1911

Carry Nation's Texas Hatchet

You wonder how we've overlooked her — this extraordinary, controversial woman. Maybe, because it seems a long way from shaded old Richmond, near Houston, to a Kansas December morning, 1900 . . . when she first went on a police blotter.

From the cold outside, she had moved on Wichita's plush Carey Hotel bar, like a black-caped, middle-aged bulldog.

All down the immense mirror, those horrified early tipplers watched her reach the distant end of brass-railed mahogony. There, where no woman came, she turned — doom in a dark bonnet. They saw it happen!

Her cane swept the bartop, splinteringly cardhousing the four-foot tier of glass tumblers. An arcing brick shattered the mirror. . .a whiskey decanter crashed the liquor case. . .she jammed the beer tubes. . .and, now by the door, ripped the life-sized canvas *Cleopatra at the Bath*. Then she was gone . . . for the saloon across!

She spent three weeks in jail, was freed in evenly-divided public uproar. Kansas was constitutionally dry; the near-hundred saloons she'd assaulted these next months operated illegally — if openly — under that state's law. For saloon-hatcheting orbit — Maine to California and ultimately prohibition — she had chosen a fine hotel for launching pad. She felt she knew hotels.

And rightly so. For ten years, ending a decade earlier, Richmond Texans called their twenty-one room frame Veranda, across from the courthouse, the "Nation Hotel". Proprietress? Square-jawed, headlong moralist Carry A. Nation.

Today, the Nation site is unmarked, and few remember its mistress. A distinguished exception is white-haired historian Frank Lane Heard of Rosenberg, whose twenty-five volume Texas notes wait for some university with eyes to see what his can no longer finish.

As a boy nearly ten, Frank Heard remembered neither a crazy trouble-maker nor a saint with a hatchet. Rather, a dignified, handsome woman who seemed always after boys to quit smoking and who prayed a lot. Long later, historian Heard would trail Carry Nation as have few others today.

Carry was a snub-nosed teen-ager from good Kentucky-Scottish family, suddenly destitute from border state Civil War. Her post war marriage to a young army doctor proved as tragic as he was war-alcoholic, dead in two years with delirium tremens.

A despondent decade later, she married Missouri lawyer-journalist David Nation, tried a new start in Texas,

204

failing in Brazoria County farming and a hotel in Old Columbia. Then Richmond's Veranda; she brought it her loathing for liquor, a belief she had failed spiritually, and hands-and-knees labor that made ends meet.

The old colony town, trigger tense in reconstruction, believed the Nations carpetbaggers and Carry, too headlong in religion. She countered, teaching Sunday school on plank seats in her hotel.

During 1887's terrible drought, she challenged prayer for rain, led it kneeling the dusty street. Cloudless blue spattered shutters about, banked dark next morning for three days' rain. Yet how could you find warmth in this stern woman who denounced any young drummer's before-dinner drink or slapped cigarettes from town boys' hands?

Was she crazy? Richmond felt sure, when sudden night flames swept on her hotel firetrap. For while frantic guests escaped, Carry sat in her lobby rocker and prayed for help. And the fire smouldered out, wind-turned, at the very walls outside.

Still it was husband David who drove them from Richmond. Writing for Houston papers, he scalded the town's Democrats, took a beating and leave-town warning. Were those men drinking? He didn't know. So, a Texas decade down the drain, the Nations began again in Kansas, Carry violently certain now that drink had dogged them to ruin.

At Medicine Lodge, she combatted it a time in restrained W.C.T.U. protest, then took the activist plunge. She rolled a drugstore's barrel in the street, smashed it. Short weeks after, she loaded her buggy with bricks and drove to little Kiowa, wrecking three saloons. Then she moved on big city Wichita's Carey Hotel. . .and national sensation.

She was egged on train platforms, handcuffed at Coney Island, knocked down in Colorado and Maine, led from Washington's Union Station bar and wrestled out by a Montana lady barkeep. Yet she packed her Chatauqua speeches; one Sioux City church filled and emptied three times while she kept talking. And this, historian Heard reminds quietly, was a full decade before American women won their vote. . .and prohibition. Some temperate leaders drew fines; plunging Carry Nation drew jail in twenty-five states. With it, ridicule and charges from meddling to insanity.

Carry came back to Texas twice. At her nation-rocking peak, she descended on the University of Texas in 1902. Intrigued, students met her at Austin's Hancock House marched happily to a Fifth and Congress saloon. There, a firm barkeep barricaded her outside, drowned her street speech with a loud phonograph, within.

To University steps she marched for a philippic against "campus conditions," then led her cheering followers toward a drug emporium — saved from her hatchet only when she realized it was train time.

She smashed one place in her formerly-adopted state. Two years later, in Houston, she assaulted a "Carry Nation Saloon", across the bayou from downtown, followed her bricks through the glass front door, swinging her symbolic hatchet.

"There she goes!" finally yelled a bartender across the wreckage. "Headin' for the San Jacinto bridge. You can still catch her!"

"Catch her, hell!" groaned the shaken owner. "Who wants her back?"

In 1911, at sixty-five, she collapsed while speaking in Arkansas. She did not recover to see her fought-for prohibition tested.

Which, if you've puzzled, isn't the moral anyhow. Nor is whether you can demand or enforce virtue. This is the story of the now almost-forgotten Carry Nation who descended on Kansas and America. . .in a way, from Texas. You can make a case that it was Texas, where Carry felt something snap and picked up her hatchet.

I agree with gentle and thorough Frank Heard, who judges no more than that we have overlooked an extraordinary woman. It does seem a long way back to her times. Maybe because the key to Carry Nation — the one she showed crystal clear in old Richmond was neither lunatic nor saint. Just relentless nonconformity.

Put on? Studied. . .rehearsed? Or rare, real non-conformity?
Hard to tell, these die-stamped days.

1900-1918

Mollie Bailey and the Circus

That was the day! The day to see, to hear and feel — the day, never to forget!

You met sunrise on the grounds, roughnecks unloading . . . bull men with their animals . . . skinners, their wagons . . . canvas and pole and plank men . . . maybe a job and free ticket! Sure, you'd haul water, set stakes. Down went the sawdust; up, the canvas!

Then parade! Crowd-bounding clowns. . .rainbow calliope's wail. . .chain-clanking elephants. . .gilt cages rumbling. . .the here-we-come racketing brass band.

And finally, time! Wet sawdust, cotton candy, earth and animal smell, raw on the breeze. Grounds transformed — shoreless faces spilling past the double-decked, wild-promising spiel of sideshow fronts. . .past the pennanted main entrance, through menagerie tent's fierce cages, to the blue-seated high vastness of the Big Top!

Now any instant, the band's flourishes, act-break whistles, caged whipcrack, the spangles, scarlets and velvets, tense long drumrolls, the spinning high-up figures and the racing, pounding, disciplined rings.

All new this year, that was Circus, come to town!

But not altogether new. Fourth Century B. C. Rome's Circus Maximus let a quarter million regularly watch seven deadly courses of racing chariots. A later, jaded Rome would loose lion on woman, thumb down wounded gladiators by thousands. Rome and circus waned.

Medieval centuries saw wandering troupes, from acrobat to minstel. But happy revival awaited the 1800's;

207

even before them, George Washington had welcomed John Ricketts' company to Philadelphia's national capital; and before mid-century, a river-opening, west-pushing nation was showboating her major waterways with "floating palaces."

Coming soon was Cooper and Bailey's 76,000 mile world-round tour, W. C. Coup's simultaneous two rings; Adam Forepaugh's first beauty contests; and the all-time showman, P. T. Barnum, introducing everything from Tom Thumb to Jumbo, million dollar seasons and four acres of canvas. . .and ultimate merger with Ringling Brothers. With a hundred shows crisscrossing the land, 1880 to 1920 was the golden age of circus.

Right through it and even before ran the thread of what became the Texas circus and, in some ways, the most remarkable director of them all — adopted Texan Mollie Bailey, circus queen of the Southwest.

Ask any old-timer; he helped crown her.

You can locate Mollie Bailey easily in two places. One is San Antonio Public Library's Hertzberg Collection of Circusana, world's largest; her old flyers and handbills are there. I stopped over in drowsy little Blum, south of Fort Worth, where Lake Whitney heads. Here, next door to a wide-eyed young Frances Assiter, Mollie Bailey bought her first Texas home and wintered her family show above Schoolhouse Creek. Those were the 1890's, but pert Miss Frankie remembers the wonderful Baileys as though it were yesterday.

Like most, she knew that though matter-of-fact and businesslike, Aunt Mollie was good to people. She was to learn that Mollie once had been an extraordinarily beautiful girl, a gypsy-eyed brunette in her teens when she ran away from her father's Alabama plantation to marry a riverboat showman, Gus Bailey.

The Baileys had scarcely begun their own acts when Hood's Texas Brigade took Gus for bandmaster (he'd write *The Old Gray Mare*, the eve of Second Manassas). Following him, Mollie turned Confederate nurse and spy. More than once, she brought medicine through the lines in her high-piled pompadour or magically changed from a stooped old lady who sold cookies in Federal camp, to a lissome twenty-year old, back on a foam-flanked horse to report what she had learned.

After the war, the Baileys riverboated briefly, then, with reconstructing South, were Gone To Texas. They launched a Mollie Bailey wagon show, out of Dallas. Under its triple banners — American, Confederate and Lone Star — this family troupe would make every little town in Texas, admission free to any Confederate veteran, expecially Hood's. Almost every stop, from red-rutted East Texas to dusty West, mushroomed into a Confederate ray-union, a balloon ascension, finally the Mollie Bailey Show.

Son Eugene had the waltzing, ball-playing precision horses and doubled with horn and clown suit. Son Allie's were the acrobat dogs, the trombone, the fallaway ladder and slack-wire. Willie managed business, and cornet. Daredevil Brad was tumbler and highwire man. Miss Minnie sang; pretty young Birda showed her educated canaries and her floating serpentine dance. It was Birda for whom Frances Assiter waited the wings, and, with her, watched still handsome, fiftying Aunt Mollie manage the busy winter; for age took Gus off the road here at Blum.

The wagons (to reach a total of thirty) were repaired, fresh-painted; the one-ring-and-stage big top recanvassed. And the other multitudinous details: refurbishing costumes, planning new acts, schooling the animals, detailing nine months' route over 4,000 dust and mud miles.

Time, too, to ponder competition from more than fifty shows—the cheaper ones razor-edged with "advance men" to wreck competitors with fake sideshows, ballyhooed hoax, with any appeal to run an audience through a fast-change mill.

By contrast, Mollie held to small towns, unknown to Barnum or Ringling spectacles. She stuck to a slogan - "A Texas Show for Texas People". No two-headed Cinderellas; she insisted on a clean, up-to-date show. And on this, she was inflexible: whiskey fired a man automatically, profanity, the second time. With this philosophy, she grew steadily, buying more than a hundred city lots, leaving them for playgrounds after the show had passed.

And so her circus grew up with Texas — a small, two wagon affair in 1869 that once frightened off Indians with Mollie inside, pounding a drum to sound like cannon, a circus that spanned fifty years to the railroads, dissolving two years after Mollie's death in her Houston home in 1918.

Maybe Miss Frankie, watching over those years, has Mollie Bailey in focus. If P. T. Barnum left the parable, "there's one born every minute," the Texas circus queen was rigid in insistence on a family show that her grandchildren could see.

"She covered the big years of circus," Miss Frankie declared. "She was the only woman to run a real one. She was more than generous to everybody, yet she lived comfortably." Then her eyes sparked. "Most of all, she proved that a clean show does pay."

That was the day, for sure.

Be nice to see it again, wouldn't it?

Part Four

Flag o' My Land!

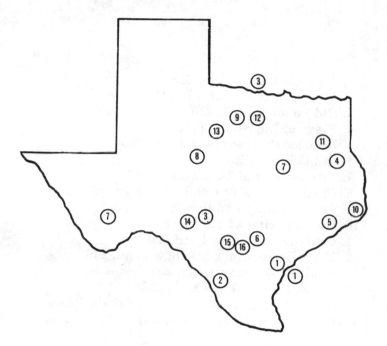

*"Proudly agaze at your glory I stand, Flag o' my land!
flag o' my land!"*

Thomas A. Daly

La Salle's Lost Fort

Chester Evans, an amiable history buff who formerly published the Edna *Herald*, periodically used to suggest the changing of his town's name. Down our coast's historic "Trail of Six Flags" from Houston toward Victoria, this trim little city would forget a railroad builder's daughter; Edna would become Texana.

The newsman had reason, old and sound. Just south, where the Lavaca and Navidad flow together deeply, was pioneer Texas' natural inland port of the 1830's. The Allen brothers very nearly bought Texana for their new city, Houston; the land was priced too high. However, consider the name for an even older reason.Close by this town was once rendezvous for one of our continent's most indomitable wilderness searches: France's flag and Spain's in death-hunt of each other. The rendezvous? Long-forgotten, two-story, log-walled Fort St. Louis, the lost, last outpost of Rene Robert Cavelier Sieur de La Salle.

The hunters missed each other, but found something else.

There is a monument to French explorer La Salle on a later Indianola's Matagorda Bay beaches, where history believes he misread himself ashore at the Mississippi's mouth. A marker near Edna generalized upon where he built his last ditch fort. Where he died, struggling back for Canada, is claimed by several Texas locales from Navasota northeast to Cherokee County.

It was Chester Evans who helped me locate Edna's nearby fort sites. One is five miles up Lavaca's timber, close to little Vanderbilt. Another is on the John Keeran's big ranch, just west on deep Garcitas Creek. Recent Spanish evidence hints that the lost fort might have been on the east outskirts of Edna herself. To many, the last bastion of La Salle yet remains lost.

But not lost are the incredible fifteen years of his coming, and what resulted from it. To comprehend those years, first fix your time: the latter decades of the 1600's. A few French dare the forest blizzards to trap beyond Quebec and Montreal. Down the lonely Atlantic coast, some English and Dutch cling, barely ashore. From Mexico City, Spain stairsteps north - a fort colony at a time. She knows that from her sierras to the northern Alleghenies is home to Indian, but to white man, howling wilderness. It is across that four thousand miles that La Salle will trigger what sends Spain and France groping for each other — finally to this ground, just in from the Texas coast.

By 1670, a twenty-seven year old La Salle that some call visionary has stalked Montreal's frontier for four years, certain of a passage to the Pacific. Black cold and white distance block him. Later by eight years, he has thrust again and again, far into our Great Lakes, each time being driven back: snow blind or starving, poisoned or fevered, shipwrecked and afoot a thousand miles through Iroquois and Seneca.

Now this strong-faced man that some call foolhardy knows something else. The Indian's "Great River" seeks the Gulf of Mexico - Spain's closed sea. His King Louis XIV listens. "Find a way to Mexico!" La Salle hears. Canada's winter of 1681, he sets out. His party walks two hundred miles of frozen river, sledging, portaging. Into an ice-clogged Mississippi go their birch bark canoes. Warming, they drift south: past wilderness faces strange to white men . . . now past the great houses of the Natchez and ceremonial feasts on buffalo hump and roast dog. In April, they breast marshy flats . . . to the sea beyond! La Salle sweeps French claim from Allegheny to Rocky, then faces the two thousand miles back. Once he is fever-felled for forty days; finally, he is in Paris.

Now it is 1684. He will take four ships, nearly three hundred colonists. Fortify the New France window south; ready the attack on Spanish Main! From France, he sails in late summer; in dismal, ship-jammed voyage, finally rounds the Florida coast, strikes for his river. In winter fog, has he missed? Keep on!

In the scuppers roll his sick; weighted overboard, sink his dead. He has lost a ship off Santo Domingo. Over his decks whispers dissension, then near-mutiny. This man that most call mad keeps on! Now lost, a second ship - his main supplies - grounding in what seemed pass to his river. His navy escort turns back. With one ship left, he is ashore deep inside - unmistakeably up no Mississippi. Near today's statue, he scans Matagorda Bay, pushes up its emptying river.

Here, among the daubed, cannibal Karankawa, the empty land, his last ship grounded, and his supplies near gone, he takes the inevitable last step: from wreckage, builds his fort. For two years from its mounting desperation he will search — west to Rio Grande, east to the Neches forests. Is he hunting Spain now . . . or survival?

Spain is hunting him! Angrily, she must break her deliberate march north. Find enemy France! From below frontier Monterrey, this early 1686, a burly, hawkfaced Captain Alonso de Leon forces that desert wilderness in search of the hidden French fort - even as French support, finally at Mississippi's mouth, spreads out to seek the lost garrison.

For five consecutive years, de Leon sets out. Ironically, he reaches Rio Grande just weeks after La Salle's desperate men have fallen back. Another year, and again come de Leon's columns, this time as far as today's King Ranch country. There is no Indian word of Frenchmen to the east. . .and rightly so: all but a dozen are dead or scattered.

A third time, Spanish search! From near today's Brackettville, they return a French captive. He can report only disaster — death from disease and starvation, Indian and finally anarchy. De Leon's force now rounds the Texas

215

coast, finds the sagging log walls abandoned: its last sight, grimly clear — massacre!

The Spaniard will not know that La Salle made his final try east for the river to Canada in the forlorn hope of help waiting at its mouth; and, on the way, fell murdered by his own men. A half-dozen survivors will find French rescue, hunting them.

De Leon knows only that Spain's sea is no longer safe; this upper territory must be garrisoned, colonized. . .and immediately! The Spaniard's fifth expedition is with priests, soldiers and Indian gifts. He has burned Fort St. Louis to the ground, buried its guns and — this year of 1690 — near today's Nacogdoches, he founds the first Spanish mission of the northeast frontier — San Francisco de los Tejas.

It will survive only in a sense, for it is too far distant for adequate support. But it will lead in short years to a San Antonio and a Nacogdoches, and ultimately — both Spain's and France's flags long earlier struck — to another river: San Jacinto.

And so you turn full circle with this fort — lost today. Its hunters never found each other alive, either side of the walls. But through them, the land found something else — the name and land, Texas.

Chester Evans had a point. For his town near forgotten Fort St. Louis, what better name than the fort's real legacy - Texana?

The Rock of St. John Baptist

Your map scarcely notes tiny Guerrero, a secluded oasis thirty miles down river from Eagle Pass. See it any how; along the Rio Grande, no town is more intriguing, and none have more significance to Texas.

You reach it on the Mexican side, an hour from Piedras Negras, handsome port of entry. Traffic is light over tolerable gravel and caliche, for few but Guerrerans know what lies at journey's end.

In the new, banner-flying *aduana* across the bridge, I asked directions. A handsome man came over from his desk and introduced himself.

"You know Guerrero, then?" He was Felix Cano, with gray eyes, an easy smile and English markedly better than my Spanish. We talked awhile of when the only road north — except for Coronado's — crossed there. His Guerrero family holds quill-penned title to much of the great gray plain, both sides of the river, dating very nearly from then.

You see, this village has extraordinary age and importance to match; for within its old shade still broods the massive ruin that, under a name other than Guerrero, made it really the now-forgotten Plymouth Rock of Texas.

The name? Presidio San Juan Bautista, the great Spanish frontier bastion: Fort St. John Baptist. The road? Before San Antonio and Nacogdoches, this was "FranceWay" — military pike to drive La Salle's French from Spanish-claimed Texas.

Until La Salle's Fort St. Louis, Spain has been content to leapfrog her settlements slowly north from Mexico City.

217

Time aplenty for outmost empire, since first reports call it endless, deadly desert. Now, in 1690, she hurdles the empty land north of Monterrey's mountains. She will line missions at today's Nacogdoches, later at San Antonio.

The major base to stage and sustain them all (and those to follow) must be here on Rio Grande. Up looms a two-mile triangle: three mission forts - San Juan, San Francisco, San Bernardo. Interlacing are miles of irrigation ditches from the river; close about, vineyards and gardens; beyond, cotton and cane; and outlying it all, the cattle ranches that will stock Texas. All this — from garrison to Franciscan base that will missionize, and thus begin, Texas — is Presidio San Juan Bautista.

Aside from El Paso's Santa Fe line, here is great gate north. It mounts the expedition of 1718 that settles way station San Antonio de Valero. Thirty years later, it bases Jose de Escandon's march downriver to found Ciudad Mier, Reynosa, Camargo and, a little closer, a town some feel may not survive — Laredo.

Aging now, this fort detains the first Anglo intruders, survivors of Philip Nolan's band of 1801 and short years later, Zebulon Pike, who has mapped to the western mountains and is enroute back to the United States.

And now, these years after Spain's missions and Spain herself, Santa Anna stays four days dictating terms against insurgent Texans he will strike a week later at one of this presidio's offsprings — Alamo.

Finally, the old walls see an 1846 American column drive south for Saltillo and three years later, upriver, stake a Fort Duncan that will grow to Eagle Pass.

By now, there are other roads. The presidio and its town are bypassed.

Unless you require neon and jukebox, you must find Guerrero a delight. As from the beginning, the road wanders from a scruffy plain into the tall shade of *nogales* and *olmos*; and, trailing beside, the patioed adobes follow. Some are raw and thatch-roofed; most have the rare Mexican beauty that age enhances. Carved doorways let to beamed ceilings and wrought iron hardware faces the fronts that tint from whites and pinks to morning-glory blues.

There is a little plaza and, off it, a splended *Presidencia Municipal*, a white, bell-towered church, a pin-neat club for Guerrero's young, and the spotless and only cantina — *El Rio Grande*. Signs and shops are notably few; one of the handsomer buildings houses the telegraph; there are no phones. Streets are the earth and bend or dip with it. You expect the two well-mounted horsemen. The sudden-crossing auto surprises you.

Apart to the north is the low hill and on it, *"las ruinas."* This is San Bernardo, mightiest of the old presidio's three, and alone remaining, the others' rock long ago having gone into walls in the town below.

Bernardo's walls rear thirty feet to a roofless nave, fully a hundred feet long and half that width at the cross-forming transepts. About are the lesser rooms, massive-walled in three-foot tufanous blocks, rising to a perfect, if mouldering, dome at the apse and sacristy. The rest are traces — refectory to baptistry and granary to corrals. Aside from the rebuilt wall to the well, this stern ruin stands protected by Mexican law, just as it has survived — and shall — for centuries to come.

But beyond the hill is one change. The fields and gardens are gone. Guerrero's aristocratic descendants are hard put to live from their land. But they stay.

White-haired Valentin Sierra Rodriguez showed me his Guerrero. It has changed little in his seventy-five years; not too much, he suspected, in its near three centuries.

"Does one know in Texas," he asked me presently in his home, "that here is the father of all your missions? Here, in truth, the beginning?"

"They will know when they come to see." Would Guerrero welcome visitors?

Yes, he said; and so did Felix Cano, who also felt it would be good if Guerrerans can prepare a small story of their history printed in English. For see it, you must.

You will know this place for the genesis — the mission and fortress, the oasis, sanctuary and hospice that opened

219

the gate to Texas. Yes, they need to tell their story in something we can read. After all, Fort St. John Baptist is a substantial part of our story, too.

1758

Old Spanish Fort

Follow your map north of Fort Worth; there is a horseshoe bend in the Red River immediately north of little, leather-working Nocona. On the riverbend is a tiny dot, ancient as Inca country maybe.

This village is called Old Spanish Fort, which is about as wrong in its name as you can get. Even Old French Fort might be a little more accurate.

If we recall there was a race of bronzed men dwelling here when France was Gaul and Spain was Moorish, and long before that, then there is a real name for that big fortress town that the dot represents — a name nobody knows.

Of course, all the ruin is under cotton and corn, a little way up Village Creek toward the Red from the hamlet that has been misnamed. And yet, with the rolling and verdant emptiness you find farmed today, there are fragments of a city nearabouts. Poking about is worth your time, for this fortress city had a substantial share in changing the course of Spain's American empire.

Drive first to Ringgold's boxy old red brick buildings and look up Gene Wilson. As well as any man alive, he can guide you to Old Spanish Fort and tell you its story. He isn't hard to find: on some job around town, fixing, or helping with the kids at the school, or, within his plain cottage, tinkering with the little museum he has made of it and of the old Indian fort-city.

Gene is tall, a little stooped; and his face is older with wisdom than his sixty-plus years admit. Ever since a boy,

220

traveling with his father — a Methodist preacher — he has been uncovering, studying and assembling what the old, old races left behind. His archaeology will stand with anybody's.

Scarcely scratching the old buried city, he yet has an extensive collection: countless perfect points, scrapers, knives, flint axes, ancient cookware, rusted parts of firearms (Spanish and French) and bits of things that even he's not sure of. Will he take you across to the old ground and help you probe around?

"Sure! Rains turn it up. You never know what you might really find."

And so, how the name, "Old Spanish Fort?"

Years ago — perhaps thousands — this seems to have been a chief stronghold of a confederacy of Indian nations. There was a long valley, fertile for crops and game, a good crossing of the river. That is was a meeting place for red men from the mountains west and those from the plains and forests — north, south and east — has been confirmed by reports from earliest day European travelers, who referred to it as the town of the Tayovayas. How long it had been there, archaeology may one day tell us.

Some experts believe that the crossroads grew to campground, then to a kind of Indian city-fort, enclosing scores of acres and surrounded by log walls and possibly a moat. The fort appears to have gone up about the time that the Indian knew he was beset: with mission and presidio, the Spaniard pressed him from the south; from New Orleans in their flatboats and overland as *couriers de bois*, the French came from the north and along the Red for trade.

Now, in the mid-1700's, hard-riding scouts bring word that Spain has pushed her line of missions along the San Saba and Nueces, in the hill country to the south.

Comanches lead an alliance of Tonkawa, and the Tejas confederacy tribes in shattering the San Saba line. That they have burned and beheaded, they leave clear-painted on the Concho cliff walls of Paint Rock — near today's San Angelo. Only the mission-fort at today's Menard survives, over two hundred men, women and children packed

221

into it. Then the Spanish remnant falls back to San Antonio.

Infuriated Spain mounts her greatest punitive expedition. Five hundred men, almost three thousand horses and mules! Artillery! All the way from Mexico, she pursues the Indian forces, defeats them once at the Brazos near today's Fort Griffin. Now, far north, Spanish arms confront what has become a bristling fortress here on the Red.

On the gray, chill morning of October 7, 1759, Spanish commander Diego Ortiz Parrilla orders assault, and will later recall the appearance of his objective: "a village formed of large huts of oval shape, enclosed by a stockade and a moat. The winding entrance road . . . enclosed in the same way, with the gate toward the river, in which water runs . . . deep. The entire stockade was covered with Indians, armed and firing muskets."

It is over for Parrilla's forces by nightfall and their remnants will later swear they saw "a French flag" and artillery on the parapets, and confronted anywhere from two to six thousand warriors. In any event, Spanish arms are routed, and survivors reach San Antonio in bleak November.

Shortly thereafter, reappraising her overextended frontier, Spain begins reduction of her mission system along this frontier, a withdrawal that will not abate until she herself is ousted from New World empire in the early 1800's.

Perhaps no Waterloo, the Red River fortress city was nonetheless a turning point in Spain's ultimate American eclipse. That it was a major city, and an old one, archaeology is already determining. That is was a major fortress can hardly be debated; try to recollect where Indians anywhere massed thousands of troops. Yet that is not what you ponder, across that peaceful swell of empty land, not so much as that time so completely erased it.

Erased it and the American causes of all who fought for it!

"I expect a lot of those Spaniards are still out there."

Gene Wilson gestured the wide country from Ringgold, twenty miles across to the old fort.

"But why call it 'Spanish Fort'?" I knew some credence should be given the possibility of France's arming the Indian bastion. "Why not 'French Fort'?"

"Why not 'Indian Fort'?" Gene Wilson countered.

"All right, why not?"

"People get mixed up with what goes on," said archaeologist Wilson. "Not one in a thousand even knows it was here. Or, today, cares much."

1778

Flags of Old Stone Fort

Set back in big pines, the Old Stone Fort of Nacogdoches is a rare Texian museum. Yet it takes awhile really to see what its aging walls contain.

Showing me through, Mrs. Hattie Smith, curator, paused; the two visiting ladies had walked outside again. They had browsed the displays, ranging from ancient Nacogdoches mound-builder pottery and points to early colonists' land deeds and muskets to hold that land, an old hand press and a copy of *Gaceta de Tejas*, our first newspaper. Now the ladies stood under the pines outside and studied the nearly two-centuries-old building.

"Sometimes, I'm afraid they expect stockades or mission walls," said the curator quietly. "Ours doesn't look exactly like a fort."

And it doesn't. It is an erect two stories of rust-colored rock, built to serve every frontier task from store to court to capitol. Its restored thick walls front on a gallery with eight hand-finished square columns. At the top of each is a flag bracket; you begin to count the banners.

Of our six flags over Texas, France's *fleur de lis* is omitted technically because — built in 1778 — this fort flies only the colors it served. There are three you don't recognize. Each proclaimed a free republic here — and all before San Jacinto.

In the story of those flags, East Texans know their Old Stone Fort has no peer.

You begin that story nearly a century earlier than the fort. Both empire-hunting, French and Spanish found the east-west trail of the relatively cultured Indian confederacy, Tejas; confronted each other across the Sabine. Off and on mission-forted, Nacogdoches was New Spain's frontier east. Then French danger seemed gone.

Distant Mexico City shrugged when hardy Captain Gil Y'Barbo built his remote trading fort here. True, there was fighting to the east, but — that wilderness world away — the foolish American revolt should surely end at Valley Forge. How could England tolerate colonies that produced farm cabins instead of gold! Yes, let Y'Barbo build his fort; time enough for a leisurely New Spain north. Let Y'Barbo trade with the Indians; it can keep frontier's mind off American revolt. Then, time enough to complete colonization.

Time enough? It is just 1800 . . . and a world in upheaval. America's revolution has struck fire from Buenos Aires to Panama. Worse, the buckskinned Yankees already are across the Mississippi. Spanish agents rumor that Jefferson's United States may buy the Louisiana that Napoleon's France has taken back from Spain. Y'Barbo's stone house is now New Spain's beleagured eastern bastion.

It is 1801 when the fort's dragoons capture, near today's Waco, Philip Nolan's Americans who hunt mustangs but also map Texas for U.S. eyes. For that handful bound for dungeons south, Stone Fort turns temporary jail for thirty days.

Now, five years later, America has indeed bought Louisiana and insolently claims it includes everything west to Rio Grande. Tottering New Spain must hold here or lose all — conceivably to the very Californias.

Stone Fort headquarters Spain's greatest army yet north — fifteen hundred troops battlelined across the

Sabine from American long rifles. The red rock walls see Spain accept a Sabine boundary and a "neutral ground" just east of Nacogdoches. A temporary arrangement!

Temporary indeed! Revolt is exploding in Mexico itself. With 1812, the green flag yonder flies over these walls. Under it has sprung a secret frontiersman-adventurer army, allied with Mexicans, headed by a West Pointer, Augustus Magee, and a Rio Grande patriot, Bernardo Gutierrez.

From Nacogdoches' Stone Fort, *Gaceta de Tejas* publishes proclamations of independence for this Republic of the North. In struggle as bloody as our Texas Revolution, the rebel allies storm to San Antonio, their republic all but won. But America, suddenly and again war-locked with England, cannot reinforce. History writes off the old fort's green banner of Gutierrez-Magee.

Seven years later comes the second assault. From Natchez to this fort's headquarters, marches the small army of Dr. James Long. Anticipating Mexican revolution's success, Nacogdoches again proclaims independence. Again the republic fails, never really penetrating beyond this beachhead and one briefly at Galveston. Yonder, too, is Long's banner.

For a time, under independent Mexico, the old fort serves as northern port of entry. Over brief years, colonist's oath will be sworn to Jim Bowie, Thomas Rusk, Sam Houston, even Davy Crockett. An early signer in the 1820's is Hayden Edwards, colonizer. His was a short-lived republic — perhaps strangest of all.

Land disputes with old titles — issues as cloudy as a second generation feud — fires this revolt. For a third time, Old Stone Fort declares independence — notably this time from the "Mexican United States."

Under the rock walls snaps the red and white banner of "Fredonia" — a republic solemnly fusing Anglo colonist with Cherokee and lesser tribes. Within the fort is struck a startling treaty: divide Texas on a line roughly from Nacogdoches west to today's El Paso. All the north, Indian; all to the south, Anglo-American.

225

Incredible? Not to Mexico, certain it is U.S. pretext for seizing her Louisiana claim. Mexico plans to land a thousand troops on the Texas coast, march ten thousand overland. An anguished Stephen Austin is ordered to mobilize his colony to help.

But Fredonia's fusion never comes off: red and white man alike hold the same fears and distrusts, one of the other. Within a month, beginning 1827, Fredonia's flag is down, scarcely a shot fired. Peace seems patched.

It will shatter again, three years before Alamo, when Nacogdoches colonists drive its fort's garrison from East Texas. Ironically, these Texans — like those smouldering to the south — ally to a rising young general who promises true democracy for all of Mexico. His name: Antonio Lopez de Santa Anna.

In the struggle yet to come, fighting will be south. This fort's gunsmoke is done. Its fort's fighting, not its men's. And not its concern with freedom flags. The next one standing here to the wind will flaunt a single star for Texas republic.

Where's a better place? There are three predecessors that only Old Stone Fort can fly. And they led the way.

1818

Napoleon's Place of Refuge

Most of us, recalling France in Texas, begin and end with La Salle's wandering ordeal. Yet one French historian and patriot, Charles De Gaulle, fence-mending in Mexico in the 1960's, doubtless could recollect another colony — a later and extraordinary one — on the Trinity River.

This was a remote place, now forgotten, where jungle presses the river bluffs below Liberty: a fort-settlement called Champs d'Asile — "place of refuge" for men weary of Europe's wars. In 1818, three years before Stephen Austin, these colonists came "to cultivate the vine and olive"; their leaders insisted they came only as free men who were totally disinterested in the politics of empire.

Yet hidden away here, Champs d'Asile really posed a major invasion of Spanish Mexico. On the throne of a treasure-rich New France below the Rio Grande, place Joseph Bonaparte! Rescue brother Napoleon from St. Helena's Atlantic rock! Then, across the New World, fling the Tricolor!

Unbelievable? Not to Spain, England, America. . .nor France. Champs d'Asile's invading hard core would be Napoleon's Old Guard!

This second decade of the 1800's, all Europe is prostrate from Napoleon's bloodletting. Spain is free, but wrecked: her American colonies up for the taking or revolt. Even England, winning at Waterloo, has lost at New Orleans. France, shattered, is royalist again; Napoleon's bitter-end officers prefer exile.

There is asylum in an America that remembers La Fayette. The exiles find a restless nation driving west to the Sabine, looking beyond, committed to ridding the continent of European rule — specifically, that of tottering Spain. But in New York is onetime Spanish puppet king Joseph Bonaparte; around him, growing speculation. The talk is of land grants; the whispers, empire.

Let Bonaparte take the sovereignty that he never renounced in Spain's colony, Mexico. Through intrigue's shadows moves tough, hard-eyed General Charles Lallemand, Napoleon's artillerist. Did he not very nearly spirit the emperor from St. Helena? Next time. . .

Conjecture grants Lallemand eight thousand men poised at ports from Boston to Savannah, from the Indies to Europe. In New York, guns; New Orleans, speculative money!

But where to begin? The new territory of Alabama has granted land blocs to French exiles, but these are too far from Mexico, and the U. S. would block their use for staging anyhow. Texas then! A vast no man's land, claimed by both Spain and the United States, occupied by neither.

Fit out a fleet at Galveston Island (speculators foresee forty French cruisers). Up the Trinity from Galveston Bay, conceal a fort to stage the troops.

By January, 1818, the island's free-wheeling Jean Lafitte hosts the first Napoleonic contingent. What else but host; Lafitte knows fighters when he sees them. He boats them twenty miles upriver to a bend in the low bluffs; the "place of refuge" is begun. By spring, four hundred are at the fort.

It is strong, a large, round log pallisade with four gun bastions, and a supporting bluff-edge redoubt. All about are the log huts, for the women have followed.

But where is the vine and the olive? This is what they ask outside. By Indian runner or freebooter ashore with a rum-loosened mouth, word leaks that there is no planting at Champs d'Asile, but drill, drill, drill!

"We wish to live as free men through our labor and in peace," General Lallemand repeatedly protests for Spanish and American ears. For French ears, through Frenchman Lafitte, he hurries word that he is ready for his recruits, money and supplies.

Strange colonists, these of Champs d'Asile. French in dragoon helmet and side buttoning breeches. Leathery, tough Poles of the Foreign Legion. Now, fiery Mexicans and cold-eyed Anglos — some scoundrels, some patriots: all, ready for the treasure that is there for the taking in Mexico.

There is a shrine in the parade center — Napoleon's statue, heaped about with captured arms and battleflags from Europe's most awesome fields. Yet here, still muster no more than the early arrivals. Where are the others? Are messages getting through?

To the wrong ears perhaps: to the south, the Spanish growl. Then let Frenchman Lafitte, a man they trust, reassure Spain that the colony truly is busy with farming. Also suggest that Champs d'Asile is a convenient block to greedy America, pressing from the east.

American War Secretary Graham comes down for a closer look. Lallemand tells him there is no reason why this projected French invasion cannot clear all of Texas for the America who claims her.

Still, one thought nags the general: what detains the recruits for his army. . .its supplies. . .money? To fellow Frenchman Lafitte, Lallemand confides that when the help does come, he will be done with America and Spain alike. All this will be just France — Napoleon's France.

Frenchman Lafitte listens. As Spanish Agent Thirteen, he must report accurately. Presently, Lafitte can frighteningly warn Champs d'Asile of an overwhelming Spanish army that approaches. Later, he can advise those two hundred forty Spaniards struggling the wilderness — the overwhelming army — that the French have fallen back to his own island. There, a hurricane takes the last French stores. Unsupported, the Tricolor streams back to Louisiana, eventually Europe. Spain burns Champs d'Asile level.

Its promise lived nine months.

It is hard to determine precisely where the log fort stood. There is a marker by the Trinity bridge at Liberty; a better guess is downriver seven miles at Moss Bluff. As children, the oldest old-timers recall tales of faint ruins. There is high ground that an artillerist would choose Beyond that, and a fishing resort, nothing.

Wherever Champs d'Asile was, it was bitter end for Napoleon's veterans. They knew no battle beat them; was it a country they did not understand? Where was the treasure, the food, even the men that — in Europe — you levied from your conquests? Were they to tax the miserable huts of Attakapa Indians? And the French who never came? Had they become dull Americans?

Napoleon's General Lallemand turned his back on the "place of refuge" and its planned gobbling of Mexico. An incredibly stupid land, not to value a Napoleon! One must conclude it not yet ready for Europe's new empires.

History-minded Charles De Gaulle could have told you that this long ago 1818 was a time of just such provincial thinking. He could name the American president who authored such thought in his hands-off doctrine — James Monroe.

In Mexico, he also might have recalled a president who repeated it to another Napoleon and his Maximilian — a man named Benito Juarez.

1836

The Gonzales Road

Could I recommend but one road in all Texas to my Eastern metropolitan friends, I know none better to travel and ponder than the sixty-two miles from Gonzales to San Antonio.

Except for expresswaying the original meanders, except for the overpassing bridges and flashing-by signs, the checkerboard fields and the whip-by of cars, the old way has changed little over the years.

Now, as then, it leaves Gonzales' liveoak shade, strikes across the bottoms of the San Marcos to its timbered rims, crests rolling land awhile, then slopes the long plain for the Alamo City. Always it has aimed for the Alamo.

I drove it one day not too long ago, a day suited to traveling it. I wanted to recall its old traffic. Not too many years ago, it was the route of thirty-two Americans. They were booted or buckskinned horsemen, taut-faced against the wind's bite and against their thoughts. They crossed the bottoms and the rolling country and the plain.

They had determined to enter Santa Anna's death ring of five thousand troops. . .

They had some neighbors in the Alamo.

Gonzales is a pretty little city in the valley where the San Marcos joins the Guadalupe. She is old enough for magnolia shade and quiet beneath her silver water tanks and out from her square with its rococo red brick courthouse.

To her east, where Kerr Creek crosses U.S. 90-A for Houston by the San Jacinto, there is a long, block-wide park that the state has given back to the city. There is a marker for Green DeWitt's 1825 colony, the sturdy old dog run Eggleston House and an imposing shellstone building. Too often, you pass it; you should stop.

This is the Gonzales Memorial, a museum and library ... and something more. For in it you can understand the road to San Antonio. Guarding its east wall is a massive red granite shaft. It memorializes this old town's just claim as "The Lexington of Texas." It salutes the "Old Eighteen" who fired their hot war's first shot, October 2, 1835, when Mexican troops demanded their cannon. In the museum is a replica of that ox-carted little gun and Gonzales' black and white "Come and Take It" flag. And the rest that makes this a good Texas museum.

But it is the west wall monument — gray granite over blue reflecting basin — I liked best; for here is suggested the Gonzales Road's story. There are thirty-two names, from forty-eight year old Jacob Darst to seventeen year old Johnny Gaston.

These are the men who rode to help their neighbors.

From the west wall shaft, you can almost see the little log house town, scattered about. What was it like, this bitter cold last morning of February, 1836?

Weeks ago, Texans figured they had a cause won. Old Ben Milam's boys had taken San Antonio, and so, like frontiersmen, they went home to tend things. Sure, they'd come back if needed. But now the land is thunderstruck. In a giant stride, Santa Anna himself is on them !

With only stubborn Alamo to block. Travis and a hundred fifty men and mighty little powder. "Surrounded!" Jim Bonham had shouted, his first long ride to warn and rally. "Maybe three, four thousand!" Then he was gone, hammering back to his fort. "Get help!"

Gonzales rode for help. Plenty, if there's time! Fannin's south with nearly five hundred. Houston promises (and delivered) other hundreds in Gonzales within two weeks. Should Gonzales' men wait for the gathering army?

In that fort are neighbors. Almaron Dickenson, who runs the hat factory by the square yonder. Amos Pollard, now army's surgeon, and the others. Far more than the rest

231

of Texas, Gonzales is already committed to Alamo. Finally, scout John Smith, gray-weary in the saddle: "Whatever you've got, send now!"

Let the army follow. These thirty-two — the men and the boys — are already heading west. Two dark nights later, hugging the *acequia* brush shadow, they are through the battalions of Matamoros and Tolucca, under the walls and in the gate.

And five days later, dead.

You can only guess what they thought, over that land we take in an hour today. It may well be, as most say, they knew they rode to certain death.

But at the same time that I know them for men as gallant as our land has ever nurtured, I feel equally certain they rode for the Alamo with the sense they would hold . . . and walk, living, from their fort. That this is the strange blessing of any man going into action is not the point. *The point is they knew their neighbors.*

The ones they rode to help. The ones who would ride to help them.

Their error was only time. The men they knew coming to their aid were in Gonzales, aimed for the Alamo, just a few days later. That Gonzales had to be burned instead; and the Texan road led to San Jacinto rather than San Antonio came primarily from time and tactics and circumstance.

Not from the uncertainty of help, called of a Texan neighbor.

You may recall the day I chose to drive the Gonzales Road. New York television had just uncovered another "author and scholar" who was ready to expose our heroes — Davy Crockett in this instance — as total frauds.

This is the city — I remembered, standing by that Gonzales shaft — where a dozen families could look down from their windows and, unmoving, watch a woman murdered while she cried up to them for help.

And these are a breed who, elsewhere, can watch a woman drown, watch her plead for help from an easy hundred foot swim's distance. I hope never to understand the breed. I doubt they could comprehend the Gonzales Road.

And so I traveled the road and it reassured me. I like to think that the land and its traffic have not changed too much in this state of mind that is Texas.

1836/79

Two Forts and Two Women

This is a story about two Texas women, neither of whom could be what she wanted. Both died because of the wanting.

A little east of Waco are the neighboring towns of Groesbeck and Mexia; between the two, in the sudden heavy timber along the Navasota, stands old Fort Parker, authentic in its restoration.

Here is where Cynthia Ann Parker was turned Indian.

Five hundred miles west, in the cottonwoods and crags of Davis Mountains' Limpia Canyon, they have restored Fort Davis.

Here is where Indian Emily tried to turn white.

I walked inside Fort Parker's log-barriered gate and talked with T. F. Bain, who cared for it as though he had cut it from the wilderness himself. The fort encloses a big compound, has high walls with vertical logs sharpened at the top and outjutting blockhouses atop diagonal corners. There are firing steps and gunports. Six cabins butt against the fort walls inside.

The cabin across the compound, the one with the honeysuckle, is where Cynthia Ann lived. Hers was one of six families who came with Baptist Elder John Parker from Illinois three years before Alamo. There was nothing north and west, little more than Nacogdoches east and San Antonio south.

She was a blue-eyed nine years old the last time she could run laughing when they called out "Cynthia Ann."

233

Someone must have called once, terribly, that May morning in 1836, when it happened. Then the Indians were inside, pouring over Uncle Ben's dead body at the open gate; and Fort Parker subsided in yells, scattered shots and screams.

Those who could walk the ninety miles of wilderness to safety at a log fort where Palestine now stands, those survivors could remember Cynthia Ann struggling in terror, swept up by a Comanche rider and vanished in the din.

Taken, too, was her six year old brother John, but it is another story that he is believed to have lived out his life in Mexico.

The two women later ransomed to freedom spoke seldom and in quiet horror of their own captivity. For a child like Cynthia Ann? They had never seen her afterwards; it was best that way.

Yet the strange frontier telegraph whispered insistently that Cynthia Ann was alive, had been seen by traders on the Canadian, had talked with hunters in the Comanche camp of Chieftain Peta Nocona . . . that she might even be his wife.

A Comanche? It would not be possible. How could she have ridden with them when they sacked Linnville, fought at Plum Creek, when they killed or when they buried their own? And Nocona? Still too crafty to corner. Cynthia Ann must be dead; a quarter century has passed, and her Uncle James has driven himself nearly to exhaustion in fruitless searching for her.

Then on December 18, 1860, Captain Sul Ross and a detachment of Second Cavalry smashed Nocona's band west of what is now Wichita Falls. Ross outrode the chief's wife, escaping with her baby girl.

She was blue-eyed. She recognized only two words . . . "Cynthia Ann."

They sent her far east to relatives in Anderson County. Her two-year old child, Prairie Flower, died shortly. Cynthia Ann, who some said had seen her husband killed by the cavalrymen, asked without hope to go back to her people. It could not be done.

Repeatedly, they reminded her she was *with her people*. She died with them four years later.

The Fort Davis story is the opposite side of the coin. The 1870's saw that western bastion in almost continual action in the last struggle with the Apache.

One sunrise attack on the fort was beaten off and among the wounded was a pretty Indian girl. She was taken in and nursed back to health by the mother of young Lieutenant Tom Easton.

She stayed on with Mrs. Easton as maid and companion. The older woman felt deep affection for dark-skinned, dark-eyed Emily, no longer a girl but an increasingly lovely young woman. Emily quietly returned that affection; even more quietly nourishing the one she felt for the cavalryman.

The Nelsons were among replacements at Fort Davis. In that family was Mary Nelson. Indian Emily stood by, part of the Easton household, and watched her lieutenant announce his engagement to Miss Nelson. She saw the happiness in him, not even looking at her.

Then she ran away.

She was gone a year. Although happy with her new daughter, Mrs. Easton missed Emily badly. Word came at irregular intervals that she was back with her Apache people. There was nothing for it but to forget the girl who had been so close to them. . .almost part of them.

That Emily had not forgotten came with deadly suddenness. The sentry standing late, dark duty, twice cried "Halt!" at the figure coming straight for him through the night. Then he fired.

They took Emily inside the Colonel's house where she called for Mrs. Easton. She told her old friend that the attack — all her people — would burst on them in the morning. She wanted Tom to live. Then she died.

Legend says her warning saved the fort; the attack was thrown back.

The sentry? He lived through the fight, as did Tom Easton. But the thing the sentry remembered most was that Injun girl, the way kept comin' through the night.

It was like she wanted him to shoot.

Chadbourne Felt Comanche Funnybone

It may surprise you, as it did me, to learn that the dreaded centaur of Texas, the Comanche, had a sense of humor.

Some time ago, enroute from San Antonio to Palo Duro Canyon, I covered a fair piece of old Comancheria, if you leave out his nether reaches: to the mountains at Denver, and down them, to the Big Bend. I stopped in Comanche heartland, at Ballinger and Paint Rock near San Angelo and, toward Abilene, at old Fort Chadbourne. Ballinger has opened a museum with excellent Comanche artifacts, and Paint Rock's cliffs made as near an almanac-newspaper as the warrior horseman ever painted.

Hard-to-find Fort Chadbourne has a quarter-mile flat that served to stage an Indian-American derby and to showcase the Comanche's little-suspected funnybone — about which, more in a moment.

Aside from the fact that this Texan was the real raw-deal minority of our era, one thing you realize after a little time in Comanche country, is that he also was a considerably more faceted man than we credit him, round and round our movie wagon trains.

To show you their Concho cliff pictographs better, the Fred Campbells of Paint Rock have studied everything findable on the formidable Plains fighter. Under the stoic exterior everybody labels as Indian, was he perhaps a man who felt the same aches and aspirations as most of us? With black hair and eyes, he was short, chunky, coppery. Not too agile afoot, he was the wind once mounted. Fearless? More nearly, an iron grip on his fears. So much for the standard man. For a quick look, what else?

He was keen on games: riding, shooting, racing, wrestling, swimming and. . .well, he had a hot dice hand for an Indian version of craps. He liked whiskey which did not like him.

He was long on shoot-the-breeze visits, longer on singing at them. He had hero songs and gambling songs. In fact, for any first rate event, from a break in the weather to the marriage of his daughter, he had a ballad and rated an audience. He was a prodigious yarn-spinner, and in story-telling, neither audience restlessness nor sensitivity bothered him. He was somewhere between Thomas Wolfe, Tennessee Williams and an outright bore.

He knew the Great Spirit had put the sun in the heavens; and to it, he addressed himself, first and last, each day. In his deep thoughts, he knew his beginnings: his body from the earth, his bones from rock, his blood from dew and his eyes from the depths of clear water. From the winds came his breath and from the storms, his strength. From the waterfalls, his thoughts; from the Great Spirit's own image, his beauty. This is the man we consider inarticulate!

Somehow, we have written off his sense of humor. Maybe in the same way it would have been hard to convince either Marine or Jap at Iwo that his opposite number had ever laughed.

South of Abilene, near Bronte, Fort Chadbourne's ruins guard the long, notched mesas much as in 1852, year the post was founded. The outpost guarded a section of the Butterfield stage route; duty was hot, dry and dull — except on one occasion. From the roadside park marker, you can see the old rock walls up the low hill; see them from here, you must for the fort has long been on a private ranch.

Beyond the hill is the stubby-grassed flat; and across this, the Comanche once let the white man glimpse what would have warmed a practical joker's heart.

237

Chadbourne's Eighth U.S. troopers relieved the monotony of duty with horse races, and they figured themselves as knowlegeable of fast mounts as any men on the frontier. They had the times, almost to a stride, of their top horses. By far their pride was a deep-chested, fine-legged Kentucky mare.

One summer day in the mid-fifties, Chief Mulaquetop and a small band drifted south into camp near the fort. They watched the troopers' time trials, aimed at uncovering some horse which might hope to challenge the mare. Diffidently, Mulaquetop opined he had a running pony.

He produced what army journalist Colonel Richard Dodge later recalled as a "miserable sheep of a pony with legs like churns. A three-inch mat of rough hair stuck out all over his body," said Dodge, "and a general expression of neglect, helplessness and patient suffering struck pity into the hearts of all beholders."

It was too easy! Chadbourne troopers showed a dun, their third best horse. Almost, they regretted taking the seventy dollars in robes and gewgaws which the Indians wagered after long, uncertain debate.

And the rider! He seemed a giant, big enough to carry that pony on his shoulders. He held a huge club. When *go* was signaled, he belabored the miserable animal from start to finish. Astonished, the troopers saw the Indian lumber in, ahead by a neck.

Out came Chadbourne's chestnut, two lengths faster than the dun. The troopers knew it was no contest now, but the Comanches were cajoled and taunted into doubling their bets. Incredibly, the "sheep" stumbled home by a neck once more.

Angrily now, Chadbourne played its trump. Out came the proud Kentucky mare. An old buck sergeant chuckled and spat. Them devils didn't know that, for this four hundred yards, the mare was forty yards faster'n what they'd seen. Along with everybody else, he laid his month's pay on the line. . .and they were off!

The Comanche rider dropped his club, gave a whoop,

and was an instant compact part of a silver lightning streak. He was opening five lengths at the finish!

Worse! He was riding backwards, gesturing assorted obscenities to the army mare.

Later, Mulaquetop showed the Chadbourne command the six hundred Kickapoo ponies he had brought from the north. Let the soldiers not feel badly; they were no more stupid than the Kickapoos.

1859

Fort Belknap's Indian Exodus

Big for frontier, rusty-rocked and stern, Fort Belknap is one of our best-preserved old army outposts. It stands alone, west of Graham below Wichita Falls, where the Brazos gathers for Possum Kingdom Lake. It also stands alone in little-known story.

Guarding a cross-timbered hill over the river's triple bend, Belknap is fifteen close-cropped acres within a breast-high rock wall. You circle the heavy stone magazine and corn house, around to the two story commissary-museum, opposite the old kitchen and two long barracks. Aside is a rock-slabbed well; across, the meeting arbor. The buildings are open for public view and use.

There are markers about, for this was hub and anchor of our 1851 northwest frontier. The easterly military road tied to America, traversing the fort towns up to St. Louis. Headed west, Butterfield's stages swapped horses for mules here, the empty run for El Paso's Fort Bliss and California beyond.

Down from Belknap, cavalry scouted the frontier fort-road that edged Texas to the west — from Phantom Hill, next below, all the way to Fort Clark and the border. And no ordinary cavalry, this; but U.S. Second, with Albert Sidney Johnston and Robert E. Lee and fifteen others to wear generals' stars after a faraway Fort Sumter.

And if Belknap's cavalry was extraordinary, so was the least-known page of this fort's history. It was here that the West Texas Indian legally ceased to be.

This takes you back to Indian treaties which, in Texas as elsewhere, were nearly always three-stage affairs: taking the land, formalizing the seizure with agreement to take no more, then frontier attack and counter attack.

In 1824, Stephen Austin moved to clear his Mexican colony coast; fifteen years later, the republic had all of East Texas. And in less than a decade, Indian and white would sight a north-south line through Fort Worth as "Where the West begins."

But there was gold in California, railroad building to get there, land, buffalo and bloodspill between. There had to be a Texas end for the west-pressing treaty line; and the new north anchor of frontier garrisons for the state — Fort Belknap — would be it.

In spring, 1854, Texas assigned two Indian reservations on Belknap's line: the eight-league Brazos, edging today's Graham for the Indian from east; and forty miles west, below today's Throckmorton, the Comanche — where the southern Peneteka would try it on four leagues of land.

The reservations would last five years.

Look on that clumpy, rolling country through Indian eyes. Your people, this July of 1859, already have traveled a long journey.

Yonder are the Caddo lodges by their maize and melon patches. Not great dwellings as the old ones tell were once in many towns by their sacred mounds far to the east. And beyond, the few people of Tawakoni Jim, who speak little of when Cherokee, driven west, took their hilltop fort and when they, with brother Waco, took last drink from their eternal spring . . . And the others, pieces of tribes — Tonkawa to Delaware — swept like broken flint west . . . like Choctaw Tom, and seven of his people killed in their blankets these few moons past, even with permission to leave the reservation to hunt . . .

To steal or kill, say the whites. To live or take vengeance, say your people. There was vengeance for Choctaw Tom; you have fought one battle with *Tejanos* when they came for braves that you will not surrender. That fight was scarcely off the reservation; where can you call land your own?

North-riding Kiowa and Comanche call you to join their fight or die. You are between two stones — both for war. From this reservation, there seems little left of the land of Tejas that was yours.

There is none at all. Your chiefs bring word: with sun, you will trail with what you can carry, leaving even your garden patch. . .and your land, forever.

The morning of July 31, these old walls see it happen.

To check impending war, nearly two thousand Indians are drummed out for the march north. The Washita Valley in Indian Nation Country, near Fort Sill, will be new home.

Escorting army reports confusion intense. Old ones sit by their vegetable patches, prodded out by chiefs, back and forth in the pony dust, shouting. Out wanders the gaunt livestock, churning the hot, rising haze.

Yonder are squaws, stolidly bundling what may be carried on their lodgepole travois. . .no way to take the crops nearly ready for harvest. . .even seed spilled behind, no room. . .little ones on squaws' backs, screaming at strange faces . . . their dogs running, barking in the dust . . . the soldier mules, braying back . . .

And over it all, bugle and drum roll to form up! *Form up!* There is no column, no order. A sweating infantry column slogs the center and, strung a sagging mile to the sides, shuffles that caravan. In blistering heat they will trudge from water to water, live off army rations or the land or fallen cattle. They straggle three miles the first day, ten, the second. A coming Union Rock of Chickamaugua, Major George Thomas of Virginia, takes them finally over Red River.

Later, meticulous Army will report two babies born on the trail, an old man dead. Also will come the report: "The last Indian is cleared of Texas."

Of course, they will be back, for twenty-five bloody, raiding years — as long as there are men to ride: back with
the unvoiced cry that a last day Indian chief will call for
them: "The Great Spirit did not make me a Reservation
Indian."

But they will come back, strangers to a different land.
As a legal entity, they have ceased officially to exist in
what was home.

At Fort Belknap, end of their line.

And for Texas, Indian exodus.

1863

Dick Dowling at Sabine

There was no way for Confederate General John
Magruder to know that his Department of Texas was about
to earn the South's one medal of honor; he was only certain
that, should Federal invasion come, they could not hold
the unfinished mud fort on the Sabine.

There was reason enough for Magruder's pessimism;
this fall of 1863 was a grim time for Texas. Her men had
stormed Gettysburg's Little Round Top and had held the
bluffs at Vicksburg. And now flew rumor that, from
captured New Orleans, Federal General Nathaniel Banks
planned a full-scale invasion of the state.

To strike Texas where? Southern intelligence could tell
Magruder little, and he had too much coast to defend.
Best, then, to concentrate what little resources he had;
he considered the little fort on the marshy southeast tip
of Texas.

The works were raw mud and rock with an end open
— really little better than heavy earthworks. Inside, six
pieces of heavy artillery: two smooth-bore twenty-four
pounders, four thirty-two's, two of the latter howitzers
that were no match for fleet guns. And to man those pieces,
only Company F, First Texas Heavy Artillery — "Davis

242

Guards", they called themselves. They were good, those Houston-Galveston dock-wallopers, but there were less than half a hundred of them.

Spike the guns, Magruder ordered. Abandon the fort.

Few Texans know it, but you can locate what was known alternately as Fort Sabine or Griffin. Below Port Arthur, the coast flattens to a lonely reach of reeds and Sabine Pass lets its Gulf of Mexico into a brackish lake stretching almost to Beaumont. Old Sabinetown is a quiet, weathered village that looks over the narrows to Louisiana and down them to the sea. There are oleanders about, some wind-bent trees, some moored shrimpers, turgid water under the cry of gulls and, outward, the gray line of breakers. On the west bank is a grassy park, a statue and granite marker and faintest traces of what once were earthen embankments. Here is where a young Irishman determined to disobey General Magruder's orders. He was in temporary command of the Davis Guards, a twenty-four year old lieutenant named Dick Dowling.

Born in Galway County Ireland, young Richard W. Dowling had come first to New Orleans, then Houston, where he opened an eminently successful saloon that featured such drinks as "Kiss Me Quick and Let Me Go." Well-liked in his new city, he had, with war's outbreak, little difficulty in putting together an artillery company — all of Erin's stock. They liked to be known as the "Fighting Irishmen", and they rapidly earned a reputation for deadly accuracy with their heavy pieces.

Now, forty-two of them stood in the muck of the fort's compound and young Dowling looked out from its walls, and debated Magruder's order. Why spike good cannon? Perhaps there'd be no assault, and if one came, perhaps not here. Besides, he didn't like to back up; he was Irish about that. Stripped to the waist, sweating and loblollied with mud, his Davis Guards tore up a small railroad siding. Instead of abandoning Fort Sabine, they worked feverishly to strengthen its walls.

Then, gun by gun, Dowling had them train in on pre-selected, close-range markers down the slack channel. Should the pass be forced, he told them, they'd ride out whatever bombardment the Federal fleet would loose on them; they'd just dig into the walls and hold on. They'd wait until those inbound ships were point-blank in their sights. He told them maybe there wouldn't even be any ships.

There would be. At three in the morning of September 8, sentries picked up flashing lights, far in the offshore blackness like big fireflies. And they were coming in.

Offshore were eighteen transports with five thousand troops under General William B. Franklin, Banks' second in command. Four shallow-draft gunboats of Farragut's Gulf squadron — the *Clifton, Sachem, Arizona and Granite City* — were in escort. Northern intelligence had been thorough; they knew of the little fort, of its difficulty of defense and, isolated across these marshes, of support. They suspected rightly that a commander as skilled as Magruder might have ordered it abandoned.

This sea-borne assault was the leap-frog element in Federal invasion plans An overland army, pressing across Louisiana, would batter straight in. This force would land behind the badly outnumbered Confederate army, cut it off, and — united — sweep from Beaumont to Houston and fan out across Texas. On the inbound ships, they knew they had the element of surprise. No part of the alerted coast of Texas knew where to expect assault.

None, now, but Dick Dowling and his men. By morning twilight, they could make out the great sprawl of ships and bearing down for the quarter-mile-wide channel, the squat outlines of the big, shallow-draft gunboats. Then bombardment hit; the fort's gunners gouged themselves into their mud walls; Dowling's orders were to hold fire.

Gunboat *Clifton*, leading, pounded the silent fort for an hour, her lookouts reporting direct hits in its center. *Clifton* withdrew to signal in the others; they'd close to point-blank range and level the fort, even deserted as it seemed. Out went signals to the transports: prepare to land. *Clifton, Sachem* and *Arizona* steamed in close, raking the fort. *Granite City*, leading the transports, was on the channel marker. But *Clifton* and *Sachem* were on Dowling's zeroed target markers; he opened up.

244

In forty-five minutes his gunners fired one hundred thirty-seven rounds without once swabbing their smoking guns. *Sachem* tried to haul about and enfilade the gap in the works; she was hit in the boilers, exploded steam and grounded, striking her colors. *Clifton*, her superstructure shattered and decks a wreck, was ripped at the waterline and went aground. *Arizona*, badly mauled put about for sea and *Granite City* without a shot, joined her. Offshore, General Franklin had no choice; he steamed back for the Louisiana coast.

Captain Francis Crocker, U.S. Navy, surrendered what was left of his two gunboats, some three hundred fifty men. He had lost almost two hundred killed and wounded. Baffled, he surveyed his captors — forty-two halfnaked, powder-grimed men. He was thunderstruck when he learned Dowling had stopped them without the loss of a man.

Even more thunderstruck was Union high command. One of its pincers disabled, the overland army turned back from invasion at Opelousas, retired to New Orleans. Banks' army of thirty-five thousand would not invade Texas this fall.

General Magruder overlooked the young Irishman's disregard for orders, had Confederacy's medals of honor struck for his "Davis Guards.".

And Dick Dowling, the war finally over, returned to what should have been a promising business career, but yellow fever took him at age twenty-nine. Throughout his short life he was never in the least convinced that his stand at Sabine had been of heroic proportion.

In a way, his modesty and his short life have left him little known to most Texans. Yet search history throughout; I doubt you will very often find as decisive result dealt by the hands of so few.

Confederate Camp Ford

You wonder what he found, exploring that park.

It is not large — grass and hillside shade where the road leaves Tyler north for Gladewater; and the gray-headed man wandered up it slowly, beneath the rows of terraced pines and beyond, into brush — pausing to poke and scuff and let his eyes search. He stood awhile up there, looking across broken land to the railroad.

Then he came down to his wife, waiting at the table by the marker. They read it again and looked about once more, at the park and low sandy hill behind, then across the highway curve to O. B. Dozier's white frame service station and the others, strung along. Presently they left, north. They had midwest plates.

"They stop by from all over," Mr. Dozier told me. "Massachusetts . . . Illinois . . . all over. Sometimes they bring an old pocket knife or a whittled out spoon, something their granddaddies took back from the war. They want to see where he was."

They stop with white-haired, clear-eyed Mr. Dozier, for he has known this glade since the 1890's. Before that, his family helped guard the long log walls that marched up that park hill and across where the auto dump is now, far as today's railroad.

This was Camp Ford C.S.A., known North better than in Texas. Biggest Confederate prison camp west of the Mississippi, it is singular to us for yet better reason.

"Nothing left to find up there," said Mr. Dozier.

Just memories, then that gray-headed man had hunted; perhaps some notion of how that prison compound must have looked. A two-block-square log stockade of sixteen-foot pines, chopped sharp atop. Outside, a guard path round from cavalry corral east to sand hill cemetery west. Inside, thirty feet of deadline nobody crossed to the walls, then prison camp — at peak over a century ago — for five thousand Federals.

Inside, ten acres of that war's debris: mud-daubed stick tents, earth-roofed burrows, junk-board shebangs for men like scarecrows: beard-matted, hollow-eyed, lousy, scurvy-ridden. Tattered men, pants roped around the ankles, a few, barefoot. Bunks? Blanket rags in sand or mud; latrines, where men stood or lay.

Yet post-war comparisons showed Camp Ford a Utopia by comparison with North's swarming Douglas and freezing Elmira, or South's pestilent Libby and Andersonville. And far, far smaller. Then why singular?

In man-for-man proportion, Ford was the strangest, widest cross-section of prisoners anywhere. Here were fragments of one hundred different regiments, from every state north. In addition were signalmen, landmen, cottonmen and sailors — captain to deckhand; even spies and a correspondent from the New York Herald.

Camp Ford, built for Confederate training ground, turned prison almost by accident. Its prisoners were part of the massive, badly-bungled expedition to capture and "colonize" Texas. They were remnants of former Massachusetts governor Nathaniel Banks' Red River expedition. Of it, they alone reached their target.

In 1862, this camp takes the name of indomitable ranger John S. "Rip" Ford. It musters Texans west for New Mexico and the Indian front, east for Hood's Brigade. But even earlier has begun the chapter to make it war-end prison. Angry, idle New England textile industry pressures for capture of Texas, division to five states, with eighty acres per man who stays to plant cotton. Volunteers rise from every state, for Banks' free land appeal is strong.

But year by year — from Manassas to Vicksburg — the Texas "Invasion" is sidetracked. Banks makes hesitant coastal jabs, holds a thready fringe of beach, is driven from Galveston and beaten back at Sabine Pass. Now, however, in 1864, South totters in Virginia, Tennessee and Georgia. From New Orleans, the Banks juggernaut rolls northeast for the Red River, then up it. Shreveport will be easy; then a month to overrun Texas. He has thirty-five thousand men, sixty riverboats and an immense supply train. By a fourth his numbers, he is hit savagely at Mansfield and Pleasant Hill, short of the Texas line. The invasion collapses; there are nearly five thousand prisoners.

Presbyterian minister John McCulloch will recall he was chaplain of the 77th Illinois less than a week before marched 140 miles to Camp Ford's log walls. He is dismayed to see all those men — Kansans to New Yorkers — guarded with him. Even more with what awaits them. No blankets, clothing, shelter! One pot and skillet for each sixteen men. An ax, grubbing hoe, shovel and a bad saw for each hundred. Food averages eight ounces of "salt horse" beef, a cup of cornmeal daily. His own plate is a flattened tomato can, his spoon, a whittled stick. There is simply nothing at Camp Ford!

In time, Preacher McCulloch recognizes there is nothing also for their Confederate guards. For how long this had been Confederate ration, he cannot comprehend. He knows only that Indiana jumbles with New York stranger, Illinois with Massachusetts — and all grapple to survive.

Ford's men improvise: checkers to ball games, make up a banjo-fiddle band for hoedowns, swap greenbacks or gold watches for anything warm, try escape. A Kansas outfit squeezes through the walls in night storm; dogs round them in the Sabine bottoms. It is the same with Nebraska, New Jersey, Ohio: you dig; they find your tunnel. Private Bob Burke's First Indiana gouges a hundred feet with butcher knives; five finally make it to Union lines at Natchez.

Then one day, this spring of 1865, they wake; gates are open, guards gone. Prison Camp Ford is as empty as Confederate hope. Union troops shortly will come and raze the stockade.

But the Illinois preacher has seen the real enemy. A

Missouri prisoner grudges food to a Pennsylvanian...or warmth ... or help, both ill. So many fragments from so many places. This is Camp Ford's singularity: so small, the enemy is easy to see.

The preacher goes home, knowing him.

You hope that's what the gray-headed man found, exploring Tyler's small park. Nothing up there? No, not a trace of the wreck and shambles of prison camp. A friendly and handsome city, Tyler has dressed old land's wound and left it to heal. Heal the scars that Preacher McCulloch went home knowing.

Scars from the real enemy — war that pits man against his brother.

1871

Fort Richardson's Strange Trial

Halfway across the low, pin oak hills between Fort Worth and Wichita Falls, Jacksboro once manned our Indian frontier west and, like others on that onetime deadly perimeter, boasts its restored army outpost. However, although little noted by our state, its Fort Richardson holds a story which few others can equal.

Here, in this privately-preserved forty acre compound, a drama came to climax involving Federal General William T. Sherman, President U.S. Grant and some other impassioned men, including three Kiowa chieftains who fought and lost and became America's first "war crimes defendants."

Turn back to May 17, 1871. The war which Sherman labeled "hell" is over. He is on West Texas frontier, sent by Grant, to see if Kiowa, Comanche and Apache are as dreadful as Texas reports.

He rides from Fort Belknap, near what is now Graham, to Fort Richardson. Halfway, near Flattop Mountain along Salt Creek, his point riders sense Indians. His little troop of twenty cavalrymen ride on; the hills lie quiet. The hundred fifty watchers wait, letting them pass. Sherman will learn next day that he was never closer to death.

A few hours behind him comes the heavy-wheeled transport wagons of Captain Henry Warren. There are twelve men to face the avalanche that screams down.

Kiowa Chief Satank, who carries his son's bones in a buckskin bag by his knee so he can remember Texans. sounds the charge on an eagle wingbone whistle.

It is over so quickly! The teamsters try to fort and fail, but the seven who die take one for one. Five make the woods. The wagonmaster, last to perish, thrusts his gun in the face of the young chief, coming over the tail gate. The wagonmaster is split and roasted like a turkey over the wagon tongue. This is what no longer skeptical General Sherman learns in the early hours next morning.

Now the man who scourged Georgia is, on that moment and paradoxically, a revenger for Texas. He moves on Fort Sill and the Oklahoma Indian reservations.

Up there are three chiefs who understand revenge, too. They have lost sons and brothers. The white man has their land. These Kiowas are Satank, Satanta and Big Tree. They face Sherman, ready to fight, but the old soldier has them outguessed. Every window bristles with American carbines. They will go back to Fort Richardson and stand white man's trial.

Satank leaves behind the son he has carried so long. Near the Red River he gnaws his wrists free, stabs at a guard, is shot dead by Corporal Johnnie Charlton.

Satanta and Big Tree stood trial in Jacksboro in the old courthouse on the present square. Since the town was explosive with angry whites and the hill rims, with reds who trailed the wagons, it fell to Fort Richardson to hold the prisoners. They were locked in the thick-walled morgue, which guards grimly behind fort headquarters today.

This was "State of Texas Versus Murder — Satanta and Big Tree." Burning denunciation of Indian by prosecutor S. W. Lanham! Satanta made his own speech: "I cannot speak with these things upon my wrists." He held up his chained arms. "I am a squaw!" He promised peace for freedom, "but if you kill me it will be spark on the prairie — make big fire — burn heap!"

In moments, the jury returned verdict: "Death by hanging."

Now, strangely, across the land come conflicting pressures—to free, to commute, to execute. The Oklahoma Indian agent appealed directly to President Grant. Old Soldier Sherman was inexorable; they should die. Old Soldier Grant commuted the sentence to life imprisonment in Huntsville. Within two years, Reconstruction Governor E.J. Davis ordered parole. Satanta and Big Tree went free — back to the reservation. A furious Sherman fought it all the way.

The parole worked halfway. Within months, Satanta led war parties on Texas once more. This time, he went to Huntsville to stay. He ended that by diving, face down, into the brick courtyard.

Big Tree? He became a churchman, a deacon, and a good one. But, as an old man, he liked to chuckle over what he had done, down Texas way.

This was Fort Richardson, site of Texas' first effort to impose judicial wisdom on the red man. Today, the fort is a museum reflecting bits of this story, indeed unlike any other.

An Indian chieftain fought for his land and the soul of his son. The South's enemy, Sherman, fought for Texans. And in and about Fort Richardson we had, in effect, our first Nuremburg Trials.

251

1880

Griffin's Mystery Lady

For some time, it disturbed me watching Kitty, Marshal Dillion's svelte and shapely firebrand in television's "Gunsmoke". You like to believe our old West had a few lookers like Kitty for the good guys to protect from the bad guys.

What bothered me was it couldn't be. Not if you've seen the anvil jaw on the real Calamity Jane and Belle Starr's rhubarb nose. I quit looking up pictures of western heroines.

Well, this will report to you heretofore disillusioned romantics that Kitty is the genuine, authentic imitation we hoped. In fact, Texas fleetingly knew a woman for whom Kitty might well have been modeled. She was the young side of thirty, a lissome, auburn-haired, dark-eyed beauty. Her clothes whispered elegance; her manner, breeding. Men? She was aloof to them. Except on one count.

She was a cold-blooded magician with cards, and gambling was her passion. The men she knew, she faced across green-felted poker tables in The Flat, old Fort Griffin's hell-roarer of a town. She went by the improbable name, Lottie Deno. What it really was, before and after her three meteoric years at Griffin, nobody has ever known.

Fort Griffin was an anchor on the Red River-Rio Grande line after the Civil War. North of Albany toward Wichita Falls, it is a state park now, its old regimental grounds and their rock-walled skeletons at parade rest atop a broad, bare mesa. Below are the bottoms of the

Brazos' Clear Fork; and there — in fainter ruin now — grew up The Flat, the self-acknowledged wickedest town on earth.

Triple-tandemed, oxdrawn freighters watered and went out for the buffalo slaughter. The endless dust cloud surge of bawling cattle drove for Griffin town. Here was headquarters for hunter and cowboy, gambler and gunman — the frontier's ragged edge until the early 1880's: last stop before the emptiness to Dodge. There were merchandise depots, Uncle Billy's Eatery, the Hotel de Wilson, four dance halls, eight saloons and three forthright emporiums where gambling was all you did.

Into this, the westbound stage from Jacksboro pulled one late afternoon. The broad-hatted, top-booted loungers at the stage station felt their eyes bug: up beside teamster Dick Wheeler — riding shotgun — was a red-headed, jet-eyed dream!

The lady — and the men she froze with one look could vouch for that — lost no time establishing herself. No question, she had money; she rented one of the better shacks, cash a year in advance.

She turned up at Griffin's liveliest — the Beehive. For its manager, she riffled a new deck of cards. Cards did things in her slender fingers. Finally she sat in on a close-to-the-vest game and broke it. She knew faro, monte, roulette, casino. She was in! Even though she remained an enigmatic mask behind her hand, who minded it so doggoned much, losing to a lady like that! And what if the name sounded contrived; looking at her, who cared?

She could sit through gunplay with calm. She was playing a fifty dollar limit the October night that the big game went on at the next table. Monte Bill, Arizona's best, was locked up with Smoky Joe, a plunging Texan. Lottie won a fair stud hand, kings wired, when her table and the room cleared suddenly.

It was deadly quiet a few feet away. Monte Bill had fanned his hand, full to three aces. The furious Texan's whiskey glass went crashing and his chair kicked backwards the same instant the Arizonan coiled to his

253

feet. . .the same instant that Lottie leaned back a little from the line of fire.

Chest to chest over the table, the two gamblers shot each other dead. Silently, Lottie stepped past their bodies, met the sheriff bounding up the stairs.

She asked him to cash her in.

For three years, Lottie lived her two lives in Griffintown. Days, she remained in her shack, shunning visitors. With nightfall, The Flat came to raucous life; and Lottie, elegant and aloof, came forth to face the men across the tables, beat them, and somehow move untouched through violence that, much more than once, saw death sprawled on the floor.

She was touched once however, and it left a legend. One bottle-throwing, chair-smashing free-for-all caught her in its vortex. Somebody hurled a cuspidor that grazed her forehead. It left no permanent outward mar, even in the eye it blinded. But it left with her, for Texana, the descriptive finality: "out like Lottie's eye."

Lottie left as suddenly as she had come. Some say she may have loved a man who followed her to Griffin, a man killed there in a brush with the law. This is legend, as is the report of the opening of her shack weeks after she disappeared. It was luxuriously furnished, runs the story, and a note had been left: "Sell this outfit and use the money for those in need."

Some say she used her winnings to restore her family's shattered Confederate fortune. Others, that her gambling paid for philanthropy in New Orleans. Still others simply generalize her as a saint in the east and a hellion in the west. All agree she must have gone back to the life she led somewhere before she opened and closed the book on Fort Griffin.

One thing is certain. In Lottie, our old West did have a looker like Gunsmoke's Kitty — an auburn-haired beauty for the good guys to protect from the bad guys. And yet . . .

Who protected the good guys from Lottie?

1883

Three Faces of McKavett

Some day, forgotten phantom Fort McKavett must be found again, southeast of San Angelo, or many an old trooper's ghost will ride back to haunt us. They will know we lost the best post, west in Texas.

Nearly all of us have bypassed the great stone ruin commanding the San Saba's hidden headwater valley; for it seems on the road to nowhere except itself, and has been abandoned since 1883. By all, that is, except the handful that cling to a town in the tumbling rock buildings today.

So we never discover McKavett's puzzling superlatives. Of all army's West Texas forts, here was one of the biggest and best built. Here strangely, the least Indian action. Yet here finally, the one that old army's hardnosed fighters prized most.

Why? Hurtling the sparse divide country seventeen miles west of Menard today, you miss that rim to the south. Its edge hides a green valley, crystal-watered... a trooper's Shangri-La.

With Menard's Mrs. Frances Fish, a plump and merry historian who grew up in the town that army left behind, I saw McKavett's three faces: the one that was, is, and should be.

McKavett wasn't selected for an army resort, as your map will show. On a line between today's Denison and Eagle Pass, space a north to south cordon of forts like Worth, Graham, Gates, Croghan, Martin Scott and Inge. In fresh-won Texas, frontier west — 1850.

255

These next few years, leapfrog to a new line, bulging deep as the Abilene of now. On this front is an old and favorite Indian campground at the three spring-fed fords heading the San Saba. Indian-fighting army has learned an axiom: last one to the water, loses. And so, a small outpost McKavett.

But forget the second line; the big war is in Virginia. Forts like Mason and Terrett, Chadbourne and Phantom Hill will see Gray briefly, never really recover.

McKavett will. It centers behind the new line of the 1870's, angling from Jacksboro through San Angelo, then far west. Where a young Virginia colonel, Robert E. Lee, bunked old McKavett's frontier, Old Soldiers William T. Sherman and Phil Sheridan order the distant Panhandle swept clear of "hostiles." A good New York fighter, Colonel Ranald Mackenzie, does it in four years. McKavett is mightily rebuilt: a strategic supply depot decreed by geography. With fifty big stone buildings and as many, frame, it vies with new Fort Sam Houston in San Antonio as handsomest in Texas. Geography also decreed it beauty.

Mrs. Fish stopped us at valley rim, where once stage or freighter pulled up. The valley reaches broad. Its low center hill hides much of the San Saba's heavy timber, bending around; and atop, the fort stands white. Climbing, you feel its size.

West, the long line of quarter-block commissary barns. South and east, officer's row, L-ing off a quadrangle bottomed on five big stone barracks. Beyond the lesser buildings about, another mall — green to fort headquarters, the commanding officer's tall two story, the spacious hospital compound. And throughout, no gunported walls, but window and floor-to-ceiling French doors. In each room, even each barn, fireplaces.

A pleasant military geometry, white on green. Wide-galleried comfort. Why not? McKavett's last Indian action was one poor devil trying to snake out a horse.

Pleasant days, too. On the mile-wide parade green under the hill, the fort's dress reviews are color-splashed symmetry. McKavett's rifles are for Target Hill, the mesa beyond, or for the pronghorn, deer and turkey in any direction. So many, you take only backstrap and ham. Fish? A half-dozen shade-sparkling holes within five miles.

Sutler Sam Wallick will charge anything from Maine lobsters to good Kentucky whiskey; and his is the best piano west of Fort Worth. The ladies like it for recitals or Sunday chapel. They like the matched races and trick riding on McKavett's groomed half-mile parade ground and the quadrangle's band concert before colors. Everybody likes the full dress dances in the big hospital building.

The face of Fort McKavett — while army — is pleasant indeed. Then it changes.

Far north, no Indian campaign to supply, army blue finally leaves. The new face is civilian, up from the flats across, determined to live on in the stone buildings left behind. But where will dollars come from?

"That was hotel for awhile." Mrs. Fish pointed to a roofless commisary skeleton. "For two-bits, you rented a clean goatskin. You could pick your place on the floor."

The hand-carved walnut furniture was gone. Year on year, a few walls fell and the roofs went to fires, with neither people nor buckets enough to fight. Today, the grocery and post office are by the tall-chimneyed shell where McKavett's C.O. cooled Madeira in his stone cellar and kept paired duns in his private stable. A refreshment emporium quarters the last standing barracks. Frank's Place is the old P.X.

For a time, they made a hotel where Sherman sent his dispatches from GHQ's wide-galleried building. Now, the fine windows are stoppered with a torn-off door, some corrugated iron and cardboard, wedged with an old tire. The original cypress sags a roof; the floor is shambles.

And all about are the other skeletons, some hanging on, some occupied. But mostly the hilltop is dying; sad, the face that is. It seems resigned to let the world, unknowing, pass it by.

"And so much could be done," said Frances Fish angrily. "Clean up a little. . .some paths. . .signs, to explain. . ."

McKavett's face that could be?

Seems to me, our usually alert San Angelo area may be missing a tourist boat. Here is a fort comparable in size and poignant ruin with nationally-monumented Fort Davis. Let us walk it and wonder.

More, there is the reason that McKavett had to follow the Comanche here: quiet beauty, game and — undiscovered by us moderns — fine, clearwater campsites that neither Frio, Nueces nor Guadalupe will top. If Shangri-La then, why not now? We'd like to camp what old army knew was best, west in Texas.

1941-45

A Quadrangle's Remembering Bells

Some say great bells have souls and old clock faces, indelible memory of their times. I doubt the lanky seventeen year old Weatherford boy thought about it then. His awareness was limited to knowing that to the right of the heavy-arched sally port, three doors past the stiff sentries, were his week-long West Point exams — inexorably timed to that clock's booming bell.

He knew, in awe, that directly above him was the office of the commanding general. He could not suspect that, nearly forty years later, that same office would be his.

He finished the Point, class of 1909. Seventying and retired today, he still looks the tall, powerful "Indian" his classmates dubbed him. His World War II Ninth Army was the final lightning bolt that split the Reich "with never a mistake" to his commander, Dwight Eisenhowever.

I asked San Antonio's General William Hood Simpson to show me the Fort Sam Houston he has known, those long years. We drove the valiant-named streets past barracks, buildings and parade grounds — a good post's always disciplined beauty. Finally, we were through the old sally port, past the stiff young sentries, to the un-changing heart of Old Army — Fort Sam's quadrangle.

It is a two-block-square, shaded park dwelt upon by everything from tame deer to peacocks, still frontier fort-walled with high heavy rock, and Fourth Army's nerve center offices patioed inward. Centering, with two brassy salute guns beside, is the clock tower — eight stories, staired like a square lighthouse. The old clock's bell tolled the hour.

We talked awhile of what it must remember.

Look down from the bell tower.

South, down the river that Comanche calls "Drunk Old Man Going Home at Night", stands the still-battered Alamo, army headquarters before this 1882. Commanding there had been men to wear Gray: Albert Sidney Johnston and then Robert E. Lee.

But now this new Southwest depot-fort cornerstones its planners: President Ulysses S. Grant, General of the Army William T. Sherman, Philip Sheridan, commanding. It bears a name from San Jacinto and, above you, the bell from the Alamo.

Below, by the north wall — unchanged today even to the gunports — is strange camp, this fall of 1886. In white army tents is last Apache chief, Geronimo. Fort Sam's Fourth Cavalry has brought him here, awaiting Florida reservation. Below really, is end of Indian war, southwest.

"We always figured that's why the deer and turkey are here," said General Simpson. "Geronimo couldn't take army rations. Afterwards. . .well, they just had a home."

Beyond the southwest walls, disarmed rockets poise skyward. They seem incongruous; they are truly at home. Look north to the long green past the barracks. Rockets were born at Fort Sam.

On Texas Independence Day 1910, young Signal Corps Lieutenant Benjamin Fulois finishes his doubtful mission. Seven years after Kitty Hawk, he proves that a Wright biplane can serve army. Over Arthur MacArthur Field, he flies a "collection of bamboo poles, more or less attached to a gasoline engine."

In Mexico with Blackjack Pershing, young Lieutenant Simpson will glimpse army's six-plane air force. Fort Sam has opened the sky door to today's Houston Space Center.

Look down on the rest: those north-wall nesting pigeons; their forebears trained here to fly World War I messages, when nothing else got through. Below, this post blueprinted World War II's airborne troops, trained them over the flat plains to Brackettville.

Finally, you see the men who also looked up to hear this bell.

Here a chunky, vital Teddy Roosevelt, down with Leonard Wood, to meld a strange blend of Western cowboys and New York's elite for their Rough Riders, hell-for-leather up San Juan Hill.

Now, strong-faced John J. Pershing, who pulls in from the Pancho Villa hunt, commands from this quadrangle, then hurdles his American Expeditionary Force from here to Chateau Thierry, the Argonne and a debt paid to La Fayette.

Others, too. An army youngster, intently studying these troops, Douglas MacArthur will train his fellow cadets at Texas Military Institute, across the hills. And those others, long later, across the Pacific.

A young lieutenant will station here a time, come back as brigadier general. In the quadrangle, December 7, 1941, Dwight Eisenhower will learn of Pearl Harbor; five days later, leave for ultimate command and destiny.

So many others, over the great clock's time. Fighting Joe Stillwell, to know Burma's green hell; Simon Bolivar Buckner, Okinawa's rock; Jonathan Wainwright, to come back from Corregidor and Bataan's death march.

And probably the greatest team of fighting American generals we have known. First Army's Courtney Hodges, smashing up the middle: Paris and beyond; the Fifth's Mark Clark, toiling Italy's spine; Seventh's Alexander Patch, bursting Southern France's beachheads; and Walter Krueger's Sixth, down the dark jungle trails of South Pacific.

And the tall, quiet man from Weatherford, whose lightning Ninth engulfed impregnable Ruhr in eighteen days, won the race to the Elbe, stood on the Berlin autobahn at dark knowing he could have his tanks in the capital by dawn. Under orders, he pulled back and waited for Russia to take the city.

What else can you see from that tower? A million and a half Americans who made those names great. While we studied the changeless quadrangle, a master sergeant came up and talked with General Simpson. They had been together at the Elbe.

Some of those others you can see from the tower...under the crosses beyond the hill northeast, like the many more beneath crosses far away.

That's the view from Fort Sam's watchtower, when the bell rings clear. And for whom rings the bell?

You. Me. Our children; our country. Lest we forget Old Army's proudest best.

Want to go listen?

1836-1971

Alamo's Flame of Travis

It is the flame of Travis you watch closest.

Bugler's taps still echo within the vaulted walls, the erect old colors retire; and quietly, you wonder. Why so long since you've come back to Alamo to reappraise your freedom? Doubtless, you've pondered other things throughout these memorial services, this day of our Texas shrine in San Antonio.

Though any day is right to contemplate the stern old mission-fort — it releases few, unmoved — a truer time here is when February slips to March: within that thirteen day long ago that spanned from siege to slaughter. In painting yonder, the last man falls, fighting; and you know that March 6 — day of final fury — is truest of all.

This once, each year — within the last-stand chapel — Alamo commemorates her heroes. Our quietly steadfast Daughters of the Republic of Texas — guardians of the shrine since they rescued it from warehouse ruin in 1905 (another story) — open these services to all. They are poignantly simple; their significance is not.

For few would argue that the candle flame touched symbolically for Travis and the rest struck, in fact, the very torch of San Jacinto. Throughout, you wonder if these rites are too little known across Texas. Perhaps you conclude that Alamo's March 6 rededication should be better marked on our calendars.

But inevitably, you search the message of that flame for William Barret Travis.

You came in from heavy-trafficked, park-patterned Alamo Plaza, all part of the original fort's sprawl: log barricade angling southwest from the chapel to today's Alamo Street, then low barracks wall across and all down the store fronts opposite, far as the distant post office; finally back, along the present rock wall line. Perhaps one rifleman each ten feet. Thin line indeed!

Inside, quiet shuts out the city; services are begun. But you sit, thinking how it was when the cross-belted, black-shakoed, blue and white wave engulfed:

Travis, killed at the north breakthrough, dying literally where today's post office windows seem infinitely far; Crockett, close beyond your doors by his Tennesseean's log wall. Bowie, knife to bayonet, on his cot in the cell-like baptistry, just within; and Bonham, fallen across his guns atop the chapel, almost above where today's speaker stands. Four flames lighted — one for each — in candelabrum there; and the fifth, for the desperate, valiant rest who took nine for one and wrecked Santa Anna's army.

Now, down the north wall, stands the long color guard with banners at ease — for the eighteen states of Alamo's defenders: from Mississippi's Stars and Bars to New York's Empire Seal; and for seven nations — England to Germany to Mexico's Texans.

Invocation and scripture reading are brief, the heroes' candles lighted, and the roll called — Alabama to Massachusetts, Pennsylvania to Virginia — as each flag snaps to attention. There is a talk, benediction, then echoing in, silver taps.

Later — or before — you walked the quiet, round the grave gray walls. Here is the bronze with Alamo's history from 1716 authorization; there, how D.R.T. has held the shrine without charge or cost to Texas; and the others, rostering Alamo's men. Spaced along are the paintings: Travis at his last sword thrust; Major Robert Evans, cut down, torch-racing for the magazine; Crockett and Old Betsy by the barricade; Dr. Amos Pollard, dressing the wounded with death nearly at the doors; a then-well Jim Bowie atop the wall; Jim Bonham Comanche-slung, galloping from his last try for help; handsome young Tapley Holland, first over Travis' line — all fragments of pattern, those last desperate days.

And in the glass cases, other bits from lives given here. They add, not as sometimes pictured, to freebooter, runaway and illiterate; but to a cross-section of lawyer, doctor, writer, naturalist — a spectrum from aristocrat Bonham to Crockett's coon-capped riflemen.

And always, inevitably, William Barret Travis and *The Letter*, timeless in bronze:

"To the people of Texas and all Americans in the World — Fellow citizens and compatriots — I am besieged by . . . Santa Anna . . . The garrison are to be put to the sword if the fort is taken — I have answered the demand with a cannon shot . . . I shall never surrender nor retreat . . .

"Then I call on you in the name of Liberty, of patriotism and everything dear to the American character to come to our aid with all dispatch . . . Victory or Death."

You look deeper in Travis' flame, there by the speaker. How steady was it three days ago — March 3, the day Jim Bonham's last wild ride told him there was no help, and he knew it was death! The day he fronted his men and drew the line to tell them?

Maybe, like me, you'll find that day inseparable from this March 6; for it was then, the lean twenty-six year old commander left us another message. His prized black cat's eye ring, he strung round the neck of little Angelina Dickenson — his last gift, to a youngster who might (and would) be spared.

That day, he wrote hurriedly a final note to friends, yet safely east in Texas. In exhaustion and cordoned in cannon thunder, Travis thought of his seven-year-old son, Charles.

"Take care of my little boy. If the country should be saved, I may make him a splended fortune; but if . . . I should perish, he will have . . . the proud recollection that he is the son of a man who died for his country." Intently, you probe this flame, standing for what he left. Was it not really a legacy to all those boys and girls yet to be Texans — this splendid fortune . . . this proud recollection?

And did he not really leave that legacy to so many young to follow? To our fathers, to us?

This is the Travis you may read in the light of his Alamo candle on March 6.

And later, in your town and mine, perhaps we'll take another look at our young and ponder how well we've guarded that legacy — "take care of my little boy!" Maybe we'll recollect Kipling:

"Lord God of Hosts, be with us yet.

"Lest we forget. Lest we forget."

Part Five

A Lodging Place

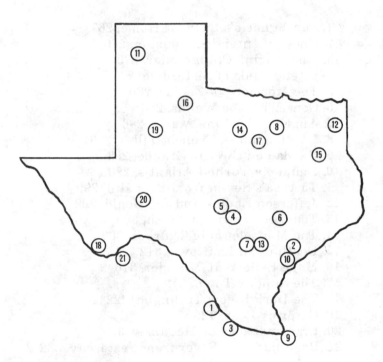

"O, that I had in the wilderness, a lodging place for wayfaring men."

Jeremiah

San Ygnacio's Star for Home

Beyond our necklaced streets and tinseled, gift-decked trees, Christmas is also the season of Yule Log and Saint Nicholas, the Child's Chair and Petit Noel, of kind gnomes and Nacimiento, for we are many, whose faiths are in Texas. Yet for all of us there is recollection of the Star wise men once followed.

As a boy in old San Ygnacio, briefly down Rio Grande from Laredo, Nacho Sanchez remembers when grown-up's eyes lighted with the miracle plays of Los Pastores, as December turned on January: a time when plain workaday neighbors turned devout shepherds, following their star to a manger.

This was always at Nacho's family home, oldest of the village; and it was by the north wall's great arched gate.

Today he is Dr. Ignacio Sanchez, who seeks to heal in Corpus Christi, but whose heart, these middle years, seeks, too, his sixth-generation village; and hopes that the Nativity again touches the century and a half of his house.

He showed me that house, where his sisters' families now live. Over the north gate, the half-block-square, stone-forted Rancho San Ygnacio de Loyola looks to heaven, in its way, as perhaps no other in our state. Weathering atop the gate is a yet timekeeping sun dial.

It has been there well over a century to remember the following of another star.

From Falcon Dam's low hills to Laredo, you miss San Ygnacio easily: a flash of simple frame, house and roadside store. The old town hides below, where just yesterday they took water from the river in barrels—all, so like it was in the early 1800's, that Marlon Brando's *Viva Zapata* chose this grillworked rock, and earthy, narrow streets for location.

Here it was, the grandfather of Nacho's grandmother took almost direct title from Spain, pushing into Texas long before any Stephen Austin. First came jacales for herd-riding vaqueros; by the 1820's, a stern rock house, forted at either door. This, in thirty years, squared immensely to the partly tumbled rock fort you see today. Gun-ported outward, buildings patioed inward, the rancho stands changeless: thick, eight-foot walls, hand-turned mesquite beams, carved stone windows, drop-barred double portals — ample for ox-teamed *carretas* — heavy doors, peg-socketed for hinges. Of houses never left by founding family, probably this state's very oldest.

But treasure as is the house, this story is of the mouldering sun dial and its star — all that, atop the house; and for that, you go back a long time.

The time is earliest 1800 and from old Guerrero (now in Falcon Lake) a dark-eyed, seven year old boy rides the river with his father. There is no fort here now; what matter? For young Jose Villareal is not a father enough for anything? "What makes the grass grow, Papa? Why does one sleep?" And riding home by night, "Why are the stars, Papa?"

One thing from his father, Jose will never forget: "That one is star of the north, son; our God placed it there for us. When you are lost, have patience. Watch the star and keep on; she will take you home." How do you tell a boy more than "Have faith?" How, explain the infinite!

And so they talk, this twilight, when the Comanche—raiding September's Mexican Moon—burst from the mesquite wilderness. For a son, the horribly impossible! His father struck, sprawling, dust-eddied...dead! And quick as terror, he himself pinioned to the greased chest of a head-feathered, fierce-eyed man. Then gone, galloping north . . . and north . . . and north — to the ends of the earth, it seems, from his home.

He can hear his father's words: "The star, son! She will

take you home!" From his soul, Jose shuts sickness; he must think of his father's star.

The boy cannot know the Comanche seeks young braves; he is to be the chief's. He knows only that, by night, the strange man armlocks him close for each sleep. If he stirs, the chief wakes. What is it? Jose must leave the robe. The chief goes, too. And shortly again. And now the boy must scratch. Sleepily, the chief holds him.

But there is little sleep for the man. For three nights now, Jose has stirred on the hour. "How does one sleep, Papa?" *Like that?* limp...unaware the boy has rolled clear of the buffalo robe? Jose crawls, then breaks, running. He hears his father again: "The star, son!" He sets it over his left shoulder. He must circle east from the back trail! That one, they will surely search!

Daylight, in the endless cold sea of mesquite, thorn and cactus, he hears the horses' hooves, lies silent the day through, then finds his star again.

And now, ordeal. The boy has slept little, and of the Comanche's raw meat, has eaten less. Three-four days' horseback; how far afoot? How far, circling as he must? By day's sun, he moves warily or tries to sleep. Always nightmare mustang drumbeat wakes him, terrified, to still-empty horizon.

Then night's cold! "The star, son! Patience and faith; watch the star!" His deerskin jacket and pants are ripped by thorns. One night. Another! Yet another! Days, he can see the deer, the rabbit. But his rocks are weakly thrown. That scuttling armadillo! He only sprawls, grasping; holds up torn hands.

Water? The pebble in his mouth no longer serves. Finally, a puddle. With his bandana, he pushes down the scum, cups enough to drink. He chews the mesquite bean, dry-gags the first time he finds the worms, then chews them anyway.

The star? There it is! He stumbles on, raked bloody, black night crouching him. Yet there is the star of his Father. "Faith and patience, son!"

"How long, Papa?"

The boy staggers into little Ubireño, below his village — a week afoot. His mother comes rejoicing from chapel, where she has never left praying. And seven-year-old Jose Villareal grows on to manhood, rightly tall among the people of his village.

He is near the age of my friend Nacho Sanchez when those close to his family ask him, this year of 1851, to dedicate the finished wall of Fort San Ygnacio. Over the north portal at midnight, he sets the stone—its hours precisely carved, each face. To cast its time shadow—one face for summer, the opposite for winter—he sets a wrought iron shaft, arrow-straight for his Father's star.

A thumbrule navigator can tell you what he did with what we call latitude and longitude. To Jose Villareal, though, his star was also something more: it was a light from his God to lead men home.

Isn't that what our Christmas season is about?

1828-36

Ghost of Intended Houston

It startled me—as I'm sure it will Houstonians—to learn that their metropolis is misplaced: 150 coastal miles east of where it was intended.

In fact, Houston's founding Allen brothers made a kind of second choice, bargain basement deal for the bayou land above old Harrisburg after the New Yorkers had been turned down on the site they really wanted.

What John K. and A. C. Allen really wanted lies on the gently rolling, mott-timbered and lush-grassed coastal prairie, inland on a waterway of enough depth and amplitude for La Salle, long years earlier, to have read its Matagorda Bay mouth — some miles to the south — for that of the Mississippi. There was no problem of clearing or dredging a ship channel for the pioneer port that flourished briefly here.

Today it is a ghost; its name was Texana.

270

Hunting intended Houston, I searched out Rob T. Walker of Lolita, an elder statesman even among old timers. In 1897, he came in a wagon from Waco: fourteen days' travel. Now he was tall and spare with white hair and keen eyes that had studied all the changes: he flew planes from 1917 to 1956, when his hands were no longer sure with the controls.

But his eyes and his memory were sure, and together we circled the land around the little towns of Lolita and Vanderbilt, which lie between Port Lavaca on the coast and inland Edna. This was where Houston was to have sprawled today's metropolis.

Mr Rob pulled us to the shoulder below a broad, long concrete bridge and pointed upriver. Above, wide and deep-running Lavaca is joined by Navidad in woody bottoms, and the land beyond their Y keeps breasting higher over the timber.

"That's where she was," he said. "The high ground there between. Keeps on, up all that slope. Of course, Texana was about dead when I was a kid and we got here. But I can still show you."

He could, indeed; and through those intent eyes, it was not hard to see the Texana that once had promised so much. Nor was it hard to see how she failed of that promise.

In 1828, Stephen Austin's colony had few settlements, but a promising one was situated at this juncture. Its name was Santa Anna, for colonists sided with him, believing he stood against Spanish tyranny.

Six years later, when that dictator was no Texan's friend, the town changed names. Dr. Francis F. Wells, intimate of Austin, chose "Texana" for the port's future promise. Downriver and across its bay was the raw, beginning seaport, Indianola, but here was protected water. Here would land Fannin's Georgians, mustering for Goliad; here, Texanans would stage and supply a campaign that could not fail to sweep the republic clear of invader...

And here, Santa Anna would take particular pains to raze his former namesake, as he marched to the destiny of another river, San Jacinto.

271

And here, immediately after the war, the Allen brothers came by way of Nacogdoches. They sought a dream city, an inland port. They scoured the republic's coast; even in rebuilding rubble, Texana had everything: drainage, shelter, deep water, rich land, and beauty (oil, yet to come).

Granted, the settlement still reeled from Santa Anna's scorched earth wrath. To purchase a site, as good a time as any! They offered Dr. Wells an astronomical hundred thousand dollars, were thunderstruck when chesty Texanans suggested they double the figure.

Furious, one of the Allens jumped atop a stump, leveled a damning finger down Texana's Broadway. "You'll see it plowed under!" he shouted. "Home to nothing but jackrabbits!" The Allens rode away and, four months after San Jacinto, bought a sixty-block site just above Harrisburg. The cost for Houston was five thousand dollars; the cost for this town, its life.

Still, Texana went its complacent way. Let the Allens clear Buffalo Bayou's snags. Here was deep water, twenty ships a week in port. Here was, in ghostly parallel, a Texana Houston to Indianola's Galveston. The obliterating hurricanes were yet to come.

Then the railroad came to Houston and branched out. Texana shrugged it off, saw a little town cluster the new right-of-way, eight miles north. That town was Edna; Texanans knew railroads couldn't beat shipping. They shrugged off Edna.

And died. Now was railroad time. Even burgeoning Houston, far away, was thinking railroad, not the colossal task she faced in ship channel clearing. Edna's railroad killed Texana.

Mr. Rob drove me along with his memories. Over in the maize had been the Red Bluff School, where the teacher handled ten grades and sixty-five youngsters and a cheroot in his jaw all day. Down the Clement fenceline, just off the bank, was where they had sunk the old Confederate ironclad to block the port. We had circled from the rusty iron bridge over Lavaca to the low concrete

272

across Navidad, completing the perimeter of what might have been Houston. Strung out along were the belly-deep Brahmas and the wells, the timber and the good land and deep water.

The old turning basin lies at the Navidad crossing. Up the hill to the right is the cemetery, all that's left; and even its cypress fence is smothered in palmetto and sleepy with honeysuckle.

We drove up the hill. Broadway was erased along that hog-proof division fence, toward the farmhouse with the pens and the heavy trees. Near the strange new microwave tower would have been the saloons and the old opera house, even Texana Academy, its walls echoing the confident tramp of Fannin's men.

Mr. Rob didn't dwell on what might have been. Did he think time had passed Texana by? No sir! There's always time aplenty for any good town: Texana, Houston, too. It isn't like you were talking about, say...Babylon or Nineveh.

Well, not altogether.

1842—

Unchanging Ciudad Mier

They had rammed rifle ports through the foot-thick adobe, all down the east side, and cleared the Mexican cannon, batteried before the cathedral. Three frontal assaults by Mier's black-hatted guard were now six hundred dead in the block-square plaza.

Bigfoot Wallace, greatest ranger of all, had picked his fifteenth man from the rooftops. But there were yet hundreds across in the smoke, and the constant bugles;

273

and commanding Colonel Fisher was hurt bad in the *cuarto* behind, with the dead; and these Texans had nothing left for fighting but *aguardiente*.

All Christmas Day, then all night and now afternoon again, it had been house-to-house and block after forted block. Bigfoot, sweating in the cold, knew they had it won—except the ammunition was gone. And no food for two days.

Canny General Pedro Ampudia, although saddled up for quits, rolled his last dice with a white-flag parley. He invented two thousand fresh Mier troops, more pouring from Monterrey. About two hundred twenty Texans surrendered; forty others were dead or wounded. But without ammunition, Alamo looked them in the face.

They had stormed ten times their number in an ill-conceived, unauthorized assault which yet must rival, for sheer audacity, the Light Brigade's charge or Pickett's at Gettysburg. They would later draw against the black beans for one in ten to die. Eventually, most would get home. Their terrible imprisonment is another story.

In Texas to avenge kinsmen killed at Goliad, Bigfoot surrendered his gun last. This was Ciudad Mier, December 26, 1842, just across the Bravo. Bitterest, deadliest day in the life of a man who never knew one without peril.

Mier—as I drove and walked it—is almost precisely as Bigfoot saw it, marching east in irons. New green, raw blue, orange and tan paint covers the bullet and shell scars. Remote until Falcon Lake came to be, Ciudad Mier is one of the most fascinating Mexican border cities facing us across Rio Grande.

This aged city is opposite Texas' Roma Los Saenz--up west for Laredo from Mission, where shortly the tall-palmed valley breaks off for desert, like a dried stick. Ancient land! Founded in 1753 by Jose de Escandon, along with his string of river missions now gone, Mier flourished with Spain's aristocracy.

To learn of Mier, talk with the gracious Felipe Ramons, who newspaper in Rio Grande City. To find it, cross six-piered, toll-free Falcon Dam with its great, rock-girt lake. At Nuevo Guererro across—the new town replacing the ancient one under the lake — visit the Villareals — "Abarrotes y Curiosidades." They will put you on good pavement down the Mexican side. Mier is thirty minutes' distance, and a little beyond, you recross at Ciudad Miguel Aleman.

Neither Ciudad Mier, nor its desperate battle is known to many Texans. After San Jacinto, there was cold war that flared occasionally hot. Texans tried for Santa Fe. Mexico countered for San Antonio. Both missed.

In spite of wiser heads, Texan temper determined to invade a country twenty times the size of this cocky new republic. President Houston, every tactic of dissuasion exhausted, allowed his militia commander, General Somervell, to lead an expedition which both hoped would finally cool off, tire, go home. All but two hundred sixty did. They crossed the river to assault Mier's two thousand troop garrison.

And so you can see Mier today as a student of its old, aristocratic Moorish-Spain architecture, or as one marveling at the reckless storming of block on solid block of butted-together buildings—the city, itself a vast fortress.

Look for no flashy signs or chrome and carpeted bars in Mier. You drive the narrow entering street. Wall abutting wall, the heavy-doored, grill-windowed buildings press against their narrow walks and pass, one and two storied, in colors ranging from the pastel to the violent.

Circling any block is the same. Occasionally, old brick and ornamental iron filigreed balcony...a few cars...a two-wheeled, rubber-tired cart—burro-drawn. The dark youngsters watching intently from the street...the quiet people studying you from behind their windows.

A little away, that high steeple...occasional tumbled rock walls with weeds beyond . . . the inevitable *Tome Bimbo!* or *Carta Blanca* signs . . . *Sastreria a de Mexico* . . . *Casino Monte Carlo* . . .

There is such air of age—not decadence, mind you, for Mier is a clean, neat city—such a feeling of yesterday, that you come to sense that it might have been just yes-

275

terday that the battle was fought. Perhaps these of the city, these who watch you, regard you still as invader...

I stopped on the plaza where the scarred old cathedral stood silent to the south. I walked here, using my map. Along the east were the new-painted old walls beyond which the Texans forted. Across had been the decimated artillery park and over the plaza—when it was finished—the four, block-long rows of dead that Bigfoot remembered when he came home.

It was just as Mrs. Edna Ramon had told me: "Mier has never changed. I don't think it ever will."

I started for my car and there, in his doorway was Pablo, dark and silent, yelling "pom-pom-pom!" over his toy tommygun.

Even the young, I thought; they're still down on us. Anyhow, face it out.

"Pablo," I said, "is this the place of the big fight?"

He told me the fight was next week at the Reynosa Corrida with Nuevo Laredo fighting bulls—very shy ones!

1847

Intellectuals of Sisterdale

To recall the staunch Texas German pioneer, there is an excellent museum in New Braunfels and another, sixty miles up the Guadalupe at Comfort, in the hills above San Antonio. But for such old time, my favorite museum piece is about midway between them—the tiny, almost forgotten hamlet of Sisterdale.

This back road village, you thread quickly — flash of neat homes, a general store, garage, some old high-roofed German stone and earlier tumbled log; and, across this broad and beautiful river valley, a checkerboard of timber and old rockwalled field.

Listed population, fifty—about as at the beginning. Yet

276

here have lived nobleman, congressman, author, editor, doctor and scholar—from naturalist to geographer and musician to philosopher.

Brain for brain, this state's most polished intellects? Possibly. All of them came at the same time. Beginning in 1847, when these blue hills were Comanche death, they were the gentlemen farmers who founded a town "where it was free to think."

Stop at Smith's store, where you check hunting or fishing about. You'll meet the kin of Kapp, Behr, Zink, Degener, Douai and the rest who made Sisterdale—deadcentering the Comanche gun muzzle—the German intellectual colony of Texas

Most of us Scotch-Irish-whatever forget the extraordinary way the Texas German opened our west. Wanderlusting, he was here with the earliest. In 1821, overcrowded Germany talked of buying Texas from Spain. Build a complete state; ship it across! Before this could materialize, San Jacinto had been fought.

Nevertheless, German aristocracy—Prince Victor of Leiningen, Count Carl of Castell, Prince Solms-Braunfels, Duke Adolph of Nassau, and a dozen others—formed a society for German immigrants. Perhaps still a chance for a new Germany overseas? There were customers aplenty, sick of Europe's tyranny and war. To these, Texas spelled a man's feedom.

From professional to craftsman, they were a wave up the Texas river valleys: the San Antonio to its headwaters above Alamo, the Guadalupe and Colorado from the coast to the hills. Earliest, in the 1830's, were the coastal settlements: Industry, Frelsburg and towns over to Houston and up to San Antonio. These were traditionally small, family-farmed about, and—outside the cities—are today.

But at the Comanche hills above New Braunfels, the settlers paused. This year of 1845 only a madman or Texas Rangers ventured that land. If their purchased land grants were beyond, so was the Comanche!

It is another story that a strong man led into that land. A baron, he was now plain John Meusebach; and he founded Fredericksburg in 1846, proving German treaty word and Comanche as well. Another story entirely, but Texas Germans were safely in Comanche heartland...something no others achieved, short of shooting their way in.

Sisterdale followed Fredericksburg closely. Lieutenant Colonel Nicholas Zink, who had laid out by-now-thriving New Braunfels, set his cabin where Sister Creek met the Guadalupe. Across, settled Ottomar von Behr; the German intellectuals had begun their home.

You can drive to the old Behr home, high over the riffles where the ford used to be. Above the deep pool is the tall rock house and recent barns that followed the first logs. Here then was Sisterdale's school: in its earliest days already one of Texas' finest. Why not? Every family along the valley boasted a library of classics from commentaries on Caesar to Sir Walter Scott. Here, Sisterdale's intellectuals met weekly for song and discussion.

Here was where Prince Paul of Württemberg, brother to the king, came visiting at mid century. This brink-to-wilderness startled him completely.

He had visited the Edward Degeners (later Congressman), across the river, happy with their land plot, with no regrets for their estates left in Germany. At Dr. Ernst Kapp's, on the hill beyond, he found the distinguished Minden author-professor extending a sanitarium for mineral baths, preparing new studies on geography, and chuckling over his just-invented "Indian door" with inch-apart spikes. The prince had heard the fiery Douai on the rights of man and had read von Behr, published in Leipzig, on advice to new Texans.

Most of all, at any home, he found it nothing to hear rich singing voices in *Morningsong* or *Springtime*, or Goethe's *New Songs* read, or Mozart, on piano and flute. The king's brother could have mistaken the wine for Bergundy, but there was no mistaking the Bavarian glass, nor the gold-leafed Meissen china. No mistaking the inside of these log walls; they were extraordinary drawing rooms.

Tonight, for example, the men of Sisterdale had worn out Voltaire and Fourier's all-for-one theories. Then, unbelievably, he had seen it. While the spade-bearded dark-

278

suited men puffed their longstemmed pipes and gestured their pilseners...there at the window, the Indian! Puzzled, listening . . . but only curious, not hostile!

"They take a little stock," someone said later. "It kills no one. Cheap rent."

Yes, he could tell his brother, the king, that the colonists were doing wonderfully—here, where nothing was beyond but the savage! Also something else extraordinary. This, of course, was German culture. *But the men who spoke it were Texans!*

As you drive past the log ruin that was Nicolas Zink's first cabin...down the pecan lane behind the store, where Dr. Kapp's sanitarium is a handsome new ranch house, and the stone schoolhouse that now stores hay, you wonder what happened to Sisterdale—the village that lighted German culture on our frontier.

With a civil war's bitterness that they knew from home, some drifted—against slavery or, for their new homeland, now Confederate. There had to be schism.

Some say Sisterdale's intellectuals failed. You can look on the valley quiet and the old stone and read desertion and perhaps agree. But really, the Texas German disproved only one theory: that of their earliest planners—that they were come over to found a new Germany. What they did was bring Germany's best...and give it to Texas. Sisterdale didn't die; she just spread out...across our land.

That's why, to recall the old German colonist, this hamlet is my favorite museum.

The Mormons of Zodiac

From almost any direction, you can drive into our Hill Country's pioneering Fredericksburg and, within its stippled hills and steepled spires, all along its long main street with the old, slope-roofed rock houses, find an immaculate town, as attractive and industrious as any in our state.

This is not uncommon with our Texas German settlements, this solid, orderly and thriving neatness. But there is a particularity about the town which Baron John von Meusebach set deep into our western hills at a time when there was almost nothing nearabout but the wary, hostile Indian. Almost nothing, and that is the particularity; in the very beginnings, there was another neighbor.

Looking about Fredericksburg, from its Kirches Verein to the old Nimitz Hotel, you can see the grip it has maintained upon old foundations. What you cannot see are the close-by foundations of another determined colony of settlers, the neighbors other than Comanche. Right beside this German town was a major effort of the Mormon faith to establish a community that could be New Zion in Texas.

Few in Fredericksburg today can take you to its ruins; they are that faint. The town was called Zodiac and once — in the mid-1800's — its founders felt it held all the promise of far west Salt Lake City.

History has been unaccountably silent about our Mormon neighbors in Texas. You may recall that the faith began in New York, near the village of Manchester in 1827. Those who believed that Joseph Smith had been led to great documentary proof of The Word, left on this continent, made a spiritual choice; the Church of the Latter Day Saints was born.

This choice, this birth of church would drive those early ones on many a desperate and often bloody pilgrimage west, then farther west: to Ohio, Missouri, Illinois, and finally to what was first called by them "Deseret," and later — as mutual forebearance prevailed — would become Utah and fringes of surrounding states.

In the wilderness pilgrimage, one group split away, believing that infant Texas might become New Zion, while the others toiled on for what was to be Utah. Each division fought for its goal, mile by mile: those west-bound finally walking behind handcarts. The Texas party, led by a tall, strong man, Lyman Wight, flat-boated the north Mississippi to Davenport, Iowa, and there, swapped boats and lumber for wagons and oxen. There was little room in the wagons for more than their goods; down over the Missouri, the Arkansas, and Canadian and Red, they struggled afoot.

Ten years after Alamo, they settled on the Colorado just above the frontier capital, Austin; a flood wrecked their mills. A year later, their scouts found land they could develop on the Pedernales, three miles east of struggling Fredericksburg.

For almost five years, the western site appeared a happy choice. There was peace with the Indian, for John Meusebach had fashioned a Comanche treaty that stood. Their Zodiac had two mills, a blacksmithy, a church, a community well and spring, and solid houses going up about a lake they had created for irrigation (even the industrious German could learn from them in this farm science). Their crops were increasingly abundant, as opposed to tales of extreme hardship in far west Deseret. This New Zion seemed ready to fulfill its promise.

True, Zodiac clashed with neighbor Fredericksburg, for neither Mormon nor German had learned flexibility on frontier; and, across America, there was a rising wave of anti-Mormonism that shortly would lead to U.S. invasion of Utah. Still, in Texas, the peace was kept and the communities grew on, side by side.

Then came a major flood, and the blessing of Zodiac's irrigation lake became the settlement's curse; the Pedernales poured down and everything went to the black, swirling waters. The Lyman Wight colony moved briefly near Burnet, then camped near Bandera, finally went on south to land now submerged by Medina Lake. There, their community effectually ended; most kept their faith, but the land absorbed them.

Close by the Pedernales east of Fredericksburg, I leaned against the Can't-Sag gate with Adolph Schmidtzinsky and looked across his land. He was in his leathery seventies, heavy-shouldered, and had eyes that took their time deciding about you. His grandfather came to Fredericksburg shortly before all this happened, and what is left of Zodiac lies just down from that gate we leaned against.

"Mormon Well's over beyond those liveoaks." He pointed across his field to another oak, tall and slick-dead and leaning on its roots. "Their church was there, too. Houses all around."

"There isn't much left," I said.

"Oh, you can find a 'dobe brick every now and then. Mill, everything else, washed away. You couldn't even find a grave now."

"Hard to figure that much flood." The Pedernales was summer-low.

"Not if you throw in a dam-busted lake. Not in a real rain." Adolph Schmidtzinsky made a gesture of finality. "We put up a monument. But it's right out in the middle of the field where the stock graze." He considered, looking at his land and what had been Zodiac, the Mormon dream for Texas. "There just isn't anything else."

So, when you reach for forgotten, lost Zodiac, you'll see only the Pedernales meadow where the Schmidtzinsky brothers graze sheep, and perhaps, far out in the field, a weathered stone.

However, it's worth your stop on the low concrete bridge over the river. Pull to the shoulder. See those shadows in the scrub up the stream bed?

They stand for what was to be Southwest's Salt Lake City.

"Wiped out," I had said to Adolph Schmidtzinsky, turning for my car.

"Not the people."

And he was right. I drove on to Kerrville. On the way through, I passed the Church of the Latter Day Saints.

1854

Gone With The Wends

Once upon a time, in what is now East Germany, between Dresden and Berlin, there was a tiny kingdom known as Lusatia. This little country reached its prime when Slavic tribes drove into the land of the Franks before the year 1000.

Charlemagne drove them out, leaving Lusatia an ethnic island: speaking the Slavic tongue of Wendish — not quite Polish or Bohemian — in a Teutonic sea.

All this is history as, one day not too distant, will be the Wends themselves. As a distinct nationality with a distinct language, they are disappearing by absorption in three areas of the world: Germany, to begin with; southern Australia, and one other land to which they emigrated for freedom of religion in the Lutheran faith.

This other land is Texas.

Specifically, the land is post oak and blackjack-timbered Lee County in Central Texas and its seat of government, Giddings. Near Giddings is almost-deserted Serbin, the first colony and wellspring of Wend culture in the state.

Of all the waves of immigrants which flooded Texas for three decades after 1836, none brought more deeply seated custom nor more indigenous folkways than did the quiet

283

Wends. You could mistake the industry of their farming for that of Germans to their south, or their often stern dress for that of Poles or Czechs, closer to the coast. It was the Wendish expression of life-style — to borrow a phrase from today — that remained unique.

To gauge it, I stopped at the Giddings *Star*, a friendly, folksy little paper. Albert Miertschin runs the composing room now, as he did when the *Star* had a sister journal, *Das Volksblatt*, which, in its German pages, carried inserts printed in the ornate Wendish characters. Mr. Miertschin is about the only American who can set his type in Wendish, and the *Star* is America's only paper with the type fonts to allow it done.

This quiet and studious newsman is not only a linguist (when he speaks Wendish, Giddings' Germans can't understand him, but La Grange Czechs can), but he is an historian. He traced the pilgrimage of the Wends from their twenty German cities to Galveston, then Houston and finally Rabbs Creek and Serbin, named for the old country. As was the case with most Europeans unready for the frontier, their first years were an ordeal of drought, starvation, illness, death and near despair.

Their spiritual leader, Johann Kilian, virtually a Wendish Moses, brought six hundred of them through to the erection of a parochial school and the mother church of all Texas Wends, St. Paul's Lutheran at Serbin. The church is there now, its cedars trimmed like box hedges in European fashion, and its cemetery monuments ornamented with porcelein miniatures. An early Wendish custom in this congregation was that its men occupied the balcony for worship; its women were seated below.

Many of their old world customs, the Wends brought here.

The two great holy days, Easter and Christmas, were celebrated for not one day but for three in succession. Recently this has relaxed to two.

Nor was any Wend wedding a hurried affair. First, all friends (which meant the entire colony and environs) were to be invited orally by bride and groom. The formal church wedding, once adjourned to the bride's home, became a three-day celebration, during which time neither bride nor groom could leave.

"But three days!" I protested to Mr. Miertschin. "That's rough on newlyweds."

"We're lucky if we hold them six hours now."

Worship modes were not all that came from Europe. The Wends practiced their form of frontier cure-alls, but these, too, were steeped in the dim past of their continental heritage. Consider some of them:

Carrying a black cloth cured cramps.

A man bitten by a dog literally took the hair of the dog that bit him. The hair was dissolved, after having been burned, in water.

Carrying a hazlenut filled with quicksilver prevented disease. So did burning herbs or cedar.

One curative that seldom failed of use was the "life awakener." This was a device that let fly a spring-driven array of needles to puncture the skin. The skin was then rubbed with oil that had been imported from Germany, and the treatment accommodated anything from mumps and pneumonia to insect bites and rheumatism.

Similarly careful was the Wend with his livestock. One treatment was to run around the ailing animal five or six times, praying on the dead run, then finishing with a stout jerk of the tail. Of course, you could bleed a horse, wind the bloody cloth around a stick and lodge it in a tree — particularly useful when the nature of the complaint was in doubt.

The Wend was less likely to take to such frontier science as treating rheumatism with hog lard and jimtown leaves or dropsy with vinegar, rusty nails and snakeroot than he was to stick with preventatives that had order and logic about them. For example, one knew he should face east feeding chickens, that he should circle a surly pig three times before putting down slop, and that he'd better retreat to the house and bar the door, should a whippoorwill begin calling.

Mr. Miertschin admitted that the Wends were intrigued and delighted by itinerant medicine peddlers and had not a moment's doubt that the pleasure was mutual.

285

I suppose all this is gone now, custom and language alike, and Mr. Miertschin suspected it's the same in Germany and Australia. Wends, like others, adapt to their adopted life style.

Here, where they have spread northwest to Copperas Cove and Vernon, southeast to Houston and Port Arthur, and heavily throughout Central Texas, the language and the style is Texan.

Yet theirs has been a distinct part of the seasoning that has given Texas its flavor.

1854

Angelus of Panna Maria

One recent Christmas Eve — nearly her thousandth as a nation — Poland heard the Angelus bells, the breadth of her bleak plains from Danzig to Cracow. Ringing from the Voice of America on Radio Free Europe, the bells were Texan.

At six of each morning or evening, and at noon, these bells have pealed Angelus a long time from a farm village south of San Antonio. They ring from a beautifully high-steepled old church in Panna Maria, just above Karnes City.

Wayside Panna Maria is where America's first Poles settled permanently, over a century ago. Beside the church is a neat school and buildings about, some rock stores and old, steep-roofed stone dwellings, and a checkerboard of good farms over the long sloping land.

By the church on the hill is a giant live oak, where the long ago settlers named their home for Virgin Mary and held first mass at midnight on Christmas Eve. This is one reason Panna Marians sent America's Christmas greetings in 1963.

The bells pealed in triples for the annunciation. Then Texans with names like Snoga, Pawelek, Manka and Djiuk and the rest sang old Polish hymns, and the scrubbed-shiny blonde youngsters sang some. To Europe's Poles, white-haired, blue-eyed Felix Mika (Polish pronounces every letter) talked about the Texas farms for which he mills feed, however the farmers want it mixed.

Mrs. Mika told that the village would begin the Christmas feast with the first star and hoped they still did this in the old country. In the name of Polish Americans everywhere, they wished the old land a happy Christmas. Then the bells played.

Any evening Angelus, the notes of those hillside bells take you a long way.

For Polish Texans, a pilgrimage in ordeal!

In 1854, Poland has been blotted from Europe's map for two generations, her people slaves to Russian and Prussian, her language officially erased. Turning their backs on Europe's endless war, more than a hundred families leave their homes, knowing this leaving is forever.

There is a new land called Texas, where a man can farm and be free.

Since it will be better than what they left, they face what they must. For nine weeks, eight hundred peasants literally cram one sailing vessel. They bury their dead at sea and again at Galveston, where yellow fever waits.

And still more burials over the two hundred mile trail inland, afoot! None who watch them know their language; they are a silent, toiling procession: the men in coarse jackets and peasant caps, the women in wooden shoes, stiff wool skirts and broad black felt hats.

How can the Texan pioneer, long toughened to frontier, recognize in these pilgrims the stamp of George Washington's freedom fighters — Pulaski and Kosciusko? How see a race capable of Copernicus and Curie, Chopin and Paderewski and Joseph Conrad? These are stumbling, mute foreigners who will never make it!

They reach this hill, earlier assigned their priest, in the howling cold dark of Christmas Eve. By torchlight is Panna Maria's first midnight mass: thanksgiving and prayer for survival. Their first shelters are simply holes — grass-lined, brush-topped, and sluiced to freezing muck in winter rain.

But slowly, mud-daubed picket huts go up and first crops are planted. To survive the wait for food to grow, Panna Marians must work for it, all the way from San Antonio north, to the already-established German settlements along the rivers east. Their language useless now, they work in silence. Scrubbing a floor for her family's bread, one girl collapses and dies without looking up or speaking.

But Panna Maria survives. Her second Christmas sees mass within a church and can give thanks for thin, first crops. Then the houses become rock and . . . over the years . . . the ordeal is ended. The Texan Pole has made good his name — *farmer*.

Felix Mika looked from the hill on the far, burgeoning fields and his brisk new mill below. It was not impossible, he said, for those who prayed and worked and stayed.

And the Poland for whom these Texas bells rang Angelus?

They heard. Felix Mika has answered a boxful of letters from every corner of Poland — the girl in Kalisz who will study her English so the twenty-eight Mika grandchildren can write her, the lady in Wrocław with the sick husband, the Gdansk student who wants American books.

"You can tell they have a very hard time," Felix Mika looked at the letters that do not say so precisely, but in classic script, ask everything about America. "Books. They want books! They will trade us books about Poland."

No, probably not Communist books. More likely Poland's history — a thousand years of struggle only to say this land is ours. The way he understands it, thirty million Poles must live today as one million Communists tell them to live.

For Poland's history is her geography — a level plain from East Germany to the sloping steppes of Russia. Since the very beginning, no boundary barriers to defend; so a crossroads for invasion. From the east, Mongol and Tatar; Bulgar and Turk from the south. From north, the Swede; from the west, French and German.

And now Russia.

Did Panna Maria's Texans feel strong ties to the old

country? About as I feel for the Scotland and Ireland of my forebears. Momentarily, I couldn't think of Scotland's capital.

Panna Maria's Angelus rang at sunset, and I left the hill with its graceful, high-vaulting church and the live oak where America's first Polish prayers went up to let them stay.

I did not talk much with Felix Mika about the old Polish legend. At some time near her thousandth year, it says, freedom shall come to her. Her thousandth was 1966. For the plains of the Vistula, maybe the Voice of America is as near as first freedom will come.

Anyway, there would be little I could tell Polish Texans about freedom. They know, first hand, what it costs.

And how about you and me?

1855

La Reunion — French Dallas

To most of us, ghost towns are eerie places, like pirate troves and curse-sealed mines, to be found by the lonely dune or the forgotten canyon. Yet there is one — and a great one, too — in the very western shadows of the Dallas skyline.

This is La Reunion, founded in 1855 by French aristocracy. It lies about three miles square, where the Fort Worth Turnpike takes off from Oak Cliff's chalky bluffs on the hard-trafficked north-south artery, Hampton Road.

Look for the great gray stack of the cement plant. Just behind it, up the cutaway bluff, was the downtown of this forgotten French Utopia-to-be; in many ways one of the most remarkable ghost towns of our land.

Its remarkability was various: it is a ghost within a city. More, its founders combined brains, wide talent, good

289

blood, courage, money, and painstaking planning. Most, even as ghost, it has succeeded in the city that swallows it.

La Reunion was far advanced for its day. The dwellings would be "dormitory" units (much like those dark brick Stevens Park Apartments on La Reunion land today). For economy, meals would be cafeteria style — pay as you could afford. Its store and its produce would operate on a stock-issue, profit-sharing basis. It would be governed by democratic assembly. Everybody — even women — would vote.

Its brainpower? It produced the great botanists, Julien Revershon and Jacob Boll, and the geologist, Emile Redmond, who discovered how to make cement of the lime cliffs. The Santerres, whose coat of arms goes back to the Fourth Century, were the farm experts. And there were the rugged ones, too, like Jean Le Gogue, who survived every battle of Napoleon's Old Guard. There were jewelers, tailors, blacksmiths. The Capys could teach music and the dance. There was a veterinarian. Monsieur Victor Considerant, who led the way, had served admirably in the good government days of the French Republic.

La Reunion, in its stone houses, was double the size of the little ragnot, buckskin village across the river — Dallas.

La Reunion's French came to Texas for just what their town's name proclaimed. M. Considerant, disenchanted with a cabinet which had sought a president for France, and got Napoleon III instead, saw to the purchase of three sections of land in the north of this new land of Texas. Here could be what his people had fought for: liberty, equality, fraternity!

As was the case with German, Polish and Bohemian emigrants escaping Europe's tyranny, there were terrible hardships between them and new home: they walked from Galveston.

But the town, which an advance guard had prepared, seemed promising. There was a central store, the apartment units, a small factory for soap and candles, the pens

290

for stock and private land for each family. The profits for everybody's effort would be pooled, then divided.

What felled La Reunion was the bleak whim of weather. Impossible, endless scorch of drought. Winters with Trinity frozen solid. Nothing alive in their fields except clouds of grasshoppers.

The buckskin men across the river had seen this before on other frontiers; these French had not. La Reunion ceased to exist as a dream, then to function as a town. Its only capital, land, was sold to those crazy enough to face the ordeal.

One was the family of Francois Santerre. Son Paul is La Reunion's last man, and now lives near where he was born, eighty-two years ago. He is a chunky, bald John Nance Garner without the owlish eyebrows and with Gallic charm. He lives in a simple white cottage on three-plus acres he could sell for six figures. He knows only friends and the determination to live out his life on the land the Santerres bought when La Reunion was a town and, from his hill, it was hard to see the settlement across the river — the one they called Dallas.

He and I drove the boundaries of his old town. They are, roughly, Adams to the south, Hampton and Westmoreland, east and west, and the Trinity River, north. Inside the bounds of forgotten La Reunion is a multimillion of today's Dallas dollars.

We swung into Adams, with its high-signed supermarkets and smaller shops and cars in four streams. He pointed at the theater. "My daddy shot thirty prairie chicken there! Oh, we could sell rabbits, three dollars a dozen and five cents each for doves, and a quarter for plover. You. strung them six to the string, across your shoulders."

We threaded the traffic surge across into Plymouth Road. On the right, Coombs Creek slashed woodland rock. On the left, luxury apartments rose in tiers with lazy swimming pools and many cars, all big. Paul Santerre stopped me excitedly.

"Right here was Mr. Rhode's apple orchard! He caught me up the tree once. He pretended not to see me, but he said very loud he was afraid he would have to shoot the next boy after his apples. I got the biggest apple on the tree."

Across from the labyrinth of apartments and the big houses beyond, Paul Santerre had hauled water, cold and clear, in barrels on a sled. He remembered how you just turned over rocks and took fat catfish in your wire net.

We drove north to La Reunion's cemetery, close by Dallas Housing Authority's massive project in the Trinity bottoms. Here are the graves of the first Santerres, the Revershons, Redmonds, even old soldier Le Gogue. For a third generation now, a Santerre has inherited the trust of its care.

He liked the bluebell flowers but he was worried over the rain-sprung grass. It would take cutting again soon. But at least the city had fenced it and now the hoodlums wouldn't come in and push over the old stones of his family and their neighbors. He had come back many times to labor the stones back in place, using a chain hoist; then once, with his rifle, he caught the hoodlums there, and they ran straight into the police car, watching them. Then the city put up the fence.

"This is really all that's left." His old hands had trouble locking the cemetery gate. "You see how it has grown up; there is little La Reunion left at all."

I like and respect guardian Paul Santerre, but I disagree. The old rock houses are jumbles, right enough; but La Reunion's French dream-hunters left their stamp on the city. It is the quality and culture which every Texan knows is a living thing in Dallas.

Ghost town? No question. But its ghosts have been good to our northern metropolis.

Bagdad on the Rio Grande

Below, the frothy beach ran empty; and up the sand shelves where Rio Grande steals to sea, the blowing dunes circled about. And nothing toward Matamoros and Brownsville, inland over the horizon. All empty, this Mexico and Texas, just across!

"And all this," I said to the fisherman, "was Bagdad?"

"Yes, all," said chunky, dark-eyed Noe Alanis, hitching his khakis and gesturing far. "And more, beyond. Large! Very rich!" He turned to his nets, hung to the wind.

Remote indeed is this river mouth that once saw great fleets, because today — fifteen miles above — ships stand in under South Padre's beach resorts, Port Isabel's old light, and make the new Laguna cut to Brownsville's docks. No longer come the sails and sidewheelers to Rio Grande's mouth; no longer to Bagdad, the once great port. This strange ghost is literally buried here by the sea.

A century ago, this emptiness was brawling, war-boom gateway for every seagoing nation — fast-dealing, blockade-running, smuggling, Babel-tongued, lusting, rich and rioutous, dirty and bandit-ridden Bagdad — a kind of hell-roaring neutral ground for four contending armies, hard-eyed traders, and sailors: English to French and Portugee, and Yankee to Kanuck.

What they left behind is still largely mired in river marsh and sand; for in Mexico, you do not dig. Yet you can catch glimpses of the extraordinary city that was, for wind and wave keeps turning it . . . and its treasure.

Old Mexican story claims a late-1700 seashore playground here, frequented by wealthy Spaniards of upriver

293

Reynosa, Mier and Camargo. Bagdad's only known painting, in Matamoros' handsome Hotel Ritz, lends credence; and outcropping the river banks are ancient brick foundations. That spa, says legend, plunged to sea in some dread, forgotten hurricane.

When Zachary Taylor's troops marched down in 1846, they found only a few Mexican jacales at the mouth. Army's tent city came and went, leaving little more than a cross-river shack cluster — Clarksville, Texas.

But now thunders American Civil War; Confederate cotton is blockaded everywhere except Texas' quarter-million bales each year: hauled across to Mexico, shipped out through Bagdad, in exchange for whatever sinews — guns to gold — that Europe will swap. Confederate sea captain, Raphael Semmes, will count over a hundred sail, riding anchor, lighters plying day and night for the cotton-piled beach. If Blue holds a Texas beachhead, above at Port Isabel, Gray holds the river, at whatever chosen crossing, for cotton.

And now into this moves France. With America deathlocked, Napoleon III revives overseas empire dreams, pours into Mexico forty thousand red-pantalooned Zouaves — French, Austrian, Belgian — to enthrone Emperor Maximilian against the sombreroed, sometimes barefoot and always furious legions of Benito Juarez.

Best Mexican eastern port, rich-booming Bagdad, is melting pot for it all.

Walking, scuffing the dunes, you can envision the Bagdad, population thirty thousand, that was known to an earnest Belgian priest, Father Pariscot. Dismayed, he walked those narrow streets and knew them for "a whirlpool of money, pleasures and sin."

Here was teamster cursing oxen, mule or burro in every tongue. Here, ten dollars a day for common labor and up to forty, if you owned a boat. Here was sailor, soldier, peddler, gambler, trader, bandit, patriot, lady and woman.

Here, ten stages a day, up the river road for Matamoros — jamful, a dollar a mile and bandits, your problem. Here was cotton, all up the banks and down the beach. Ironically, here were New Orleans men to sell; New Englanders to buy. And here, inevitably, was champagne in French glass, whiskey in gallon crocks; here was faro, monte, women, and more often than not, gunfire.

The priest heard that gunfire now: Juaristas, hitting the Maximilianos, struck in turn by a U.S. Federal detachment, which was, itself, attacked by Confederates from across the river. Utter confusion, then quiet, with whatever military in command of Bagdad's garrison. Father Pariscot knew what really commanded Bagdad was not guns, but dollars. For that city that was a forest of seaborne masts, that town of every tongue, that trading post built on war, he saw no good end.

It came with war's finish. The Gray was gone, and his cotton. Then the French. But, most decisively, was gone the trade. War-rich Bagdad was at a standstill.

Before it could wither, hurricane struck. In October, 1867, the sea and sand buried it.

It is not easy to reach the river mouth where Bagdad now lies buried; there are no direct bridges. You drive through Matamoros, out to La Playa — Washington Beach. From there, it is ten miles up dune and scudding shore that can bog you with the running tide. I went up with Mrs. Ila Loetscher, who explores every direction from her beach home on South Padre and who, incredibly, is one of the very few South Texans who even know the existence of this once great port. Most believe it legend.

We took her beach buggy and skimmed the raw, hummocked sand. Finally, we stopped close by the river mouth at the three small houses of Noe Alanis and his friends, who take pompano, *truchas* and *colorados* from the sea. Shortly, Noe showed me the treasures of his buried city.

To your imagination, I'll leave the dollar value of what he has found, his fifteen years-plus on that lonely beach. You can get a notion, however, stopping in Los Fresnos with longshoreman Galen Massey, a genial, inquisitive man who has probed the Rio Grande mouth (Texas side, of course) about as long. Massey has a wall of rarest hand-turned bottles and every oddment from an ancient anchor to wrought brass. The gold and silver that ran like the river when Bagdad boomed? I never ask a treasure hunter to show me his real strike.

However, what Noe Alanis prizes most, he told me.

"The sea, *hombre*, the sky, the air . . . the fishing. Man, who needs more?"

"You don't miss the city?" I asked.

"I have one!" Noe spread his arms wide.

1875

Indianola Turned Atlantis

In addition to a splended straight beach, almost-forgotten and tragic Indianola offers the wayfarer some strange and varied contemplation.

Below Victoria and Port Lavaca, on Matagorda Bay's deep-watered coast, you look on the solitude, northwest from old Powderhorn Point, and wonder how, in all our coastline, nature could have selected this one spot to promise so much and then shatter so completely.

For here lived and died what was to have been one of America's greatest ports and, at her sophisticated peak — the fall of 1875 — the recognized "Queen City of the West." Instead, she became Atlantis, hurled into the sea.

Powderhorn, where the bay reaches like its name behind the shell beach — almost islanding it — is where Indianola began, where they are rebuilding today, and where you can puzzle over many things: the irony of Indianola's past and the possibilities of her future.

History leaves no question on nature's bounty with Matagorda Bay. So sheltered and vast it was, La Salle read it for the Mississippi's great mouth. By Texas Independence, it was considered the finest harbor between Florida's tip and Panama. Here landed the great German immigration of the 1840's.

On the point here grew up Prince Solms-Braunfels tent city, first Carlshaven, then Powderhorn, and finally Indianola that grew swiftly, handsomely, "permanently" in oystershell concrete as America's sea-gate west. What started as Runge's tent bank handled land sales at four thousand dollars a city lot, at a time when Texas population numbered but fifty thousand.

In thirty years, Indianola overcame disasters that would have destroyed a lesser city: four terrible plagues of cholera and yellow fever. Federal bombardment from sea, occupation, recapture. Indianolans rode out the hurricane of 1866, fought off the great fire of '67.

She had grown lustily. She had brought ashore Jeff Davis' U.S. Second Cavalry Camel Corps. She had harbored brigs and schooners. Now, to her half-mile T-headed piers came the slick sidewheelers. Indianola marched her new railroad straight out the pier to meet them. The shipping giants, Morgan and Vanderbilt, fought for her cargo. What could stop her?

She had grown in sophistication. Along with sixteen muleteam freighters and ox-tandemed wagons, came Austrian physicians, English engineers, German craftsmen, Irish merchants, French musicians, New Zealand meat packers. All recorded by Philadelphia lawyers, reported by a New York editor and observed by Americans from everywhere.

She had built well. Up from the point — Huck's Lumber Yard, the stretch of one and two story buildings to the square. There, the customs house, the handsome, three story Cassimire Hotel, the surrounding thriving business houses, and beyond, the new courthouse, homes and churches and the magnificient beach and lake drive.

That was the city, the hot, glassy September morning when, on the square, the Indianola *Bulletin's* printer locked his forms and in the saloon close by, the barkeep cleaned up and checked his imported stock.

Now you can locate these two places. Recently, they uncovered the rusted old type slugs that once printed the *Bulletin* and, nearby, row on row of antique bottles —

just as they had stood in their cases when entombed September 17, 1875.

Permit yourself random conjecture. Little things, say like . . . who was at the bar for Indianola's last drink? How long did that newsman wait to go to press?

How long, for the story he saw coming? Until the wind grew to a solid thing with an animal cry? Until the ocean was an eight-foot torrent pouring far inland? Until houses melted, exploded, collapsed; and boats and wagons were hurled; and babies and cattle crushed under.

He must have thought, the way you do, "Can it really be happening?" and then, "Can I make it?" Then he tried.

Last man at the bar? Was it the awful moment in the night when the wind reversed and threw the tidal wave back to sea? Could he have seen the locomotive plucked like a toy and flung into the bay; then his own walls, caving in?

Or was it next morning when what had been Indianola, living and dead, was a raft of wreckage seventeen miles long? Did somebody stumbling, looking for his kids, find his brother, try to lift his head and pour whiskey between his lips?

Or did somebody look back at what had promised so much, take a last bitter drink and walk away from the city's three hundred dead?

Jim Carter, veteran Victoria newsman who knows the Indianola story as do few, believes that neither this nor the hurricane and fire eleven years later necessarily finished Indianola. No more than did Carla, which smashed a budding resort.

I think Jim secretly believes Texas resortmen are overlooking perhaps one of the state's most singular opportunities. Rebuild the square of the sea's greatest ghost city. Return a modernized elegance of old Cassimire House. Restore pleasure-excursioning sidewheeler *Belle of the Bay*. Bring back an old drug store, saloon, livery stable for moonlight hansom cab beach rides. Stock the old fashioned Emporium. Republish the old Indianola *Bulletin*.

And surround the whole with a resort that takes advantage of the fine beach, the moderate surf and, farther out, the good fishing.

Another hurricane?

Has that stopped Corpus Christi, Houston, Galveston or, even more afield, Miami?

You take it from there. Perhaps the most intriguing conjecture on all of Indianola is what might yet be her future.

1880

Tascosa's Seven from Boot Hill

Of old Tascosa, northwest of Amarillo, nothing really is left except Boot Hill. Maybe that's the way it should be.

It seems ironically proper that the ghost of Texas' deadliest guntown should leave behind no more than this somber hillock by the cottonwoods of the Canadian, where they laid only the ones who died with their boots on. In all the raw west there were few real boot hills; and this was one.

To ponder Tascosa's restless ones who stayed behind, go up at night. The hill is low and bald by day, but by dark it listens to the big whispering trees below; and the violent little town once more is down there. In the wind and dim heat lightning from the west, you can almost see it.

You can see the twenty-seven markers inside the barbed wire plot on top. The first row, just over the stile, were the men who paid for the Hill.

The town you look down on?

There was always a crossing here, and there had been dim, coppery people first, and later the great plains Indians and the Comancheros who traded and herded over from New Mexico. There was a sprawl of adobes — Plaza Atascosa, for the bogging sands—when the buffalo hunters roared down. Then came the cowboy's cattle, and the village grew and boomed and became "Ol' Tascosy"—in the 1880's, prodigal queen of the Panhandle.

Amarillo newsman-historian John McCarty recollected she reached nearly eight blocks square—a kind of general store-warehouse-stable-hotel-saloon spread that a few TV westerns have captured. Every few paces down Main, either way from Dodge trailend at Spring Street, a palace like Equity or Captain Jinks' would kill your thirst and deal you cards, women or trouble.

There were gambler gunmen like the Catfish Kid and girls of a special breed: Rockin' Chair Emma and Boxcar Jane, Slippery Sue and Midnight Rose. It took a real belt of red-eye to face up to a lady like Gizzard Lip.

There would come the steady law and order builders of the Goodnight-Littlefield brand, but first came the deadly ones. Billy the Kid, with his curly hair and boy-quick, bucktoothed grin. Here, Bat Masterson saw Billy lose a draw-shoot match for fun. Tascosa's district attorney won it — brilliant, volatile Temple Houston, old Sam's son.

Others saw Billy driven by cold-eyed Panhandle lawmen, who chased him west to New Mexico and, with lanky Pat Garrett, killed him there. For a time, Garrett hammered down outlawry and rustling and Tascosa breathed easier.

But as always with the west, Garrett moved on and the wars came back. Between big ranch and little, between barbed wire and open range, between men angry over women, or a slight or a big thirst. With it all, came Boot Hill and the strange roads that led to it.

Those seven markers on the Hill with you? So much alike under the dirt, why use the names? Why think about their ever having been boys?

Take Grave One, there by the wire on your right. He rode in, a cowpoke, got him a wife and, to stay near her, ran a saloon. His showdown came from talk about her.

It was a chest-to-chest gun-snatch from a table top; and the last thing he knew was he was too slow! *Too slow!*

Grave Two was no easygoing waddy. He was a whipcord-tough, cat-fast trail boss with a big thirst and the recklessness it gave him. Twice when they tried to take his guns, he dared them, laughing, scorning. The third time, he dared a shotgun in his face. He vaulted his saddle and, rearing, almost cleared his draw; but he caught two barrels of buckshot.

Grave Three? Killed while he slept. Relatives left his grave "unknown," but in Boot Hill's row behind is the barkeeper his brother picked for revenge. Those other graves — the lesser ones by the Hill's grim standards—sheltered others, like the Dutchman, gunned at one-foot range, and paradoxically, the man who died, falling from his horse, and still others who must have belonged there but are forgotten now.

Right in front of the stile, Graves Four, Five and Six —and the one yonder by the far-left wire strand—these, Boot Hill remembers best. They came in a dark night shoot-out that, for close-quarters desperation, matched the O.K.Corral.

In the time it takes you to read it and think, Grave Four stepped into a shadowy saloon porch ambush, was blasted off it and, dying in the dirt, was finished with a Winchester rammed against his neck. Grave Five was his friend and so was Grave Six, and both came running, furious and fearing, through the night.

They riddled two men at the saloon's back door, hammering them back inside. Grave Five charged the door, flung it open, and took a rifle blast in the face.

Grave Six, crouched at the building's corner, shot a man through the forehead in a dark doorway opposite and died in his own gunflash, rifled through the chest. Of the perhaps ten who fought blind in a dark little bigger than your living room, two were desperately wounded and four dead. With him, Grave Six took the one yonder by the far left wire strand—a bystander...maybe.

Up there in the night, you wonder briefly what they

fought for. But that's a question nobody ever answers at a boot hill—by whatever name.

When you go down and daylight comes later across the High Plains, Tascosa is gone, her two decades done. The railroad passed her and barbed wire ended her open range.

Down in the cottonwoods where the violent town stood, a boy's ranch today makes first rate citizens of youngsters who, in those days the Hill remembers, might have tried their luck with Billy the Kid.

But don't see the ranch to feel Old Tascosa. There is no bridge between the two—a good thing.

Nothing really is left except Boot Hill. That's the way it should be, all right.

1882

Jefferson Ladies and Jay Gould

The Dallas couple had come from the chandeliered grand ballroom and now stood looking out on the antique brick patio, fountained and trumpet-vined. I crossed the lobby to the old registers where U. S. Grant and Rutherford Hayes and John Jacob Astor had once signed into the Excelsior House.

"There's Jay Gould's signature," said Mrs. Dan Lester, studying it like an annoyed Barbara Stanwyck. "And his curse."

At the bottom of the page dated January 2, 1882 — in the arrogant Spencerian of America's most feared and envied robber barron — "End of Jefferson, Texas."

Presently she took me on the tour of this bayou-forested, northeast Texas river town that was supposed to have been our Memphis-New Orleans combined.

A must for any Texas wayfarer worthy of his curiosity is a tour with the soft-spoken ladies of Jefferson. You see most of the city's historically-medallioned homes and buildings — the most fascinating bit of Old South in our state. Through their eyes you see her almost as she stood

302

— at thirty-five thousand, challenging for Texas' biggest city — the day Gould damned her!

You also see how Jefferson's redoubtable ladies beat Jay Gould's curse.

Under her iron-red, pine plumed hills, Jefferson began with the republic in 1836. From the days of Indian legend, a giant log jam had backed Red River's waters across dark Caddo Lake. Here would be upper port to outfit the drive west for villages they talked about as Dallas and Fort Worth, and for lands even beyond.

War between the States peaked Jefferson's boom in block on block of permanent three and four-story brick, with packeries, mills, foundries, splendid hotels and, most of all, great, gracious homes.

This was a far-sighted city, too: manufacturing unheard-of's like artificial ice and gas; and a busy one, her wharves mooring the side-wheelers up from New Orleans and her red roads west, six miles deep in cotton wagons.

She was crinoline and frock coat in the gas-lamped streets, with the surreys and hansoms out for Queen Mab's Ball, already rivaling Mardi Gras. She was elegance in the cherrywood, tiger mahogany and Italian marble of Excelsior and Haywood Houses. If you came to Texas, you came to Jefferson.

Jay Gould came, the man who could juggle American currency and topple European thrones. Nobody said "no" to Jay Gould, and he told Jefferson he wanted his Texas and Pacific tracks smack through the middle of an elegance anchored solidly on river shipping. Under the pressed metal ceilings of Excelsior's grand ballroom, they told Jay Gould "no."

"Jefferson, " snapped the slight, weedy man with the terrible eyes, "pronounces her town's doom. I will build around her, grass will grow in her streets and bats dwell in her vacant houses."

Circling, the railroad drove west. The following year, U. S. engineers noncommittally blew the log dam below Caddo, and Jefferson's port sluiced out to sea.

The wharves rotted, the walls sagged and fell with the years, and the great, empty-eyed houses watched the forest creep back and the red dust settle. A quarter century ago, Gould's curse was all but fulfilled. Except for one thing.

The thing about a Southern lady is she can attain her ends by looking helpless as a kitten or working like a Trojan on a winning streak — or both — which the redoubtable ladies of Jefferson did, to the hilt.

In a do-it-yourself restoration equalled only by San Antonio's decades-ago saving of the Alamo, Jefferson's Jessie Allen Wise Garden Club borrowed twenty-five thousand dollars, bought the about-to-close Exchange House and dived into the business of saving their city by running part of it. Did they want federal aid to make a Williamsburg? No thanks; they lived here.

Literally on hands and knees, they scraped back to white marble, scrubbed to raw bronze and French gilt, sanded off cracked paint and hand-finished the four-posters, armoirs, bird-cage tables, re-polished Sevres crystal and French beveled pier glass — the pieces brought up by riverboat in the halcyon days.

Twenty years ago, they began to show their houses. Recently at the club's annual spring pilgrimage, the Dan Lesters showed their *Guarding Oaks* — one of our most beautiful homes — to twenty-three hundred visitors one Sunday afternoon. So many came, Dan Lester introduced himself to his sister from Shreveport.

Yes, it's working. The Jefferson ladies have gone to everyday tours now, and their jewel box, white brick Excelsior is one of the state's best traveling addresses, at surprisingly modest cost. . .but make your reservations in advance.

Even if you're as intimidated by antiques as I, you will find an unexpected thrill in discovering, in Jefferson, the era when we designed our homes instead of our automobiles.

There is the classic Greek simplicity of *The Manse*, Jefferson's oldest — from 1839; and across, the stately, widow's walked *House of the Seasons*, with its magnificent inner dome. There is the proper brick Presbyterian Church and the Methodist steeple that hung the silver bell. There is shadowy *Haywood House* with its secret tunnel, the vine-wrapped old Masonic Lodge, the splendid French Colonial Freeman Plantation, and the dozens of others whose names — like *Falling Leaves, Catalpa Villa* and *The Magnolias* — suggest themselves. You see these by arrangement at the Excelsior.

Along the bayou are the old brick buildings and back in the press of the forest, the faint lines of forgotten streets and markers, the old brick furnaces and block-long foundations of Jefferson's limitless industrial future — before Jay Gould.

More than forty homes and buildings carry the Texas historic medallion — more than any other city. They could very nearly put a medallion on all of Jefferson. They should. The soft-spoken, redoubtable ladies rate it.

Let them show you my favorite view.

Directly across from the Excelsior, where you can look down from the upper grill-work, the ladies have restored what they found abandoned on a weed-laced East Texas siding.

It is *Atalanta* — the sumptuous private railroad car of George Jay Gould.

Toughest Town on Earth

Half way between Corpus Christi and San Antonio is the county named for Sam Houston's intrepid scout, Captain Henry Karnes. This pleasant land, gently valleying the San Antonio, is notable for its black waxy farms, its peanut-growing loams, its flax, its uranium flurry of 1955, and its steady oil play of today.

And, to my notion, for a strange-storied piece of country eight miles northeast of Karnes City, where the San Antonio makes a great bend just below its juncture with the Cibolo. This wooded valley-head held a mission fort, dating back to the Eighteenth Century. It bore and saw die Spanish ranchos and a Mexican trail-crossing village.

Finally, it produced a town that boomed so rapidly it promised to rank among the state's largest. This was the self-proclaimed "toughest town on earth", and it achieved a distinction afforded no other. The frontier's grisliest kind of duel wore its name.

And this town, at its lusty, hell-roaring prime, was killed by one unbending man because his son met death there.

Almost killed at least. Abraham Guerrerro runs a service station where the maps show "Helena". He can show you the remnant, in the mesquite off to the east.

There are ruins near Helena where the Spanish established a way camp in 1735, and, in 1771, a small outpost, Arroyo del Cibolo. Comanche attacks drove them out in two years. Until 1800, a succession of Spanish incursions with garrison, chapel and rancho forts was met by attack and massacre.

But by 1830, a vestige had clung — a tiny village, Alamita, where the long Chihuahua Trail intersected the San Antonio-Goliad-Indianola cart road. Alamita's huts sheltered Jim Bonham for a few hour's snatched sleep on each of his two reckless rides for Fannin at Goliad.

Twenty years later, a pioneer San Antonian, Thomas Ruckman, saw the future for this great crossroads of Texas — a freighting and trade metropolis. Streets, blocks, alleys were laid out. The town was named for Helen Owings, the wife of Ruckman's partner. Nearby Alamita shriveled and died; Helena mushroomed.

And with Helena's prodigal growth came the naked edge of frontier existence, whetted by the smouldering struggle between Mexican and Gringo and honed fine by the running fight between freighters lumbering from coast inland and back and the Chihuahua rigs over the looping trail from Mexico's mine-rich sierra.

Helena became number one truck-stop, jut-jawed and chip-shouldered, wide open with sky the limit for living, dying or envisioning. San Antonio? Too settled! Helena was booming!

Its board-fronted narrow streets were jammed with freighters, and long columns of dust marched to town from four entering roads. There were four saloons, a cantina, beanery, two hotels, and all the rest, including four lawyers to argue trouble, and two doctors to bury it.

These latter were busy. Law already was on your hip or in your knife. For litigants, where wrong was not at once sufficiently clear for the plaza's hanging tree, an innovation in trial-by-combat was devised. This was the Helena Duel.

The duelists were stripped, their left wrists lashed with buckskin. Each had a Helena knife, bladed about as long and sharp as your razor: too short to reach a vital organ. It let the whirling, howling fight run until the loser bled to death; and each drew crowds and betting, for with a well-matched pair, the outcome was interestingly delayed.

By the time Helena's impressive two story court house was built, law was more settled: just hangings to watch now, but often several at a time from the mesquites outside the county seat of law. By nightfall they were generally cut down; court had to be cleared. You went up the long steps to the second floor courtroom for Helena's dances.

By the 1880's, the city had a college, two newspapers and the launch pad for the great trail drives. So the railroad was coming? Through Helena, then; her three thousand popuation was only her beginning!

Then it was that a stern and powerful man changed history. He was Colonel William G. Butler, as direct and as pliable as a ramrod; and his lands were empire, south and west. With his sons, the Butlers made a clan that rode hard and knew how to use their guns.

At four in the afternoon, December 26, 1884, there was the not unusual gunplay in Helena. But among the dead was Colonel Butler's son, Emmett; and the shots which felled him had come from a saloon crowd. That was Friday.

Twenty-year-old Emmett was buried on Sunday. On Monday, Colonel Butler landed in Helena with twenty-five men. The streets were empty; the Friday crowd had left town.

The tall man rode his horse up and down Helena's main street, brandishing his rifle, shouting at the town to produce the killers. Then, tell him who! Where were they? No answer.

"All right!" Butler cried out, wheeling his horse. "Then I'll kill the town that killed my son!"

And kill it, he did. The railroad was nearing his land now. Immediately he gave all right of way across the vast ranch with but one stipulation. The road would go nowhere near Helena!

With the rails came quick growth to Karnes City and Kenedy, well on the other side of the San Antonio River. Helena tottered.

Shortly thereafter, a county election moved the seat of government to the railroad town, Karnes City. Helena's court house looked on, empty-eyed, as its town died.

Well. . .almost. The remnant Abraham Guerrerro can show you, just off your highway in the mesquite, is the grim, ghost-like Helena court house. Nearby had been the duels, hangings, shoot-outs, dances — all of Helena's prime.

The street Colonel Butler rode when he laid his curse? It's creeping back to the cactus and scrub that were there when the Spanish came looking for a fort.

1886—1922

The Mausoleum of Thurber

They say you cannot see ghost towns but must feel them; and if this is true, then each of us may come upon forgotten Thurber by a different path. Mine led me to the strange and tragic tomb of its founder and his family.

Half way between Fort Worth and Abilene, where the roll of country breaks to big crouching hills, quick-passing signs alert you that just ahead is the spectre of a once-promising industrial city of almost ten thousand.

A mile beyond are a few weathered red brick buildings and a tall brick smoke-stack. The two story fronting the highway is a combination cafe and service station — Thurber's only business activities today.

Perhaps you can visit in the cafe or with E. W. Dunn in the station and get the feel of the Thurber that lived crudely and flamboyantly and elegantly by turns. Or you may see only the neatly-kept, though abandoned property of the Texas and Pacific Coal and Oil Company, which owns the hundred million tons of bituminous coal a few hundred feet beneath you. Thurber was the coal capital of Texas.

Perhaps you'll poke deeper: at the cut-away hill and the ruins of its great brick plant, or at the dark pocks on hillsides where the shafts probed to a peak of three thousand tons daily in 1919.

309

You can drive up New York Hill and climb the ruins of handsome brick steps that once mounted to brick mansions. Here, and along rutted and overgrown Silk Stocking Road, a World War I clothing drive netted four dozen mink coats, while over in the shafts, sweating miners fed their mules bananas to keep them going, and down in the saloon, gamblers practiced dealing in front of mirrors. All about are brick foundations and forgotten roadways and out beyond are scars which earlier miners' shacks left.

Perhaps you can feel Thurber even better, come July 4, when some of the old timers hold their annual reunion and swap tale and legend.

Or, as I did, you may search out the tomb of William W. Johnson, a few miles north. Johnson found the coal that gave birth to Thurber.

It was in the early 1880's when the Michigan man moved to nearby Strawn and studied the surrounding hills. His first shaft hit big and shortly he sold out to Texas and Pacific.

In came miners from across the world: Italians, with their round, outside bake ovens and wine cellars; Poles with choppy accents and bounding dances; silent Welshmen, volatile Mexicans, stolid Chinese. . .Slavs, Bohemians, Germans, English. . .a racial potpourri such as Texas had never seen.

Also came labor troubles, violence, Rangers, and quiet, in cycles. One strike cost more than a hundred thousand working days but won labor's point: recognition of union and establishment of a man-sized saloon in the company town. The Snake had a horseshoe bar big enough for hundreds at a time; and Thurber was the first totally union town in the nation.

Fortune had only begun. Thurber clays made excellent brick, brought a giant plant and a thousand new workers. Austin's Congress Avenue was paved with that brick; Galveston's seawall buttressed with them. The city boomed.

And matured. She had an opera house, a library, schools; of course, a railroad. Before 1920, she was five times the size of a couple of villages west, Odessa and Midland, combined.

Then a sudden chill! Thurber's locomotives — the ones hauling her coal — had switched to oil. But fortune wasn't through, it seemed. The big McClesky blew in at Ranger, ten miles west. What matter if the miners moved away? Thurber would follow oil now. And literally, she did, as the play moved farther west and north.

What had seemed a blessing was really the beginning of the end. T. & P. moved to Fort Worth. Thurber? She didn't die; she moved away, brick by brick.

And what of the Michigan man whose discovery had brought Thurber to life? It made him wealthy, of course, but there was to be a macabre parallel between his town and his life. For the very year his shaft struck big enough to promise a town — 1885 — that year, he and his wife Anna watched their three-year-old daughter, sunny, bubbling Marian, die.

Distraught, the mother rebelled at burial. A little "house" was built for the child. Embalmed and marble-like she lay for a time while her mother dressed and redressed her daily. When the coffin was closed, it remained in Marian's "house."

Two years later, a son, William Harvey, took away some of the pain. It came crushing back when death took him at age seven. It may have been then that the Johnsons made their incredible decision. The boy joined his sister in the "house".

A decade passed and the childless Johnsons retired to the solitude of their ranch a few miles northeast. A new "house" with windows was built and stands today, Another decade passed and the father died.

His will was simple. He would join his children and wait for wife and mother. On June 22, 1922 — thirty-seven years after little Marian had begun her vigil — Anna F. Johnson joined her family, and the last provisions of the will were carried out.

The four caskets were placed inside a massive, windowless mausoleum of native stone, high on a point overlooking the Johnson ranch, high enough to look toward the Thurber hills. Then the entrance way was sealed forever, as man counts time.

Thirty-seven years from Marian to reunion. The same thirty-seven years since Thurber's birth.

The practical life span of this city. For it was 1922, the year of Anna Johnson's death, that T. & P. left left Thurber for Fort Worth headquarters.

It would take time to show — another decade — but Thurber had joined its founder.

1891

Death of an Irontown

Among all our ghosts — from rowdy Thurber to lonely Terlingua — none is more poignant than the ruins that dwell the high pine and red hill shade, close by drowsy Rusk in East Texas.

This is New Birmingham, known or seen by almost no Texans today, but once queen city of the great East Texas iron rush of the early 1890's.

Some will say — and with reason — that she is not dead at all, but waiting. That, as with Lone Star Steel just north, the toolmaker's metal will come increasingly from the iron red earth of Cherokee County, below Jacksonville and Palestine. A few old timers will say the sad thing about New Birmingham was the way she boomed and busted — from forest to city's promise and back to wilderness again — all in a five year flash.

But why singular, this ghost? In strange fashion, her death came — by accident — from the Panhandle's high plains. The man who felled her was a native son of her own rolling hills. And he did it, almost unaware, helping Texas grow.

In the splendid woodlands south of Rusk, you can find her faintly traced today: from the maw of her iron foundry and her street shadows to the foundations that once were among the most magnificent of the Southwest's hotels.

312

On Texas maps, New Birmingham appeared quietly enough at first. In the late 1880's, an Alabama sewing machine salesman, A. B. Blevins, drives his hack south from old Rusk and sees the iron ore crust in Cherokee's red hills. He knows of the earlier, small Confederate foundries here and north near Jefferson. The state of Texas, fighting poverty, poorboys one herself, nearby.

What if real capital came in? Can he reach the proper ears?

Blevins knows his Genesis: ever since Cain's son Tubal fired his forges east of Eden, man's ears have heard the anvil. Nothing tops the lure of cities built on iron. Blevins figures he will be heard and, to a degree across America, he is.

By early 1891, the New Birmingham *Times*, handsomely housed in brick, will quote to the world its city's startling prospectus:

"On November 12, 1888. . .not a single house. . .entirely in the woods. Today. . .nearly four hundred buildings completed. . .lighted with electricity. . .streets graded and lighted. . .brick business buildings and school. . .a street railway. . .the new Tassie Belle (for Blevins' wife) and nearby Star and Crescent, puddling fifty thousand tons of pig iron annually. . ."

And the magnificent Southern Hotel — this new city's crown jewel! Some few are bigger in Atlantic City, on which hostelries, the hundred-room, four-story Southern is modeled — but none, more elegant. Dinner is full dress to string ensemble; the soirees, sheer beauty. The bricklaid walkways wind the magnolias down to mineral spas. Grover Cleveland and the ubiquitous Jay Gould, more than once, have registered.

There are titled British names on the registry, too: Victorian peerage who, for the first time see England's industrial might challenged by a United States that now fights for leadership in iron and steel.

As heavy as English investment in the new lands of the Texas Panhandle, is English interest in Texas iron — specifically, the New Birmingham Iron and Land Company's twenty thousand acres. British chemists and geologists like what they've seen.

What have they seen? True, nearly five million dollars already invested. Yet nothing compared with the U. S. Steel colossus that still declines to look south and has the power that shortly will select eight thousand barren acres edging Lake Michigan and decree upon it a multi-million-dollar Gary, Indiana.

Perhaps a British colossus south? Is that what they've seen?

New Birmingham, shunned north, has reached the plateau of no return: go big or go bust. Which is to say, go British! In the Southern's grand ballroom, they will discuss the roadblocks for both. A technicality, perhaps, in Texas law?

Also registered this night is the state's first native-born governor — big, full-bearded James Stephen Hogg. He was elected to curb monopolies and to protect Texas families heading west to homestead the now open Panhandle plains.

Foreign syndicates, the deliberate governor knows, buy up West Texas land at fifty cents an acre, then townsite it at spiraling profits. To block that, his first legislature enacts the Alien Land Law. The struggling West Texan is protected. No foreign ownership of Texas land!

Now he must meet with the British syndicate who seem the only major capital interested in New Birmingham's imperative expansion. And to him, much more than passing interest, this meeting, this expansion.

Jim Hogg had grown up, running the very hills where the Southern now stands!

To trace New Birmingham today, see George Goldsberry who surveys for the Highway Department and, like all surveyors, knows his land's story. Or see W. C. Tucker, at his store in Rusk. As a boy, Tucker sat astraddle the Southern's gutted walls and cleaned bricks at thirty cents a hundred. For fire took the Southern in 1926. Long, long before — in 1893 — she had seen her town stone dead, five years after starting.

314

You find the ghost south, where the Atoy road leaves the new four-laner for Alto. On the second hill to the right is the brick school's foundations and far into the pines across, the immense brick pit of what was Tassie Belle's furnace. You can see where the slag spilled down the hill and where the molten iron ran the trenched sand sow and off to the side-cut pigs.

Behind the highway office, old Dallas Street's fence line intersected Broadway — the red lane squeezing into the pines. Far over the hill toward Atoy, New Birmingham reached her four thousand, out to where they stripped the earth for promised empire. It's all gone now but an occasional foundation laced in weeds.

Even across the Y in the long empty lot against the tracks, it's almost gone. You can still find five twisted old magnolias, a deep bricklined cistern and well, and some foundations that suggest an elegant walkway, out from the Southern's great entrance. It was here that Jim Hogg walked out to look at the night when it was over.

There had been no choice but tell them the land law was just and right — to protect Texans homesteading west. And a law has to read the same, all parts of Texas.

So. . .no ownership. . .no investment. He could see the rest coming. No Irontown!

It is here, by the old magnolias, looking through the eyes of Jim Hogg, come home for a banquet, you can feel the real sadness of New Birmingham's ghost.

Make Believe at Matador

Next time you're bound northwest, toward Lubbock, look closer at the big country and little town that is Matador. Nowhere else is a truer legacy from the Texas cowboy. The town centers the lonely rangeland of the upper Pease — a heaving sea of mesquite and grass that hides tangled red arroyos and heaps up low hills where the windmills catch the only sound. Old empire of the big spreads — the Spurs, Pitchforks, Four Sixes and Flying V's!

The town is a sprinkle of roofs in pools of cottonwood shade. It is frame, adobe-colored stuccos and plain brown brick around a neat square. With the quiet of a line camp awaiting its riders, it is somewhat like other range towns about, Spur or Guthrie. But there's a difference, and therein lies the legacy.

You see, this town came overnight — twenty business establishments sprung from the prairie where the square drowses today. Somewhat incredibly, they were not built; they were "invented" — a cowboy's baling-wire make believe.

Most singular of all, they were not intended to change the land to city, but rather to hold it exactly as it was ... and very nearly is, today.

Talk to soft-spoken Doug Meador, Matador's gifted publisher-philosopher. Nobody knows those Flying V cowboys better.

In the beginning, Matador's rider very deliberately built his big ranch. After Confederate ebbtide, he had drifted

316

west — buffalo hunter, scout. . .even trooper. He stayed to ride the range he took from the Comanche; and where the Pease broke the prairies under the Cap Rock rim, he threw in with a Texas cavalryman, Henry Campbell. Paint Campbell headquartered a dugout at the old hunters' camp on Ballard Springs, but he had plans. Talk was, his Matador spread could go as big as Chisum's or Goodnight's outfits.

It did, with capital, as always in reconstructing Texas, from elsewhere. For a time, it meant little to Matador's cowboy that his real range bosses were Dundee, Scotland bankers.

What meant much was room to ride — sixty miles from the tortured Croton breaks to line camp north, forty miles from old Comanche Tee Pee City, west to the mesa walls.

It meant a reasonable minimum of red-eye, shoot-outs, busting jails or hangings; there was no town to catalyze these things. It meant some rustling to check or to manage. After a time, it meant scoffing at, but tolerating, barbed wire.

It meant helping Paint Campbell build his dugout into a fancy White House spread (where the wide-galleried, deep-shaded headquarters stand southwest of town today). And presently, it meant accepting old Paint's Miss Lizzie as lady boss, when a rope burned off a wrangler's finger and she stuck it back and made it grow. And particularly, when she gave the Matadors their first Christmas ball — a couple of fiddles and five pretty girls, the nearest from a hundred miles east.

And so many other pleasant things. Early morning cool, when you waked to smell coffee and took your bearings on your back, in the lay of the stars. . .sunset's flame, when you watched a way-off wolf lean into it and knew what pulled him. . .even restless night guard, when lightning sheeted the sky and spooked your herd into crazy millrace. . .

And other, hard things! The two droughts of the 'eighties when the holes dried; and the skeleton cows walked until

317

they fell. . .the '86 blizzard — the stage driver pulling in, still holding the reins but high and stiff-dead; the herds drifted to frozen walls against the south fences. . .

Partly it meant belonging to Matador — one of the few, tough enough to make it. Mostly, it meant room to ride, with the sufficient company of your thoughts!

Those thoughts never fully understood that Governor Jim Hogg's Alien Land Law of 1891 was designed to check foreign land speculation and, conversely, that the Scots now had no choice but to move across and run Matador themselves. The law was clear: if you own the land, come live on it.

The Matadors only understood that Paint Campbell was out as ranch boss. The men who had built this 450,000 acres had to start over and build again.

To ranch their country now, explains Doug Meador, meant that these riders must learn to live with the laws of an established county. For a county seat, you needed a town; for a town, Matador's cowboys figured twenty business establishments enough. On Paint Campbell's section, they invented those businesses.

On the bald prairie, planks made sudden tables — stores. Inventory? Borrowed from the ranch commissary.

"Bill Tilson had a sack or two of feed," said Doug. "That was the feed store." Jim Briscoe managed a few cans of tomatoes, a sack of shelled corn and a bucket of speckled peas — one grocery. Tom McAdams rolled out a wagon sheet and a few pairs of California pants — new Matador's dry goods emporium. Hugh White and Walter Walton were other "merchants", where a spool of barbed wire was hardware; and a pile of fence posts, lumber yard.

Paint Campbell? Duly elected county judge.

Later, the ranch — skeptical of a county that might begin to levy taxes — got into elections, too. At one time, Matador's Motley County had two sheriffs, one trying to arrest the other. That, says Doug Meador, is another story. The ranch — American-owned for some time now— and the town live together in the country little changed.

This story is simply how the cowboys kept it from changing.

I didn't ask Doug Meador what they saw, to want it unchanged. That is asking what a man sees in wind or rock, night sky or day's far horizon, asking what beauty he sees in the old frontier symbols — the strength of a dugout's rooftree, the human warmth of a sod hut, the beckon of horizon and challenge of first winter wind, of man's unwavering quest to be left alone.

Of course, those old riders made up a town so their country would be left alone. Just as it was, just as they knew it, their country showed them beauty.

And what, this beauty? What you can see — left alone, perhaps wherever — given time and room for the company of your own thoughts.

Why not give it a try, on a hill over your Matador?

1893—

The Sunday Town

No state can claim a more unusual town than Keene, Texas.

This little community is known in South Korea and West Berlin, in Florida, California or any other state and most countries; and, where known, favorably so. It is almost unknown in Texas; yet is is an intensely friendly town.

Like you, I've driven U.S. 67 — the Dallas-Cleburne stretch from blacklands to cross timbers — time and again, only to miss the turn-off sign to what is hidden behind the low hills just east of Cleburne.

A mile north of the highway is a neat, industrious, prosperous village of some two thousand souls, home of a million-dollar modern campus in Southwestern Junior College, whose six hundred students come from all over the world.

Keene has bustling industry far beyond what you'd expect from a village: printing, plastics, furniture, textiles. Quietly efficient, the plants serve a large market, Mondays through Fridays.

On Saturdays, everything closes but church.
On Sundays, everyone is back at work all day.

The sign you miss, slamming by the paved turn-off, reads: "The Seventh Day Adventist Church Welcomes You to Keene, Texas."

I picked up a clear-eyed, burr-headed young man who was on his way to Cleburne. He was Charles Bennett, whose family moved to "The Village" from Chicago. As you'd tell of anything in which you felt quiet pride, young Bennett told me about Keene.

We circled the campus, watching the pretty, white-socked girls and the lean, Texas-looking boys threading between classes or making for the corner drug. It was like the drag fronting your campus or mine, maybe neater, maybe newer and smaller, and with another difference — tobacco's just one of the things you can't buy.

"Those license plates?" I had already counted nine states. "Your students really come from all over?"

"Pretty much," he said in clipped midwest accent. "Two from South Korea. A boy from West Germany. Even one from East Berlin; his family made it and moved to Houston. I'd say half our students are from out of state."

"Why? Aren't there Seventh Day Adventist colleges elsewhere?"

"Oh, yes. There's one a few blocks from where we lived in Chicago. But we moved to Texas. This is the best and most practical and economical. You see, everyone gets to work."

I looked at the gleaming campus, the neat houses of "The Village," and the quiet quota of Cadillacs. We turned back past the massively graceful new church.

"Nearly all the money has been raised by the families right here in "The Village'," he said. "We'll finish two more buildings and everything will be new — about two million dollars in everything."

He told me that, in 1893, Keene had started as the college alone. There was a five-story frame building out in the lonely pin oaks. The village just grew up and kept growing. I could see it; we had passed two of the new industries.

"Is everybody in Keene Seventh Day Adventist?"

"Maybe ten families aren't."

"And everything stays open Sunday? I don't mean to offend you."

"You don't at all," he said. "We believe what the Old Testament teaches. Saturday is the Sabbath Day. Everybody goes to church then." He thought awhile and then guessed that was one of the main differences in his faith.

We drove down the spur road toward the highway. "I'm Presbyterian," I said. "How do you get along with the other denominations? How do you get along over in Cleburne?"

Young Bennett took off his heavy-rimmed glasses and grinned. "If you're from Keene," he said, "your credit's good anywhere in Cleburne." He gestured back at the neat town dropping under the hill. "We don't have a jail. Oh, we finally got a constable, because a town this size ought to have a constable. He doesn't have anything to do."

I worked around to asking him how many of his class would be missionaries.

"Some," he said. "About the same per cent as from your church schools, I guess. I'm studying engineering."

"Then, where to?"

"Well, I hope right here in Texas."

I let him off in Cleburne. I hope he'll stay in Texas, too.

The Dark Below Terlingua

Austin's Bob Cartledge would be first to tell you he's getting along in years; but just once more, I wish he'd go back to his Terlingua, remote and lonely in Big Bend's vastness. Just long enough to remember everything and then to tell somebody.

West of the towering Chisos, the town lies just off the road from the national park to Presidio, upriver. It is a strange ghost that some have glimpsed, few have really seen . . . and silver-haired Bob Cartledge has known, half a century, like his hand.

From its yellow, rocky, greasewooded hill, you look across to Casa Grande's high fort, Emory's pinnacle, then far south to the many-colored Gibraltar of Castolon. Between is long malpais, splotched in devil's pastels.

So Terlingua's highway turn-off is dwarfed; but the town follows, climbing, hiding hill-colored: scores of roofless, tumbled rock, melting adobe . . . up to the iron-steepled church and tile-roofed school. And to the gaunt white house at summit, an empty, hollow-eyed house.

And an empty town, this once American quicksilver mining capital of nearly two thousand.

Yet not quite. On a flat, nearly atop, is the long-porched Chisos Oasis, a cantina and curio shop. It used to be, you could stop here with Warren Davenport and his mother, friendly folk who invariably warned that beyond their building and all over that hill lurked the deadly danger of deep, open shafts. They could tell you most that is known hereabouts of the Terlingua you are able to see.

This town was born with the mother-ore cinnabar strike of the 1890's. A short and wiry New Englander, Howard Perry, developed and ran his Chisos Mining Company from Chicago. He ran it close-fisted, tight-mouthed and seldom-appearing. His was the now-collapsing white mansion above; and all below it, he found what promised to be America's bonanza for this all-purpose mercury. But, over-extended in the 1930's, he sold. In the 'forties, straining to meet World War II demands, the mine flooded to seven hundred feet, and its town died after the war. About then, Perry died at eighty-six and, still a stranger here, left mystery for his legacy.

The man who knew Terlingua for nearly half a century was Perry's right arm — a soft-spoken Walter Brennan. Home now in Austin, Robert Lee Cartledge was Terlingua's everything: from general manager to constable and justice of the peace. This deceptively mild mannered man ran the town, the store, the jail . . . and the fifty-mile labyrinth that is Terlingua under the hill.

Outside the Chisos Oasis, town center then as now, is where best to see old Terlingua as she boomed in 1911, when young Bob Cartledge came out to work for the Yankee his father's Austin law office represented. Look at the country as he did then.

It is three days by stage to Alpine, the road a dry wash. They have checked the ninety-nine miles with a rag round a wagon spoke, counting the turns. The seventy-six pound iron flasks of quicksilver freight out by canvas-bonneted Studebaker wagons to six Spanish mules. Heavy stuff comes in, high-sided, teamed in twelves.

Below, the town is much what you see today, except the better dwellings are iron-roofed and there are scratchy garden patches by the ocotillo corrals. And as too much water is enemy below, lack of it is enemy above. From the downhill tank, old Ursalo Seguin spigots it out, two pails a family per day. The girls carry it, shoulder-yoked. For an extra dime, they can balance a third luxurious pail on their heads. But a dime comes hard.

Behind you is company store: sugar, beans and flour, or calico and denim. You pay from your check, a punch card in colors from the six-bit blue to the two dollar green. You make up to two dollars a day. The real mine is not quicksilver, but the company store.

To the right, the plastered adobe theater — roofless now — came later, as did the six-pew church and the school across the tailing hills. In the draw between, marched broad-sided tents and barracks when the Villa border troubles kept Chicagoan Perry certain he must sandbag and machine-gun the parapets of his great white house.

Take those men down the hill, the hard-looking ones hunkering by the water tank shade. "Hire *them*?" the old man would explode. "They're bandits!"

"Only when there's no job," would reason young Superintendent Cartledge.

The jail of Justice of the Peace Cartledge is just outside the Oasis. A practical man, the J.P. knows that Saturday night's *sotol* will fill it. Also practical, Superintendent Cartledge will insist on windows so his jailed workers can watch Terlingua's movies.

Over the hill beyond the house is the mine's industrial heart, worn and stopped now. There is a five-room assay building, clotted with thirty-year old papers carrying Cartledge's "R.L.C." The close by road circles up to the shafts.

The big one is boarded over with bolted twelve by twelves; it is Number Eight, and it handled two cages: one up, the other down. Off its straight drop, as with all the others, a lateral lets at each fifty foot level. And it is deep, deep! Drop a rock; you wait a frighteningly long time.

Up here came the heavy red rock to be crushed, nut-sized, then furnaced to vaporize its mercury into a tandem of condensers — each big as your garage. All are gone, but Bob Cartledge still remembers that mercury with awe. With all his strength he could drive a fist no deeper than six inches into it. On its surface he could float a wrench. That was the quicksilver that went from the kettles to the flasks to the wagons to the railroads.

To get it, men gouged an incredible anthill beneath you. There are sixteen shafts like Number Eight.

They let nobody in that mine, probably not to interfere. Possibly, because Terlingua's miners sweated naked into those black tunnels (below the church and the Oasis, and the far below cemetery, and all the hills about). They gouged a face the old-fashioned way, single or double jacking, depending on whether there was room for another man to hold the drillbit you sledged. If there wasn't room, you lay on your side and drilled the black powder hole yourself. Then you blew it, and if the roof didn't entomb you, you carted what came down. Later, of course, came air hammers.

Sure, men got killed down there; and some got sick, just being down there so long, and they died. It was a big mine.

Fifty black miles down there! The carbide light you carried fingered the shoulder-wide tube you walked, and it died quickly, both ahead and behind. Probably nobody ever walked all that man dug down there, and certainly nobody ever really got a clear look at what he had dug. It was a dark mine.

Toward the end, government-pressed for another war, they hit water. The water flooded; they left the mine to its darkness.

That's what you walk over at Terlingua, the real ghost, the one you don't see.

So, of course, I wish Bob Cartledge could go back and experience total recall of those fifty years. And then leave notes.

Well, he can't. So the rest of us will have to guess at all that lies down there in the dark below Terlingua.

Gateway Post

It's a sign you wish Charlie Post could see today.

It reads simply "Welcome to Post — Gateway to the Plains," at first glance little different from most others outside friendly, prospering towns and cities of our high country, Panhandle way.

It's just east of U.S. 84 for Lubbock and beyond it, oil pumps work the red gullies, and the distant grassy breaks still range cattle. Ahead is a pin-neat city with wide, clean streets and handsome homes under grown-up, planted shade. Walling the city, west to north, is the gray-red Cap Rock cliff; atop it, an unbroken lush green sea, on and on to all horizons.

In downtown Post, population some five thousand, they boast of water to spare now, with White River Dam completed east. And all this brings you back to the sign.

Long before it went up, two riders for the Currycomb scanned that expanse — what any cattleman knew could never be more than a hundred acres per cow.

"What you reckon Mr. Post bought all this country for?" asked one.

"He's gonna plant it," the other rolled a Durham, "all out to grape nuts."

Erect, handsome, intense Charles William Post you may remember as the dynamo who rewrote America's breakfast menu. What is less known is that he was a Texianized Yankee, down for his health as early as 1886.

New England rooted, by way of Illinois, Charlie Post at age fifteen had lost patience with college and, by seventeen, had doubled a thousand dollars capital in

326

hardware business, the midwest plains. Then he skyrocketed and, over the next thirty years, would prove a genius in any field to which he set his hand.

He would invent: from a sulky plow to a player piano and an electricity-generating water paddle. He was artist and writer and business man whose drive broke his health by his mid-thirties. It was then he came to Texas and, ranching where Fort Worth's Forest Park now stands, predicted America's greatest future for this southwest.

In Fort Worth, theoretically recuperating, he launched a woollen mill and a new process to manufacture paper from Texas cottonseed and, by times, explored west as far as Panhandle country, scarcely clear of Indian and buffalo. His health broke again and this time he went to Battle Creek, Michigan, and international fame.

By 1891 he had formulized a wheat, bran and molasses "coffee" that he named Postum, followed it in five years with Grape Nuts and by century's turn, a cornflaked health food he called awhile "Elijah's Manna," then changed to Post Toasties.

Literally, he had found vitamins before they were named, had laid the foundation for the empire of General Foods, had perfected an honorable management-labor policy based on care for his men. And he had achieved titan stature in American industry. Yet, under his pyramid-peaked white Stetson, he was first and last a Westerner and his last determined project would be to create a model city on those plains — a city where every man could own his home and farm.

He bought over three hundred square miles of ranchland, atop and below the Cap Rock: what early explorers had known for the Great American Desert. Here would be America's model Post City. It sprang in white tent clusters, March 1, 1907. Railhead was Big Spring, 100 miles south, with six-mule freighters rumbling up supplies. Big town north was Lubbock, population, three thousand. Almost nothing else.

But at Post City, a man could buy a 160-acre plot, complete with four-room house, barn, well, windmill and tank for twenty-five dollars an acre. By 1910, the new town topped a thousand, boasted a fine general store, thirty-room hotel with dollar-a-day rates, a railroad and big cotton mill coming. Also coming was that little city's first terrible drought.

From his London or Washington offices or from Post City, where he laid stone, repaired machinery, and knew every man in his town, Charlie Post faced the enemy this country had to beat. He remembered reading of the rains following great battles; he would turn to rain-making — pluviculture, they called it. Direct Charlie Post just called them "rain battles." Cannonade the atmosphere with enough explosion, you'd compress atmosphere humidity to rain.

In March, 1910, he tried two pound dynamite sticks tailed to kites; it proved too dangerous. The following year, he regrouped his battle for water on different lines. Save all bath water from the hotel, sluice it to the trees planted down the streets. Wet down all streets with exhaust water from his mill. He had wells up the Cap Rock and reservoirs; and his sub-irrigation and dry-farming techniques had already proved crops as startling as cantaloupe and strawberries. But what he really foresaw for those plains was an endless sea of cotton and grains.

Along the high rim over town, Post set his rain battle lines. Stations, eight to a mile, would fire two pound dynamite charges in battery. Ultimate refinement would shield a two-man team: one running for a one-minute fuse and back, the other making ready the next. A dozen stations blasting two hundred fifty rounds each, one each on the minute. No peacetime American city ever shook to such a barrage — a dozen each summer for three years.

On a cloudless June 30, 1911, Post's rain battle satisfied him with a ten-day sluicer. A 1912 April battle was too early: it hailed hens' eggs. Over the three years, perhaps Post's thunderings did no more than break even; but his crops came in and, down in the embattled town, the building went on.

In 1914, C. W. Post died, short of his sixtieth birthday. His rain battles ended. Yet where he had put water, the Plains burgeoned green.

Above the town today are traces of the old dynamite magazines by the twin cap rock fingers called Chimneys. And most of them in Post can show you the old Double U Store, the C. W. Post home, and the rock gate that Charlie Post laid out on that desert before he brought it to bloom.

Also, with the dam, Post's water is assured without the battles — just as the plains above have lushed green from shallow wells and irrigation.

And so you come inevitably to the sign. Maybe Charlie Post made rain and maybe not; but he proved the limitless crops that our Panhandle harvests today.

Once you've crossed that great, green growing sea today, the sign takes on full meaning. You just wish Charlie Post could drive up in his 1908 Pierce Arrow and see it. "Welcome to Post — Gateway to the Plains."

True enough.

1933 —

Diamondbacks of McCamey

From the day the first Indian chewed his popotillo weed or sweated the race between his cactus poultice and the fang poison, Texas folk have sudderingly shown off the king of our snake family, the burly western diamondback.

Your adventurous appetite can sample a rattlesnake sandwich in San Antonio. With enough skill and nerve, you can milk the reptile at the Sweetwater rattler roundup each spring.

But nobody again has reached the skin-crawling heights achieved by oilboom McCamey in its heyday. Most old timers there still shake their heads recalling the day that Slicker won the First World's Rattlesnake Derby in that West Texas Pecos River town. Slicker was a lusty five footer with twenty-two rattles, and he beat a fast field in as bizarre a race as you'll find since the tortoise took the hare.

Cuthbert Carll told me about McCamey's swashbuckling days. He publishes the McCamey *News* and looks too young to have watched his town explode from a desert way stop to a city with a half-inch phone book, then subside within a settled four thousand population and a neat, modern-looking community.

Not too long before Calvin Coolidge did not choose to run and the Great Depression would haunt the name of Hoover, McCamey rested unknown in the solitude of its on-stretching mesa country. On November 16, 1926, Baker Number One roared in with the beginnings of the fabulous West Texas play. McCamey took off!

Next day, graders were slashing streets across greasewood flats, a step behind the hurrying surveyors' lines. By daylight of the second day, the new townsite's first lot was sold, provided a building was begun in an hour. It took thirty minutes. The boom that followed saw population soar to almost fifteen thousand, prices rocketing with it. Water brought a dollar a barrel.

By the Thirties, McCamey was shaking down into a hustling resemblance to a circus, set up in the middle of nowhere, yet doing a standing-room-only business, thank you! For a couple of years, McCameyites were too busy with money to bother with a jail. They anchored a chain to two deep-driven posts and snapped the unruly to the chain like you'd hang charms on a bracelet. What matter if occasionally the jail was uprooted and marched en masse to the nearest beer emporium?

Ultimately, most boomtowns slow down, and more than others, says Carll philosophically, they need a man born a promoter. McCamey had P. L. Brown, who kept things from getting dull and who was destined for the handle, Rattlesnake Brownie. Brownie staged the first derby in April 1933.

In early March that year, he set about harvesting his diamondbacks. This took an ingenious pool cue arrangement with a hook to extract six-footers from crevices in

330

the rocky country about. The cue held the snake down until Brownie could reach behind its flat, triangular head and snip the fangs.

"He had a couple hundred in no time," Carll recalls. "Then he thinned 'em down to about fifty of the biggest and strongest. They ran up to seven feet long."

Brownie's snake collection had McCamey talking from the Braley Hotel to the never-closing Oil King Cafe. Travelers drove in for a beer and a look at the writhing mass of reptiles in their big circular pen inside Brownie's place downtown. To keep things lively, he would single out an occasional curious and unsuspecting lady, toss a limp rubber hose under her feet — from behind — and yell "Snake!"

Derby time approached. The track went up on the high school football field, where stands would handle the hundreds come to watch, maybe do a little side-betting. The starting gate was Brownie's invention: a wide, low box with sides that collapsed when triggered by the starter.

The box was the exact center of a big circle, measured precisely, then staked around the circumference with evenly-spaced wickets made of wooden pegs, each bearing a number. The snakes had corresponding numbers, and the trick was not only to drive your racer over the line first (any direction was as short as another), but to go for the extra bonus by maneuvering him through the appropriate wicket. It was a kind of rattlesnake bingo. The jockeys steered their entires with pool cues: no handling or helping was allowed.

The snakes, ignoring the starter's gun, immediately experienced a second Brownie innovation. The box was wired. The racers got the word to go with an electric wallop.

The awestruck crowd witnessed the spectacle of a quivering, twisting mass one moment, and the next, a surge of racers literally electrified into action. Flat, ugly heads reared for the sky, then took off for the barriers, their handlers laboring to steer them for their numbered wickets.

Rosie was the entry for Oasis Picture Show, while Esmeralda was a common favorite under Grand Theater's silks. Some of the smart money went for V-8, the Hildebrand Motors entry, and for Airflow, wearing Allan Motors' colors. Drain Pipe appropriately raced for Acme Plumbing. But Owl Drug's Slicker took that first big race.

"It came off so well," Carll reflected, "we planned it for a sure-fire annual event, each April . . ."
"And you quit? . . ."
"I told you; it takes one guy in every town. It takes a guy like Brownie to pull off a rattlesnake derby . . . and he moved to El Paso. I guess maybe he lost interest."
Well, now, *that* is surely something I can understand.

1971 —

Boquillas — A River from Yesterday

Manana, they say, the jagged and wild sierra beyond the Bravo will become one with Big Bend. Gray-gold desert, blue-deep canyons, and mountains changing tint with the sun's mood — all in a vast international park.
This will come; and when it does, I hope in a way, they will not build that bridge at Boquillas.
Boquillas, as it is today and seems always to have been — pinned there to the river by the ten thousand foot purple and red cliffs of Sierra del Carmen to the east and by the rearing Fronteriza to south and west and by the crouching ghost mountains, Chisos, behind you in America — possesses an eloquent loneliness that a bridge should not destroy.
It is said by the old ones in this tiny village of mud-packed river cane jacales and small, blocklike adobe structures, that one can see — from the surrounding peaks — the day after tomorrow, deep in Mexico.

332

How much more true it is that you span more time, just crossing the river. In Boquillas itself, you step back a century.

You get there by horse, belly-deep in the Rio Grande. Or you catch a fluorspar ore truck. If the water is low, you may with care wade or make the raw ford in your own car. Any careful tourist can cross; few do.

Juan's horse, *El Pinto*, took me last time, the dark-faced, serious boy leading the way, saddled and splashing. The night before, it had rained high in the mountains, and the water was over the stirrups.

Once across, we left the trail where it wandered into mesquite and canyon wall and 150 miles of emptiness toward pavement and the interior city, Cuatrocienegas. Had Juan been down that trail to the Mexico beyond the mountains? No, one did not venture such a journey without a vehicle of much strength. Even the Coca Cola man might take a week or not come at all, and he was a constant man.

We crossed the mud flats under Boquillas' chalk hill. In big cans, village women scopped coffee-colored water from the rain pools, for thatch-roofed wells like this one, now, were for the drinking. We passed the well and the rusting Chevrolet truck body, topped the rise, and were in town.

Outlying are the jacales, then the single street, a broad space between facing adobe dwellings and establishments; here you dismount. To the left is *Cantina Por Los Pobres*, its bar, two planks; its hospitality, genial. There is a patio behind the Poor Man's Saloon, and from it, a magnificient view of Boquillas Canyon, easternmost of Rio Grande's three great gorges.

Across is a neat, whitewashed adobe, *Juzgado Auxiliar*, Boquillas' courthouse. It is no bigger than your bedroom and, indeed, why should it be? Are not the crimes of this village, themselves small as well?

Perhaps a *borracho* or two when the Saturday dances encounter fine weather and extend themselves late. The dancing pavillion? It is the concrete floor of what was to be a filling station, there below the courthouse. Two pumps stand rusty sentinel, waiting for walls that never went up.

Farther along is a more elaborate cantina. Its bar has a front. There is a gas icebox and a calendar picture of Manolete dying. It abuts a general store which displays staples like dried pintos, things for hand sewing and mending, a shelf scatter of dusty cans and candy for turistas to buy for the children. At the other end is an open air casino where Boquillas' men and boys play poker and monte bank with soda pop caps for chips. At the far end is the village school and then little else but a thinning of dwellings and the closing-in country beyond.

There is a sign over Boquillas' most imposing building, the one with uniformed *oficiales* inside. The sign tells you not to enter that forbidding country beyond, not without first properly stamping your visa.

The country that pins Boquillas to its river? Some of Mexico's wildest, and unchanged since Villa bandits stormed across here. Unchanged since the Comanche and long before.

Somewhere in the hazy and distant Picoteras, where even a burro takes care, is Lost Nigger Mine. Upriver, toward lonely, deep-slashed Mariscal Canyon, lie the ruins of old Presidio San Vincente, which never succeeded in protecting Spain's treasure. Ironically, runs the legend, you can locate one great lode from the fort's very doorway. On Easter morning, stand there and the rising sun's rays touch faraway Lost Mine Peak exactly where the Comanche entombed the mine forever.

Except that the Indian's shadow has faded, Boquillas country is the same, sealed there in its mountain fastness. You leave the village as you came, with perhaps a few little ones running out in good weather to call "nickely-nickely," and the old ones scolding them back to their packed yards, nodding to you in the dignity of the poor.

Across, on the Yanqui side, the country imperceptibly leaps a century. There are the properly-spaced winter campgrounds of the park, near the river where

334

temperatures are moderate and camping is warmer than summer nights on the cliffs over Yosemite. The paved park roads . . . neat directional signs . . . the forestry green of park rangers tending an empire and talking across the mountains with car radios. Even on winter days, the tourist with camera, all the way from eastern Boquillas, far across to the great gorge of Santa Elena, and to the long reach of quiet spires toward Mariscal.

Behind you, Boquillas, as it seems always to have been; and, mountain-walled against the river, must always be: a forgotten century ago, yet just a river away.

I'm quite sure of it: I hope they don't build that bridge.

Part Six

Ghosts and Treasure

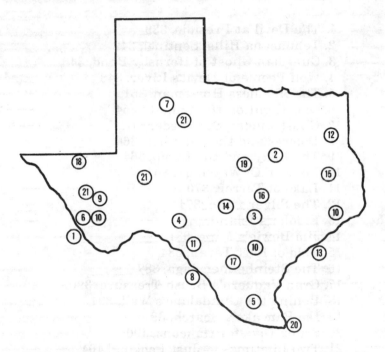

*"Take care lest ye fetch ghosts, aye, and treasure
For ghouls do guard gold in darkly hid measure."*

Sea Chantey

The Devil at Presidio

"*Los pobrecitos!* They have fear of the Evil One!" The priest drew his cassock closer against the night chill, for they were high up the ridge.

"Perhaps," said the other in the darkness, "it is because they are close to him. Truth, they are *primitivos*, violent ones." They were shadows against the cliff rearing above; they were shadows down the *cerro*. It fell steeply to where the river cut between the broad plain and the sierra.

"It is the violence of children," said the priest. "They cannot yet understand that the Evil One waits within them, as within all men." He studied the Indians, silent by the great brush pile on the glowing fire for the torches.

"And so, for them," he said, "I must lock the Devil in his cave. Then they will remember and come with fire each year to keep him there. For awhile, we must teach by parable; finally they will learn."

Then the priest held up the cross and gave the order. Presently the ridge flickered, flared, then flamed against the night. Later, as it dimmed, a tracery of torches wound down from the mountain toward the crude stone mission.

And so, into legend. On the night of May 3 last year, you might have looked across the Rio Grande at Presidio, in Big Bend's mountains, and seen the distant fire rites up the shoulder of Sierra Santa Cruz. There is a tiny chapel high on the trail, since it is not too distant from the chapel to a hidden cave where the long ago priest imprisoned the Devil, the long-memoried fire rites are very proper.

Now, if you're thinking, as I suspect you are, "what

an appropriate place to lock up the Devil!" then you are a victim of weathercasters who, each summer, libel as this nation's perennial hot spot one of the most intriguing towns in Texas.

Presidio has fine weather in fall, winter and spring. It enjoys spectacular mountain country, fresh-cut by Camino del Rio, a hundred miles of highway to Big Bend National Park, judged one of America's twenty most magnificent drives. It has the feel of dim and storied age.

It still possesses the flavor of old border and old Mexico, just over the river at Ojinaga. And there, it has the excellently appointed and scenic railway hurdling the western Sierra Madre to Topolobambo and the beautiful Mexican Pacific coast, which that road brings five hundred miles closer to anything east.

Unless you take the soft line on neon and chrome, you will have missed a rare treat until you look in on this completely overlooked and weather-maligned little city of a thousand souls. That it has escaped discovery so long is baffling, except for one thing. . .and we'll get to that shortly.

You come down on Presidio from high-ranched Marfa to the north. For a time, the big spreads tilt up toward a blue rampart of mountain. Then the land breaks in the rough country of the Chinatis, the country of roaming phantom lights where you pass canyoned and ghostly Shafter, its adobe skeletons astride the silver lodes no longer mined.

South of Shafter, the tableland spills to a fan-shaped valley speared with cactus and ocotillo. Far across, against the Mexican mountains, lies Presidio, and, within the twenty intervening miles, you drop fifteen hundred feet. Up looms a mountain ring: the Burros to west, Chinati and Black to east, the tiering Sierra, south.

Presidio's principal street ambles generally toward Sierra Santa Cruz, across the river. It is up there that the fire rites are held with annual unpredictability each May. Up that rocky ridge, too, the penitents walk barefoot to atone. The long mass to the west, like a great wrinkled lizard, is *Viejo* – the old one. Through it, cuts Rio Conchas, out of Mexico; and here at the juncture of the two rivers, the earliest Spaniards built their first missions and laid down the oldest highway of them all — the Chihuahua Trail.

Here, in 1571, Antonio de Espejo — mindful of Coronado's pilgrimage — was the first white man to lead a determined exploration of Texas. He found an old Indian pueblo civilization waiting at the rivers and pondered its beginnings. Today, archaeology believes they were more than eight thousand years before Christ.

And so Presidio must be numbered among the oldest continually occupied sites in America. Something of merit was found here for a long, long time.

Along Presidio's main street, visit with Oliver Harper, who runs the big hardware store and knows that his weather is pleasantly bracing most of the time. He shrugs off the July-August 110's; the air is dry. "We've never had a death from heat prostration; compare that with a lot of other cities — the ones worrying about our summer temperatures." Harper knows temperatures, too. For Presidio, his were official for many years.

East of town, Walter Millington has come back from California after eighteen years. On his considerable acreage under the shadow of Santa Cruz, he scents a one day Palm Springs in the Presidio wind. The new Mexican railroad. . .the not-too-distant highway that will link Chihuahua City. . .

For a long time, downtown, Juan Rivera edited a two-fisted paper, the Presidio *Voice*. His was a salty, bilingual demand that Presidians get off their siestas and prepare for the progress that was bound to come to this yet undiscovered-by-moderns frontier. He was fed up with the general notion that this country was a never-never land bordered by inferno. But now Juan's old and he's not too sure the progress will come.

Well, I'm sure. Maybe not right away, but it will come. And I have a suggestion.

Sure, the Devil laid a curse from that cave across on

341

Santa Cruz; it's time to break it. Next fire rites, pile some rocks in the first cave you find; get the word to the weathercasters that their Devil is forever sealed.

And thereafter, send out only your September to May temperatures; they're a delight. Nuts to those summer numbers; it gets hot in Miami and Palm Springs, too.

Arriba, Presidio!

1820's

Tehuacana Hills' Sentinel

Lately, I've wondered what has become of the legendary ghost of Tehuacana Hills. Morning and evening twilights for so long, old story had him waiting and watching from atop this low range, forty miles east of Waco.

And so, not long ago — at sunrise and sunset both — I watched from the hills and asked about in little Tehuacana, near Mexia, toward Hillsboro. You see, this is no ordinary spirit.

He was last chief of the Tawakoni, latter-day west wall guards of a once strong and civilized Indian confederacy: mound builders, all to the east and north. He perished with almost all his people, battling, not the invading Anglo, but strangely, other Indians. On the highest hilltop here, legend says he fell.

And so here, at first and last light for well over a century, the old Texans looked up to see him watching them, sometimes as though to warn. However, I could find no one who admits to seeing him recently.

I had gone up because Texas archaeology, carefully threading our past, had just found his village site. According to Indian history, that village was wiped out by the Cherokee in the late 1820's. And if the legended village was real, perhaps also, its ghost.

Was he, as old story said, yet coming back to wait for his son?

Gray and easy going Robert D. Carter knows of the Tehuacana ghost. He runs the little grocery near the once-silvered dome of what was, at one time, Trinity University and is now Westminster College. Long ago in Tehuacana, a very young Bob Carter heard the story from his grandfather, who helped settle this country.

The Tawakoni and their brothers, the Brazos-dwelling Waco built their beehive thatched huts on these hills when the Cherokee were a great Carolina nation. Inexorably hammered west, the Cherokee retreated finally here, where the once mighty mound-builders' empire long had held firm line against the savage plains. But here now was empire remnant, its people withered under Spanish, French and now Anglo settlement. Little more than Tawakoni stood guard; and instead of their common enemy, the Indians fought each other: once near today's Waco High School, and finally on the highest of these hills. The surrounding Cherokee fired the hill's high grass; the Tawakoni were virtually annihilated.

That last stand would go into the records years later, struck from the memory of Indian scout for old Second Cavalry. He was Tawakoni Jim, by nature trailing the Plains Indians, but this time for Earl Van Dorn's troopers, west on the Washita. Tawakoni Jim could remember when his father fell, far away, on a flaming hilltop. His people had smuggled Jim from the holocaust so he could reach manhood, as their chief. His father, though, had been last chief on the hills of their land.

Drifting back to those hills, the story let old Texans recognize the Indian who came with sunrise and twilight. This must be the father, waiting for his son to come home.

Yet the years turned, and finally the son was dead; still, the sentinel ghost came back.

You can see far from his lookout hill, west of the little town. The highway drops its ribbon to the rolling prairies toward Waco, and all about the crest is a camper's secluded park where, in summer, the breeze is lazy and the katydids doze in the hackberries.

Far around this shoulder is the site where archaeologists located the Tawakoni village. They traced the sunken floors and their central fire basins, and the lodgepole marks for the circular and oval dwellings. They

343

found a sad story in the few artifacts recovered: nearly all, trade from the white man, beads and gun parts. There were, however, enough pottery sherds for identification; this was the Tawakoni village, and in its latter days, it was poverty-stricken. Empty, its granaries and storage bins; and this, for a people whose ancestors introduced yours and mine to most of the vegetables in today's supermarkets.

In short, here was evidence of a destitute end for a once far-flung and affluent society which had long since learned to control war and had eliminated most crime, including quarreling. This was a last village before captivity in the Babylon of Indian reservation, far west.

And, of course, the searchers found the village totally burned.

An end in battle? Here, archaeology must check you to history, in this case, primarily Indian story: a blazing hilltop and its last stand. It's hard indeed to argue that story.

Then what of the ghost?

I think he's there, but not waiting for his son. Any good red man can tell you that his ancestors await him, not on the hilltops but in his hereafter.

I think Tehuacana's ghost stands guard in a kind of sentinel penance. Surely, at the end, he knew that a nation fighting itself, rather than a common enemy, must fall.

He must have known that all his people — too long complacent, too long affluent and soft with it — had forgotten how to mount guard until too late.

So he's still there.

With silent warning.

And we may see it yet. Provided we can recognize what is demanded from each of us, if we are to guard our freedom.

Guardian Ghost of Hornsby Bend

These dark eves of All Hallows are for phantoms — always, somehow, fearful things. So this, instead, is about a guardian ghost, though you may be awhile recognizing the story for more than that of an Indian fight.

It was east of Austin, down the tranquil valley of the Colorado, today hardly land for haunting. There is airport's glitter and the outspilling geometry of new homes, and finally the river, lazily wandering its meadow and timber for Bastrop.

To explore it, take the old Webberville Road; it hugs the river north. Above the road, edging the airport, and again, nine miles out by Blue Bluff, you'll discover granite markers. These tell of Kentuckian Josiah Wilbarger and Georgian Reuben Hornsby, and a Comanche ambush where a man survived his scalping. Nothing of ghosts.

History recalls these two for westernmost frontiersmen, log-forting their riverbends down this trail, three years before the first shack went up where Congress Avenue crosses the Colorado. Properly, history seldom admits ghosts in granite.

But look again over the long valley. There is no capitol dome, nor university tower: nothing but grass and timber to the violet hills west — Comanche fortress this 1833, when Stephen Austin considers the land for new colonies.

From his remote Blue Bluff fort this August morning, wiry, fortyish Reuben Hornsby looks out very nearly where Farm Road 973 today crosses his bend for the river. He watches five men ride from his clearing to scout

345

west, for in that direction lies the beauty that Mirabeau Lamar will seek for frontier capital seven years later.

To lead these young scouts is downriver neighbor Wilbarger, whose fort guards the bend near today's tiny Utley. At thirty-two, that handsome buckskinned horseman, like himself, fears nothing but Judgment Day.

As you measure their ride today, they trail the Webberville Road to Walnut Creek's crossing near the airport. At its southeast edge, they flush an Indian. Up the creek, they pursue to its head near today's expressway for Georgetown and Waco.

Then? Only silence from what seem empty oak-motted slopes. They backtrail down Pecan Spring Branch and, in a thin clump near where the jets now touch down, they hobble their horses and noon it. Cold spring water, cornpone and jerky tastes good to men who fear nothing. They stretch lazily; how fine to be alive!

Moments later, the ambushing Comanche hit!

Wilbarger sees one man dropped, screaming; another, hip-shattered, sprawled outside their fort of trees. To drag him back, he darts for the wounded man, twisting low as he runs. He goes down, hit in one leg, then the other; but he reaches his friend, fires for him, and about him, looks desperately for help. He sees the other two running for their horses.

He pushes up, reeling, shouting for them to wait. He takes a ball through his neck and out his chin.

In shaken horror, this is what the escaped two relate at Hornsby's fort. They saw Wilbarger crumple, dead, the Indians already swarming the others . . . then down upon him!

Wilbarger is not dead — by a shadow's breadth. He is paralyzed and near-blind in shock. On his back, he senses the Comanche finish his companions: their screams pitch high, then choke off. Now they are above him, the dark faces expressionless as death.

They rip his clothes away. He knows his naked body rolls dead to them. Is it? No, he sees the knife! the hand reach to grip his scalp!

His brain hears distant thunder when something wrenches. Then nothing.

The sun is low when he feels again. Away somewhere, the coyote calls, and the owl. Surely above the circling buzzard. But the Indians are gone, and he has waked to something. *Something!*

His sister's voice? In his vise of naked pain, he hears her speak. Hold on, she keeps saying. But his sister is far away in St. Louis. He crawls to lave in the cold water below and presently collapses naked on the bank. He feels the cold sear his head. He has one sock on his body. The cold pounds his brain! He stretches the sock. Then he pulls it on his tortured head.

Hornsby's fort is seven miles. He crawls a quarter mile of it and fetches against a big live oak. Nothing left, but to die.

Again he hears his sister, Margaret. *Hold on!* His friends *will* come!

His friends wait grim inside the fort's log walls. They will gather every settler northwest of La Grange. Enough then to dare the ride for the three dead men. By firelight, they ponder their frontier. Finally they sleep.

But not Sarah Hornsby. Suddenly she stirs her husband. Startled awake, he hears her whisper urgently that their friend is yet alive. He hushes her; she is dreaming.

She wakes again. *That man lives!* He is propped against a live oak, naked and scalped. But he lives! He is holding to life, waiting for them to come! Hornsby's men must go for him!

This time, Reuben Hornsby listens. Before first light, his thin column of riders trails out. Under the oak that Sarah Hornsby described, they find Josiah Wilbarger, waiting naked with his sock over his head.

His friend Reuben Hornsby holds him, riding in. Days, they soothe his head with bear oil. And though, for a dozen years, he will always wear a fur cap like that sock, he will live: his last home still standing in Bastrop.

In delirium, those first days, he talks of his sister, Margaret. It was she who held him between the twilight that is dream and the midnight that is death.

347

Sarah Hornsby tells him finally of the twilight of *her* dream: *it had to be Margaret she heard, telling her again and again to send the men!*

They must write his sister.

Then the letter comes. Far away in St. Louis — the day *before* he rode into ambush — his sister Margaret had died.

1834—

The Wolf People of Devil's River

Since I shortly intend to camp and fish the beautifully remote Devil's River, canyoned and crystal above Del Rio, it seems time to dispose of foolish rumors that, now and again, suggest sub-human monsters still at large in our back country.

No one really believes the *Thing* glimpsed in South Texas brush near Alice not long ago, nor the creature whispered to be a *Manimal* up in Red River's lonely woodlands. Nor the half human in Edna's Navidad bottoms that old timers used to recollect.

And what if otherwise sound men as far back as Herodotus and Virgil tried to explain a wolf-man? Let them believe from the drear forests of the Balkans to the Ardennes and the Scottish moors, as from Pakistan to Africa and Java today, that man changes, under certain conditions, to animal. Well, not in Texas.

What connection has this with the Devil's River? Not just that its gorges and those of the Pecos, west beyond, gateway a wildly-unchanged land of spirit lights on phantom mountains, of lost mines cursed by Apache ghost, of forbidden canyons. Rather that there, where the gray wolf still leans to the moon, this phantasy should end, where it seems to have begun.

Some years ago, a lore-minded writer, L. D. Bertillion, trailed some wolf tracks out of history, as far as the Devil's

348

between Sonora and Comstock; then left us guessing.

Almost lost, you see, in the explosive years just before Texas Revolution, was the fact of Mexico's greatest land grant—an empire reaching from the Nueces River beyond today's El Paso—to an English-managed colony under one Dr. John Charles Beales.

Beales' Rio Grande colony struggled briefly, beginning in 1834, to anchor its tiny capital, Dolores, downriver from today's Eagle Pass; but drought and Indian withered the settlement, sending the first stragglers back by groups. Invading Santa Anna finished it; Dolores' last handful, fleeing ahead, were wiped out by Comanche beside brooding Lake Espantosa on the old Presidio Road near today's Carrizo Springs. Only two women survived for later Indian ransom at Santa Fe.

Only two? Or was there a third? Bertillion thought so.

He found Beales' colonists to have been men of various inclinations. One, an Englishman named George Dent, had the trapper's instinct for loneliness and desire for the wealth of beaver pelts. Up the San Pedro (later change from St. Peter's to the Devil's by Ranger Jack Hays) Dent took his wife and trap lines. Near today's Juno and Beaver Lake, he contrived his stick and rock jacal and his willow-wand frames to salt and stretch the pelts.

Fall turned to winter, with trapping good. Far west of Dolores and civilization's real fringe at Bexar, Dent toiled on, conscious only that his race was against time. In a few weeks his wife would bear a child. Just a little longer, and they would wagon back to become wealthy . . . and a family.

But misjudging, they had waited too long! No mistaking those pains, surging more rapidly. For one horrified moment, Dent felt the grip of his isolation; he considered the thunderheads massing west, the wilderness miles east and south. Then he flung to the saddle. Closest help was forty miles west, where Mexican shepherds grazed the Pecos valley.

Out of night's wild storm, the shepherds' camp saw him ride. Yes, they would bring one of the women; yes, even now! Saddling feverishly, while thunderbolts shook the hills and lightning flashed in lances and chains, the sheepherders fell stunned in one near-crashing bolt. The Englishman was struck dead.

It was morning before the searchers reached Dent's camp. Under a brush arbor lay the body of his wife, dead in childbirth . . . but obviously delivered.

Merciful Father! they saw more! Under that arbor, tracks of lobo! The woman untouched . . . but the child, gone. For this poor family, all was over.

It was not over, said Bertillion. A decade passed, and the military road for American El Paso swung north up the Devil's and across to the Pecos—close on Dent's old route and past his now-forgotten beaver camp. Along that trail, the waystops, then thin settlements grew; and with them grew the shepherds' tale of the lost Dent child.

More years passed, and the tales had grown to dreadful proportion. Travelers had glimpsed a creature resembling a half-grown girl, running crouched with a wolf pack. Seminole scouts out of Fort Clark and Camp Hudson, here on the Devil's, read wolf sign and in it, the clear print of human hand and foot.

Finally, goes old story, that frontier massed to cordon the pack. Back over gorge and rock they trailed, circled and closed . . . and cut out their quarry.

There was near-human form and face, something capable of rising almost erect, yet more agile on all fours—a snarling, cowering, hairy creature—its nearest human sound the long, cold wolf cry. Something, even as they barred it in the shed-room, that left a woman distraught and trembled a man's hands; while, round the cabin in the night, the gray wolves closed in . . . you could tell it from the rising frenzy without and . . . from within that shack!

Then the wolves were in the corral and pens. Out rushed the settlers to save their stock, yelling hoarsely at the darting blur of forms and, all at once, at the dead silence of night. Gone was the pack . . . with their prize. She had torn loose a plank and crawled free.

Over the years, reports of the wolf-girl lessened; finally none spoke openly of having seen her. Yet the story persisted, half-a-century and more, said Bertillion. From deep in the wilderness back from the Devil's, some few old ones have seen them yet: the sudden frightful watching wolf, studying you a moment, then gone . . . but watching with eyes in a fearfully human face.

You may inquire, as I have, from the wayside store at tiny Juno, and among the lonely ranches along that tiptoeing stream, and as far as Comstock and even Del Rio. Ask what is known of the Lobo Girl of Devil's River.

Since I intend to camp and fish that country soon, I think it's time we dispose of such foolish rumors. Obviously Bertillion was way off on the wolf-people. I can find nobody to back him up. I may not even ask around before I make camp this time.

I don't suppose you've heard anything, have you?

1845—

The Headless Horseman

Something!—the nicker of his hobbled horse, a whisper of wind or the smell of it—waked him in dread where he lay black-camped within the scrub along the river bank.

He rolled silently, leg-spraddled under the cedar. In the same moment that he slid the Spencer up to sight, he felt cold on his spine, and he saw It.

Across the dark stream, the big mustang drank, pawing. Gaunt in the thin moon, his rider waited, leaning on his pommel with all the patience of Death. God have mercy!why not? Even the faint light showed just the stump above his shoulders. His sombreroed head was a restless pendulum swinging from his saddle horn.

El Muerto! The headless one! The mustang started toward him.

He squeezed his shot, centered on its chest. The mustang reared, plunging with the ricochet whine. He levered two more, sick with knowing the first could not have missed.

351

El Muerto was gone in the dark at a gallop, his head bouncing against his thigh.

And he? Fumbling his bedroll, clumsy with the saddle cinches, he was praying and cursing in Spanish or English, depending on whether he were vaquero, cowpoke or trooper. At a dead run momentarily, he knew he had left behind his hat, his cookpot and maybe even his gunbelt.

What he knew, most of all, was you couldn't stop *El Muerto* with a bullet.

It's really not so long a jump from that man's fear-driven ride to Al Kennedy, who can build you a gun in Ingram, then outshoot you with it. Al likes lore and knows the story of the Headless Horseman as well as anybody except those who occupy the three widely separated graves he can take you to.

One is within the old state cemetery in Austin, gray granite marked and still secluded from the near-passing expressway. Here, Bigfoot Wallace finally rests.

One is the old Knoxville graveyard north of Kerrville, where the sometime ranger, sometime "outlaw", always dangerous Creed Taylor "died from cigarettes at right near a hundred," according to Kennedy. Creed and Bigfoot were friends.

The third is the almost time-erased marker in La Trinidad's *rancho cimintario* just south of Ben Bolt, near Corpus Christi. Here, the Headless Horseman lies. Creed Taylor called him Vidal; it isn't the name on his stone, but let it do.

Connecting these three distantly separated graves in the fact of Texas' headless horseman is a simple matter to Al. Vidal had a fancy for other men's stock. He erred, one fall morning in 1845, in selecting a string of Creed Taylor's horses.

Taylor and a rancher named Flores picked up the trail from the hills, ran into Bigfoot Wallace ranging near the Nueces. Bigfoot was looking for the outlaw in general and any convenient excitement in particular. They joined, rode hard into the night and came on the bedded down outlaw camp.

Taylor crawled a half mile to the *caballada* and after midnight was back: one guard pacing, three men asleep, the herd quiet and upwind all the way. Before daylight, he, Bigfoot, and Flores had bellied through the grass so close that the waking men stumbled to their feet only to die.

One was Vidal, who had terrorized settlers from the border to the hills. There was a price on his head, but Bigfoot's grim humor declined it. Besides, he could remember old Ichabod Crane and that pumpkin. The three beheaded the outlaw.

They selected the strongest, wildest mustang in the herd, roped and saddled him. They lashed the headless man to his mount, bound his hands to the pommel. Carefully, they replaced his hat with leather thongs worked through the chin and jawbones, then tied it all, swinging to the saddle horn.

They cut loose the mustang. For five full minutes he fought his rider, but the grisly horseman was up to stay—as the three avengers figured: a warning to rustlers. The mustang broke for the horizon.

"It's legend from there," says lore-minded Kennedy. "He was *El Muerto del Rodeo*—the wandering dead you couldn't kill."

He panicked everything from Corpus Christi to Eagle Pass. Soldiers from Uvalde's Fort Inge, rangers, vaqueros, even Indians fired, then fled. One cowpoke, riding a lonely late trail, heard company galloping up, waited long enough to see his fellow traveler, and kept going to Kansas.

"Finally," says Kennedy, "they got the horse at a water hole. Some say with a rope, some say, a gun. Vidal's body was pretty near a mummy, and it was a sieve with bullet holes."

That, Al Kennedy took from Creed Taylor's own account, long later recalled.

Driving the long rolling brushland, we stopped between Alice and Ben Bolt. It was the remotest service station we could find. We knew—as the old timers know—what Vidal's real name was, but why reopen old wounds? And

353

after all, *El Muerto* was the name that really clung to the man.

Al asked of him from the man coming out of the station. "The one with no head?"

The swarthy man filled the tank. "He is spoken of. Mostly by the old ones."

"They say," said Al, "that he still rides at nights."

"Perhaps."

"They say," Al persisted, "that even now, some see him ride at night."

The man counted back the change. He supposed the world still had its fools.

Not fools to believe. But to stay up.

1870's—

Ghostlight on the Chinati

They have many names for it in that high and handsome land around Marfa, north of Big Bend's mountains, names like "Marfa Light", "Smuggler's Light", "Ghost Light." And witnesses they have by the score, for three generations now. An explanation, they do not have. Not one they can agree upon.

Nine miles toward Alpine from Marfa, you can look toward the ranges south on many a night and, high in the dark Chinatis, see a phantom-like light that flares and flickers, but that always extinguishes if you approach too closely.

For a long, long time in that rugged country, the light has let itself be seen. It is often so easily visible from the old Marfa air base that World War II pilots tried to buzz it for a close look. They brought back an unvarying report.

It was of variable size, sometimes a pinprick, sometimes big as a searchlight. It appeared always within the mountains, generally on a high point as though to signal. And there was a ghostly beckoning about it: it lured you right in, getting brighter; then at the last moment, it snuffed out, and you had to peel away from those crags in a hurry. *But it was there; it stalked those empty peaks.*

Phlegmatic Air Force totted up various theories of the lights' source: from reflecting minerals, from someone burning sotol up the lonely heights, from maybe even smugglers as some old timers contend (the border is close). In any event, pilots were forbidden further buzzing.

The flyers, of course, continued to peep, as do the curious today. Fully a dozen dogged pursuers have come close enough to try for photographs; for an inexplicable reason, the film will not record what the eye sees.

One Austin researcher, H. E. Berry, calls the phenomenon "Alsate's Light", and his explanation is perhaps as valid as any. Little known Alsate may have been last of the Texas Apache chieftains.

He was born of Mexican parentage and, as a boy, was captured in a mid-1800 Apache crossriver raid. He grew up Apache and by the latter 1880's, when the Mescalero and Chiracahua were effectually finished, Alsate's band held out in the ghostly Chisos. They clung to the peaks and the caves, dodging, doubling back, starving literally; but they remained free.

Mexico's Porfirio Diaz finished them with a trap, dragged the captured remnant south to Chihuahua City and decreed their scattering across that land. Because his family blood reached back to Spain, Alsate was heard. Passionately, he asked only that his small band be left free to breathe their last air from their mountains.

"No!" came the answer, and on pre-arranged signal, the Indians broke. Most were cut down or recaptured. but not Alsate. Shortly thereafter, about the little settlements of the Bravo's mountains, there appeared a solitary Indian watchman: from a crag yonder, a shadow high on that hillside. And always by night a signal fire, now here, now there: from whatever direction Alsate's people might yet come home.

He harmed no one; he seemed simply to wait. Big Bend's new Anglo explorers waked more than once to find moccasin prints close by their burned out fires. Finally, they found a high up cave in the Chinatis. In it, preserved by the dry air, a mummy sat backed against the wall.

There was a certain set to him, an expectancy even in the skeleton of him; he seemed still waiting. And by the ashes in the cave was a supply of fagots for torches yet to be burned.

From little Sundown in the Panhandle, Mrs. W. T. Giddens has a version which, while not ruling out the light of Alsate's torch, does suggest a more unearthly source.

"I've seen the Ghost Lights all my life," she declares (for she was raised in the Chinatis), and I can't remember their ever causing harm other than fright. They are just curious and want to investigate things that are new to them, as the air base was, during the war. For example, they liked to follow you out in the pastures at night; they seem drawn to people or stock, and animals don't fear them at all."

Mrs. Giddens recounts an extraordinary experience of her father's, long ago. Night and a sudden blizzard had caught him afoot, high up the mountains and some miles from home. For hours, he fought on, hopelessly lost as the storm increased, hopelessly aware of the increasing certainty of his death by freezing.

Blind in the night and ready to collapse, he stumbled around a howling point of rock. *They were there, close on him; they were blocking his way!*

They seemed to flare and flash, his memory would tell him later, they were like pulsating, solid things that glowed, and there seemed several of them, all about him. At the time, looking into the lights in that night, he knew he was dead.

"But the lights 'said' to him (he could never later explain how he could 'hear' them) that he was three miles south of Chinati Peak," Mrs. Giddens says, "that he was off the trail and heading the wrong direction, and that he would surely die if he didn't follow them."

He did follow, for they seemed to extend some hidden strength to him. He sensed that he was high and on thin trail, but the night was black and bitter and the lights danced about, blinding him yet leading him. He was almost unaware that finally he had entered a small cave.

There, he found sheltered warmth; it seemed to come from the largest light, the one that had stayed closest and that now remained beside him.

"Before he slept," Mrs. Giddens adds, "my father was 'told' that these were spirits from long before, that they wanted to save him, and that he could sleep now and would not freeze. With morning, both they and the blizzard were gone."

And sure enough, he was off trail, heading for precipice; and three miles south of Chinati Peak.

1880's

Ghost Riders' Stampede

Northwest, between Crosbyton and Spur, the high, lush green plains break off sharply at the Cap Rock cliffs; and below, the land heaves — dull reds and grays — off to rims and hills of a sameness as though pasted there, low against the sky.

Down within, the land has changed little since John Chisum trailed his Jingle-bob herds across, and Loving, Goodnight and the rest drove this way. It is a lonely land; you can sense the ghosts of old cattle country. And across it, there is a back ranch road where the sense is very strong; this road crosses the jumbled canyon of the White River near remote little Kalgary. Up the canyon to the north, you can make out hunched hills and mesas in the haze.

You are looking directly toward the ghost ground of "Stampede Mesa", recounted long ago by cowboy folklorist John R. Craddock. Away in that swim of heat and mirage,

357

the White jags along the back Cap Rock breaks of the L-Seven Ranch; here is as close as the highway will take you.

From his Crosbyton Phillips station on U.S. 82, Tilman Reeves can direct you much closer, and so can Spur publisher Grady Joe Harrison, a little to the east. For you can saddle and ride to the mesa itself. . .but you may want to think twice about that, particularly since you'd reach it about nightfall.

You see, ghost riders still herd a long ago night stampede up there. And they'll try to take you over a hundred foot cliff.

Craddock believed the story of Stampede Mesa one of the strangest on Texas trails, and that covers a lot of country. Of the ten million longhorns driven north in the two decades after Confederate cavalrymen turned cowboys, few indeed were the herds that did not, at least once, explode in blind, thundering terror.

Near Gatesville is a Stampede Creek; another, above Belton. Early Stephenville was flattened by one red-eyed herd. At old Doan's Crossing, north of Vernon on the Red, thirty-three thousand head made a hundred mile chaos for nearly two weeks before lathered, exhausted riders could sift out their original eleven herds.

Old Matador riders, bound to a strict daily journal by their Scottish bosses, could write "stompead" across two days' entry with nothing else needed; a cattleman knew that as little as gust-blown tumbleweed could spark the explosion. A hat blown sailing, a sneeze, a sudden yell or laugh. . .a gunshot. More, a smell of wolf or the scent of panther or Indian in the night. Even the nearness of water, even the morning start of birds.

When he sang his *Old Chisholm Trail*, a cowboy recalled that he did no more than "popped my foot in the stirrup and gave a little yell. The tail cattle broke, and the leaders went to hell!"

And, of course, there was lightning, thunder!

Then you rode the blue-white and black nightmare. Wet backs sleek, eyes orange in the flashes, fireballs on the horns; and the trembling ground gone beneath in the bawling, thundering tumult. You bet you rode! You rode like a "likkered injun" and you tried like hell to mill 'em to the right. And you cried to God to bring the morning light!

Now, no lightning spooked the stampede up that White River canyon.

Call the drover Jones, which wasn't his name. He came through in the 1880's with something over a thousand head, gaunted from the dry pull over the flats and breaks below and spooky with it. Jones was making for what promised a fair bedground for his herd.

He called it a mesa; it was really an extension of Cap Rock, with water across a small neck of land that opened to a gradual slope which, in turn, widened and came to an abrupt end in hundred foot cliffs. You could water and bed down on good grass up that slope. And, the cliffs being there, you could hold them through the night with scarcely half your riders.

Short of the mesa, a nester drove out of the brush. He hadn't many steers and they were poor; he flanked them right into Jones' cattle. Whether he did it purposely to pick up some extra head, the trail boss didn't ask.

"Cut 'em out," demanded the nester. Then he threatened.

Jones stared him down over his rifle. They'd be cut out in the morning; right now he was heading to bed a herd. And up the mesa he pushed them, just ahead of dark. It started like a good camp.

But in the night, all the herd stampeded, not for the water, but for the cliffs. They turned a few; two riders went over. One who didn't, tried to remember the blackness when he waked. He thought he'd seen the nester waving. . .shooting. Or was it lightning?

They rode the man down, tied him to his horse, and blindfolding both, pitched them to writhing agony on the rock below.

After that, old timers shunned that tableland, particularly for night camp. Some who didn't, said the nester came, calling for his cattle. Some saw him, fighting his ropes and choking his gag. They saw him plunge from

359

the cliff, along with the cattle he took from them. A stampede not long later took two more riders.

The last one was about 1900, says Craddock. It was a small herd with a hard-headed boss. The moon had set to hard dark when one of the night guard saw it happen: a sleeping, rested herd, all quiet until something came through: "floatin'," the way he recalled it. The herd exploded.

They were milled and held, short of the cliffs. Yet those shaken drovers saw the strange floating ones, riders and all, sweep right on, right over the edge.

Nobody camped the mesa thereafter, although the grass, they saw, is still good and the trail is clear, right up to the water.

So, if you want to ride up — arriving by night, of course — you may have trouble getting directions from cattlemen out there. Sure they know that old story, any of them from Crosbyton to Spur. They're just not sure they could find the place.

I don't blame them.

Dolores and the Searcher

With a certainty, he knew it for the ghost light! Swinging, as one who walks a lantern, it retreated a step . . . another, then taunted him to follow: into the chaparral . . . into the night, away from the little lamps of his village.

From where he stood, just up the shoulder of tailings from the mine, he could see the horizon glow flat, where Laredo hid to the east. The tailings made a dark mountain beside the dimness of his village; and all about was night, even across the river in Mexico.

And this beckoning light? Which ghost, then? He knew of two.

It could be *the searcher*, spoken of by the old ones. This would be the one who hid his treasure in the old mine shafts and died, not telling where. It was warned that one did not follow such a ghost. But a brave man might. . .and be rewarded!

Equally, this could be Dolores. That lovely girl who loved so much and waited and died for her lover! The mescal made one sad for Dolores. A kind man should comfort such a sorrowing ghost.

The old ones said she wandered the low hills crying. Or was it only the cold wind's song? They said *the searcher's* lamp showed only his form; never look on his face! But was that not just the shadow of mesquite behind the light?

No, it moved! Slowly it went into the cactus and rocky flatness toward the far hill that marked the abandoned mine. He regretted that the mescal was finished.

Still, he followed. Was he not sufficient man to encounter either?

Such ghost tales, we skeptics know, are pieceworks of legend. However, twenty-five miles west of Laredo, some strange pieces are still there: ghost mines and their ghost towns. Not long ago, Rancher Ted Scibienski showed them to me on the fifteen thousand acres where he feedlots graded Herefords.

His river ranch overlies a bonanza of bright-burning cannel coal.

In 1880, when coal was king, a former Colorado governor, A C. Hunt, opened the first mine, six miles upriver. The tunnels were a two-layer labyrinth, a hundred feet deep and reaching two miles back from the bluff. Governor Hunt called his first town, a sprawl of adobe and river cane, Minera.

As veins played out, Minera followed the new railroad downriver in two mile steps. The ruins stayed in the brush; the dark shafts in the bluff. Minera drew new names; she was really the same, just booming bigger: by the 1900's, possessing a population of five thousand, and still moving with the coal shafts. Then came the Twenties and oil.

Today, in the rolling brush, she is almost gone: collapsed shafts and river bluff entries, concrete foundations and piers, rusting pipes reaching for now-sealed galleries. The big, stained hills — really tailing piles — tell you how much dark tunnel lies beneath. The five-foot air shafts are covered; they drop ten stories.

So all you really can see from the road (and this is a private working ranch) is where Minera's last headquarters stood. By a tailing hill and a blue silo and two silver grain storage tanks, the old mine commissary is now storage barn for the ranch, named for the last shaft sunk — Dolores.

Dolores was the name of an eighteen-year-old servant girl in Governor Hunt's "White House", headquartering first Minera. She was a miner's daughter; she was also a lissome, dark-eyed beauty.

To the White House came a handsome young Pennsylvania graduate engineer. He and Dolores fell in love. What at first had seemed amusing to the others, now was incredible. Those two intended marriage! The young engineer was sent home.

In broken Spanish, he told Dolores he would come back; in broken English, she told him she would wait.

He wrote. She could not read, nor trust another who could and who could write him what remained in her heart. But she could save the letters. Then they lessened; finally, they stopped.

Dolores sickened with grief. She wandered the bare hills they had walked together, crying hopelessly. Eventually, as the old ones knew they must, they found her at the bottom of an air shaft.

And, as the old ones knew they would, they saw her come back to walk the hills after twilight. In the dark, in the black, windy dark, they heard her crying for her love to come home.

And the other, who also walks the night near old Minera? What is he seeking?

Of course, these mine shafts — the scores, crisscrossing in the dark down there — are where one hides treasure. Every bad man, pistolero or gringo gunslinger, used those shafts for hiding. As they were abandoned, the better the hiding.

Some say *the searcher* is an evil old man who had hoarded or had discovered what others had hidden. Others say that the gold was bandit, and that it is guarded by the ghost of the most terrible of all those bad men. Still others say that *he* is not searching at all, but tempting where you must not go.

All know *the searcher* carries a lantern, swinging as he walks slowly. Sometimes you can see the form, even the dim hand. But not the face. *Never the face!*

It was pleasant to talk with Ted Scibienski, a quiet and friendly man with good eyes that know this country of Dolores.

We talked about his new feedlot operation, a large one in Texas; and about the feasibility of strip-mining cannel coal with huge new equipment that can move two hundred tons an hour.

We visited the old graveyard at Dolores, where the plastic flowers stand fresh by the crosses, and where some of the old ones, the ones from Minera's mining days, still come back on Sundays.

We didn't talk about the ones who come back by night.

We would have had to finish the story of that long ago man who followed the ghost light. They found him in the morning, goes the story, a broken, deranged man. All he remembered was that it finally waited for him, *and he had seen its face.*

Why talk yourself into believing those things? Then you'd have to watch the night and follow that lantern and see for yourself.

The Lady and the Lamp

For lofty-spired Fort Davis country, it doesn't seem much mountain: just rock and brush-rubbled mesa a little south of town. Yet you marvel, if you try as I did, how she climbed it each Thursday twilight, those thirty years, to build that fire for her lover.

Of course, she died finally, doing it: rubber-legged, prematurely white-haired, yellow-faced and haggard where once there had been so much beauty. Maybe, as some old timers said, she just grew old fast, went crazy and finally gave out. Or maybe her heart had died long ago, and she drove her body to catch up.

I've the notion that this last is what Fort Davis' graying, perceptive Barry Scobee thinks. He has quizzical eyes that look deep on the Davis Mountain country which he loves and knows better than anyone else.

He took me outside his court house office and showed me the unpretentious mountain just beyond the town and told me about Dolores. That was her name; it is now her mountain's name. Her mountain has changed little since the time she named it.

The time is the latter 1800's. Fort Davis, with its Irishman Eighth Infantry and Buffalo Soldier Tenth Cavalry, is our biggest, most important frontier post. It must be; it lies in our most beautiful, remote and contested land.

Apache, who knows he owns this land, swaps dead for dead. Almost nothing gets through an Overland's Concord stages: almost nothing that isn't shot up. Davis' hard nosed troopers know there are no patrols, only ambushes, and very little of anything but empty land between the villages of San Antonio, thirty-two water holes east, and El Paso, two hundred deadly miles west. But if we are to reach burgeoning California, there must be a Fort Davis. And so there is.

Just beyond the fort, under the cottonwoods along Limpia Creek, there is a little settlement. Chihuahua is a welter of adobes and jacales, but in it lives a girl of incredible beauty and goodness. With her father lives the girl Dolores, slim, yet full as a woman should be. She has that luminous quality that sizes her homespun with the sheen of grace. She is a happy and much loved queen of her little town.

She is beloved, first and always, by a sheepherder named Jose Chavez. And he is man enough for her: his rifle is as good as any Tennesseean's. He can fight like a Texan or a devil, take your choice. He can ride his gray mustang like a Comanche. And he has as much fear of the Apache, waiting at the water holes and behind the templed rocks, as he has for any man — which is nothing. Painstakingly, and with great happiness, he and Dolores have built their adobe home, mud brick by brick.

All is finished. They are to be married Thursday next.

Jose has chuckled over Dolores' dread of his work. It takes him down deadly Musquiz Canyon, where so many have died. Being an accommodating man, however, and amused with her, he has humored her whim.

The nights — hot summer ones or biting winter ones — he has, these many months, agreed to her fire signal. To show her concerned love she will, each night, climb to the point of the little mesa above Chihuahua, and she will build a fire.

Somewhere on the slopes of Musquiz where his flocks graze and drowse, he will light the answering fire. How can you refuse such a thing, even though it is not wise to backlight yourself to the Indian?

And so it goes, each night. She toils to the summit and throws her beacon to the stars. Then she stares across the emptiness where, out there somewhere, he camps alone.

The fire comes back. There? No, far over on the more distant slope.

Just before the Thursday they are to be married, it does not come back.

They found him, riddled and scalped. Instead of the altar, for which she had only now finished her wedding dress, Dolores, the young and beautiful, follows her betrothed to his grave.

Imperceptibly, she changes. There is no laughter light in her eyes. With the unfathomable stoicism of woman, she works regularly at her tasks in her father's home. But on Thursday nights, she toils that monstrous path up the mountain and builds her fire for Jose. Somewhere, where the good God lets him be, he will see it.

This she will do until she dies — about thirty years to Barry Scobee's recollection. That would make many hundred trips up the mountain.

"In the fall of 1893 some folks visiting saw her last fire." Barry nodded toward the barren top of the headland. "It was kind of weak. But she got it up. Then they found out in a day or two she was dead.

"I went up there lots of times. Used to be charcoal all over the place. Wind must have got it; you know how the wind blows up here in the winter."

I've tried to consider how it must have blown up there, how it must have been for Dolores. The coldness of that height! I'm not sure it is comprehensible for me.

Maybe the last time, the fire warmed her a little; she must have known she was going to join Jose.

Still, I don't know how she climbed that mountain, faggot-burdened, the many hundred times before they buried her in a tangled grave in a forgotten cemetery below her mountain.

No, it isn't much of a mountain, that little height of Dolores.

But all in all, it's the best named summit in all our state.

For U.F.O. Watchers

As previously stated — if you're reading along — there are some "lights" flitting about our western mountains, and a singular lack of explanation for them. And to all this, I have given not a little thought.

Frankly, it's hard for me to understand the fuss over these short jaunts to the moon when it is obvious that some extra-terrestrial gentry have been giving our little Earth the once-over for some time. Now, I think the Pentagon people have not quite leveled with us. They are worried about U.F.O.'s in Washington or they would not already have them alphabetized. Yet they pretend there are no such things as unidentified-flying-objects.

Accordingly, I am constrained to reveal some of our Texas beachheads where a watchful eye may observe the infiltration of our state by visitors unknown. My witnesses, too numerous to detail, are credible. It should be pointed out that our voyageurs-from-afar are full of cunning, always selecting out-of-the-way places in which to appear. And this has been going on for quite a spell, as you shall learn.

Near Saratoga, in Big Thicket's wilds, is shadowed Bragg Road, an old siding that runs narrowly, forest-walled for miles. Almost any Thicket man can tell you of what visits Bragg Road some nights. A kind of luminous, pulsating ectoplasm it is, restlessly patrolling that lonely byway.

It is not seen so much now, because some years ago it was molested by young couples who drove up the lane on spring nights to talk about life. It responded, as might be expected, by frightening them away. They, in turn, rallied car squadrons from as far as Houston and sought to run over it with automobiles, at least bump it or photograph it. This, of course, it eluded, changing in form, tint, movement, disappearing if necessary. A coherent description was not easy to come by, but I pinned down young David Hughes of Saratoga, who likes to shiver and watch the occupant of Bragg Road.

"Sometimes," he said finally, "it gets little, like a panther with headlights."

In the Thicket, I avoided those offering only vague references to fireballs, foxfire, and the like. This is claptrap; I prefer a forthright ghost-believer, misled as he is.

For example, there are some valid ghost-believers in the brush country below San Antonio; though, over the past, they have reacted with an insensitive vigor, reaching for firearms or clubs. Take the old moss-bottomed bridge between Kenedy and Runge and what stalked below. Kenedy's Beauregard Moye, who looks like a white haired cowboy and is, took me out.

Long ago, he and the other boys chased the *Thing*, night after night, toward the dark timber edging Pleas Butler's pastures, trying to get between it and the river.

"It kept changing size," Mr. Moye reflected. "Big as a wagon in the trees, then above them — like a barrel on fire. Get close? It'd turn off like a light."

Otto von Schroeder, a fast, dead shot and strong as they came, got it down once and tried to stomp it. In the confusion, he might have thrown a couple of shots, but he never could get a real grip on it.

It retaliated angrily, soon after, by drifting right through three-strand wire, burning too bright to look at, and chasing Mrs. Sallie Ricks' buggy into a ditch. Miss Sallie wasn't hurt, but she was considerably put upon; and Mr. Moye has kept an eye on that bridge for her ever since. But he still doesn't understand.

He didn't know, you see, about what stalks around the mountains south of Marfa, didn't know it has worried three generations, didn't know that almost everybody in Marfa and a lot of Californians have seen that light, and that most have tried to track it down and nobody has.

I could see no reason to tell him about the Air Force's settoos with that *Thing*, nor the theories about a lost Apache chief. I started to tell him about the way it saved an old timer from freezing to death, started to tell him it had shown itself quite friendly, but then they'd had that trouble under the Runge bridge. His might not be friendly, and besides, you can't be sure about these transients.

In the same sense, I haven't told those Marfans about some other theories concerning what they believe to be just a ghost light.

There are those, nearer the Chinatis (where the Marfa light prowls) who believe they are perhaps wiser about such things. This is Big Bend, where Mexico stands across in the mountains and leaves strange lights alone. The old ones say they are warnings from the Indian departed; and other *viejos* smile, for is it not true that all lost mines glow by night?

To Crescencio Sanchez, whose family is of this land for many generations, the light on San Vicente Mountain is left, as it should be, undisturbed. Certainly, he could show you; he has lined it, sighting from his house corner on bearings marked with sticks. It hovers about the steep side, well up the sierra across the river.

Long ago, when there was little more to Texas than the trail from here, there was, beside the mountain, presidio and church. Time and the Indian brought abandonment. Legend decrees a treasure that went up the mountainside to a cave, where it was sealed by vengeful Indian.

Such a treasure glows. It is, like the light on Dead Horse Mountain, just away, a warning not to defile. There have been those who tried and died; and all this is known to those of the river.

They I must add, approach the entire matter in an open-minded fashion more to my liking. Let them call their phenomena ghosts!

369

You can see from this that the Pentagon's secretive behavior is producing rather considerable confusion among us and, to say the least, ineffective countermeasures. Assault by automobile, wrestling, skylarking by young pilots, digging around in mountains, surrender to the supernatural along the border canyons.

You may draw your own conclusions. (If you look in on them — and the sites are not impossible to find — I will appreciate any reports you may send me). However, although I am specializing only on the Texas phenomena, I believe you can see that I know what they are. Despite the Pentagon.

To hearten you, let me report a recent small success in repelling one craft attempting to land on the bluff opposite our river front. It was twilight, and I snapped off two good rounds at the glowing object just above the high cedars.

If at all, I missed narrowly. This was due to my bifocals slipping in irritation with my son Bill's nonsense about the planet Venus.

1750's

Lake of Terror

Among our multiplying and various lakes, this one, almost hidden off the Crystal City-Carrizo Springs road in the lush greens of Rio Grande's Winter Garden, at first impresses very little.

It lies dark, thin and listless as an aged man. It seems singular only in that within this ever-treeless land, its banks crowd jungle shadows upon six miles of narrow, slack water. At some forgotten time, it was the Nueces, now away to the east. Even the fishing promises little; you dismiss the opaque water.

Better look again. In Texas, there is no other like this one.

You reach it off Farm Road 1433, up a slight hill crowned with a high line of palm. Under the hill is a silted rock dam (long later added), and a marker. The granite tells that this was the best-known campground on one of the oldest highways of all — Mexico's from-1700-on Presidio Road to Bexar. The marker also suggests why wayfarers finally shunned this water and endured dry camp in the brush.

A curse, they'll tell you — the really old ones about.

A curse that has lived on in the lake's name? The name is *Espantosa*. Freely translated, it is "Ghostly Lake", or perhaps more precisely, "Lake of Terror."

Since the lake and its crossing here are as old as the missions and the ox-drawn, wood-wheeled *carretas* plodding to them; then aged, too, the lake's name and the tales from which that name grew.

One relates a wagon train of the 1750's, northeast for Bexar. Three nights beyond the safe walls of the Rio Grande fortress, San Juan Bautista, camp was made in this welcome wood and water. One of the women went to the bank of the dark lake. She was scarcely beyond the ring of campfire's light when the wagoners heard her frightful scream.

Later, from their shock, those nearest the water could recall fragments: the yawn of gigantic and awful jaws, a horrible thrashing at the reedy bank and finally, the terrible blood spoor.

"*Lagarto!*" said one grimly. "A giant alligator!" Look at the water; it could have been.

But the others knew it truly for something terribly larger. . .something fearful, dwelling that dark lagoon. Then and there, they laid their curse in the name, "Espantosa."

Yet the mission years continued longer than we have been a state, and memory is short. Wagoners, smiling with the foolishness of legend, camped the lake again.

One train arrived late on a moonless night. Drovers had pushed the parched wastes two days for this water and grass. Now, wearily, they slept in their wagons. At some small, dark hour came the thunderclap and blinding flash. Oxen, wagons and the very ground beneath . . . all sank, leaving only sullen boggy ground. One poor fellow wandered, half-crazed, to Bautista, to tell what had happened.

The old tales told, of course, that this had been a treasure train.

Of a certainty, the tale tellers would say, you can hear the ghost wheels rumble to the lake, any dark night, then stop. It is a stifled, strangled stopping. And then a terrible sound of the very ground sucking them down. And so those who tried for respite by Espantosa heard groaning wagons and the strangle of bogs. . .or something from the lake itself. There was no more camp.

Except, as recorded inscrutably in granite, when an outlaw band found the empty banks and shunning of Espantosa a practical haven. It was 1876 when Texas Rangers wiped them out. Legend says the west bank dead limbs hanged the last of them; and by then, the old ones knew that it made no difference to this accursed lake how it destroyed those who came to it.

Of course, these are old tales with perhaps no place in proper history. However, there is a history of those who farmed this land before it was Winter Garden. It is tragic and for a long time was forgotten.

While Stephen Austin, Green DeWitt and the rest were working at modest grants to the east, a distinguished English surgeon (and naturalized Mexican citizen) amassed an incredible grant of seventy million acres — from the Nueces to New Mexico. His name was Dr. John Charles Beales; the capital of his empire was named for his wife — and prophetically so — Dolores. That tiny settlement was down Presidio Road, near Eagle Pass.

By 1833, he had brought a vanguard of fifty-nine colonists — mostly English, wagoned west from Copano Bay. Theirs would be empire west — beyond El Paso. But history skips Dolores, for it died. Its death came in a kind of void, and historians dislike voids.

A hard land and the Comanche, drought and time itself stood against Dolores. Irrigation failed. Cattle died. There was no fort, as the Mexicans had, over the river. By dwindles, Dolores faded. Finally, those last sought a road home to England.

They looked south: at the Rio Grande fortress of Bautista, Santa Anna's army promised one thing for Anglos north — death. Eleven men, two women and three children — the last of the colony — turned their wagons from Dolores. In the tumult of war north they disappeared; history forgot them. It was long later that two women were ransomed in Santa Fe.

They could remember. They had hidden from Santa Anna's army. Their men drove the battered wagons along an old trail north. One night they found what seemed an excellent camp — by a lake.

It was by that lake that the Comanche had hit them, killed every man, taken them and the screaming children. No, they hadn't seen the children again. Yes, they remembered the lake. It was long and thin, boggy and timbered, three days up road.

They described Espantosa.

Looking for Espantosa — for it isn't easy to find, I ran onto Granville Howard and his family, weekend-fishing out of Carrizo Springs. He is a big, jovial man who works heavy machinery and — a native — knows all the legends of the old lake. He got me down to the old campground crossing.

Sure, if anybody'd tell him where the treasure wagons went under, he'd take a look. But who goes for those old tales, anyhow?

He just prefers to fish the upper end — away from that ancient crossing where the wagons sank and the creature lives in the lagoon, where the outlaws and an empire died. You know: all the kind of stuff you hear if you ask around.

Well, you ask around. If you can find anybody down there. I couldn't; se.ned to me, they avoided that place. So I left before dark.

The Silver Lake

Swarthy, sleepy-eyed Jean Lafitte, Galveston's last of the big-name buccaneers, hid all things well, including finally, himself. And old story persists that his richest cache, two million dollars in Mexican silver bars, still waits finding in Texas.

One school of the hunt sifts the northerly dune range of Padre's long white island for a legendary "millstone", beneath which is fortune. Another, including treasure-diver Harry Rieseberg and many a scubaman, believes that broad and multifingered Matagorda Bay holds the treasure, still in its ship.

Yet two hundred miles from sea, an East Texas group periodically pursues what must be the most dogged and, except to those wise in pirate trove, least likely search of all. It probes a narrow, mile-long, eerie swamp of a lake in the jungly Sabine bottoms north of Carthage, at the Rusk-Panola line.

Find the right bottom, says the legend — close beside where an old smugglers' trail once fringed that lake — and you'll find Lafitte's treasure. "With all that blue gumbo down there," say old timers like Carthage editor Clabe Applegate, "the trick is finding any bottom at all." In a century, nobody's beaten Hendricks Lake.

Far-fetched? Not to keen-eyed, fiftyish, drawling Barney Waldrop, a television repairman in the deepwoods little town. In treasure hunting, Barney putters with electronics and has found more loot than he'll admit. But

Hendricks? From oil explorers to water witchers to plain nuts, he's seen "anyway, fifty of 'em" beaten by the lake's bottom. "Try to gouge blue gumbo working ten feet under water!" he says laconically. "Tough ain't quite the word."

But Barney continues to try Hendricks' bottom. You see, he knows the legend of the Spanish treasure ship, *Santa Rosa*. Should he believe it? You judge.

On an early spring morning of 1816 (some say 1812), wind and tide sets fair off Hernando Cortez' old harbor of Vera Cruz. The Spanish brig clears the fort guns and, heeling seaward, the outer rocks of Sacrificios Islands. She'll ride the trade round the Gulf by Havana, and out Bahama Passage for home.

She is heavy-ballasted with hundred-pound, two foot silver bars, burro-packed down from Zacatecas' and Guanajuato's mountains: she makes a dangerously solitary prize! But this is a desperate Spain: her new world tottering from the Horn to the Amazon and over the mountains to distant, empty Texas. Get while you can!

Santa Rosa, suggest the vague old registers, gets as far as Matagorda Bay. . .and is somewhere inside Pass Cavallo today. Here sea story picks up the thread. Out of the islets slashes a low, fast schooner, breaking Venezuela's red-striped ensign — or any convenient revolutionary's. She ducks the high guns, rakes her swivel cannon. She rams, boards, clears the Spaniard's deck.

But this prize is too big, too easily recognized as Spanish, to moor off the Galveston that Jean Lafitte has scarcely settled — certainly, if he and partner-brother Pierre are to continue as Spain's trusted Agent Thirteen, to fend against America. They must sink the *Santa Rosa!*

But not before her holds reveal the silver stacked below.

The treasure went down, say the Matagorda divers. Some got off to Padre caches, insist the dune sitters. Yet the strange East Texas thread still survives.

Today, East Texans can show you marks of the old smuggling trail their forebears knew as Trammel's Trace. It cut the wilderness north from Nacogdoches, near today's Carthage, Marshall and Texarkana. Then it made for America's back door at St. Louis, a buckskin town that would fence anything from horses to hot silver.

Ingenious Lafitte, who formerly used the back bayous before New Orleans was closed to him, saw the contraband trail loom large in his plans. He commanded a half dozen fast coasters and five hundred men under lieutenants like Cochrane, Lambert, Gerol and Lopez. He discussed schemes to seize Texas for the United States, for struggling Mexico, and to sabotage all revolts for Spain — all with the appropriate authority.

Meantime, he worked Trammel's Trace to the ruts. Up it, this late 1816 spring, he hurries a long wagon train. Aboard? Musty sources claim the *Santa Rosa* swag. San Antonio's Spanish cavalry have no doubt. They hammer up *Camino Real* to intercept the wagoners before they can escape, too far beyond Nacogdoches.

Camped along the Sabine on the banks of a pinched-off lake, indelibly described as today's Hendricks, the loot train has but minutes' warning before the jackbooted dragoons hit. Just one thing to do! Into the dark water and the bog below goes every wagon. Later they can return.

But only the Spaniards return, to San Antonio. They intercepted no treasure, but they cut down a ruffian pack beside a lake that also recalls Hendricks. No survivors, they report. But Lafitte legend says two pirates got away.

They couldn't return. Hurricane, the onrush of frontier and finally the U.S. Navy drive them from Galveston.

Over the years, out of Mexico, straggled the first few searchers. They poked the edges of the dark water, but the sucking bottoms turned them back. Finally, in the 1880's, Uncle Fox Tatum, who named the town nearby, attacked in earnest. He rigged a steam engine bucket-belt and "nearly dried her up", but the rains beat him. Ten years later, a Mexican group, trying canal drainage, lost to seepage. Some contend that it is not Lafitte treasure at all, but a Santa Anna payload, buried down there. Skeptics say there's nothing on Hendricks' bottom but mud.

Barney Waldrop pretends a *que sera* attitude about what's under the blue gumbo. *"Quien sabe, amigo,"* he says in solid East Texas Spanish. Yet he has helped increasingly-determined exploration over the years. Not too long ago, Houston oil operators assaulted Hendricks with a long-boomed dragline and finally a floating dredge. The grim bottom gumbo stopped them.

Is there a bottom? More than that, Barney's answers suggest: something still gripped in that bottom. If they can reach it. At last report, off the old Trammel Trace high bank, he had staked six locations with a new combine — from Milwaukee and Los Angeles.

Now I report all this, not to excite you with an old legend that probably neither of us believe. But wouldn't it be a shame to let those outlanders get our Texas pirate money? And, I'd join you in a minute; but it's like today. . .

I've got to stay ahead on writing.

1816 —

Fiddler's Island

Crossing from Houston toward San Antonio or Corpus Christi, most travelers today overlook the San Bernard; for, along its brief upper reaches, it is a thin stream, and it gathers to full, dark flow only near the old Brazoria coast, a hundred miles from its head.

But trace its final forested course to the mouth. Of all our Texas rivers, none glides legend more mysteriously to sea.

You can take a boat or the back country shelltop where Farm Road 2611 plays out, off the Brazoria-Freeport highway. You flank ten miles of San Bernard's wooded west bank, first past pleasant homes, green-lawned to water's edge, then thinning timber with stilted cottages set back, finally the reedy, open coast and the Gulf beyond.

A long two miles inland is a land's end cluster of beach houses. . .and Nettie's Place, a jaunty, weathered story-and-a-half frame with a bottlecap drive-up. Whether you fish or hunt something else, here's end of the line.

Inconspicuously behind is a low, triangular river island, hip-high in an acre of salt grass. A worn wood walkway crosses; most fishermen regard island and slip between for no more than well-sheltered moorage at Henry and Nettie Overbay's place.

It is quite something more. Despite today's seashore jollity, you are at center of an old, old circle of haunted ground where something is ghost-guarded by music that no one, perhaps, has dared to hear to its end. What kind of music? Hard indeed to describe.

But you're looking at Fiddler's Island.

"What really makes the sound?" I asked Henry Overbay who, shrimping or ashore, knows this coast as few others. When he frowns he looks like a graying buccaneer.

"Could be drum feeding," he said without conviction. "They feed in the shell." Others suggest oyster shell itself, working in the tide, or the dark night wind, perhaps. Or, if they're real oldtimers confronted with newcomers like us, they may change the subject.

But the old ones know that, to those who seek it or what it may guard, it wells up from the water, any dark of the moon. You sense it, funereally thin at first. Then it swells to something you hear, all through you, and — if you face it out — floods to an enveloping crescendo that you know, in an instant, you can reach out and touch . . . even see!

But turn away, it dies in the darkness.

"Just fish," assured Henry Overbay, "you don't hear anything at all."

Years ago, the old Freeport *Facts* lorist J. W. Morris uncovered only mystery when he searched for why the first settlers called this reach of San Bernard, the "Singing River." One legend with a dozen variants centered on a young musician, back in the days when this was Stephen Austin's colony land. The man was a violinist who lost his bride-to-be, just hours before their wedding.

Grief stricken, he shut himself away in a shack on a then-larger island. Nightly, any frontier wayfarer could see the pinprick of his lamp and hear the wind-drifting, echoing cry of his violin...even the long years after death took him; and time, the last traces of his cabin.

Other even older story has an 1816 pirate sloop, hurricane driven for San Bernard haven, but crushed instead in the storm's fist. Yet . . . one survivor! And he knew the treasure in the wreck-buried chest. Perhaps it was part of the incredibly rich *Santa Rosa* swag taken that very year in Matagorda Bay to the west.

Was that man the recluse that yet another legend brings back to a hut on the island at San Bernard's mouth? That one fiddled the nights away with his jug and old chanteys and searched through the days when few but Karankawa Indian looked from the trees and, looking, saw only a lone, crazy man. Him, it might have been, they found on his pallet, head and fiddle split; and all about, scoured by angry search. That one, too, they buried in the dark waters . . . with his fiddle.

But not his music.

Half a century ago, any old timer could remember a group of strangers who once rowed the bend past the island, just to wait out the windy dark, they said, and to listen. Had they really intended beaching somewhere below . . . and searching for something? Whatever their intent, they came back badly shaken and were never seen again.

But those are the memories of old timers, and they are about gone now. Old Blind Lee was one. "Deckhanded some," said Henry, looking round at his white-haired, merry-faced wife. "How old was Blind Lee, Nettie? Musta been a hundred and twenty-five." It was coming in, late nights, that troubled Old Blind Lee.

"Why he'd go straight up the mast and yell: "Lawd! Mr. Henry, git outta here quick! Lawd God, he's fixin' to fiddle ag'in!""

Then Henry Overbay starts to tell you about their recluse friend they called Sandy — down from the East, alone down there before much of anything was built up. But he seems to skip parts of the story, and finally he stops.

Once or twice, Sandy showed the Overbays some of his crude-minted *reales;* and you get the feeling that this loner not only dared the music. . .but found what he hunted, before he died not so long ago.

"You'd have figured him poor. . .mighty poor. He was smart. Ane he was rich. You wouldn't believe how rich that old man died!"

I asked Henry Overbay if he thought that somebody's finding the treasure might have ended the music off Fiddler's Island. He shrugged and changed the subject.

Well, you can find out. . .if you wish.

Just above Freeport, take the Churchill Bridge road, paved west as far as Angie and Cowboy Risinger's Totem Pole Cafe. They'll get you on down the shell to Nettie's Place. The Overbays will let you over on Fiddler's Island . . . even to spend the night.

Or to boat out and fish the river. The San Bernard ghost won't bother a fisherman; after all, maybe the strange music really is gone

I didn't camp the island; couldn't get my camper over that catwalk. And I didn't stay the night to fish; my reel had begun to snag. Anyhow, it's all legend.

But. . .well, let me know what you hear, will you?

Jim Bowie's Mine

It was hard dark and the wind came gusty with rain sheets. August Oestreich, lanky and muddy-booted, peered at the depression and its pit within the mesquite clump — bullseyed in his pickup's headlights. He welcomed the rain: first good one in ninety-two days for their rocky two hundred acres, sixteen miles southwest of Llano.

Sodden and sloshing, I didn't mind too much either: this was my fourth try at finding the place. Maybe here in the shinnery and old granite hills, I really was looking into the original shaft: "*Los Almagres*," the "Lost Jim Bowie Mine." The big one!

Now, a lot of us know that most of the fun is believing the legends. Most lore-loving Llanoans, high in our Hill Country, believe that, if there is an old shaft where Spaniards stacked their silver bars, it is here and not seventy miles west, at Menard, where Bowie searched and fought. And they have reason.

Inside the barrier brush, the shaft is a five-foot black circle, piercing the rock like a well, straight down, perhaps forty feet. Crisscrossed bars, rolled wire and brush top it. The Oestreichs think this is only a ventilation duct, for it drops to a maze of tunnels, collapsed and stoppered, as must be the main entrance far beyond and still secret down one of them. It was worked by the Spaniards; old Castillian writing is cut in the tunnel walls below. Up one lateral they found ancient Spanish coins and men's skeletons.

Lightning flared, and I stepped closer to look down.

"Watch it!" said August Oestreich. "It caves in. I don't go down no more."

The last time he went down was 1947. At shaft bottom, rotting beams held a boulder that held the roof leading to all those passages, some already collapsed, any of them ready to bury you. Living there a quarter century, he never passed the boulder, not even for the solid silver bars up one of those pitch dark galleries.

And what about the silver bars?

In 1756, Don Bernardo de Miranda, Spanish Lieutenant Governor of Texas, rode to Llano country. Some say it was to red-cliffed Packsaddle Mountain, a long pickaxe echo northeast, which he mined. But wherever his shaft, Miranda reported great treasure. Spaniards began to dig for Apache and Comanche silver.

Miranda asked for a fort. Presently one went up seventy miles west, at what is now Menard on the San Saba. Though its Franciscans went out to Christianize the Indian, that presidio made a convenient kind of "bank" for treasure-seeking Spain. Maybe the ingots came from the mountains west. Or maybe, as everybody relentlessly believed, they came from these oldest of rocks, Llano's granite.

In any event, there followed the searchers. Secretive Indian, map-studying Mexican, money-hungry American. Harp Perry, a roving filibuster, smelted silver up the Llano in 1834 until Comanches drove him out. He came back thirty years later, an old man, to search for silver he'd hidden. The country had changed.

And there were others by the score; other places by the dozens. Scotsman George Gordon found and lost the treasure — this time near Fort McKavett in McCulloch County, farther west. A ranger captain named Johnson saw it as a young man and could have found it as an old man, but he was blind. Some of Ben McCulloch's rangers stumbled on it near Packsaddle, could tell you of the old pick still stuck in the tree, pointing to the sealed entrance. They couldn't find their way back.

The Dixon expedition, out of San Marcos, traced old

Spanish maps into the bottoms of Silver Creek, above Menard, found every marker on the map — everything. Except the elusive silver.

Inevitably, you come to Jim Bowie. In 1830, he spent a year living with the Indians until he had threaded up their secret. He took eleven men into one of our frontier's most incredible fights — the one near the San Saba — survived it, knew the great treasure trove was really west, near the old mission at Menard. Some figure he really knew, and if he did, he took the secret with him into Alamo.

The Lost Jim Bowie Mine has been sought doggedly, urgently and with certainty in a half-dozen Hill Country counties. A mine? A cave? Or a cache, like Lafitte's buried treasure?

A hard-headed San Antonio lawyer spent eighty thousand dollars, together with a Comanche chief's granddaughter, scouring around Menard. Only recently, one young man with secret knowledge came to August Oestreich on his granite-hilled Llano pasture. The silver was in those tunnels; he could find it! Did he have money to work the shafts? No, he would sell stock. Oestreich said no.

The Oestreich pasture is not easy to find, or we would not have been standing in the night rain. It is nine cattleguards west on gravel from the Riley Mountains between Fredericksburg and Llano.

If you are sightseeing only, don't bother. The gate is locked; the dogs are out. If you really intend to find those silver bars, and you have the means to do it, you can find farmer Oestreich easily enough. And you'll like him.

We dodged the sudden night trees and boulders, looming in the rain across his pasture. We talked awhile in his house.

"What do you really think is down there?" I asked him.

"I am a stock farmer." He scrubbed the water from the sandy stubble on lean jaws. "I don't know about old mines. What do you think, Mister?"

I think the silver's down there, hidden somewhere. But then I'm not a miner either.

The Gold of Fort Teran

Northeast of Houston, the Neches comes from the forest to cut the Woodville-Lufkin road. Hidden, just upriver, is almost-forgotten Fort Teran — a strange place known to legend but hard to find in history or in fact.

This 1832 outpost, which Mexico vainly hoped would check onrushing American colonization, is dismissed by most guide books as "inaccessible." Baffling is a better word for, by boat and forest trail, you find not only a marker but, some distance away, three separate ruins, each insisting it stood as a fort.

"Inaccessible" better fits Teran's legend, specifically, its Mexican gold that men have hunted for more than a century: a cannon rammed full, gold-packed deerskin bags. And somewhere down the old trace for Anahuac, a buried, brass-bound chest. That heavy-timbered land is pocked with holes from the long, long search.

From the bridge, I drove the forested lane for three winding miles and came out on the river cabin clearing that is John Wilson's camp, a fine, remote place to fish, hunt, or just listen to the quiet. Mr. John is a graying, thin-faced man with patient eyes, an East Texas drawl, and such an honest pity for city dwellers that he changed his posted signs to welcome. He knows the Teran treasure legend, because his great grandfather was here when East Texans drove Mexican troops from Nacogdoches, three years before San Jacinto.

Ignoring Fort Teran, history says the Mexicans retreated down the old San Antonio road. But a few slipped south with a loaded wagon, held the crossing by Shawnee

Creek long enough to plunge a cannon from a high, forted bluff into the river. Down the trail, their pursuers found only the wagon, wrecked and empty.

At that time, they could not have known the cannon was loaded with gold and the wagon, with the deerskin sacks and the chest. Nor could the Mexican guard know they would never get back as an army; so their map was crude — triangling the marks of a cow's head, a turkey track and a scorpion. Those who did return, came long after — a furtive few searchers. The last was a very old man who gave up and left behind a deerskin map, the one his father had given him. A very young John Wilson saw it.

"That deerskin was so old, it was yellow as gold," old Mr. John recalled. "I found the cow's head and the turkey track. Never found the scorpion. I remember it was all measured in varas."

We took the eighteen foot longjohn upriver, landed across under a cypress and walked the woods, cutting the horseshoe bend to the old crossing. Above it in a brief clearing, a granite marker announced the site of Fort Teran, named for the general who came up to hold the Americans in check. Nothing is there now but the old holes left by long ago searchers.

A quarter mile west as the river bends back, the bank rose abruptly in a sandstone hill. On the river side, the rock opened in a low tunnel, rubble-strewn and caving in. Thirty feet inside, it made a Y and disappeared each way in darkness.

"It's blowed in the middle," said Mr. John. "Other side's blocked the same way. Used to go in when I was a kid. But not any more."

I climbed to the flat top. From the half dozen old shafts sunk from up there, you could trace the line of the tunnels far below. The shafts had sought them but had halted far short. The deepest had pierced thirty feet but was abandoned some years ago when well damp killed one of the diggers.

I crawled down the other side where the collapsed shaft once sallied on an elevated flat. About the edges seemed traces of earth parapets. From river or forest, cannon here would command the approaches.

"That river bluff," I said to Mr. John, walking down. "If that's the only height near the crossing, it's where they had to dump the cannon."

"That's why it's Money Hill, Mister. The cow's head was south, turkey track west. Like I said, I couldn't find the scorpion, but didn't you see those holes, all over?"

As natural a fort as is Money Hill, it is not the only one, nor the only place men have dug. Across the river is the collapsed and sealed entrance to an eleven-room cave, old as five generations' memory. Passages, three by six feet, once led to ten-foot square rooms, brick-lined and shelved. A very young John Wilson had ventured here, too, until the wild hogs made it risky. It was dynamited.

Two miles down river is the other elevation comparable to Money Hill. A half mile in from the bank are some tumbled rock walls that suggest a small, unfinished presidio. That made three of them, three places where a man could have stood his ground, could have felt he'd built his fort . . . And so it isn't that Fort Teran is hard to find; it's hard to guess which: old Money Hill's collapsed Corregidor, the blasted caves on the Neches' north bank, or the rock walls back from the river.

The treasure? Mr. John figures that, over the long years, somebody found the chest and forever left that forest. Then what about the cannon? It had to hit the water right under Money Hill's bluff.

He showed me his high water trot line. It crossed, twenty feet above our boat.

"When she gets up," he said drily, "lots o' water comes down this river. Where you reckon that cannon'd be by now?"

And so you figure that Fort Teran isn't inaccessible; only it's treasure. And you think of the incomprehensible grubbing of those who have looked for it so long.

On the way to his boat, we had stopped to examine what John Wilson predicted would be a good fall and acorn crop. Good, fat deer, he judged from their tracks.

"Remember that hill by the rocks," he said mildly. "That one where you said there was maybe a third fort?"

"Sure," I said. "There was some digging all around it."

"Well," said John Wilson, "that's Buck Hill now. And you know why? An old man sat there in a rockin' chair one afternoon. He shot him seven big bucks without movin'. He could just as easy gone down to that good hole and caught him a mess o' catfish."

"Good," I said. I was irritated because, as always, we'd missed what we had been so close to. All that treasure.

"You miss my point," said John Wilson. "A man gets him one o' them machines, digs around and all. When he could be really huntin' . . . fishin', anyway."

1838 —

The Steinheimer Saga

Because years of treasure hunting have both lured and troubled her family, we'll call her Mrs. Jones; she prefers anonymity for herself and her farm home southeast of Waco. For over three decades she has wrestled with the possibility that her land hides the legendary fortune of a shadowy, strange early adventurer, one Karl Steinheimer.

Steinheimer's somewhat obscure saga, as often ridiculed as recalled, depicts a German youth disappointed in love and thus 1804 runaway to successive careers as a Lafitte pirate off Galveston Island, a slave ship captain, finally a mining prospector in northern Mexico. Twenty years prospecting the Sierra Madre near Monterrey, Steinheimer became wealthy; his was a silver bonanza.

In 1838, he looked across the Rio Grande: Texas claimed republic status; in that new country his wealth could acquire vast land holdings and open a future as wide and secure as the horizons. More important, he had word that his boyhood sweetheart was now free, living in St. Louis.

387

They could share that future. For Karl Steinheimer, decision was easy: take what treasure he could manage inconspicuously, leave for America.

He packed ten jackloads of silver bullion, took his two most trusted men, and pushed north over the upper Mexican desert, into Texas and her guerilla fighting that pitted Texan, Mexican, Indian and plain renegade in the troubled times following San Jacinto. Traveling awhile with an irregular Mexican force (Manuel Flores' contingent of the Cordova Rebellion), Steinheimer escaped from one Texan-Mexican clash near today's Georgetown and hurried on alone. Passing themselves off as traders, he and his men journeyed north up the old Indian-Spanish trail that is approximately by today's San Antonio-Dallas highway, but his party was too small, his cargo too obviously inviting.

Some accounts say he knew he was followed by renegades or fugitives from the earlier fight; in any event, near the three-stream headwaters of Little River, south of today's Belton, he cached his treasure, marked it and pressed on. But pursuit was on him; in the wooded Little River bottoms, his party was wiped out and he, with a gangrenous wound, stumbled on afoot.

Shortly, some travelers overtook him. Whether or not the very renegades who had attacked, Steinheimer must have felt he had no choice; the travelers agreed to send a courier north, and the near delirious man wrote his sweetheart a detailed letter. If he did not appear within three months, she would know him dead and the treasure, hers. It was carefully buried, just so: by the trail, this big live oak and in it, the brass spike he had driven. On its head were amplifying directions, and the wealth was hers alone; he had laid a curse upon it for anyone else. And here, the trail ends for Karl Steinheimer.

In due time from St. Louis came treasure hunters; the lady sought her legacy. They ransacked the trail, the Little River woodland, but finally rode away empty-handed. However, they left a century of legend to taunt many a scouring of those bottoms. Not long ago, a highly publicized search took place near Salado, its backers certain of a strike. As had scores of others, they failed.

Of all who have searched, Glen Rose's R. E. Shackelford believes he was closest. Years ago, after studying accounts of the cache, he and his partner determined to try Little River once more. They knew of the live oak and the brass spike. Close by, the treasure was buried, at least by Steinheimer. But finding the tree? Little River folks just shrugged; too many had looked before. The two men found the terrain as old story had described it, but no more.

They went back again and again. "Finally," says Shackelford, "we found the tree, the spike imbedded in a limb about ten feet high. We started to dig; it was like looking for the proverbial needle in the haystack. Then my partner got sick and we had to quit. But one thing I'm sure of: there's truth to the Steinheimer treasure.

"I have the brass spike, had it checked for authenticity. It's old and on its head, some kind of map had been carved. But it was too faint; we couldn't make it out."

Searcher Shackelford overlooked another piece of the legend. As persistent as the brass spike clue has been the conviction that the treasure had been found, likely by the renegades, moved and hidden again, perhaps not too distant. And that brings us to Mrs. Jones; her land is not far away.

"Working the farm in 1936," she recalls, "we began to turn up things and then we began to search in earnest. At depths of from three to ten feet, we found a map carved on lead, another on rock, some Austrian and Mexican coins minted in 1804 and earlier."

Her most extraordinary find was a protectively sealed diary, a haphazard and illiterate set of notes by a nameless diarist, all of which she concedes could be hoax. But if they are valid, she reasoned, here indeed could be the renegade cache, moved from Steinheimer's original hiding place.

The notes seem to indicate a strange mixture of renegade breeds with a tyrannical, half-crazed German for their chief. The diary suggests that, one by one, the original band had been killed off. Two caves had been dug.

The smaller one, "for provisions", was found by the searching Jones family . . . empty.

The sealed treasure cave? When last I heard, the search continues, but warily. Mrs. Jones halfway believes the treasure's curse. And the diary, incoherent as it is, ends with an entry substantiating this lady's concern. It was written apparently by a last survivor in the camp. "Cannot get to cave to get money, he watch it to close," the scrawl finishes, ". . . let him have it all . . . leave tomorrow . . ."

And so, after thirty-five years' hunting, record-searching as far as Germany, and two deaths in her family, she has still found "only what we can call junk. Many believe this is all a hoax," she concedes.

But not all. At last report, at least two reputable firms have volunteered their services in her search. The outcome? At this writing, I do not know.

She asked two things of me. One, understandably, is anonymity for name and home. The other?

What did I think: hoax or not?

I think, Mrs. Jones, that — perhaps like Steinheimer — legends die hard.

1873 —

Gran Vaquero's Brush Treasure

In lonely Tilden, where big mesquite shades the brush country, all from Laredo toward Corpus Christi, they were talking about how the rains had brought out range grass . . . and big rattlers. I asked if there was any new treasure sign.

"Those old treasure stories!" The court house lady replaced her map and fixed me over her glasses for a prospector who had dry-camped too long. "Folks don't set much store in those stories."

390

Of course they do, and they should; for across his rough and rolling home range, J. Frank Dobie left such treasure to all of us. This state's *gran vaquero* of open-eyed searchers and far-seeing writers waybilled to his brush country, more secreted lodes per cactus-thatched mile than almost anywhere in the Southwest.

That it is unlikely for silver and gold — this arroyo-twisted, lean thorn and gray grit and choppy mesas called "mountains" — is unimportant. The old Laredo-San Antonio trail wandered this way; and up its heat and shadow, Frank Dobie knew the troves. By hilltop and cave, by forgotten tree and parched spring, by shifting river course, he trailed upwards of a dozen hidden hoards, largely all within Live Oak and McMullen Counties.

I followed him to perhaps three of the best known — the flat-topped Mexican pyramid that is San Caja Mountain, Loma Alta's long notched mesa, and over the sea of brush that somewhere drowns the ruins of the "Rock Pens".

San Caja is easiest to find. It stands lonely and quick-sloped above the dead-fingered mesquite, ten miles east of south from Tilden. It was a far-seen way marker on the old Mexican trail; and those early ones, hiding or chasing in the early 1800's, named it "Holy Box" or, some say, for some coffinless-buried wayfarer.

Up its west side, a couple of miles from the back road near the river, is a cave. Legend has bandit treasure — gold candelabrum to silver bullion by the jack load — in a hidden room, deep within. The very old ones of the border can warn that a fearful monster stands guard; the more practical ones fear a rattlers' den.

San Caja's treasure? It is all about: nine jackloads of bullion atop, two cowhides of doubloons down the south face, off east in the knobby rock, a hidden entrance to the deep room. Over a century, San Caja has been pried, dug at, blasted and cross-lateraled. It has yielded "sign" in uncovered holes and rock cairns, nothing more.

In the Cajitas and Las Chuzas north are other legended caches, as to the south. At the McMullen line, you can see a newer treasure in the distant tanks of Seven Sisters'

391

field. Close on you is the country's highest hill, Loma Alta; and somewhere down its long base should be seven round rocks.

Once they were in line, pointing to fortune. But now, if there at all, they are scattered under the mat of pear and thorn.

Even richer — and, of course, harder to find — are the baffling "Rock Pens", west toward the great bend of the Nueces. Those pens, known to a young cowboy Frank Dobie and hunted hard for a century, have a taunting fabric of fact with their legend.

The treasure was looted from Mexico, and its bandits, saddled hard for San Antonio, found themselves pinned near the river by a Comanche war party. With hopelessly open country ahead and behind, a train too rich to leave and too slow to run, they forted a ravine fed by a small spring. They shoved up two low barricades.

Buried in one, went their treasure; in the other, the remains of their last stand where, as always with forbidden loot, only one man survived.

Frank Dobie found a waybill from a long later Austin deathbed of one Daniel Dunham: "At the foot of the hills, at the mouth of a ravine, there is a large rock. Under the rock, there was a small spring of water . . . due east . . . there is a rock pen . . . and due east a few yards there is another pen of rocks. In that pen is the spoils of thirty-one mule loads . . ." Dunham's date was 1873.

Over the years, searcher Dobie trailed every brush country old timer who thought he had glimpsed or very nearly found those pens. They were here . . . no, there: far as La Salle or Live Oak Counties. Time and the brush took the country; the treasure yet lay hidden. Frank Dobie went on to treasures from Arizona's forbidden canyons to Durango's trailless chasms, and to true statue in Southwestern letters. But of all the treasure left to us, I suspect his favorite was the wealth of his youth — the brush country lodes.

W. C. Rutherford, who ranches east of Tilden, sketched me a map in the dirt by his tractor: San Caja, below the river; and beyond it, Loma Alta. Then he passed his hand over a hundred square miles of the rough land where the Nueces bends round the hills. Somewhere in the rocky arroyo, thorn and chaparral, are the pens.

"Some say ... up the river about ten-fifteen miles. Some say, on the Two Rivers Ranch." He grinned when I asked if he had hunted. "Couple of years ago, my son-in-law flew a small plane all over that country. Figured to see from the air."

No, he hadn't looked at San Caja. He guessed the one who searched hardest was the fellow forty years ago who ran a shaft clear through and out the top, trying to hit that lost room. Under his pulled down hat brim, Rutherford squinted a smile:

"That feller had to believe. He was a banker."

They're still sure, today's searchers. Stop with Roy Wheeler, who runs the white frame variety store opposite Tilden's court house. San Caja is on his brother's ranch.

Two weeks earlier, some boys came in from Fort Worth, asking permission to hunt the mountains, maybe look round for the pens.

"I told those boys they'd make more money digging ditches," said Wheeler. "But they had to try."

Probably we'll never really know how many, beside Frank Dobie, will find that brush country treasure.

I never pass the low, squared-off hills away east from State 183 that I don't think of a young cowboy's beginning his search. Then I realize it's all still there, waiting over the hills for the finding ... when you take a notion. And finally ... how much treasure has been found, just thinking that way.

Which is to say that Frank Dobie made a lot of us rich.

Behind the Guadalupes' Wall

"Just old mountains!" The tourist lady craned from her car window. "National park? What's so special up there?"

She had glanced along the east battlements of Guadalupe Peak and El Capitan, below the southeast New Mexico line. Then, bound south from Carlsbad Caverns, she was gone down U.S. 180's steep-curling pass to drum the desert's salt flats far below, toward El Paso. Like most of us, she'd scanned only the stern outer walls of what will be Guadalupe Mountains National Park, second to be designated in Texas. "What's special?" seems fairly asked below, for until the park opens, you see only the edge view of ramparts that wedge thirty miles into Texas. You cannot see what lies behind that wall: a sea of mountains, our highest and a dozen loftier than Big Bend's.

Atop those high crags, the green tufts are forests that spill to chasm-slashed labyrinths, beginning with spectacular McKittrick Canyon, north of El Capitan's towering bastion. The park service has compared the Guadalupes with any American wilderness, noting that the hidden interior is magnificently unchanged from the days of Geronimo's Apache.

To almost all but Apache, that wall has guarded the Guadalupes' secrets: a mighty and beautiful maze of mountain and chasm that could lose a U.S. cavalry patrol and perhaps still hides a legendary fortune in gold.

While you await the park, you need not pass, unseeing. Stop with the Bob Wests, just under state line at Nickel Spring. He is a strong-faced former lawman, and she has

394

known mountains since a youngster. And you may meet longtime ranchers, in for coffee. They'll be reticent or may pretend to scoff at Guadalupe legend, but as well as any, they know that hidden park: its sheer gorges, its lofty slopes standing Ponderosa pine and Douglas fir, bighorn and elk. They know the high, fragile trails skirting canyons that are well-named Blue, Devil's Den and, of course, the close quarter Yosemite that is McKittrick.It is in these and in the hundreds of shallow-pocked caves that the Guadalupes best hide their secrets like "Old Ben" Sublett's Apache gold. And these are true secrets, for geologists can tell you that these mountains were once barrier reefs heaved upward in prehistoric cataclysm. Gold simply can't occur there. Yet. . .

You had better begin by visualizing this range in an earlier perspective. See it as did the Forty Niners, gold-rushing California. From St. Louis and Memphis, the trail crosses Arkansas, enters Texas above today's Sherman... Abilene ... San Angelo ... the Pecos' Horsehead Crossing ... looping north for El Capitan's far-seen way-marker ... on to El Paso ... and, for those who got through, the golden West.

Here, at the Guadalupes' southmost tip was one of the Apache's deadliest points of ambush. East or west-bound wagons were looted and burned; the Indian faded into his mountains. One pursuing cavalry patrol lost itself so completely, its troopers destroyed their horses and came down from the heights by compass and afoot.

By the 1880's, the old Butterfield trail is fast fading to memory for, to the south, Texas and Pacific drives its iron rails to junction with Southern Pacific at Sierra Blanca on a lower El Paso route.

T. & P. road-ganging is an old time prospector, almost worn out from dead ends in Arizona and New Mexico. He is William C. Sublett and he shacks his children in tiny, desert Monahans where womenfolk will care for them. He has one more try left in him and periodically from the thread of track now nearing Van Horn, he disappears. The rail hands and townfolk know him loco, for when very drunk, he mumbles of an Apache who has told him where a fortune in gold lies hidden. More than that, he invariably strikes out for the Mescalero's very home range — the Guadalupes — where no sane white man travels.

They call Bill Sublett "Old Ben", try to shame his weeks' long disappearances: "who's to look after your kids, Ben?" Yet now, in the Odessa saloon that knows him dire-poor and crazy to boot, he turns up for drinks all round. He spreads a fistful of gold nuggets, pebble-sized. What about his kids now? he can buy 'em anything! They stare at the nuggets, then the old prospector. *Where, Bill?*

Again and again, as time turns, "Old Ben" disappears in the desert and turns up with more gold. They try to worm out his secret, souse him, threaten him. His old eyes haze; an Apache friend showed him. They trail him, circling always for the Guadalupes, run always onto a cold trail or into his rifle barrel. He hardens toward his "prosperity friends"; he'll take his secret with him.

Will he share his secret for, say ten thousand dollars? The old man snorts.

He can take that much from his "mine" in a week!

He takes an Odessa friend once, then celebrates their strike so completely, the other man forgets the trail. In 1887, he takes his son Rolth (some say, Ross). The boy remembers a wild trail near El Capitan, on and on beyond to a chasm of from forty to a hundred feet wide, almost a hundred feet deep, a cave at its bottom, a knotted rope down from a cliff-edge tree. He remembers all that, but he is scarcely fourteen; he cannot remember the trail.

On his deathbed in 1892, Bill Sublett tries to tell his son. The old eyes fade with strain. "You'll have to find it like I did, son," he says finally.

And from Carlsbad country, Rolth Sublett tries, almost to his death not two decades ago. He could see that quick gorge, the upheaved land about. But the trail?

"A hundred canyons like that!" Bob West looked toward the east rim of the Guadalupes. "A hundred more that you can't find."

Bob knows geology says gold's not up there. Yet old Santa Fe archives claim Spanish mining in the 1600's. Geronimo boasted that here was America's greatest gold lode. And gold, from Japanese coal to seawater, is where you find it.

So what do you do? You shrug it off. Maybe there never was a mine . . . but a cache. Perhaps California gold on the way back, ambushed, hidden, forgotten. Did he believe it's still up there? Bob West just gave a slow smile.

One thing he does believe. That hurrying tourist lady didn't know what she passed by.

1920

Ike Pancake's Search

It's a puzzler, all right: Ike Pancake's mine. At first glance, just some holes in Horseshoe Mountain, one of those easy-going hills above Gatesville, toward Waco from the pretty valley of the Leon. I suppose it's a matter of how you look at treasure.

To most Gatesville folks, who have looked since they were young, it is a collapsed Indian cave in a hillside behind the Pancake place. They feel it was sad that merry, burly old Ike paid it his last forty years, one at a time, and died at eighty-six and never found it. They liked Uncle Ike.

You stand in the shinnery on top, beside the fallen-down gin boom, and hear Ike's son Jud "certaintee she's in there, all right!" — from platinum to Jim Bowie's gold — and you try to look from under Ike's big white hat, through his gray eyes, and see the treasure the old man knew he had, right where he lived!

Some old timers see that mine as the hard way life has for some men. There was Ike, a born cattleman on a big homestead spread. He could have built a fine ranch; instead, he poured everything down those holes. The irony

397

was, he never budged on his treasure. He had it; he died, knowing he had it. And now here was Jud, sixty-two, and just as sure.

Of course, for the skeptical, Jud has a formidable shack full of old things that insist they were all here — Indian, Spaniard, and old prospector. Fly a plane over that unassuming hill today; your instruments will go crazy.

Everybody knew that young Ike Pancake, soon as settled down, was a natural rancher. He was a stocky bull of a man with set-in-his-ways features. He could outride you, outshoot you, tell a taller story and read sign you never saw. He had the land's feel and the land, too. He could ride family range fourteen miles in any direction.

But he rode restlessly, looking for something. Finally, when his son Jud was old enough to ride along, something settled him down, as Gatesville had hoped. But it was the last thing that cattletown had looked for.

Ike and Jud cantered down the sand road from the hills one day. They had discovered a filled-in sink on Horseshoe. It let into a cave. There was a rock below with Bowie's name carved and also the date, 1832. The rock said Jim had buried three thousand pounds of gold and the gold-crowned Comanche wife he had married for the secret.

They had really dug some then. Now they had a boxful of Indian signs, some Spanish, and some heavy black ore. The cave? Sealed, but they'd find a way in.

"Jud and me are gonna be millionaires," Ike Pancake said with confident tranquility. "Ain't that right, Jud?"

"That's right, Pa," Jud said, as he would for the next forty years.

Gatesville wondered why Ike Pancake didn't just make his million with the ranch. Nevertheless, Ike's friends dug, too, to help along. Then, dead-ending, they dropped out, one by one. They waited for the spell to wear off Ike. Embarrassed first, then worried, they waited over the years while the family land went slowly. It didn't wear off. Instead, father and son seemed happier each day, just with the hunting.

Those years crowd up on Jud now — what was real and what they thought, maybe dreamed about finding. Platinum with the first assays. Silver later, five veins thick and straight across Horseshoe. Gold, too; and the mother iron, if you wanted the bother. Finally, no telling; the doodlebugs jumped and rattled with what was in that mountain: maybe gee-ranium, like Ike figured.

The outfits that came never seemed to have enough stake to finish. But they turned things up. Nuggets thick enough for Jud to whittle. A silver bar someone had smelted long ago. A friend got off with that and another lost the Bowie legend-rock.

Demanding piece work on the side to keep on hunting, the mine didn't really taunt them, though; it gave something to think about while you worked. Besides, the Ike Pancakes paid their bills; their search was free and clear. When Ike died some years ago, Jud kept it that way, cedar-cutting until he could go back to looking, the way Ike would have expected.

Did he miss his dad? Jud waited awhile on that.

"We had a right full life," he said presently.

Jud will show you part of an old shaft uncovered by an unfinished quarry. It has been there a long time as has, perhaps, "the original Bowie shaft" nearby, a wandering sink that drops forty feet to water. By that is the old boom and hoist they used, trying to reach what Bowie's rock had promised. There is an abandoned fifty-foot tunnel. "Came in too high," Jud told me, stomping out echoes in the passage. "Cave's under us; you can hear her."

Later he showed me his shack of artifacts. They would excite a museum curator; a list would take a catalogue. There is a Spanish lance head, a prospector's pack saddle. The Indians left markers that zeroed in on Horseshoe's shafts. Jud is indifferent to selling these treaures; he'd rather give them to someone who understands what's in that mountain. And that is why he'll show you Ike Pancake's mine. One of you, ultimately, will understand.

Does he care if he ever finds it? Not really. That would take away some of the fun of looking and finding just enough to keep you coming.

"That silver bar I let my friends take," Jud reflected. "Fellow told me I was a damfool because I'd never see it again. He couldn't understand I don't care. I already had my fun, findin' it."

At Gatesville live the Jim McClellans, who took me to the mine and whose families go back to Coryell's founders, much as Ike Pancake's did. They do not altogether share Gatesville's well-meant pity for old Uncle Ike. In a way, they think he found his treasure the only way his kind of man could have found it.

If Ike had a dream, it was a happy one. He was beset by neither stroke, coronary, nor ulcers. He had nothing but friends. He loved his family and that love was returned. Maybe he even figured anticipation beats realization all hollow.

Anyhow, he was certain the treasure was right where he lived. However you look.

Of course it was.

1960's —

Scuba Dive for Galleons

You clear the slip, make the bending channel where the shrimp boats nest white against gray-shedded docks. Now, the blue, choppy openness of Laguna Madre, spanking up spray. Padre's building-splashed dune line rises, nearing, then astern; and you're beyond the jetties in the long swell, anchored at thirty feet.

Calvin Jarvis puts over the diving flag, white-slashed red warning to keep curious or careless boats away. He twists into his rubber wet suit, dusting powder to ease it on. He helps you, adjusting your aqualung harness and your weight belt for quick release. You pull on long blue flippers, clear your face plate, then work the mouthpiece

400

flange under your lips and grip the teats. So far, so good: the air's there.

"Okay?" Jarvis is watching your preoccupation with breathing.

"Okay." Port Isabel's old lighthouse seems far away now. Now that it's time, your biggest concern is what might wait below, even this shallow; and how you'll react to the unexpected. In that order. You tell Jarvis so.

"We'll just get wet first. Remember: stick close to me; do what I do." Then he checks you out on hand signals again.

Make no mistake; Padre is a real treasure island, with more than two million dollars known to lie somewhere beyond the surf line down its long coast.

There are two ways to seek that treasure. One, rewarding enough, is to dig and scuff at the endless dunes where the ocean has tossed small change, or harassed free-booters have hidden it. Any truly patient hunter will turn up old coins.

The other way is to dive the ocean for the mother lode. Each year, more adventuresome aqualung Texans do (offshore depths to sixty feet), where the old treasure routes have scattered sunken hulls from galleons to side wheelers.

Harry Rieseberg, America's great salvage diver, cites scores of bounty-burdened ships — a graveyard of them near storied Brazos Santiago Pass at Rio Grande's mouth — and a long string up the bending coast to Matagorda Bay and beyond.

Near the pass, as recently as 1914, the little *E. P. Wright* went down with $100,000 in specie. Not far away are the 1874 hurricane victims with their treasure: *Little Fleta*, $30,000; the steamer, *S. J. Lee*, $100,000; the *Jessie*, $100,000. From *Ida Lewis's* modest $20,000 in the master's strongbox to *Santa Rosa's* 1816 cargo of two million dollars in silver (off Matagorda) and to those forgotten ones of conquistador days, the list is long. With aqualung's recent depth breakthrough, this vast but not-too-deep floor conceivably can be explored. Diver Rieseberg rates it high for treasure searchers.

For a quick glimpse of treasure diving, Texas has no better place to start than instruction under Brownsville's Calvin Jarvis. He is a friendly man and a rugged one, an expert salvage diver who makes light of his long acquaintance, dating from Normandy, with danger's bright face.

Among the state's best is his Scuba diving school (not skin-diving with snorkels, but self-contained-under-water - breathing - apparatus: the kind Lloyd Bridges bubbled across our T.V. screens and that Hannes Keller took, plummeting a stygian thousand feet down). Jarvis is chosey, careful with students; when he's through, they're ready.

Finally, Jarvis knows what he's hunting. He showed me the two man wet sub he will use to explore a chart on which his long study has reasonably located fourteen wrecks suspect of treasure. Two, he believes, are certainties.

Would he show me the chart? He broke it out. We'd be diving in the general area of something marked "Huckleberry", but in shallower, closer-in waters.

"No strain if you're careful," he said. "It's on television that everything happens. On T.V., a man can't get wet before he's in trouble."

You duck under the ladder. A few feet down, you're over the big hurdle: you can breathe. You feel like an awkard bellows; then it settles down.

You follow Jarvis, feet first this time, down the yellow anchor line. Sensations come fast: his watching eyes behind plate and gushing air bubbles; all about, the world gone silent, dim, wafting dreamlike to a wall of nothing. Sound? In-out rushhhh of breathing — yours.

Which way is up? There . . . the bubbles angling in an unexpected direction. It's the way they said: watch those bubbles! Sharp pressure in your ears. Over drifts your hand; fingers clamp your nose. Blow! . . . Clear the pressure! Jarvis signals "Are you okay?" Signal back "Yes." Wait, the mask's filling . . . go slow, take it easy . . . hold that plate top like he said . . . tilt back . . . exhale sharply . . . ! It worked fine; the water's gone. Try it again. Look

402

up; can you see surface? No? Yes, you can; it's wandered off, over your shoulder again.

Jarvis signals up. Slow! *Go slow!* Stay behind those bubbles so your lungs adjust. There's surface, a silver sheet; the boat's bottom, a white sliver. You're at the ladder, head out, face plate back on your forehead. Pull away the mouthpiece.

"How deep?"

"You were on bottom. You kicked it. Didn't you see it?"

You do next time. Stark clarity of boulders basing the jetties, shells, spiny sea urchins, delicate yellow-stemmed plants. Dim, away there, the other two divers, speargunning a sheepshead. You can go straight down with Jarvis, follow his signals better, maneuver a little. Out, your throat's dry from bottled air. Head rings a little, but you're all right. It's over too soon.

Back at the slip, you feel heady. Sure, you just peeped the edge; but it's the exultation each of the state's quarter million divers knew, their first time.

With Jarvis, this summer, working where it's deep and the old hulks stir restless mud to blind you . . . well, that's for the pros. Some of his worst times have been dark salvage when you couldn't see your hand before your face plate.

"Something brushes you then," he said drily, "sure, you get edgy; but you don't leave. You wait and it leaves. You're down there to hunt."

If you're down there hunting around "Huckleberry" this summer, you may run on Jarvis and his sub. You won't find him from the chart, however. Rightly, he doesn't like to show it. And even if he did, you wouldn't know where to start. "Huckleberry" is coded.

But you can bet your bullion that it leads to treasure.

403

Two Lifetimes — Just Looking

"My problem's time. I *know* where it is!" He spoke with
urgent certainity, as he had for a half hour's long distance
from Fort Worth. I listened; I like treasure hunters.

"I've got it located, give or take a hundred yards, maybe
fifteen feet of over-burden. But that's a lot of hill to move.
It's private property, you understand, and my option's
up to thirty days; I'm out of money." He needed perhaps
two thousand dollars for earth moving equipment; to finish his search, he'd go partners with anyone reasonable.
Couldn't I help him find backing? He'd already assured
himself that I knew of the legendary Maximilian treasure,
that I knew the ground.

I'd been over it. It's the endless mesa country just east
of the Pecos on a line from San Angelo to Fort Stockton.
This is the lonely land of Castle Gap and, on the river,
fabled Horsehead Crossing; and, a little below, the old
Fort Concho to Stockton government road's pontoon crossing. Iraan, Rankin, Crane and tiny Girvin make a roughly
surrounding rectangle.

From old time, Castle Gap has been a doorway south
to Mexico's treasure-freighting Chihuahua Trail, or west
for California's Forty-niners. A deadly doorway, its
windowed battlements have seen Indian and outlaw
ambush of many a rich-cargoed wagon or stage. Legend
has it that Maximilian's collapsing forces smuggled great
Mexican wealth as far as these hills, and that silver for
the embattled Confederacy reached the end of the line
in Castle Mountains. How many run of the mine high-
jackings, nobody knows. Nor where the hiding, across that
same-looking country.

For a long time have come the searchers and by various roads, some quite by accident. About the turn of the century, for example, an old Mexican paused, exhausted atop a ridge looking west on the Pecos pontoon crossing. Twilight was near but, pursuing down the Concho stage road, rangers were nearer. The old man hid in one of the countless shallow caves along the hillsides. In the morning, he waked to find a pile of silver bars where the cave bent and closed off.

He memorized everything: the far off crossing, the lay of the Y-shaped valley sloping toward the river, the nearby burned-out wreckage of a wagon. He took two silver bars and still had them when he was captured later that morning.

Jailed in San Antonio, he knew he would outlive neither his sentence nor the sickness in his chest. The jailer had been kind; for him, the *viejo* painstakingly traced a map. For almost twenty years, the jailer intended to follow its promise west, but time ran out on him, too. He gave the map to a friend who ranched near where Sheffield is today, about twenty miles south of the hills where the old Mexican had shared hiding with the silver.

Some time ago in Sheffield, Allen Graham showed me the map. He's a wide-shouldered and friendly West Texan who doubles as deputy and general storekeeper, and to whom the map is a pleasant puzzle: thin tissue, brown and brittle with age and filled with penciled landmarks. The San Antonio jailer had given it to his grandfather.

"That's Government Hill. See . . . the old road came down for the crossing . . . there." He put his finger on a cluster of marks. "Granddaddy followed it that far, found the old wagon iron and some rusted guns and a packsaddle. He looked a long time."

"What about caves?"

"Behind every rock. More like potholes." He laughed. "In every hill . . . and nothin' but hills. Jim Jones, over at McCamey, looked for twenty years."

I asked about Horsehead, on up the river, and its eastern gate at Castle Gap.

Allen Graham laughed again. "Man could spend a couple of lifetimes, just looking."

I spent awhile in the mapped valley that is four miles north of Iraan. There, the big Noltke ranch sprawls out, and the flat top hills are all the same and go on forever; and below its distant rims, the Pecos is narrow and sullen. There is little difference northwest at Horsehead and at Castle Gap, between McCamey and Crane, except the latter's canyon rock bears out its name. Both sites are posted; you can no longer just walk in and look.

A lot of that was in my mind — a man's spending two lifetimes just looking — when I talked with the Fort Worth man. I know of two spent just that way.

To the northeast, for example, the Spanish Spider Rock treasure was hunted a long, long time. It hides, says story, near old trail town Aspermont, on the high rise between the Double Mountain and Salt Forks of the Brazos, above Abilene. That rugged, broken land was said to have claimed a mid-Eighteenth Century Spanish way station on a road Spain tried hard to link from San Antonio's missions to Santa Fe's mountains. History knows the road failed; this story claims the upper Brazos outpost wiped out and its treasure lost.

A web-like map carved on rock was believed key to this cache and, for over a century, well into this one, many a searcher has felt close indeed to Spider Rock's New Mexican treasure. Some believe it long ago discovered and spirited away.

One who believed it still there was a solid midwest farmer named Frank Olmstead. Converting everything for finances, he began searching about 1920. Mostly he worked alone, pick and shovel, cross-trenching and shafting the shale breaks above the Salt Fork. He built a hillside dugout to live with his search.

For thirty years he dug, dropping a crude ladder, bucketing out empty dirt, then moving a little and digging again. At seventy-two, he died, still certain he'd been just a shovel blade's distance from his dream. His Aspermont friends remembered him as a good, gentle man who made ends meet with odd jobs when his lifetime's money ran out.

As he asked, they buried him in one trench that had missed.

Long lean miles west, in the spiring Davis Mountains, historian Barry Scobee can trail an even grimmer hunt. It takes you twenty-five miles west of Fort Davis, where State 166 magnificently circles Mount Livermore, and where an old army outpost fronts a brief canyon. Its springs, dwindling today, took the name 'El Muerto''; close above them is the troopers' rock and adobe ruin. Farther up is a collapsed, near-filled shaft and a legend that one West Texan followed to rainbow's end.

A combine of bandits had robbed a Monterrey cathedral, galloped north to cache their Mexican treasure and, as often with thieves, dumped most of each other into the deep shaft they had used to bury their loot.

If any, few ever came back. However, a curious man from dusty little Valentine trailed one hunter into the mountains and came out, visibly excited. To piece together what he suspected, he then backtrailed from Arizona to Mexico; finally he was certain. A hundred paces up the little canyon from *El Muerto*, he began to dig. He was Bill Cole, then mid-fortying, friendly, down-to-earth, and quietly confident. He went down and down, year on year, eighty-five feet through rock. He hit water, moved his shaft.

Much like Olmstead, north on the Brazos, he had rigged a tripod hoist and toiled alone in his pit. Across the mountain country, they joked with him at first, then they kept quiet. He kept on. Kept on for the remaining forty years of his life.

Age slowed him, moved him to his old home place in Valentine. Eightying now, he was too frail for the mountains, too deep in his quest. He dug at home. He had worked to ten feet, just by his porch, when the years caught him and never let go.

I hope my Fort Worth friend found his treasure, but I passed.

What stuck in my mind was his remark that his problem was time.

And Allen Graham's, about spending two lifetimes just looking.

407

Part Seven

A Number of Things

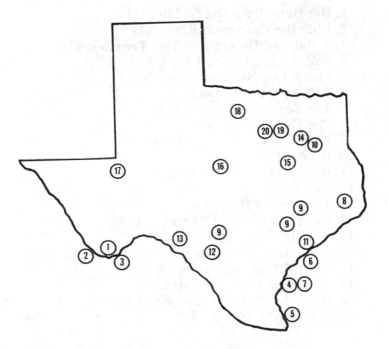

*"The world is so full of a number of things, I'm sure
we should all be as happy as kings."*

Robert Lewis Stevenson

Big Bend From The Saddle

From the rearing, jagged rims of the Chisos, you look out on space and mountain, tumbled away blue. Cupped behind you, Big Bend's mile-high Basin is a thimble, there below. Those tiny dots are corrals.

Down beside, they *were* big. They are the red, heavy-planked corrals of fifty sleek-muscled, short-backed mountain horses — the Chisos Remuda; and the two-story block and siding building is headquarters for one of America's best horseback adventures. That is, for tenderseats like you and me.

You're as safe over the mountains on those sorrels, bays and pintos as in your rocking chair. This string of mounts is so exceptionally trained for the non-experienced, they have carried fifty thousand riders over the mountain trails with no injuries and only one complaint at this writing. The complaint, in a moment.

All the Chisos — its coppery crags and hidden, timbered canyons — and the hazy outlands beyond their rim is your fenceless, million acre range for an expertly-guided, saddled-up spectacular. And high here, you are looking down on the land of the Big Bend Pack Trips — three to seven-day saddle horse journeys into elsewise inaccessible mountain back country during its most exhilarating season — October through spring.

Certainly you can make it. Riders age five to sixty have, and many have stayed a day or so longer than they had planned.

To visualize your trip, think of the Chisos as a towering

411

island of bunched peaks, thrust from a sea of lesser mountains, all bounded by the south-circling gash of the Rio Grande gorges.

Packing in, paced not to tire the least-experienced rider, you can circle the center range in three easy days or swing deeper, with more time, to points as remote as broodingly beautiful Mariscal Canyon at the national park's southmost tip.

Each day's ride, anchored on eye-popping meals (steak once a day and biscuits each breakfast) begins and ends on shelter. Refurbished ranch houses of Big Bend's rock and adobe days sleep you comfortably cool or warm. Also, they give privacy to the ladies (a surprising sixty per cent of the pack trip riders).

I visited with remuda hoss boss Jim Johnson, a lanky, younger Will Rogers who can ride anything four-legged and can't remember when he started. I asked him to sum up his advice for this fall's riders.

"Relax and let the hoss do the thinkin'." Then he added. "We size up each rider in advance — age, experience, weight, scare an' all. When he goes up next mornin', he's got the exact horse and saddle.

"Take ol' Freckles. I guess you could spook him if you blew up the mountain. Freckles carries the youngest, frailest kiddo."

That's the way it works each early morning at the corral. The denim-jacketed lead wrangler stands above, thumbing the cards on thirty riders who will be up in exactly thirty minutes. The night before, each horse and saddle were selected for the right rider. The big pinto, Geronimo, would take the heavy, middle-aged Dallasite, long out of a saddle. Tigre, the sure-footed dun with small, mule's hooves, would carry the edgy East Texas lady. The black-hatted Abilene rider would draw Karo, a cutting horse money winner.

Then they're saddled, one each minute; and motionless they wait, breathing early high smoke. They move out only when the lead wrangler clears the gate; and long later, they are a far off Z, climbing the easy switchbacks toward high and green South Rim.

412

Your pack trip will move with early sun the same way, except the X-saddled mules will string in, carrying bedrolls and groceries. A meal ahead, a camp cook will be building mesquite coals beside a six-foot rock outdoor oven and shoving the ten gallon water can over for boiling. Your first lunch will be fried chicken.

Before that, you'll have trailed down from the Window, under cliffs as sheer as Royal Gorge's, crossed a high, silver-distant hogback and dropped beside a hundred foot high Cattail Falls, spraying up its box canyon.

Later, there will be the painted riot of Apache Canyon, with its pictographed caves and old Mescalero campgrounds; then the high, rolling openness of Burro Mesa, and the long clippyting trail through remote Blue Creek Canyon, as weirdly figured as Utah's Bryce.

Long later, you may be under the half-mile cliffs of South Rim, or atop them, or possibly down past wild-colored Castolon Peak toward the old cavalry post on the river, or deeper beyond where desert crags twist in high torment toward Mariscal, or you may be up the slopes of Lost Mine Peak where the topmost rock makes a pastel-striped cliffside that juts over blue void and somewhere hides a legendary Spanish gold mine.

Finally, you'll climb and climb to the big stands in Pine or Juniper Canyon, past deep Boot Canyon and down the switchbacks ... where the Basin looks like a thimble and the corrals are dots. And it's over.

And sure, you're stiff.

I mentioned a complaint. It was not cost; Big Bend is one of the country's thriftiest trail rides; you'd spend as much, any fun-hunting weekend. Nor is it a crowded ride: one, eight or thirty can pack in, and there's distance enough for solitude and always room for company. Nor is it the pace. A day's ride can be five or twenty-five miles, depending on your saddle inclination. It is neither bed nor board; both have all of outdoor's zest.

You won't guess it. One lady's horse stopped too often to eat grass.

413

Ride the Canyoned River

In late fall, 1899, Texas' great geologist, Robert T. Hill, took five men and three heavy boats to explore for a month the three hundred fifty miles of mountain-barriered Rio Grande, from Presidio, around Big Bend all the way to lonely Langry: first, thus, to record from within, our mighty triple canyons — Santa Elena, Mariscal, and Boquillas.

Each year now, scores of outdoor families run one or more canyons and, with care, find them excitingly safe. The river and the mountains have changed little, yet it is axiomatic that peril lurks closest to the first man into the unknown. Here then is the canyoned river road as seen by explorers then and now.

Until Dr. Hill's epochal journey, the Rio Grande's upper Texas reaches had been considered impenetrable — an awesome, dark-gorged barrier that no man dared venture. True enough, steamboats — flat-bottomed, shallow-draft things — had plied the lower waters regularly from Brownsville to Camargo, from as early as Henry Austin's 1829 *Ariel* to 1907 *Bessie's* last run, from Roma to Brownsville. Camargo was head of navigation although Laredo was occasionally reached and an 1850 Fort Brown quartermaster's report claimed that keelboats had struggled upriver thirteen hundred miles to impassable white water — a feat that would have pushed them close to the forbidding western mountains.

Still, it remained for intrepid, forty-one-year-old Dr. Hill to pierce the barrier.

414

On October 5, 1899, Hill's little flotilla put in below the prehistoric crossing of Presidio, where Rio Conchas comes from the Mexican mountains and renews an almost dry Rio Grande. On their first day they were below the outlying huts and Ben Leaton's adobe-walled Fortin, where scarcely half a century earlier, this first Big Bend Anglo had subdued Apache and Comanche alike with cannon. Beyond this point they would see almost no living being for weeks.

Pushing southeast, they maneuvered the white water of the Bofecillos Mountains and the first of the river canyons in which "they were to be entombed for weeks." On they pressed, day after day, as the barrier ranges rose successively higher, past today's Tapado and Close Canyons and one they named Black Rock, "hemmed in by vertical walls, rising a thousand feet to plateau tops." Days were hot, over 120 degrees; nights were frosty. Night camps were guarded; this was yet bandit country. But it was the great wall looming ahead like some monstrous mirage they really dreaded.

Hill estimated they had come a hundred miles when they were confronted with "the awesome gash" in the Santa Elena Range, half a mile high and nearly fifteen miles wide. Dwarfed by such a portal, the stream looked to them no more than "a mere thread reach-into abyss."

"In almost the twinkling of an eye we passed out of the desert glare into the dark and silent depths of gigantic canyon walls, which rise vertically from the water's edge to a narrow ribbon of sky. The flow is so silent as to be appalling," Hill would recall. "For its entire length, there is no place where this cliff can be climbed by man." More and more, they came to dread a sudden flood within those walls.

Little over a mile inside the gorge, Hill thought his expedition doomed. From the southern wall, a gigantic rockslide, boulders big as houses, appeared to block their boats, promising to crush them and suck their occupants under. For three days, hand over hand and dreading any missed step, they portaged, climbing almost two hundred feet over the rushing river.

Camp Misery behind, they ran the rest of the canyon, noting as elsewhere the high-perched river wall caves. Hill made no note of one, three miles from Santa Elena's mouth, that has come down as one of that country's most persistent legends — a dark passageway that crosses under the river from Texas to Mexico. Any hydraulic engineer can prove that such a cave must be water-filled, yet there are Texans today who "know" men who have negotiated that under-river cave.

Hill's voyagers found the mouth of Mariscal Canyon, bottommost of the triple gorges, "a seething hole without visible outlet," and they found the imprisoned river more twisting than Santa Elena's. What they noted most was the almost total absence of any form of life and the utter stillness of their passage, for they had long grown accustomed to the rushhh of the water.

Below Mariscal they paused at the rock and adobe ruins of Spain's Presidio San Vicente, the 1750 fortress that was to protect treasure mines, but that failed and fell to the Indian and left only the legend that named Lost Mine Peak, away to the north. Hill may have stood in the crumbling doorway of San Vicente and watch sunrise color the crags of the peak, where the treasure was sealed. Yet, a practical scientist, he must have known that only on Easter morning does the sun work such a miracle; the treasure was lost to him, and nothing remained but to return to his boats.

Two days below Mariscal, Hill's flotilla, still intact was into fifty-mile-long Boquillas, deepest of the three, and his party was as awed by it as by Santa Elena. Night in that canyon moved the explorer most deeply, for there was a near full moon. "Gently," Hill recorded, "the moonlight settled from stratum to stratum as the black shadows fled before it, until finally it reached the silent but rapid waters of the river, which became a belt of silver."

Finally they emerged from the canyon and the lesser ones beyond in Maravillas country, which Hill found to be a horrible desert, ultimately to arrive at the railroad waystop of Langtry and civilization beyond.

They had conquered the impassable river.

It is easier now, as my friend, Dr. John Redden of Kerr-ville recounts. An inveterate and skilled canyon boatman, Redden maintains that a rubber raft is best for such travel and for Big Bend country recommends any period from fall to spring.

"Santa Elena and Boquillas both require overnight camps enroute, unless you're an excellent and fast canoer (and canoes, wisely, are not Big Bend-recommended). The rewards," says Redden, "are generally fine weather: crystal nights that allow a winter view of heavens rarely seen elsewhere, yet such nights aren't too cool. Sunrise and sunset defy description.

"Take fishing gear," he recommends, "for channel cats hit at dusk. You'll enjoy a batter-fried camp supper and breakfast. If firewood's scarce, use dead ocotillo stumps and stems.

"Boquillas is best to start with, though the longest water trip. The going's not hazardous and good campsites are plentiful. You put in at the park's southeast edge, end at Adams Ranch or at the International Bridge below Blackgap Wildlife Refuge. The only white water is between the ranch and the bridge.

"Santa Elena is the most difficult and rewarding. Chief problem is that massive rockslide one mile inside the gorge. Officially it calls for a difficult portage; but with enough water, you can float through. Four-man-size or larger rafts (two men each) make it, safest. It's best to stop and study this one before floating through.

"Waterproofing all gear is a must; you'll ship water, this trip. The best camp site enroute is the Mexican side, one half mile of white water before entering the canyon and a good day's trip from the launch point of Lajitas. You'll clear the canyon next day.

"Once inside," Redden reports, pausing to reach for the right words, "there's a cathedral-like stillness, interrupted only by the rush of water, so closely confined by those towering walls on both sides. Occasionally you'll hear a crow, but that's about all. The ride's like a conveyor belt; the river drops uniformly . . . like a downhill highway,

417

with the sky just a blue slit far above. Light and shadow make photography tricky.

"Mariscal," he finishes, "is the shortest trip and the most difficult to reach, driving. Jeeps or pickups are best. It's possible to make the run in one day . . . but who wants to rush it?"

All necessary information is available by writing to the Ranger Station, Big Bend National Park. A park permit, at headquarters, is required. And bring all your own gear, Redden warns, best including a car for either end of your run.

Floater Redden compares the three: Santa Elena, a mighty, sheer-walled gash; Mariscal, more open-walled, yet a more twisting run past cream-colored giant columns and terraces and overhanging walls. Boquillas combines some of each — brilliant colored cliff gashes, interspersed with great, distant-walled, quiet valleys.

Safe for you? "More and more so," says Redden. "One Thanksgiving we rode awhile with a flotilla of forty-one Lubbock explorer scouts. They'd made all three canyons in one trip."

You think about that and then about that first, dark journey of Robert Hill's heavy boats. And so, as you ride safely through this next trip, pretend just for one moment. Pretend you have no idea what lies within that chasm entrance to Santa Elena, what lies beyond that next blind turn of Mariscal or Boquillas.

Then you will have traveled with Robert Hill, the first man through.

A Painted Desert and Two Treaties

Near where Mariscal Canyon slashes Big Bend's remotest southern tip, a thin graveled road threads the mountains to Glen Springs Draw. Our national park people would do well to identify this forgotten spot and to show you there.

"Draw" is classic understatement. It bursts, sudden as Palo Duro, from below a shielding ridge and flings out in wild-colored, hill-strewn *malpais*. It is a hidden painted desert.

An unmarked spur leaves the Boquillas park road to circle Nugent Mountain and meander south between the peaks of Chilicotal and Elephant Tusk. Hiding west of the ruins of the old Ellis ranch house there, the view rewards your half hour each way.

But it is on the broad shoulder, where the ranch lies, that the view really should be marked. It tilts, lowering to the distant river haze. There, walled by Mariscal to the west and Boquillas' greater depth to the east, an ancient ford crosses to the blue Mexican mountains. Binoculars let you pick up the tiny specks both sides of the river that are the adobes of San Vicente, under the loom of their patron's mountain. In 1750, where the Comanche rode this loneliest crossing of the Rio Grande, Spain thrust an outpost. Presidio San Vicente failed and fell; and the great ghost mountains which the presidio claimed took back the mines it had tried to guard.

What you see is land of unchanging legend: the curandero's healing, the lost, ghost-guarded mines, the crops that must receive St. Vincent's blessing before planting.

419

And a land involved in two strange treaties. A marker should tell of them.

One treaty, drawn far away, will not quite come off, but it teeters destiny. Across in Europe on this May 5, 1916, Kaiser Wilhelm's junker staff is forging the lightning that will blast Russia from the war and that may, along the Second Marne, smash French and British before American aid can reach them.

Mexico is ripped by revolution that ultimately will mend her. President Venustiano Carranza, trying to fend off Pancho Villa's hosts, still studies a secret German treaty offering everything from Texas west, if Mexico will league with Germany against the *Yanqui*.

This, Villa knows. American-Mexican war intrigues him; it could topple Carranza. Two months earlier he has attacked Columbus, New Mexico and drawn a pursuing General Pershing deep into Mexico. Now, however, he is thwarted. Only days ago, General Alvaro Obregon met the *Yanqui* chiefs in El Paso. Pershing will leave; the Federales have made a promise to pursue him, Pancho Villa! This is a bad thing.

This night of May 5, two hundred Villista cavalry take the old San Vicente crossing. Out of the cover of Glen Springs Draw, they hit a U.S. outpost, bivouacked near the Ellis ranch candelilla sheds. Three American soldiers die, the last to fall on this soil against invasion. U.S. patience snaps.

Pershing halts his withdrawal. He is attacked, this time by Federal troops in southern Chihuahua. The Mexican state of Sinaloa independently declares war. German Foreign Minister Zimmerman's plan to split the Americas almost works. Almost.

The entire U.S. National Guard is mobilized and moves on the border.

Mexico declines the German offer. Pershing, gradually withdraws from Sierra Madre. America's six-plane air force has been tested (and nearly abandoned), and U. S. marines will attack at Belleau Wood the last moment before midnight for the Allies.

It was that close at remotely beautiful, little-known Glen Springs Draw.

San Vicente's other treaty? Paradoxically, it pitted Indian against Indian, down this same long slope between Chilicotal and the crossing. It was an earlier time, the early 1800's, when September was known to every Comanche as the month to raid south—the time of the Mexican Moon.

Somehow, Mexican ingenuity in Chihuahua struck a solution with the raiders. Let the state of Chihuahua join Comanche against western Mescalero Apache. Let Comanche raid the other nearby Mexican states, but not Chihuahua. Fair enough? Then done!

Chief Bajo del Sol — "greatest under the sun" — took the treaty literally. He struck hard beyond Chihuahua, but riding near San Vicente, he was a friend. With only his wife and her young brother in company, he came one day on an Apache war party on the slopes near Glen Springs Draw. There were thirty Apaches and their captive, a San Vicente youth, Domingo Parras.

Despite his wife's entreaties not to go to his death, the Comanche chief made her ride on. It would never be remembered that Bajo del Sol broke his word. Bow at the ready, shield thighed up, he rode alone on the encamped Apache. Treaty, he told them, demanded that they free the boy and surrender to him. Otherwise he must attack. The Apaches deployed and, from rock to rock, the battle was fought several hours.

Bajo del Sol died in that fight, as he must have known he would. But he took such a dreadful toll that he left his name mightiest on the Comanche Trail.

It was not that he cared so much for his allies across the river. It was that a Comanche traveled light: only his weapons and his word, and they were both good.

District Park Ranger Rod Broyles, who looks like a Virginia-born Jimmy Stewart and knows Big Bend's every rock and peak and hidden vista, drove me to Glen Springs Draw. We stood and considered the grandeur of that desert, and the long slope to San Vicente's crossing, and then we poked around the flagged walkway that led to the old ranch house foundations. There is a rubble pile near the traces of the old candelilla works. Near there, Zimmerman and Villa nearly got us in a war, but the treaty never came off. Only the Comanche's did.

"Ought to mark this place, Rod." I looked over at Mexico. "Any reason why not?"

Rod regarded me like a ranger concerned with his park, not politics.

"Come on," he said. "I'll show you the old tent line. Army's been in here several times."

1970's

Padre Island Auto Log

Once Deems Taylor, a thousand words at his disposal, struggled to describe a work by Wagner. He finally wrote: "The orchestra then played *Prelude to the Third Act of Lohengrin*, the most brilliant music ever written."

So it is with Padre; throw away your adjectives. Here is Isla Blanca of the Spanish Main, 117 miles of magnificent white island, from Corpus Christi to Brownsville: in America, unmatched. And so, these are mile-by-mile notes, somewhat like the old Auto Blue Book. I could snatch at the vastness no other way.

Across Flour Bluff causeway, checked loading at French The Beachcomber's (shell shop-lounge extraordinary): tools and emergency gear; weather promised rough beach driving. Gentlemen beachcomber Gene French, a younger, handsomer Richard Widmark, driving his Betsy, cabover, four-wheel-drive pickup. Bait and surf rigs at Bob Hall Pier, *Mile Zero*, noon.

Mile 0.1: 20 m.p.h., fringing surf on west-smooth, packed sand. Broad, fine beach. Storms have erased first two dune rows; they'll be back. Offshore Texas towers look like pygmy scaffolds. Rising dune line is low, long white endless bluff to right. Sounds: surf roar to left, engine, wind from astern, so watch overheating. *Mile 2.0*: No cars. Beach buildings, specks behind. French already brokenfield-running Padre's daily gift from the sea. *Mile 7.2*: Oil rig, tank battery behind dunes. Already inside coming national seashore, planned to remain splendidly lonely, its roadways back in the dunes.

Mile 8.1: Variety of beach loot! 100-foot length, 4-inch blue nylon hawser, many bottles, some ancient, rare. Bits of orange plastic from shrimp boat markers. First of several channel buoys (one, a slim, carved and crusted South American river marker.) Once French salvaged complete dugout canoe, hand-gouged from one log. Timbers to 8x8's and larger. Japanese shoring timber, beveled 3x3's, stenciled Jap characters that spell firm names. Want a unique fence?

Mile 11.5: Holding 30 m.p.h., dodging spiked timbers. Extraordinary inwash of lavender balloned Portuguese Men-of-War, staccato popping under wheels like firecrackers. (Don't handle; theirs is mild version cobra venom). From dune-top, island surprisingly wide. Toward mainland, Laguna Madre is silver horizon rim. Whoever described this as "pencil thin island" only saw the map. *Mile 13.9*: Dunes, higher steeper; vegetation, salt grass, sea oats like wheat fields. Unaccountably, many light bulbs. Rough surf; forget swimming today. Green Hill ahead; Little Dagger behind. *Mile 16.2*: Wreck of old shrimper. *Mile 19.4*: Beach and dunes tinting orange, means treacherous Little Shell ahead, trickier than more famous Big Shell.

Mile 20.1: Hit first shell bank, heaped-over mush. Low-low, four wheel! Backed out, crawled higher for dunes. Inwashed timber: mahogany, cherrywood, some bamboo thick as fence posts. (Bahamas, Yucatan?). Shell hunters' bonanza begins here, also beachcombers': nylon, polyethylene rope, whole creosoted pilings. New door from shrimper. Battered ship's ladder, first of many life rings, their ship's names inscrutably erased. *Mile 21.3*: Heavy going, 3 m.p.h. French towed out 28 bogged cars at this mouth of Little Shell, one afternoon. Hulk of one still there.

Mile 25.6: Good deep surf fishing hole. Beach edge, high lip, will collapse and trap a car. *Mile 29.1*: Betsy heating. Edge of Whelkland. Beautiful big spiral shells. Spiny Murex, delicate Scotch Bonnet, Sunray Venus, Sundials. *Mile 33.3*: Barge wreck. Old stake markers (to what?). Pole with electric meter still attached, old wall telephone, basketball goal. Still sweating 3 m.p.h. Occasional short sprints ending jarred in shell banks. French fighting clutch and gears; breakdown near surf here; you can forget your car. *Mile 36.0*: "Green Pastures", highest dunes, heavily grassed. Engine block and steering column in surf, once 3-ton flatbed truck. From atop dunes, counted 40 head cattle grazing long valley. Mighty sandpile of dunes 3 miles across valley, resembles faraway yellow mountains in late sun.

Mile 39.5 Rested Betsy. By accident, uncovered at dune edge, lip of 150-lb., 3-foot diameter, perfect circle concrete slab, 6 inches thick. Treasure hunters note. Meets specifications for Lafitte's legendary Padre millstone. We dug like terriers, even skeptical French, found nothing. Lafitte's treasure, believed a five figure fortune, was cached under a millstone. . .how many sand-shifting hurricanes back? Nearby, rusty ruin of old time jukebox, new rubber Voit basketball, 150 lb. block of beeswax from long ago. *Mile 41.5*: Wreckage of recent shrimper; white gulls, salt water mudhens, some ducks. *Mile 45.5*: Two marker posts to ruins of 1845 Zachary Taylor army camp far inside dunes. Dunes lowering, beach widening, tires crunching louder; into Big Shell and past "Fido" — French's point of no return. Big Shell plows like deep, soft gravel; Little Shell sucks like quicksand. *Mile 47.5*: Fishing shack, walled with service garage checkoff blackboard.

Mile 49.4: First of many delicate glass fishing floats: 10-inch blues, greens, browns — Jap, Russian, Portuguese. We netted six decorator's treasures. *Mile 51.1*: New L-shaped lake inshore, hurricane-carved. Found bottled note

No. 596 from Galveston Biological Laboratory for tide-testing. Bottle 06982, half mile south. Also two-foot block styrofoam, plastic U.S. float, new shipboard fire extinguisher. *Mile 55.0*: Coyote Lake: quiet, board expanse, beautiful at sunset, distant dunes gray gold. *Mile 57.8*: Once spacious sheet-metal beach lodge tossed to dune top, sanded to eaves, full of night-nesting birds flying in our faces.

Mile 63.1: Ran an hour into night, moonless, trying for fishing camp beside S.S. Nicaragua, wrecked in 1916. Only spotlight showed surf or dunes; headlights in beach mist catch strange shadows, make for ghost land. French's first flat in six years' beach running. Camped. Padre nights chilly; campfire easy with driftwood, extravagant with mahogany log. Morning showed tracks from two coyote night visitors. Tire change tough. Salt-frozen lugs make you appreciate penetrating oil. For a sweating hour, contemplated 20-mile trek for Mansfield cut and help called down from Corpus. (Breakdowns this remote are serious; injuries, more so.)

Mile 70.9 Surf-fished at Nicaragua boilers, 200 feet offshore. Too rough. Against dunes, 150 yards across beach, found three weathered refrigerators. One mysteriously held 150 pounds of block ice. Behind biggest dune, where blowout had cleared sand to clay base, found 3-foot deep seep well, recently dug. Water slightly brackish but okay. Rain water is cistern-trapped over salt water base. Ironic that many have died of thirst when almost any place on Padre (at clay or packed sand base) a scooped-out well finds fresh water.

Mile 73.3: Beach widening immensely and flattening. *Mile 80.0*: First man since Corpus end. He reached cut by boat, hiked down island, searching where many old Spanish coins have been found.

Mile 81.3: Granite jetties at Port Mansfield cut. Noon. Waited for Mansfield boat to cross the new channel and meet South Padre cars, coming up for the last 35-mile leg.

Beachcomber French? He went back to Corpus with a truckload he valued at over $200. Inventory? You'd have to see it to believe it.

425

Padre Log Number Two

If you could whisk them back — Conquistador Alonso Alvarez de Pineda from his 1519 Texas coastal charts, and bluff Colonel Diego Parrilla from imperial Spain's military road staked in mahogany driftwood two and a half centuries later — Padre Island's Mile 81.3 would startle them both. It would halt Parrilla's march; it would shelter Pineda's ships.

Here, two thirds down from Corpus Christi to Port Isabel, the broad tan chest of this — the world's longest barrier island — is lanced with Gulf blue at Port Mansfield's recently-cut ship channel. Ultimately a ferry will join island-long dune roads for the more adventuresome. Now, however, the cut takes some doing to cross; a Mansfield boat put me over.

North of the granite jetties, Corpus Christian Gene French churned his yellow pickup into four-wheel and made for the dunes' white-cliffed, long loneliness, heading home. Across, I joined a convoy of South Padre Islanders who had trekked up with Chamber of Commerce president John Richards — typically, for the fun of it. We logged mileage backwards, the way you'll read it driving out from Queen Isabella Causeway at the white island's southern tip. Thus, north's Mile 81.3 reads south's Mile 35.2.

Mile 35.2: From Mansfield's cut, Padre is a giant knife thrust due south, broad enough here at its hilt for an average Texas city, then tapering to its resort-playground tip where, from any breezy window, you see white sand and blue water — Gulf or Laguna Madre. This low-duned

426

beach is among the best for shell collectors. Experts all, the South Padre conyoyers had arrived early and collected enough to open a shell shop. Realtor and host Bill Greene was still disappointed; he had expected to add a few ancient Spanish coins, for they are there.

Mile 31.1: Aboard a fire engine red Scout, in company with blue command car, green jeep. Passed Coast Guard's World War II "dog cavalry" post behind dunes. From here, sailors patrolled against night beach landings from offshore U-boats. Shifting sand almost has it drowned, recollecting that our mightiest war effort is fast fading from memory. *Mile 29.4*: Rusting tank, wrecked shrimper staring at three others working offshore. Far out, big freighter outbound from Port Brownsville, hull down at horizon. No strain at 30 m.p.h. Beach loot? Same incredible variety as lonelier north's (whatever traveled the timeless ocean is somewhere on or under that sandy vastness. And it is vast; almost anywhere along its length, a hundred men could explore a square mile of Padre's ocean of dunes, unseen to you and to each other.)

Mile 25.0: Site of Padre's tantalizing Lost City, quarter mile inside dunes, thence far across to Laguna Madre. Alternately buried and uncovered by the big winds, here lies the layered legend-story of Padre's life. In the early 1800's, Spanish Padre Nicolas Balli fled mounting Mexican revolt, founded Rancho Santa Cruz with the island's first cattle. Padre's land title tottered in free Mexico, his heavy, driftwood-timbered buildings fell to the 1844 hurricane. For the island, he left only his name. Then came successive layers from Zachary Taylor's army. Santa Cruz regrew as a Taylor base camp in 1845. Two years later, a shipwrecked sea captain, John Singer, rebuilt the conglomerate ruins, prospered remarkably until white island became hit-and-run Confederate-Federal battlefield. Like Balli, Singer fled. In a big stone jar, he buried sixty-two thousand dollars in gold, silver and treasure, four feet deep and bottomed on two silver bars. But five years of war, wreckage, water and wind hid his home from even him, and the 1867 hurricane buried everything under new sand mountains.

You stand in a now broad valley, fringed far south with green scrub, all surrounded with big, shifting hills, gold in the sun, blue in the shadows. Ten feet below are the battered ruins of something, story says preceded even Padre Balli's Santa Cruz. Legend whispers a forgotten Indian city and of a Lafitte camp. Archaeologists have uncovered threads to the ancient Aztecs and shadow races that long foreran them. Even prehistoric mammoth and mastodon knew what is now this land. Yet where to dig? And it is ever-moving.

Mile 17.4: Here was Padre's mysterious fresh-water lake. Two miles around, it confounded marine biologists. Salt water drum and skipjack survived in a layer of fresh water floated atop the salt. Hurricane Carla took the lake as she built others.

Mile 14.0: Surf fishermen dotting the beach now. *Mile 10.0*: Site of old Money Hill. From here came many coins dating, indiscriminately from early 1500's to late 1700's. Wind took Money Hill in 1916, but not the conviction held by treasure hunters that the mother lode yet remains . . . somewhere.

Mile 7.8: Wreckage of shrimper, recently grounded. *Mile 7.0*: Stopped to photograph fisherman's one-hour surf haul — three fine reds, largest, 40 pounds. *Mile 4.8*: Pavement at Cameron County's Andy Bowie Park. Fishermen in force; auto licenses from six midwest states.

Mile 4.0: Carefully careless-appearing beauty of South Padre Beach all about. Undaunted by storm is bright colored, delicately fluted architecture that catches the seashore feel better than the square castles of Fort Lauderdale and West Palm Beach. From here to the tip of the island, there's the smack of future Padre: clean as raindrops, jaunty as a beach hat, easy-going as the drifting dunes, pretty as those girls in the surf. Most of all, content as that Mile 7.0 fisherman with his three reds.

Mile 00.0: Foot of Queen Isabella Causeway, crossing Laguna Madre's pale blue to Port Isabel's racket of new color under the old lighthouse.

428

Here's where you get off. You, not me. I want to stay awhile.

Toll From the Sea

Far down the wide beach from Port Aransas, the two plump ladies with an Ohio license, walking shoes and pulled-down sailor caps were at first furtive with their basket of seashells and "things".

"They're used to being told 'no!' " Bill Ellis said as we left. "Rocks, plants. . .petrified wood: things you can't strip from a national park. They don't realize a seashore renews itself. Almost every wave, something different washes in.

"Toll from the sea," he called it.

We drove back up Mustang Island, the broad, silk-sandy bar across Corpus Christi's glittering crescent bay. We went into the many-colored, jaunty-buildinged little resort, where the game tarpon brings Texans to the boat docks, where others come to splash or fish the jetties or just to look.

We talked about the looking. Tall, gray crew-cropped and squinting with a seaman's eye from here and U.S. Navy, Bill has studied the beach-watching for the fifty-plus years that Port Aransas and Tarpon Inn have been his home. Antique bottles to pieces of eight, old-crusted beeswax blocks to shiny polyethylene hawsers, obscure life rings and brown glass Russian fishing floats, delicate seashells to sculptured driftwood: all have hidden in the shifting dunes down Mustang's twenty-five miles to North Padre — a loop drive out of Corpus.

"Toll" is a good word. It varies incredibly with the sea's humor.

Sometimes that humor is rollicksome for Aransas, as in a spring of 1928 that Bill remembers, with Democrats

429

about to nominate New York Governor Al Smith in Houston. The oratory will be lubricated, this year of prohibition, with a thousand cases of Canadian "Old Hospitality", maneuvered in from Mexico.

Each pint bottle is sealed in a flat can to resemble insect spray. Twelve tins, bound in burlap, make an insignificant, suitcase-sized bundle. Should the rum-runners hit trouble, the deceptively drab treasure will also float.

And float it must; somewhere in the dark off Port Aransas, a cutter bears down. Nothing to do but deep six the cargo! Night and the tide take it, straight for slumbering Mustang Island.

Two of those who are asleep ashore are an age-weathered and poor couple in their tidal-flat tarpaper shack. Too old now to hope for a boat, they live by what they can sell from their seine. With morning twilight they are out and working the lee below South Jetty.

They see a burlap shape, foaming in on the surf. The old man retrieves it; you accept anything from the sea. He opens it. Offshore, he sees another tumbling in.

The secret leaks fast. By daylight, Port Aransas is deployed, far down beach and dune. Here comes more of the miracle burlap treasure; yonder, even more! Dozens! Maybe scores, hundreds! *Man, this is bonanza! Here, take a quick nip and hide this case, and we'll get that one, way out!*

Craftily, they hide their booty, splash out for more. Returning, they find the first cache disappeared. *Well, now ...! Lemme have a snort and we'll really hide this one! Wait ... here comes another ... Lordamighty, two!*

Their watchers, who have re-hidden the first, now dart out and back with the second, only to find that they, in turn, have been watched from another dune. Through the day, all the ingenuity of adult hide-and-seek, mellowed progressively with "Old Hospitality", fills Mustang's dunes with scurrying and, in time, lurching figures where finders are seldom keepers. Even those watching the watchers are watched; the turnover is prodigious.

But not with the old couple. Close to their shack and stone sober, they labor through the day and into the night.

When he is done, the old man has cached, inside that shack, two hundred fifty cases. He will touch only one pint; and that considerably later.

Before he sails away with his wife, he pours it in a bottle, then breaks it on the bow of the new boat which the good sea has brought him.

And the other mood — the cruel sea — and its toll?

As a boy, Bill Ellis rode out the 1916 storm aboard a tug, come to take off islanders. Her steering fouled, the tug drifted, then grounded, but survived the ocean's fist. Daylight found them still boated, but high and dry back on Mustang.

Northeast off the coast, the night had been deadly different. The little packet boat, *Pilot Boy*, and her crew of twelve were caught in the sea's wild, black mountains. The superstructure splintered and tore away; then the wood hull broke in half.

When sullen morning came, Aransans counted that sea's toll from the jetties up to St. Jo Island. Six bodies washed in. Six others, clinging to wreckage, lived to make shore.

It was the last man that then-young Bill Ellis remembers. Naked from the waist up, he must have been last to abandon ship before she was crushed under. Despairingly, he must have caught at the frail hope of a ripped-away ship's ladder. He locked both hands to a rung; were one to dislodge, he would be torn from his frail raft.

On his back leaped the ship's big, fear-crazed cat — claws driven deep into the man, deep as animal terror. To live, the man must hold, both-handed. To live, the cat must hold, with every claw a ripping spike.

Into the thunder, five miles to the beach, they were hurled: pounding, soaring, strangling, screaming over the storm. Somewhere out there, the ocean wrenched the cat loose.

In the morning light, the man staggered across the sand, his back laid open and salted. He was insane.

Bill and I talked awhile about our gleaming coast, and about seawise Texans who shake off storms and keep growing. We talked about Port Aransas, bustling to ready for fine weather by late March, about Money Hill down the dunes and whether Lafitte really used a millstone over his cache. . .even about the old days when we hunted the Pacific for subs.

Inevitably, though, you get back to the ocean — the living, moody thing that is out beyond the drum-rolling surf line. Beyond all the fun and frolic, it comes to the beach each day for toll.

Some it brings. Some it takes.

1970's

The Seashore Search

I have never forgotten meeting the man, nor his seashore search. He had discovered either a formula for tranquility or, perhaps, a human riddle that drove him to seek it.

He was well down Padre Island from Corpus Christi, where the wet-packed, wide beach stretches on and on between clifflike dunes and blue-green ocean — all of it far down a pounding white surf line — to the horizon haze and beyond. His car was by the dunes; his family was weekending our coast as its best time, before or after the summer rush. These are times when the swimming, fishing, sailing or diving equal Florida, mile for mile, and beat her badly, dollar for dollar.

If you want to relax.

He did. Lanky in rumpled khakis and a Mark Mitscher cap, he was ambling from high sand to water's edge, poking around the cast-up timbers and ancient bottles, driftwood, hawsers and colored glass fishing floats. If he came on Spanish gold, fine.

What he appeared to hunt, though, were seashells.

Don't underestimate the seashore search these days. From Sabine Pass around to the Rio Grade tip, it has become increasingly absorbing for thousands and something more than a beachcombing hobby for many of your age, mine, and older. There are experts who can look at a beached and sea-worn buoy or cask and, from its marine crust, tell you where it has journeyed and very nearly how long. And, of course, there are beginners, for Padre is a shell-hunting trove.

Many searchers catalogue shells as they would coins or stamps. Some hunt them simply for their intricate beauty. Any can tell you how to begin.

You start with a paperback handbook from almost any beach shop. Don't look near your hotel; the remoter the beach, the better. Specifically, South Padre's shell banks improve from eleven miles above the causeway to the Port Mansfield cut. North Padre's begin twenty miles below Bob Hall Pier and run to the cut.

More specifically, you don't drive those far beaches without checking in advance. You can mire a car and lose it to the rising tide.

Now what to seek?

The easiest are the orderly scallops, flared in off-whites and burnt oranges; the spilled-over, ribbed cockles; the delicate pink tellins, and the spiny jewel box.

Rarer are the sleek, lavender lettered olives, the miniature Aztec sun calendar that is interchangeably called staircase or sun dial; and the fragile, lipped Scotch bonnet. So are the calico clam, the radial-banded sunray venus, the spiraling moon shells, whelks and conches. Boiling water cleans them, and you buff up the color.

These, you should find with luck and reasonable search.

One shell collector found quite something else.

In her *Gift From the Sea*, Anne Morrow Lindbergh saw truths for her life. The channeled whelk, spiraling gently inward, was the beauty of simplicity. Thus, this mystic would seek the uncomplicated life.

Her double sunrise — your sunray venus — reflected the second glow of middle years, just as her gnarled oyster shell suggested their utility. She looked into the eye of your moon shell and saw an island of solitude: an aloneness not to be feared but, quite often, sought out. Remove complication and confusion; find reflection and peace of mind.

All this, she saw in a handful of shells you can gather, like sorted thought, any quiet afternoon along a sufficiently solitary beach.

Yet I have a notion that each of us may hunt our beaches a little differently. You may sense that it isn't the shell you seek at all, but the primitive pull of the sea: the surge and might and low thunder man has heard since he first knew sound. Walking the sand for anything or nothing would be enough reward for you.

Or you might contend that an Indian-summered shell beach — like faraway mountains or a quiet camp — means a solitude and inner stillness which, in time, brings peace. That you really look for the shell to find the solitude, as — to see Seven Sisters' faint stars — you never look directly at them.

And what of the beach searcher I encountered. He sells out of Waco; he manages to keep up; he supposed he did as well as anybody, better than some. With getting "things" he kept pointing out.

And at this point, you will have to determine whether he reported formula or posed a riddle, peculiar to man.

"Oh, I get fed up with the rat race," he told me. "Then I poke around a couple of days. It unwinds me."

He had tried just sitting and looking, just walking, not even smoking, not even a beer. It didn't work as well as hunting around.

"I need something *to keep busy*," he said, "till I unwind."

He didn't seem altogether satisfied that he had summed it up for me. He had a shell in his hand, and for a time, he simply stood there looking at it as though the answer or the question was somewhere within it. It was a sleek, spiraling conch, a beautiful thing. Once, a snail-like creature had lived in it. Suddenly, he held it out to me.

"You know, this was really a house. . .a home!" He

434

gestured it toward the sea. "He built it somewhere out there. Friend," he said, *"that must be a real rat race out there*. Under all that water. . .

"Well, he's gone now. How long's he been gone? God knows!"

He put the shell away with finality.

"But he sure built something to leave behind. . .didn't he?"

1970's

The Big Thicket

I have skirted swampy Everglades and Dismal and fringed some sullen edges of Okefenokee; and I can accept the late Lance Rosier's flat statement that, wild mile for mile, there is no wilderness in America more unyielding than the Big Thicket of Texas.

The Big Thicket is the vast, impenetrable forest (more woodland than swamp) that has barriered much of the southeast corner of this land in exotic beauty, unreachable depth and mysterious legend since before the white man.

To me, the Thicket and Lance Rosier were synonymous, inseparable. The years that I knew him, he was a slender, gentle, seventying man with eyes that were quiet from study, all his life, the plant species by hundreds, the bird and wild life families and tall and old trees by scores. His house was in Big Thicket's capital, the remote village of Saratoga, but he considered his home to be the endless botanical crossroads, the half-million acre Thicket itself. Whenever I went down, he showed me that home or told me stories of it.

Once a sweating lumberman stopped him deep inside, asked what he was doing. He was searching out a rare plant which some botanists had asked about.

"I'm looking for a flower," said Lance.

"Hell, Slim. You can do better'n that with your time!"

Well, he couldn't. He was the one man you couldn't lose within its labyrinth. He was its Daniel Boone without gun.

He guided scientists who came from as far as from Venezuela or Switzerland. Or just curious travelers like you and me. I could never determine which he enjoyed most.

Your map will trace the rough circle around the Thicket: north from Liberty through drowsy Moss Hill and once lumber-milling Rye to Livingston; then east past the Alabama-Coushatta Indian Reservation into quiet Woodville. Then south through Kountze to pick up U.S. 90 between Beaumont and Houston.

This is by no means its historic perimeter. Once, they defined everything south of the old San Antonio Road —down from Nacogdoches—and west as far as the Brazos as Big Thicket; grudgingly its outlands yielded to settlement. Old timers know you can drive the Thicket back with your axes, but it has relentless life and will return, again and again.

You can nick a little of its interior along thin, jungle-walled crossroads. There are the old, sawdusty lumber mills, the little towns standing against the attack of forest, the quick-passing garden patches, the trucks crouched under mountains of new-cut logs, the strange flashing-by of shiny tank batteries where the drillers and pipeliners have penetrated, and — most of all — the sense that this wilderness waits just off the road shoulder and goes on and on and on.

"And all you want to know?" Lance repeated, "is how easy can you get lost?" It was my first visit with him; he looked at me incredulously.

However, we agreed that this is the Thicket's first, overpowering impact on a stranger; perhaps intruder is a better word. We had talked about the men who didn't want to go to World War I and simply disappeared within Big Thicket's vault. We had talked about the more awesome Kaiser Burnout, when a hundred men who wanted no part of Confederate or Federal arms, disappeared in the wilderness to live out the war. One legend says they were burned out, south of the Indian Reservation, shot down as they ran from conflagration. There are other, differing versions.

At length, Lance Rosier pinpointed the remotest wilds within the wilderness as the triangle between Saratoga, Honey Island and Kountze. He also told me about John Hendricks, to underscore his point. Hendricks lived in Saratoga for fifty years and for most of them ran the ice house there.

"John's house," he recalled, "was . . . oh, mile and a half by road from town. He had a back trail, quite some shorter. One morning he took a wrong turn on that trail, and he got lost."

"That close to town!"

"He stayed lost eight days. Helicopters, all of us, huntin' him."

I asked how you survived in country that could lose you that quickly.

"John didn't have any trouble on food and water." Lance gave me a slow smile. "But he did say that when he ran out of chewin' tobacco, he like to went crazy." After they found him, Hendricks just skipped the hospital and went back to work. And . . . was a little more careful on the back trail.

"If they were to set you down in one place, Mr. Rosier — the one place that would be toughest to get out of — where would that be?"

Lance Rosier thought awhile, considered the deep country up the old railroad cut which is now Bragg Road and is haunted by foxfire. He discarded it.

"It would be . . ." he reflected, thinking back to 1936 when he helped survey the whole Thicket, ". . . three miles northwest of Honey Island. You cross Bad Luck Creek in the swamps of Panther Den. You have to crawl the last mile; you just can't stand up at all. Palmettos, big as a house. Everything interlaced."

Crawling is hard, so much of it bog. Did I want to go up and look?

I thanked him, just the same.

We had talked about just one of the wonders of Big

Thicket: its ability — almost its calculated intent — to lose you instantly.

"Actually," he told me, "all you have to do is walk a hundred paces away from your car, in any direction." I tried that later and got out quickly. Just off the road, blind jungle is that close.

When they make a National Park of it, as they must, I hope it remains just that way. And I hope they have a little plaque for Lance Rosier, who died not so long ago. An unostentatious little marker; he wouldn't want anything else.

Maybe in that wilderness northwest of Honey Island?

1970's

Bluebonnet and Paintbrush

Across the land, each spring, wind our wildflower trails. It is a good time to go out and see the dust-red splashes on fields blown frosty blue. And perhaps, these latter days of our country, a time to contemplate old parable.

From Brenham to Yoakum, inland from the coast, and up toward Fredericksburg in the hills, and beyond, the Garden Club ladies can tell you the bluebonnet and paintbrush legends: from when the fairies chose them prettiest of all, to the time Cactus Jack Garner earned his nickname, helping decide our state flower, back in 1901.

But look closely at the fields this spring. Perhaps you will find — as the Indian knows — how the bluebonnet and its companion paintbrush really came to be. And therein lies the parable.

Once upon a time, there lived an aged chief and his tribe, in a land of ice and mountain rock. It was a time of starving and suffering; and the chief climbed to a high place and entreated aid from the Great Spirit beyond the cold sun.

From afar, he heard the voice of his Father telling of

438

a plentiful land beyond the sunrise. The chief told his people they must cross the forbidding mountains — farther even than their boldest hunters journeyed — and though they feared, they followed him, for such was their faith in the Great Spirit he had heard.

Over mountain, then plain, bare of all but the terrible ice wind that screamed and beat them, the old chief led his people and buried them where they died. Finally he called his son to him.

"This good land we seek," spoke the chief. "I shall reach it before you. Tomorrow, you will be chief. But I shall wait and watch for you in the good land, and you will know that I wait."

How did one know this land? In each season of the bud, it will be covered with blossoms, as many as falling rain, and all of the sky's pure color.

The young chief buried his father and faced his council. "Turn back!" they challenged in the mountain cold. And long after, in the endless desert fire that choked the tongue and split the mouth, "Turn back, before all our people die!"

But the young chief had heard his father's wisdom; he forced them on and yet on. And finally, one day, the winds smelled of water and of growing; and from a valley rim, they looked upon a meadow, blue to the hills across; and down the valley in the trees, a clear stream with game about and good soil. And here, they set their village.

They were a grateful people, for as it was told, the flowers waited because the people had trusted and labored. And for all the new chief's life, they were unwearying workers and hunters and builders; and the flowers returned like blue flame, each season of the bud, as a sign that it was so. The people gave thanks and prospered, and their chief grew old.

One night his father stood before him. "You are to join me with our ancestors," he heard his father say, and replied, "Then I would summon my son, as you did me, for he will be chief."

"Let him never speak it," said his father, "that the Great Spirit permits us, as these blue flowers, to look upon our people for this short time each season."

"My son will say only that the flowers return for a sign that our people have remained true and just and honorable."

And so the chief told his son and was gathered to his ancestors. And his son told a son. And he, a son. And for sons as many as the flowers, it was known that the blue blossoms were friends of a good and diligent people.

But with the time of the full belly so long on the land, there came a season when the flowers paled, and an old chief warned that the fields looked on laziness. But his people laughed, being too wise to believe in ancient sign.

Even spoke the chief's son, "What we have, old father, we have made for ourselves."

And now, from other lands came enemies, hungry and fierce, and the people, grown soft as squaws, took fear and fled; and there were few to stand. Then it was that the old chief climbed to a high place and stood as though listening. And his son, following to watch, saw him go down into the flowers and — with a rich earth and oil and a brush fibered of the wind weed — paint many blossoms red. And the young brave followed to the tent to learn what had been done, and found his father dead.

And now, with morning sun, came a great battle and the young chief saw strange faces, fighting for his people — warriors as many as the flowers of the valley. And when the enemy fled, the strange warriors disappeared. The young chief walked among the red flowers in the blue and found his father's brush.

"Can it be that he called back all the strength of our ancestors?" the young chief asked of himself. But he thought no more of it, for the people were close about, praising him.

The people came back, dancing and exulting indeed: "Now, truly have we a power that no others possess. We have the brush and the red earth and the secret. We can create all we need to defend us."

And they became full of talk and song, all the days through; and even the young chief forgot that his father

440

had not spoken of what had been done among the flowers. But what matter? Had he not watched it happen? Could he not also do it?

The blossoms continued pale in the valley and forgotten in the festivals and games. Then one day, the sun rose in dark thunder, for a new enemy marched down.

Into the fields ran the people, first with brushes, then splashing from bowls in fearful haste, calling on their warriors to rise. Dumbly they stood in their blue fields and red; and the enemy came down.

And when the enemy passed, few were left to flee.

Far across the land they scattered; and always the blue flowers waited. And the people wept, and died in the blossoms they had made red . . . but nothing more: no Spirit rose to help.

Only by night were they seen at last, then all were gone — even the last chief. He fell, clutching one blue blossom. Across its face streaked a faint white mark — like an Indian's tear from long ago snows.

When the moon is right, this season of the bud, the old ones say you can see them out in the dark. You can hear the last despairing chief across the plains and by the water and over the meadows as he bends among the blue flowers he paints red.

I suppose it was my imagination, camped along the Guadalupe one night not so long ago. I don't mean about seeing them; they were out there, of course — across the fields in the moon. But they looked so little like Indians.

More like you and me.

Roses of Tyler

If Tyler were all mine to direct for one day, I'd make mighty few changes, but one would be to do something about those signs. They are too small. They are also too matter-of-fact; they intimate they are directing you to something as prosaic as a turnpike.

So, since you're already humming six-lane concrete that loops downtown, and since the homes and wooded hills have the clean and fair look that you like in cities and, thus, all your spare attention, you push on and never see the signs make a discreet turn and leave you.

And you miss likely the most beautiful twenty-seven acres in our land.

This is Tyler's municipally-owned rose parkland, where thirty thousand bushes — in four hundred different colors — blaze and bank a terraced, piney hillside, frame its fountains and dapple its reflecting pools.

Maybe Tyler's restrained sign-makers believe that, with the rest of us, roses are just for beautiful women: that men may go for them, cut and boxed, but not on the bush.

This is not true, and Tyler men are not alone in regarding this blossom as the olympian of the flower world. There are plenty of square-jawed males the country over who, like me, may know only that roses come in red, pink, yellow, white and mixed, and that they smell better than campfire coffee at sunup. . .but who can be entirely comfortable around a growing rose. We may not go overboard for violets or geraniums or orchids: but, like a meadow of bluebonnets, a rose is something we can understand.

442

Putting over in Tyler recently, I determined to hold a sort of contest: to explore the garden and, with no experts around to confuse me, to pick my ten favorites of all. I recommend this for your first free hour in East Texas.

Right away, Tylerites warm up to you. They all have their private rating systems and want to tout them. At my motel, for example, the Abe Hoyts must have had two hundred bushes: floribundas, grandifloras, hybrid teas — some twenty-eight varieties. Learning of my mission in the rose garden, Mrs. Hoyt made me promise to come back immediately and compare lists.

"Do you know which is the Yellow Rose of Texas?" She looked mysterious. "Don't say; I'll tell you when you get back."

You will not have time enough along the gravel and grass walks. The beds, all double-rowed with each row in one labeled variety, stretch on and on in a geometry of color.

You pass the dark red New Yorker, the black-red Mirandy, the yellow Eclipse and Golden Charm, the pink Doctor and Tiffany, the White Knight and K.A. Viktoria; the sprightly riot of color that is Circus, the orange Montezuma.

You see the freak green rose, a bud that opened green and kept on. There are some miniatures with blooms no bigger than a nickel. Others, you can't cup with both hands. And no matter where you determine to stop, the crimsons on the hill or the yellows just down the slope look a little prettier than those before you.

Afterwards, I talked with Bob Shelton, who directs Tyler's excellent park and recreation system and is a driving force behind this roseland. Many years ago it was bald clay, gully-slashed. Growing Tyler made it first a park, then two decades ago put in the initial three thousand bushes.

"We think it's different," said Shelton. "We wanted beauty but not the kind that makes you afraid to walk around. You notice the kids?"

Actually, that garden is a growing catalogue for today's roses, all of them: a showcase to browse. Tyler's three hundred fifty growers, who market thirty million bushes a year, provide the window display. Whatever rose, it's there.

"What's the Yellow Rose of Texas?" I asked Shelton.

"Lemon Chiffon. We brought it out the year of that song." He told me of other Tyler introductions. Speaker Sam, a vari-colored member of the Peace rose family, was the latest. He phoned a lady who reported she had cut one that morning, eight inches across: opened wide as a sheet of paper.

"How many people see the garden on an average day?"

"Through the summer, say eighteen hundred. In October, toward Rose Festival time, more. That's our season climax."

I suggested that if they'd grow signs to match their roses, they'd double their number of visitors. Then I asked if any garden in the country would beat Tyler's. He wanted to be fair with Columbus, Ohio and Hershey, Pennsylvania.

"I think I'll say that no garden will compare," I suggested.

"You'd be safe."

After that, I showed him my list of favorites. He had some different opinions, but I disqualified him since is a past Rose Association president, and this is for amateurs:

Red: Crimson Glory and Christian Dior; pink: Charlotte Armstrong, Tiffany and Queen Elizabeth; yellow: Buccaneer; white: White Knight. Blends: Peace, Mojave and Helen Traubel.

Of course, Mrs. Hoyt's list differed. Probably yours does, too. With four hundred to choose from?

"What about the Yellow Rose?" Mrs. Hoyt asked finally.

"Lemon Chiffon," I said with authority.

"Technically, but not with tourists," she said. "All out-of-state people want to know which is the Yellow Rose. The very first thing, the Yellow Rose."

"And?"

444

"It's the nearest yellow rose at hand," said Mrs. Hoyt, pointing to a Golden Charm.

Blithe Afield to Birding

This is written under some difficulty. There is a bird in the live oak outside my window. Large and black, it used to be a crow or blackbird, whichever amind first. But once you've become knowledgeable about bird-watching... well, let's look at that raven's picture again...

Maybe, like me, you once knew the only really tough aerial identification was aircraft — ours or theirs. Only eccentrics watched birds.   Yet here we are, I found recently, with hundreds of otherwise sound Texans each year taking up "birding". *Why*? Deciding to start at the top, I went down to the marsh and jungle of Aransas National Wildlife Refuge, up the coast from Rockport. Why not start with a look at the great Whooping Crane?

Why not indeed? North America's biggest white bird, slowly recovering from near extinction, he summers below Great Slave Lake within Canada's Arctic Circle, then each fall hurdles high heaven, trumpeting home to these haven bays.

Hunting this start at the top, I discovered some other things. Texas has more birds than anywhere: four hundred eighty-seven species from the ruby-throated humming-bird to the bald eagle. Also, the growing army of Texans who watch birds for fun have something in common besides good minds, wide interests and insatiable curiosity.

Regardless of age, they stay young.

Connie Hagar is a delightfully young seventy-eight, as pert and pretty as the birds she knows better than anybody. She is Mrs. Conger Neblett Hagar of Rockport, with its beaches, bays and wind-leaning trees, a major American bird capital.

Only leading ornithologists know enough to gauge Connie Hagar's research since she identified her first half-dozen birds at age six. She has literally remapped migratory patterns and holds every honor that Auduboners can bestow. One day in Rockport, she pinpointed an incredible two hundred and four different species between sunrise and dark.

Her published checklist of Texas' central coastal birds is a watcher's must. And, for beginners like us, she can open the world of birds with such understandables as: bird parents rear their young more wisely than do people ... the cardinal is the hardest-working father (and the cowbird, the laziest). . .Lord Baltimore saw his colors on an oriole, named it. . .the brown-winged gray shrike probably taught the Indians dried "jerky" by spiking his own food stores on the nearest thorn. . .the colorful insect-hunting warblers save American orchards millions each year. . .her favorite songster is the mockingbird (whip-poor-will, Inca dove, white-eyed vireo, close).

She also likes the question, "Why bird-watch?" "Ye have eyes and see not," she quotes and adds that looking on beauty brings tranquility; and knowing precisely what you see demands discipline, utmost concentration, and determination.

"You'll see." She checked my binoculars, loaned me her Peterson's *Field Guide to the Birds of Texas.* "I want to know the first bird you positively identify."

I would bring her the whole list, I said; and drove to the refuge, thirty miles east.

Laced with waterways, Aransas is thirty-five miles of winding shell road in a blackjack and sweetbay thicketed peninsula — a pleasant retreat. But begin identifying birds and it is instantly something else — an all-at-once torrent of sound from trees about, their birds invisible; the hundreds of others that you can see, all diving, darting, soaring, wheeling wide, out of binocular range.

446

For the first time, wings have intricate marks: bars, bands, splashes, fringes — none still, long enough to distinguish. You're to find diagnostic marks on heads, bills, tails. You see color flurries instead. The motionless ones, stilted in the water, or watchful on the branches, are too far. . .too far. The very close ones watching you? They're gone, the instant you see them.

You're not sure of gull or tern now, or whether that distant one is hawk or owl and, if owl, which of fifteen. You work in behind thickets on the beach for what must be sandpipers. You find fourteen in the book, move closer to determine which. . .and they skitter.

From the tower at Mustang Lake, those must be whoopers far out on the tidal bars: the two great white birds . . . but too distant in the glasses. Those darker ones, closer in? You wait long later, one is close enough.

Some time after dark, I reported one bird to Connie Hagar. Yellow bill, purple-white neck, yellow stilt legs, what looked like bushy black eyebrows, a silver blue body, about four feet tall.

"You got one," she said. "A Great Blue Heron, all right."

"Well, what about the whoopers? They were right where the ranger said."

"At a quarter mile," Mrs. Hagar smiled, "you could tell positively that they weren't egret or heron, even ibis?"

So, being the bird-watcher that Mrs. Hagar encourages me to be, I can't count the whoopers you better believe I saw. You also better believe my one bird was a day's work. About as pleasant, though, as I can remember.

I am now willing to agree with Connie Hagar that the way to start "birding" is not at the top, but with what you see every day in your back yard.

I will have some feed out, and water. I may build a window feeder, once I explain things to the neighbors. I have my field book and am getting my old Navy glasses worked over.

In a year, who knows? I may be up to a hundred identified

species. I have a cardinal and bluejay for sure and probably a red-bellied woodpecker.

Go ahead and laugh. We birders have an eye on tranquility that doesn't come by prescription. I confidently expect five additional years from my new hobby.

Of course, there are some drawbacks. I have had to leave this copy several times to have a look at that raven outside my window. It has a sleek purple body, yellow eyes and a long, round-ended tail.

Anybody for boat-tailed grackle?

1970's

Ney Cave's Tiny Bombers

You true spelunkers, whose ventures — like those of mountain climbers — I esteem with awe, wonder and steadfast disinclination to share, can break out your grotto records and prepare to dispute the statement I'm about to make.

Here in Texas, we have perhaps the world's most remarkable cave.

It isn't Natural Bridge (near New Braunfels) with its mighty bronzes and purples and golds, nor is it the delicate, diamond-dusted, silvery mist of Caverns of Sonora. Nor Cascade, Century (Boerne), Inner Space (Georgetown), Longhorn (Burnet), Wonder (San Marcos), not even Rocksprings' awesome Devil's Sinkhole.

My nomination for cavern nonpareil is not on the tourist list; it's not even pretty: just a fifty-foot gape that downgrades steeply into a long hole-in-the-wall in the hills above Hondo, west of San Antonio. It is even hard to get in that cave, because it is owned by private interests.

And thirty million bats.

This is Ney Cave. Its remarkability lies in its three-war record beginning with the Confederacy. Its incredibility lies in its third war, when its denizens were ready and unwittingly able to destroy Japan . . . except the Atom Bomb beat them there.

To find the Ney Cave, as I first did as a youngster in my father's Model-T, you begin at Bandera or Hondo. Between them, just before the hills give way to brush country, there is a squat, bald mountain that is part of the Middle Verde Ranch.

You climb the low mountain with the relative ease of your age. Near the top is a yawning hole. Out of it comes an acrid, musty smell, and when you are inside on the deep sloping floor — forty-five degrees at points — you find no delicate stalactites nor massive stalagmites. But up on the ceiling, broad and high-vaulted, you can see myriad clusters like close-bunched, throbbing black grapes. These are the little animals whose arms have wing-membranes between their fingers, and you would see them thus in the winter, when they are sleeping for the spring. From spring to late fall, they will be sleeping only for the night and you won't want to be in there at all.

You negotiate the steep slope with difficulty, at times knee-keep in guano, which is the manure from the night-feeding forays of Ney's inhabitants. The guano is mined; it makes splendid fertilizer, several freight cars a year. It also makes the pungent smell that takes you out of there quickly.

If you wait for the summer hours of sunset and early night, the bats come out, too. The experts say that Carlsbad's bats are a relatively small colony compared to this metropolis. Ney's bats pour a titanic hose stream, black into the sky. By thousands a minute, they come out four or five hours with a rushing, watery noise. They fly incredible distances to find their insects — far as the coast — and are home by dawn.

As recently as 1940, American experts knew no greater bat cave in the world.

A century ago, when Southern armies had scant resources, the guano furnished potassium nitrate for crude gunpowder. There are Confederate-cut ledges in the rock

449

where guano could collect. The guano exploded again in World War I.

But it was in World War II when Ney Cave achieved its then-secret record in fantastic weaponry. It was blocked off, Marine-guarded, Army-Navy controlled. There was no need for the guano's crude explosive power; there was need for the bats.

Scientists believed that this creature, with its radar sense for seeking land and hiding places, could provide a horde of incendiary bombers which would burn out Japan. Ney Cave became the major cavern in the undertaking known as "Project X-ray."

The free-tailed Mexican "guano" bats would be captured, chilled to dormancy and freighted with tiny but devastating thermite "bombs". They would be airborne to striking distance of Honshu's paper cities, dropped in "bomb clusters" of five thousand bats each. Descent would spring each canister and warm the bats again to flight. What radar could detect them? What could stop them, coming by the hundred thousands? Who could prevent their hiding in the crevices of the cities?

There, thermite would take over and conflagration would follow. Provision was even made for the bats to fly clear first.

That the bats could deliver their bomb load was no question. Desert tests proved it. One mock-up "city" was annihilated with one attack. Perhaps even more impressive was the performance of one errant bat: he accounted for an air field building.

The A-Bomb reached Japan before the bat armada was readied, but post war observers, noting that the effects of standard bomber-delivered fire raids approached the devastation achieved by the Bomb, scratched their heads.

They had to ponder what might have happened, had Ney's creatures struck.

The Devil's Hole

There may be more awesome sights in Texas, but offhand I can't think of any that can conjure with Devil's Sinkhole, near Rocksprings in the high and lonely land of Edwards County north of Del Rio and Uvalde.

Oh, there's South Rim on Mt. Emory in Big Bend, or the Guadalupe peaks, but the impact from these is the sense of great height, majestic distance.

The Devil's Hole . . . well . . . this is dark depth, unreachable abyss — a forty-story elevator shaft immense enough for a mountain at its bottom. Bottom ? Even with real cavers and scuba divers who've sought it in Emerald Lake (four hundred and seven feet down and reported at least sixty feet deep), nobody's found real bottom yet.

To separate wild tale, legend and what little fact is known, you see Clarence Whitworth, an amiable, bushy-browed man with some seventy years, the hard frame and easy humor of a divide country rancher. Since 1927, he's owned the four thousand acres that homesteads whitefaced cattle, sheep, goats . . . and the Hole.

"I've been in that hole forty times," he told me. "There's a way out of that big room, got to be. Got to be a lot of cave somewhere . . . beyond it or below it. But I've never found it."

It is the looking down into the "big room" that turns you inside out and makes you want to lie bellied flat and clinging to anything immovable. You look over the edge of an almost circular seventy-five foot wide mouth. You are on an overhanging ledge, six feet out over the void. Beneath you, everything falls inward to a second overhang, dizzyingly below, then cuts inward again and again like an overturned funnel.

The bottom looks deep and darkly flat. Clarence Whitworth saunters to the edge and heaves a rock. You watch it, and the real depth reaches for you, for it keeps falling, falling. The bottom isn't flat either; the rock hits and bounds to the side, finally disappearing in the dark.

"Mountain's a couple hundred feet high: one big rockpile, about a forty-five degree slope." To point, Whitworth leans out over that void. "All we see is the chimney. Where it ends, the big room really spreads out. Takes you a good half day to work round the base of that mountain." Finally he steps back. "Of course, it's dark, it's rough, it's up and down, and it's tight in spots."

Comparatively speaking, few but experts dare the fearful drop to the mountain top. Even these use well-drilling rigs or enough boom to lift them up the center of the chimney, through the eye of the Hole.

In the early days it wasn't like that. When Whitworth made his first drop, back in the Twenties, he tied a rope to the center of a three-foot limb, had a couple of young friends take a turn around the base of the little tree, straddled his sapling and slipped off the edge into space.

"Rough part was coming out," he recalls. "Ride up a rope over the edge, and you'll get stuck under this last overhang every time."

"This last overhang" thrusts out in every direction at the lip of the Hole. It is slab limestone about three feet thick: just enough ledge so that — with you jammed at its base — your up-clutching fingers cannot quite reach the top edge.

"What you'd finally have to do," says Mr. Whitworth, "was stand up careful on your trapeze and not look down. Then you could get a grip on something and pull over the ledge. Thing was, not to look down."

I asked him what had ever fallen in, the way the ground came level and then just opened up.

"You can't get a horse within a hundred yards. Cattle either. Goats . . . well, they'll graze a little closer."

452

In thirty-five years, Rancher Whitworth has yet to find human or animal bone inside the Hole. Even the dark, cold nights when the bats don't fly, the pit exudes some warning sense of peril.

There are two questions that confront Clarence Whitworth with his Devil's Hole. I asked him the first: Why doesn't he drop a small cage elevator from a boom and winch? Why isn't this an excellent and unusual tourist attraction?

He countered with the second: Where does the cave go? Somewhere, for sure. They've never even found where the bats come from, and the Devil's colony is believed bigger than Carlsbad's.

And it's a reasonable assumption that Emerald Lake comes up where the Nueces River begins, about nine miles south down the watershed.

"There are forty-fifty passages leading out of that big room. Some say they get too tight." Mr. Whitworth cocked a bushy eyebrow. "One bunch claimed they followed a passage to where they could hear my windmill valves clickin'. That's quite a ways."

"Anyhow, I'm a rancher," he said at length. "I'll wait'll somebody finds something really to show folks when they get down there."

I repeated that I thought folks'd pay for a good, safe, scary ride into the pit, and a walk around a safe, scary path. They'd talk about that ride for the rest of their trip.

"We'll find where the big cave goes," said Mr. Whitworth with some finality. "Maybe the lower rooms they keep talking about. Under the mountain. I'll take on a partner then, one who wants to run a cave."

If they find the lower rooms and keep looking, Rancher Whitworth may already have a partner in his cave.

A guy with horns.

Grand Caverns of Saline

I suppose you'd call it a mountain: its three-mile height would dwarf anything in the Rockies. Yet its circular top, a mile across, hides two hundred feet below the wooded marshes south of Grand Saline. This mountain is solid, marble-like salt.

Exploring the fragmentary part of it which man has reached takes you on a weird and fascinating journey, seven hundred feet deep, through a succession of huge, dull-glowing caverns. These galleries are wide enough for an expressway and high enough, almost anywhere, for a six-story building.

Somewhere inside, I had stopped my guide, husky and pleasant young Bill Buchanan. Down the recession of vast rooms ahead, I could see the vaulted dimness of right-angle crossing laterals: one. . .two. . .three. . .maybe a fourth.

"A man could get lost down here," I suggested. "Say the lights went out?"

"Oh, that's not very often." He showed me his flashlight. And anyhow, he knew it all by heart. The twelve and one-half miles of it!

This is Morton Salt's Kleer Mine, seventy miles east of Dallas; of our nation's few that you can see, not the biggest, but — say miners — "about the nicest." Which should set a record for some kind of understatement.

If mining schedule permits you to go down, you're there promptly and by advance arrangement.

All about, the gray mine buildings shoulder up massively. Above the seven-hundred foot elevator shaft stands a tall tower, taking the inch and a quarter steel cable up and high over the yard to a winch house. As you go down, more than six tons of salt come up.

A barred gate closes. Your cage is strong steel and wood, safe, elevator-sized, but without frills; and there is a certain zest in descent, since your door is open on the sliding-by concrete casing of the fourteen-foot-wide shaft. You can see out the top opening, wide enough for a man to manage repairs if necessary. The queasy void beyond is where the salt elevator runs.

Down you go, dim and cool, about ten feet a second. There's a squeal or two if there are youngsters along, and, if they are, you concentrate on looking casual and on Kleer's perfect safety record, not the pit that lies under the floor beneath you. It's a long minute down.

You aren't prepared for what waits. There is ample light, but vastness thins it. The cavern stretches straight and far. But the width! The height!

The broad, level floor wears a blanket resembling dirty, crusting snow. The ceiling, cut away parallel, has a frozen sheen. Along it march heavy cables clustering big naked bulbs in threes. All about is the sharp, not unpleasant salt smell, some bright-colored safety signs and, to your left, a heavy-roofed station from which a man watches you and smiles to himself.

Unawed after five years' mining down here, young Buchanan finally motions you toward a string of colored lights well down the gallery. Beside them is a lateral arch, and from distances beyond come muted, methodical sounds. Far away, heavy machinery is working.

Down receding corridor upon corridor, you follow Buchanan through a brief portion of Kleer's precise labyrinth. You are in a kind of checkerboard of pillars and rooms, support and void of equal size. One room is a hundred feet high and seven times that long, and you try to conceive that all that emptiness was once solid salt.

At the end of a gallery, several rows of benches front a kind of auditorium stage with a brown canvas curtain that reads, "Welcome."

"Had a banquet there once," Buchanan explains Farther on is a cubicle with benches and tables that is lunch room and beyond it, a first aid station. You come up on the barriered edge of a salt wall that overlooks a lower work level, descend a broad ramp to reach it, then turn beneath the level from which you had entered.

At the active mining area, a loaded shuttle car grumbles by, big as an earth mover and bound for the salt hopper and its quarter mile of tunneled conveyor belt that loads the "skip" — the salt's elevator out of the mine.

There is racket here. A crew is drilling to set charges. Another operates a squat crawling apparatus that extends big claw arms to scoop up the salt which is collapsed when explosives shear it away. There's a bulldozer to tidy up and a bright yellow jeep to hotshot couriers, a stratotower that cranes up a man to work the high walls. Buchanan dwells on its importance, so you ask him who operates it.

"I do," he says and presently leads your return journey. You pass some closed-off, deep-shadowed galleries, and Buchanan is firm about them. They are off limits: the old shafts, miles of them, and stygian dark. Then you are back to blue sky.

When I went through the mine, Reid Lesser, a graying, courteous, onetime Utahan, was Kleer's top executive. He was not its first.

In 1845, frontiersman John Jordan blazed a trail from Nacogdoches to the remote marshes where Cherokees evaporated salt. Jordan brought two big iron kettles, and Jordan's Saline was in business. It would later and appropriately exchange "Jordan's" for "Grand". It has been mined by various owners by various methods until Morton sank the big shaft in 1929.

For everything from tanning to table use, salt has come out in millions of tons. It isn't hard to comprehend those millions, thinking of the great galleries down below. Yet with what remains, Kleer could season the world.

Vast as are those caverns, they scarcely nick the mountain.

1970's

The Old Store

The farmer bought some flour and a sack of Durham and his towhead's ,red sodapop, and somebody dominoed on the vine-shaded porch outside, and I contemplated the solidity in point of view that is lent by an old-fashioned nail keg seat in a country general store.

I could watch almost everything from my vantage, beside the high-backed rockers just inside the door of Stewards Mill Store. The store is tucked where a south breeze stirs the big oaks, back from the Corsicana road, out of Fairfield. And what a seat that chunky keg makes! It takes a kind of fitted grip on you, gives you a foresquare base for argument, or lets you tilt back easy — visiting, as they have for a century here, lets you swivel, not to miss anything going on.

I'd had a look around, into the cool dimness past the old spool case, the sausage stuffer across, down the hand milled counters with the bins behind and the stock up the high shelves, past the old signs and calendars about . . . back where the horsecollars and hames hang as they always did. The musty, sweet smell is part of what you see.

I already knew the outside: barn-pitched roof, weathered heavy siding around to hand-made brick in the chimney, to porch rockers and bench notched by long ago whittlers. Beyond is the big grove that stretches from the small white church across to where the old mill worked the spring branch.

Presently Mrs. Frank Bragg came back with the store's first ledger. An opening entry showed that this stout old establishment had gone up for $529.20 . . . in 1867. She believes this fourth-generation country grocery Texas' oldest to have been run continually by the same family.

But what delights, from that nail keg view, is that it's run just about the same way.

Stewards Mill, now just the store and church and rolling stockfarms about, came a decade after San Jacinto, when Dorothy Bragg's great grandfather, George Washington Steward, came over from Mississippi. Up went the best grist mill between Houston and today's Dallas, and presently church, gin, saw mill, brick kiln and a store where you traded, shook hands on a deal, and swapped news.

Civil War's backlash burned it, even the cornfields, well after the formal shooting was over. From the pit of reconstruction, this building rose and kept up with its neighbors' needs, including the county's first telephone exchange — that wall box yonder. It never stopped being where neighbors got together, however hard the times.

The hardest time? Dark-haired, soft-voiced Mrs. Bragg gave a slow smile. "I guess the beginning over. We used to hear how my grandfather was in the field by four each morning. And how grandmother learned to be an expert on patching. She had only one rule: 'Never patch over a patch.' "

But hard times didn't stop them; they kept on, made their comeback. She wasn't sure how many thousand family acres they built back to, over the years — all up to Tehuacana Creek. The store grew, too. An extraordinary inventory shows in twelve thick ledgers, scrupulous in detail and a Spencerian hand that an engraver would envy. Day-to-day, perhaps a quarter million entries in those ledgers.

Consider a random sample: "1 pair shoes for wife . . . $1.75; 42½ yards bleached domestic . . . $6.75; 3 yards buckskins . . . $3.00; shots, caps and powder . . . $1.15; 3 violin strings . . . 40c; 1 bottle quinine . . . $3.00; 1 quart whiskey . . . $1.00; 73 pounds bacon . . . $9.19; 1 hoop skirt . . . $1.75; 1 set buggy springs . . . $9.50; 2 coffins . . . $25.75.

Because the Frank Braggs are as proud of Stewards Mill Store's service record as they are of its founder's, with Waul's Texas Legion, they keep a virtual museum of fragments from those early days. In easy clutter about, you'll find a barrel spigot and bung starter, a shingle frow close beside a Brown's Mule plug-cutter, a ladle and mould for lead shot, apothecary bottles, still full, brass-toed starter boots, a mustache cup, a Peaberry Coffee Tin: scores of old things.

"I couldn't begin to show it all." Mrs. Bragg pointed to a brown snuff jar. "Was it a black gum brush they used?"

"Elm's better," came from the domino game on the porch.

Outside the door, I asked about whittling these days. Well, they don't use good pine boxes for shipping any more. Nor can you pitch silver dollars out front, and horseshoes aren't as handy. But the easy visiting and the tempo, a tranquil one, stays the same.

It was outside that I found perhaps the most remarkable in all Stewards Mill Store's inventory: that of its struggle to survive — as always in farmland — against the elements. Down the board front under the shed porch roof is penciled, year by year, an almanac of that struggle.

"Grandfather began it," said Mrs. Bragg. "Droughts ... floods ... cold."

There are scores of laconic entries, fading now:

"July 31, 1893," I picked one at random, "Hit 109." Below, several topped 110.

"Frost — a.m. — Nov. 2, 1897." She showed me the 1889 ice that came as early as October 9: that was a cold that cut their five hundred steers to a hundred by spring. One faded year read: "12 hours rain, Sept. 13. First since June 2."

I began to scan those years for a real record breaker. One of the domino players cashed a double five for twenty and recalled it, without looking.

"September 3: Creeks all dry. Fenced to mouth of Caney for cattle to water." He glanced up, pointing and read the next entry slowly: "September 4: All damn cows drowned. Water over top of fence. 20-inch rain." The year read 1932; the toll, three hundred cows. *All of them?*

"Aw, he saved a few." The player pushed his hat forward and dominoed. "He was jus' mad enough to stretch the count some."

Inside, we talked about customers. Had they changed much? Mrs. Bragg shrugged.

"Those ledgers you read. That was nearly all credit, had to be. Never lost a penny, my father said."

Well, you determine if we've changed much from those old-timers.

If you want a good view, try the one from my nail keg. It beats a T.V. stool.

1970's

Little Girl Lost

For a little girl lost, it first seems the loneliest of monuments — a weathered shaft and solitary, back up a brush hillside in southwestern Comanche County.

To reach it directly, you drive, walk and climb from the out pastures of rancher Jesse Williford, near where Brushy Gap cuts the mesas south of Comanche. I took a different route, the one that brought it here almost a century ago.

Then, you looked out on no green reach of valley, timber-dotted to the rims, patched with sheep and dappled where cattle graze. You saw the brush forest of frontier, barely scant of Indian — a wilderness, thin-rutted by tar-pole wagons and hiding far-distant log shacks. The South Leon valley, heading below you, was all postoak shinnery, laced in briar and catclaw. The wild hog and cat knew the way best.

Little Frances Ellen Spraggins knew it; the monument is to her. She was a pretty, barefoot toddler in a plain linsey dress; age, twenty-two months.

460

I went over the real trail to the monument with veteran Comanche newsman Don Carpenter, who knows this Comanche country, for he walks and studies it like an Indian.

The real trail begins east of Brushy Gap, at Harmony Community. There is no handful of houses by a quiet, wandering valley: erase all that. Instead, the old timber is here, dense about the cabin, pressing close on the quarter-mile path to the spring branch under the hill.

In the cabin, Frances Ellen busies her doll about her house under the rawhide bed. From the cabin, Ellen's mother hurries bonneted and thin-lipped into another Wednesday. October smoke chimneys from the breakfast fireplace; the sawed-in-two barrels bubble the wash outside; the oldest daughter plunges the churn. The mother starts with buckets for the spring.

"Ellen, don't get dirty!" Then she calls back automatically. "Watch Ellen!" And she is gone, down the wooded path.

With buckets empty, she takes the steep side down. Filled, they carry easier the long way round the hill. She picks her way, pausing to rest, presently is back. The doll is on the bed.

"Ellen!" she calls, then again. She is off down the path and, a long time later, is up from the spring branch once more, her face deep-lined. "Get your daddy! Hurry!"

"Ellen!" The wind rattles browning leaves, a sudden wall all about. Her call breaks on a scream: "Frances Ellllennnn!"

Now the trail begins, over all the darkening hills around.

A man leads his horse from the sorghum press, looks up at two riders, shadowy by the pole corral. "Kid lost down the mountain," he hears, "bring your lantern!"

From her kitchen, a woman scolds children back to bed, packs her husband's sack with meat and bread, then carries the lamp in the bedroom to reassure the count of her own sleeping heads.

Into the black thickets around the spring branch, more and more lanterns move out in pairs and threes, winking out into the shinnery wall, trailing back shouts, echoing to other shouts, "Frances Ellen!" Then long silences.

461

And out the trails where a horse or a child can go, they ride and stop to listen, call out and listen, and ride on slowly, lanterns bobbing. And by the far off houses and in the clearings, the beacon fires start; and down to the women waiting, drift the distant calls; but they are always: "Ellen . . . Elllennn!" and no more.

And long later, with first light east, the women talk strained by the low fire in the cabin: "She's most out of her mind . . . callin' Ellen out there . . . she won't come in . . ." And they think of their own babies, and the dark wilderness surges back to stretch out forever.

It is the same, Thursday: into another night and through it; and Friday. Three hundred search now, but the faces are haggard. They have combed from Comanche to the gaps. But now, they have pieced a faint trail, east down the draw . . . on and on, the miles to Mercer Creek — a tiny bare print, a snag of cloth on briar. And yet south, down Mercer for incredible miles. Can she have struggled all the way to the Leon? A dozen miles; more, the way she'd have to round those gullies! A baby not just circling, close by? Going on and on this resolutely?

She has reached the Leon and turns up it, returning west. That *will* circle her twenty miles and will pass her scarcely two miles below where she started. It is good her mother sleeps in exhaustion, not to know how close Ellen passed.

Circling with her trail, Don Carpenter figured it must have been some dark hour Friday, the third night. The valley on the J. B. Hilley place is much like where she started. Beyond it a few miles, the Leon plays out against its heading hill above Brushy Gap. A mile of men, strung six feet apart, found her there Saturday morning.

"No more riverbank to follow," Don Carpenter said briefly. Then he added, "Got to remember she went to the spring to find her mamma. She had it in her mind." Somewhere down that riverbank, her mother would appear and would scold, then laugh and splash her from the buckets.

They cut the stone above where she was found. They

carved a delicate five-foot pier where she played out, and the last thicket caught her tattered dress and held her. That last should have been worse than all the nights you wouldn't let yourself think about her facing. Worse, knowing there was nowhere else to look for mamma. By the marker, you shake your head. It becomes lonely indeed.

Yet they insisted there was no sign of terror. She had gone, sucking a little thumb.

There are initials and dates carved way back in the old stone. You can't read what they first wrote for Frances Ellen.

You have the feeling it was what was said before an Easter, long ago.

"Suffer little children to come unto me . . ."

A little traveler isn't so lonely that way.

1970's

Ghost Planes of Pyote

Whenever All Hallows' moon is full and the wind is high, some say they come back. Across that lonely long land, west toward El Paso, it would be an awesome sight, the way they were—the ghost planes of Pyote.   Remember Pyote? The thin town you thread beyond Monahans on U.S. 80? Not so many years ago, remember, a sea of anchored planes covered the earth out there. Wingtip to tip, they reached all horizons, bent them and went beyond. Remember?

Superforts and mediums and fighter-bombers and those shark-like Mustangs, far as you could see from the highway. Waiting silent, tired and deadly behind that Air Force fence that said "Keep Out."

Days now, there seems nothing, far as that distant windmill speck; they seem gone. Most of them, planes that flew the million sorties that last year, they were awaiting cremation.

463

This is where they died. Four thousand were clipped up and furnaced: melted to aluminum bricks, finally your engine blocks. The Big Ones with the crazy names, the bullet and flak holes, the Jap and German flag and bomb rows, neatly painted on.

And some say they come back . . . the way they really were.

Beyond the cavernous five-story hangars is the Line, concreted two blocks wide and miles long. With the moon right, it is not cracked with weeds nor overgrown with scrub and greasewood, out along its vast crisscross of asphalt runways. All about is the endless, close crowding armada of '25's and '29's—the Big Ones: Seven Eleven, with the dice; Belinda and Jo-Jo and Hell's Angel there; and Aces and Eights, the dead man's hand. And by the red brick shed, guyed to her mooring bars, Enola Gay! You can hear her engines now!

It is morning, August 6, 1945, Japanese time; and far below is the toy checkerboard, and Enola Gay is bumping in close-bursting flak; but you are not sweating because of that. It is for that city of 343,000 souls who do not yet know that the Atom Age has come for half of them. You have made the drop.

Then the visual shock! Against your black glasses, the overwhelming, never-to-be-forgotten visual shock; and when you can look again, everything below is boiling dust, with fire at the edges.

"My God!" somebody says on battle circuit, and somebody else finishes, "have mercy!"

And you are back on ground in the Mariannas, and they tell you the mushroom cloud was at forty thousand feet five hours later. They tell you reconnaissance planes saw the flash nearly two hundred miles away. And the awful knowledge grows that you have loosed the dragon and opened Pandora's Box; and you have looked on the Gorgon.

Beyond the Line are the ones with camels. You earned a camel each mission over the Hump—the Himalayas, higher than the sky. Before you fought the enemy, you had to fight the mountains. There's one with thirty camels . . . And a splintered hole, bigger than your fist, straight

464

in front of the pilot; his seat smashed, most of his co-pilot's. Yet they got her back.

Far across is Swoose, last of MacArthur's B-17's at Manila. Swoose and Enola Gay went on to Washington. But the others . . .

You pass Sally Ann, the beautiful blonde with almost no clothes and probably dead waist and tail gunners. You pass Copperhead and Crazy Jake and Wheezy and Denver Express and on and on, till it's all one jaunty name and a woman painted up front, and the bombing missions you lost count of . . . in the thousands.

Any of them can put you up.

You're high, where the blue black sky is laced with vapor trails. Maybe you'll stay high for a fire raid on Tokyo; maybe lower with heavy stuff for the camouflaged plants in the Saar; maybe right through the flaming black middle of Ploesti, so low you can't miss; it's just who gets out.

You can hear the captain: "Close up. Close up! Charlie, Dan . . . close up!" Then he says test your guns; you're going in. You feel the plane buck with it.

Then all the others, slashing, lancing; and the sky and battle circuit goes crazy: "Many Zekes! Eleven o'clock! High! Watch your tail, Dan! F.W.'s at five. Here they come!"

That one, get that one! He's coming through! He'll ram! No, he's hit! *No, he's on you!* No, he's gone, flung apart in the tin-roof splatter of what was left. Across, Charlie, sagging to starboard in the strange, polka-dotted sky. Tipping over like a tired building . . . wings fringing fire . . . engine falling off. Jump! There's time! Jump!

Dan's gone straight in. They're going in, all over: yours and theirs. But you're over target, tracers stitching up below and all the sky puff-smudged. You can see the march of black trees across what was target . . . strings still going down . . .

Then you're coming out for the run through the hurt, furious enemy; and that is where gun stations four and five get it. A rent in front of port waist gunner, and you see him on the deck with no arm before you see his head . . . and here they come again . . . !

Then you're down. You're on the tired runways at base. No, it's Pyote, where they'll clip your ship with cables and smelt her, because she's served her turn. It's Pyote, cracked, weeded, deserted except for the wind. The moon is down.

When it is suggested those planes come back, nights like this, some laugh. This is not to argue. Maybe it is not so much — on nights like this — that old wisdom divides the years and lets you see between. Maybe it's who looks.

Go out beyond those empty hangars, out beyond the Line with a man who flew one that fought. Particularly, if his was buried in the wind out here.

Ask him what he sees.

1970's

Windthorst's War Grotto

It was over. They had taken the bad grenade splinters, and Third Marines had taken bloody, smoking Guam. And he would see Texas again!

On the hospital ship, they didn't have to tell him his outfit had caught it by that high-banked creek with the Jap caves under the ridge. He remembered the flamethrower get it, there beside him, and his buddy's cartridge belt explode him like a string of firecrackers. He remembered the creek turn red.

But his hammering, chopping-down automatic rifle had them stopped if he could just get those . . . *and those* . . . and come left . . . *left faster!* before they were on him, screaming . . . and he saw the grenades arcing right for his gun; and the sky splattered black, and the earth slammed him out.

The hospital ship corpsman shook his head once, the way they do when you'll be good as new, and all the rules say your ticket was sure enough punched. Punched? He should have got it in the surf by the amphtrac. And the sniper he never saw . . . and the Jap seventy-seven that went off in his face . . . and . . .

Before he went back to sleep, Marine Pfc John Hoff said his prayers, as he had from the very beginning, as they all had; and he thought about how that shrine should look. He'd have to wait, though, until they all got back home to Windthorst.

That was the pact between them, wherever they were across this crazy, shot-up world. When they had left, they made a petition to live by: "Our Lady of Perpetual Help, Pray for Us!"

Then from this tiny German Catholic community below Wichita Falls, listed population, one hundred twenty, the incredible number of fifty-nine Texans went off to World War II . . . and knew somehow they'd come home to build a shrine.

Above Jacksboro, you see Windthorst a long way off. The land rolls out to hazy rims and across it dot the neat dairy farms which German Texans built around their Benedictine church in the 1890's.

It is the church you see, a great red Romanesque basilica, square-steepled atop its hill, the village white-scattered below. Closer, the old clock faces become visible and, down the hill, the lesser buildings: schools of the St. Mary's establishment, for the Benedictines have been teachers since bringing Germany's first church and long before that, when their patron founded Sixth Century Monte Cassino Abbey below Rome.

A blond, freckled-faced boy came off the hillside Playground to lead me round to Father Cletus Post, St. Mary's pastor; and the square-shouldered, strong-featured priest took me through his church and its grounds.

Inside is delicacy in pastel blues, vaulting to arches above the nave, and all around are the sculptured stations of the cross behind the columns. The pews march down to the chancel, with statuary to either side. Recessed in the heart of the sanctuary is a shrine to Our Mother of Perpetual Help, for it is through her that the village has found its way, down the years.

Outside, from the front of the church, a walkway slopes

the hill, then drops in broad steps to the grotto built by Windthorst's men who came back. It is a replica of Lourdes, arching high and deep-recessed in rough stone. The fields that sent Windthorst's men also sent the rock that remembers them. That the Windthorst men remember, too, is cut in red marble across their shrine: "Our Lady of Perpetual Help—Pray for Us." She stands behind, in white Italian marble.

It seems no more remarkable than other handsome grottos, until you study the bronze plaque at the right.

There are fifty-nine World War II names, and eighty per cent of them saw action. Reading down the Berends, Gehrings, Hoffs, Koetters, Lindemanns, Wolfs, Zihlmans and the others amounts to calling the roll on battle action in every branch of service and nearly every theater of the Great War.

Since the Benedictine order teaches by example, the lists begins with Father Francis Zimmerer, then pastor, who went off to hold mass at Guadalcanal.

And as Windthorst's young John Hoff passed close by death on Guam, these others saw their inferno—Normandy's grim hedgerows, Bastogne's red snow, Patton's race to smash the Bulge. And on gallant, battered decks, too—like Hornet's and Franklin's. Bougainville's fetid jungles and Okinawa's death winds — kamikaze and typhoon. Anzio, and the torturous spine of Italy.

Convoying through the submarines and under air attack, clearing a burning ammo ship, crouching those last terrible minutes before the barge ramps hit the beach, it is incredible that one tiny Texas town could have sent so many sons so far . . . and into that narrow passage between quick and dead, so often. Incredible!

You select the word for the simple line over all these remembering names:

"In gratitude to Our Lady of Perpetual Help Who Returned Us Without a Single Fatality from World War II."

I doubt if Windthorst's men will talk much to you about their war. It's an unwritten rule: you simply don't want to.

468

I left big, easy-going John Hoff readying for a Colorado elk hunt and slim, bespectacled Ed Zihlman fixing up his new house. I drove back for a last look at the grotto before leaving; it was on toward twilight.

I hadn't even asked Father Cletus, or any of them, if ever — around this shrine — you sensed the breath of miracle.

Why ask?

1970's

Home for Christmas—Hobo Ranch

This is a Christmas story though it began for me in the dog days' heat of September, south of Fort Worth, when I picked up the old man, trudging and bent with his bindle, and drove him to hoped-for work in Waco.

His first name was Bruce; he gave me the last, too. His jaw stubble was whitening, and his back troubled him some from sleeping under bridges. His blanket roll was cracked oilskin, guarding one clothes change. He had a plastic soap box with a couple of cigarettes, a pack of matches, a stub pencil and a yellow notebook.

Very little else for more than sixty years' living. No family, no home, no pension. Just the recollection of jobs and weathers in forty-eight states ever since he gave up trying to get ahead enough for that Arkansas farm; and that was a long time ago.

He wrote my name in his book, caught me trying to read the print on its cover. "Hobo Ranch," he said. "Up near Dallas. They let you work at whatever you can do. Ones that can't do much get board and bunk anyhow. Good folks . . . mighty good!"

He told me there was no other place like it in America. When presently I asked him why he didn't go back now, he studied the long hill ahead until we got to the top, and you could see the country was the same on the other side.

"Might go back Christmas," he said. I let him off in Waco.

Shortly afterwards, I visited Hobo Ranch and its owner, Henry Zollner; alert at seventy, with keen blue eyes, he is third generation of his family to run this remarkable adventure in kindness. Before I left, he gave me one of the yellow notebooks. It tells that the ranch was established by his grandfather in 1876. It tells new men how to check in, draw blankets, pay.

The back side says simply: "A hobo is a transient worker of varied occupations, and not to be associated with those classed as bums, beggars or tramps. We are proud of our men who work with and for us from one day to fifty years. Make this your home—it is not your past, but the future that counts."

What has this formula produced? Outwardly, twenty-three acres of good black farmland, four miles south of the highway, about midway between Dallas and Greenville in Rockwall County . . . a spread of plain white frame buildings (bunkhouses, commissary, the big barn-like dining hall which has fed two hundred men at one sitting, the small chapel that was once Grandfather Matt's home) and the homes of the Zollners and their son-in-law, daughter and grandchildren—the David Brooks.

What else? Jobs for the jobless, home for the homeless. Hope for the hopeless.

"Every time I ask myself why I don't retire in town and hang onto my money," said Mr. Zollner, "I think about what my daddy told me." He looked at the little chapel. "He said he couldn't preach the gospel, which he considered the highest calling of man. This was the next best thing he *could* do."

Right then, with things slack, Zollner Ranch could make it easy with ten hands. But sixty men would sleep there tonight. Tomorrow they'd eat three substantial meals (seconds, if they like) at the long tables: the same fresh foodstuffs the Zollners eat. By spring, Hobo Ranch population would easily top a hundred; by fall, nearer two hundred.

470

Year after year, more than five hundred names go on the books. Some stay overnight; one old timer was nearing his forty-fifth year in the family.

Who comes? There have been doctors, lawyers, a man who built a Houston skyscraper, a judge's son. Some who could read Latin as easily as you read English. Some, scarcely literate. Some, to lose themselves or to find themselves. Who leaves? Anyone, when he wants to. A later state senator, some successful men today.

"They come back, too. Man cooked for me," said Mr. Zollner. "He got a good job cooking in Las Vegas. Kept it a few years, came back home. Another man left to marry up in Arkansas. He came back twenty-five years later when his wife died."

Some never leave. There is a wooded plot on Hackberry Creek, another in Rockwall Cemetery.

"So how can I leave? You lose money . . . like this year." He glanced at the old adding machine and the books open on his desk. "But these men are as much this place as I am. You don't leave your family."

The Zollner family ranges on the elderly side. Not many are younger than forty. The older men, too, are preferred. They can't turn out the work of a younger man, but they're reliable, and the hours they turn in don't cheat. Hobo Ranch is run on the honor system: from serving your own deep tin plates to keeping your hours and drawing your pay.

It has a few other simple rules. No drinking. No trouble. At least one bath a week, clothes boiled. Decorum in the dining hall. "You could bring your wife and the kiddos," Mr. Zollner reflected. "We do."

Recreation? Dominoes and television. They had a pool table, but it wore out.

And for the soul? Radio and T.V. gospel. Occasional visiting preachers and sometimes volunteers from the men themselves.

"The best sermon I ever heard," said this Presbyterian-educated, Sunday school teacher-rancher, "was one a cotton picker preached years ago on 'Hope!'"

I didn't ask to see the men, because a man deserves privacy in his home; and it was late enough that the bunkhouse lights were winking out. I asked about Christmas. Like Thanksgiving and New Years's, there'll be turkey and the fixings. There'll be little gifts from the commissary like tobacco, candy, fruit . . . or essentials like a new pair of socks.

I asked if there were anything a man could do to help out. Mr. Zollner shook his head. Hobo Ranch makes its own way . . . its own way.

Finally, I asked if Bruce had come back for Christmas? I described him. They placed him immediately; he hadn't come back yet.

I hope he does. I hope he stays.

Because, on Hobo Ranch, the gift the Christ Child brought us is not limited to our calendar. It is given every day.

The gift is love, hope . . . live, itself.

1970's

The Lord's Supper

Doubtless each of us carries away something different: perhaps handsome Bartholomew shocked half erect; Judas, frozen between greed and fear; burly Peter, leaning across in fierce question, Thomas Didymus, doubting finger upraised. Of what struck me first, I am not altogether sure.

I am only sure that this Easter, or as soon as you can, you should experience "The Lord's Supper" in Fort Worth.

This is the name of the magnificent, life-sized and unbelievably lifelike wax figure interpretation of the world's masterpiece, "The Last Supper," painted by Leonardo da Vinci on a chapel wall in Milan, Italy, the year of our Lord, 1494.

You find it, as have nearly a million other searchers

from over the world during the decade of its existence, in a quiet building in downtown Fort Worth.

After your particular contemplation and, if you wish, hearing its story—recorded quietly in English or Spanish—you eventually leave it. However, it very likely will never leave you.

You will have entered The Upper Room above a Jerusalem hilltop, as da Vinci saw it in four years' inspired painting. Entered at the climactic instant when Jesus, with less than twenty-four hours to live mortally, has revealed to his twelve disciples that He is the Christ and has, that moment, said simply:

"One of you will betray me."

You see on the faces of the tableau such real shock, dismay and fear that you wait moments for the burst-out words, "Is it I, Lord?"

The Scripture and its great painting have inspired reproduction in some few other American cities—stained glass in Glendale, California; mosaic tile in Lake Wales, Florida; woodcarving in Nashville, Tennessee; and a wax tableau in Santa Cruz, California, which led to the Fort Worth sculpture.

The Lord's Supper was commissioned through the quietly reverent philanthropy of the William Flemings of Fort Worth, and is open to all, daily and Sunday afternoons. It was executed by two German artists—a mother-daughter team: the Katherines Stubergh, whose family have been masters of this art since a century before Mme. Tussaud's wax museum captured Parisiennes and Londoners alike.

There is a dimensional eloquence that a painting cannot explore and warm color denied to stone or bronze. There is delicacy, epitomized in the implanting, one by one, of some forty thousand strands of human hair to each single head.

Perhaps a Stubergh figure elsewhere is merely magnificent craftsmanship, but about this table in the muted light at the far end of a small chapel, there is the breath of the Easter promise as recorded by St. John.

Walk close to this soft-lighted table with its pewter plates, its fruit and fish, its symbolic broken bread and cups of wine. You will not again forget these disciples as you study them, from your left.

Green-robed Bartholomew shares incredulous. *Traitor in our midst?* Clenching the table edge, he has arisen so suddenly his feet are still crossed beneath him.

Grave, quiet James the Lesser, leans forward, one hand reaching perhaps to restrain impetuous Peter, perhaps to inquire. His clear blue eyes lock intently on the Master.

Modest, warm-harted Andrew, who brought his brother Peter from their fisher's nets, thrusts calloused hands against the horror he has heard.

The headlong Big Fisherman already has seized a knife. His eyes tell that he seeks a human solution: he will grapple the traitor! He will yet learn Calvary must come as he, transformed, must found the Church.

Involuntarily, Judas has overturned the salt and clutched for his silver. Look closely at his eyes. Are they a mirror to a part of all of us?

John the Beloved sinks in stunned grief. Young and beardless, his delicate face now reflects acceptance of an end to things from which nothing can arise. Yet he will live to write the thundering Apocalypse.

On the left hand of Jesus is His cousin and John's brother, James the Greater. Ten years from now his iron faith will face unafraid the headman's axe, but now his outflung arms ask one dismayed question: "Who?"

Behind him, questioning finger upthrust, Doubting Thomas asks, too. Later, impelled to see and feel the wounds, he will believe. And he will hear Christ's blessing on those who, not seeing, also believed.

Young, soft-spoken Philip leans forward. Of them all, he cannot question the devotion of his closest friends, now these three years. His is the quick innocent response, "Not I, Lord!"

The last three have turned to each other in amazement. Methodical Matthew, this once, has no answer. Next to him, Thaddeus (da Vinci's self-portrait) broods on a guess he has already made. At the far right, Simon the Zealot, his old hands upraised, seeks reason for the impossible he has just heard.

In crimson and royal blue, in their center, Jesus will yet tell them, "In my Father's house are many mansions; if it were not so, I would have told you. I go to prepare a place for you."

What lies deep in His eyes is not to be seen. Da Vinci knew it was beyond his brush to look there.

Immortal is a word we Americans brandish on encountering any work of reasonably lasting merit. Immortal is a word to take care with.

Yet it is a word to seek, come each Easter; and, apart from the place you pray—your church or by your bed—you may feel the whisper of its promise in this quiet place, within the busy downtown of Fort Worth.

Index

Index

Note: Texas cities and towns are included in bold face type.

491

Spider Rock, treasure, Aspermont, 406, 407
Spindletop, oil, Beaumont, 122, 132
Spur, 316; stampede mesa, 357-360
Stamford, cowboy reunion, 197-200
Stampede Mesa, Spur, 357-360
Stampedes, 130, 357
Steamboats, 88, 208, 400-403, 414, 415
Steinheimer, Karl, treasure, 387-390
Stephenville, stampede, 358
Stewards Mill, Fairfield, old store, 457-460
Stinnett, Adobe Walls, battle, 174-177
Strawn, 310
Sublett, William C., treasure, 395-397
Sulphur River, Rio Roxo boundary, 88
Sunday School, first, 151
Superstitions, See Part Six
Surfside, Velasco, 90-93
Surveying, 43, 88, 181
Survival, Big Thicket, 435; Bowie, 158; Jane Long, 144; Jefferson, 302; Kiowa, 32; Poles, 286; Villareal, 267; Westfall, 171; wolf girl, 348
Sweetwater, rattlesnakes, 329

Taft, William Howard, 132, 134
Tascosa, boot hill, 183, 299-302
Tawakoni Indians, 46, 159, 240; ghost, 342-344
Taylor, Creed, 352
Taylor, Zachary, 72, 104, 109, 294, 424, 427
Teaselville, Cherokee war, 38
Tehuacana, 143; hilltop ghost, 342-344
Tejas Indian, 16-19, 20, 46, 30, 240, 342 (See Caddo)
Terlingua, mines, 322; ghosts, 354-357
Texana, 41, 213, Houston site, 270-273
Texarkana, 374, 376
Texas, U.S.S., Houston, 135-138
Three-Legged Willie, 167-170, 201 (Robert McAlpin Williamson)
Throckmorton, Indian reservation, 240

Thurber, ghost mine town, 133, 309, 312
Tilden, treasure, 390-393
Tillman's Lane, trackless railroad, 106, 107
Tonkawa Indians, 44, 46, 240, 148
Trails, Butterfield, 394; Caddo, 79; Cherokee, 36; Chisholm, 128; Chihuahua, 307, 341; Comanche, 421; Dodge, 128; France Way, 217; Great National, 128, Indianola, 307; Presidio Road, 371; Shawnee, 128; Trammel's Trace, 375; Western and Kansas, 128; (See Camino Real)
Treasure, See Part Six
Travis, William Barret, Anahuac, 92, 163, 166, 80; Alamo, 230; Letter, 261-264; San Felipe, 152
Treaties, Adams-Onis, 88; Guadalupe Hidalgo, 93; Indian, 18, 37, 45-48, 148, 240, 420, 421; Velasco, 92 (See Louisiana Purchase)
Trinidad, massacre, 84-87 (Spanish Bluff)
Trinity River, 290; Napoleonic refuge, 226; Spanish Bluff, 85
Tyler, Camp Ford prison, 246-249; Cherokee war, 38; roses, 442-445

U.F.O., Texas "sightings", 367-370
University of Texas, Austin, archaeology, 11, 13-16, 23, 342; Carry Nation, 206; Memorial Museum, 3, 30
Uvalde, Ft. Inge, 171-174; headless horseman, 353

Valverde Battery, C.S.A., ordeal, 112-115
Valentine, 404, 407
Vanderbilt, La Salle, 213-216; Texana, 270-273
Velasco, Father Muldoon, 163; fort, 90-93; Strap Buckner, 148, 149; treaty, 93
Vernon, 286, 358; cattle drives, 128-131
Victoria, camels, 111, Comanche raid, 40, Indianola, 296-299, La Bahia, 154-157